ELECTRICAL SAFETY RELATED WORK PRACTICES

Based on *NFPA 70E*® 2021 Edition

electrical training
IBEW · NECA
ALLIANCE

Electrical Safety-Related Work Practices: Based on *NFPA 70E*® 2021 Edition is intended to be an educational resource for the user and contains procedures commonly practiced in industry and the trade. Specific procedures vary with each task and must be performed by a qualified person. For maximum safety, always refer to specific manufacturer recommendations, insurance regulations, specific job site and plant procedures, applicable federal, state, and local regulations, and any authority having jurisdiction. The *electrical training ALLIANCE* assumes no responsibility or liability in connection with this material or its use by any individual or organization.

M74549

Contents

Contents

Contents

About the Authors

Principal Writer

Palmer Hickman
Director of Safety, Codes and Standards
electrical training ALLIANCE

Contributing Writer

Thomas Domitrovich, PE, LEED AP
VP, Technical Sales
Eaton's Bussmann Division

Text Contributors

The *electrical training ALLIANCE* wishes to thank the following individuals for permission to reprint materials in this edition.

Steve Abbott
Stark Safety Consultants

Vince A. Baclawski
Technical Director, Power Distribution Products
National Electrical Manufacturers Association (NEMA)

Scott Brady, PE
Western Region Manager, Technical Application Support
Eaton
Electrical Engineering Services & Systems

Electrical Construction & Maintenance (EC&M) Magazine
Penton Media

Michael Johnston
Executive Director Standards and Safety
NECA

Dan Neeser
Field Application Engineer
Eaton's Bussmann Division

Wesley Wheeler
Director of Safety
NECA

Acknowledgments

The *electrical training ALLIANCE* wishes to thank the following companies and individuals for submitting photos for inclusion in this edition.

Boltswitch
Jim Erickson
President

Charles Stewart & Associates

DuPont Engineering
Daniel Doan

H. Landis Floyd, II
Corporate Electrical Safety
Competency Leader
Principal Consultant—Electrical
Safety & Technology

Eaton

Eaton's Bussmann Division

Fluke Corporation
Toffee Coleman

General Electric Corp.

IBEW Local 98
Jim Dollard, Jr.
Retired Safety Coordinator

Ideal Industries, Inc.
Tony Randolph
National Account Manager

Institute of Electrical and Electronics Engineers (IEEE)
Jacqueline Hansson

International Brotherhood of Electrical Workers (IBEW)
Jim Spellane

Klein Tools
Todd Tatara
VP of Channel Sales

Milwaukee Electric Tool Corp.
Joel Petersheim
Senior National Account Manager
- Electrical

National Electrical Contractors Association (NECA)
Michael J. Johnston
Executive Director Standards
and Safety

NECA
Wesley Wheeler
Director of Safety

PACE Engineers Group Pty Ltd.
Robert Fuller

Salisbury by Honeywell
John Lynch

Saporita Consulting
Vince Saporita

Schneider Electric Inc.
Philip Santoro
US Contractor Segment Manager
Partner Projects Division

Service Electric Company

Stark Safety Consultants
Steve Abbott

Westex by Milliken

The *electrical training ALLIANCE* also wishes to thank the following who participated in the photos that are courtesy of NECA.

Wilson Electric Co.
Ryan Hand
Michael Maffiolli

Morse Electric, Inc.
Brad Munda
Kyle Borneman

Larry McCrae, Inc.
Jeff Costello

J.P. Rainey Company, Inc.
Dave Ganther
Bill Inforzato

Carr and Duff, Inc.
George Novelli
Tom McCusker

Northern Illinois Electrical JATC
Todd Kindred

Acknowledgments

NFPA 70E® and *Standard for Electrical Safety in the Workplace®* are registered trademarks of the National Fire Protection Association, Quincy, MA.

NFPA 70®, National Electrical Code, and *NEC®* are registered trademarks of the National Fire Protection Association, Quincy, MA.

QR Codes

Eaton's Bussmann Division
National Institute for Occupational Safety and Health (NIOSH)
Occupational Safety and Health Administration (OSHA)
Stark Safety Consultants

Introduction

For years, many in the industry only considered electric shock when contemplating worker protection and safe work practices. Today, however, the industry recognizes numerous additional hazards associated with work involving electrical hazards. These include, for example, the hazards associated with an arcing fault, including arc flash and arc blast. Workers are exposed to these and other hazards even during seemingly routine tasks such as voltage testing.

Working on circuits and equipment deenergized and in accordance with established lockout and tagout procedures has always been the primary safety-related work practice and a cornerstone of electrical safety. Only after it has been demonstrated that deenergizing is infeasible or would create a greater hazard may equipment and circuit parts be worked on energized, and then only after other safety-related work practices, such as insulated tools and appropriate personal protective equipment, have been implemented. Examples of additional concerns that should be considered include: worker, contractor, and customer attitude regarding energized work, comprehensiveness of an electrical safety plan, appropriate training, the role of overcurrent protective devices in electrical safety, equipment maintenance, and design and work practice considerations. These are a few of the issues that play an important role in worker safety, and are among the topics examined in this publication.

Electrical Safety-Related Work Practices has been developed in an effort to give those in the electrical industry a better understanding of a number of the hazards associated with work involving electrical hazards and the manner and conditions under which such work may be performed. These work practices and protective techniques have been developed over many years and are drawn from industry practice, national consensus standards, and federal electrical safety requirements. In many cases, these requirements are written in performance language. This publication also explores *NFPA 70E: Standard for Electrical Safety in the Workplace* as a means to comply with the electrical safety-related work practice requirements of the Occupational Safety and Health Administration.

Features

OSHA Tips, Caution boxes, and other boxes offer additional information related to electrical safety.

Blue **Headers** and **Subheaders** organize information within the text.

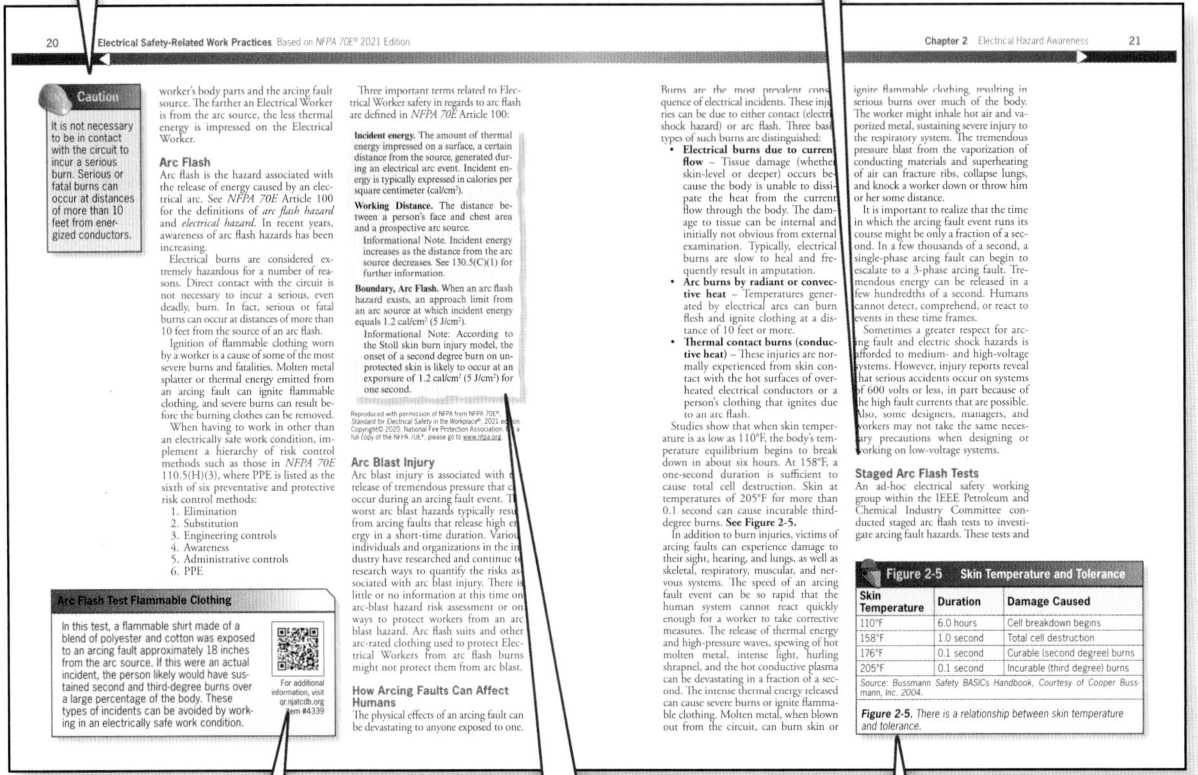

The following is the sample two-page spread shown:

Caution

It is not necessary to be in contact with the circuit to incur a serious burn. Serious or fatal burns can occur at distances of more than 10 feet from energized conductors.

worker's body parts and the arcing fault source. The farther an Electrical Worker is from the arc source, the less thermal energy is impressed on the Electrical Worker.

Arc Flash

Arc flash is the hazard associated with the release of energy caused by an electrical arc. See *NFPA 70E* Article 100 for the definitions of *arc flash hazard* and *electrical hazard*. In recent years, awareness of arc flash hazards has been increasing.

Electrical burns are considered extremely hazardous for a number of reasons. Direct contact with the circuit is not necessary to incur a serious, even deadly, burn. In fact, serious or fatal burns can occur at distances of more than 10 feet from the source of an arc flash.

Ignition of flammable clothing worn by a worker is a cause of some of the most severe burns and fatalities. Molten metal splatter or thermal energy emitted from an arcing fault can ignite flammable clothing, and severe burns can result before the burning clothes can be removed.

When having to work in other than an electrically safe work condition, implement a hierarchy of risk control methods such as those in *NFPA 70E* 110.5(H)(3), where PPE is listed as the sixth of six preventative and protective risk control methods:

1. Elimination
2. Substitution
3. Engineering controls
4. Awareness
5. Administrative controls
6. PPE

Arc Flash Test Flammable Clothing

In this test, a flammable shirt made of a blend of polyester and cotton was exposed to an arcing fault approximately 18 inches from the arc source. If this were an actual incident, the person likely would have sustained second and third-degree burns over a large percentage of the body. These types of incidents can be avoided by working in an electrically safe work condition.

For additional information, visit qr.njatcdb.org Item #4339

Three important terms related to Electrical Worker safety in regards to arc flash are defined in *NFPA 70E* Article 100:

Incident energy. The amount of thermal energy impressed on a surface, a certain distance from the source, generated during an electrical arc event. Incident energy is typically expressed in calories per square centimeter (cal/cm²).

Working Distance. The distance between a person's face and chest area and a prospective arc source.

Informational Note: Incident energy increases as the distance from the arc source decreases. See 130.5(C)(1) for further information.

Boundary, Arc Flash. When an arc flash hazard exists, an approach limit from an arc source at which incident energy equals 1.2 cal/cm² (5 J/cm²).

Informational Note: According to the Stoll skin burn injury model, the onset of a second degree burn on unprotected skin is likely to occur at an exposure of 1.2 cal/cm² (5 J/cm²) for one second.

Reproduced with permission of NFPA from NFPA 70E®, Standard for Electrical Safety in the Workplace®, 2021 edition Copyright© 2020, National Fire Protection Association. For a full copy of the NFPA 70E®, please go to www.nfpa.org

Arc Blast Injury

Arc blast injury is associated with the release of tremendous pressure that can occur during an arcing fault event. The worst arc blast hazards typically result from arcing faults that release high energy in a short-time duration. Various individuals and organizations in the industry have researched and continue to research ways to quantify the risks associated with arc blast injury. There is little or no information at this time on arc-blast hazard risk assessment or on ways to protect workers from an arc blast hazard. Arc flash suits and other arc-rated clothing used to protect Electrical Workers from arc flash burns might not protect them from arc blast.

How Arcing Faults Can Affect Humans

The physical effects of an arcing fault can be devastating to anyone exposed to one.

Burns are the most prevalent consequence of electrical incidents. These injuries can be due to either contact (electric shock hazard) or arc flash. Three basic types of such burns are distinguished:

- **Electrical burns due to current flow** – Tissue damage (whether skin-level or deeper) occurs because the body is unable to dissipate the heat from the current flow through the body. The damage to tissue can be internal and initially not obvious from external examination. Typically, electrical burns are slow to heal and frequently result in amputation.
- **Arc burns by radiant or convective heat** – Temperatures generated by electrical arcs can burn flesh and ignite clothing at a distance of 10 feet or more.
- **Thermal contact burns (conductive heat)** – These injuries are normally experienced from skin contact with the hot surfaces of overheated electrical conductors or a person's clothing that ignites due to an arc flash.

Studies show that when skin temperature is as low as 110°F, the body's temperature equilibrium begins to break down in about six hours. At 158°F, a one-second duration is sufficient to cause total cell destruction. Skin at temperatures of 205°F for more than 0.1 second can cause incurable third-degree burns. **See Figure 2-5.**

In addition to burn injuries, victims of arcing faults can experience damage to their sight, hearing, and lungs, as well as skeletal, respiratory, muscular, and nervous systems. The speed of an arcing fault event can be so rapid that the human system cannot react quickly enough for a worker to take corrective action. The release of thermal energy and high-pressure waves, spewing of hot molten metal, intense light, hurling shrapnel, and the hot conductive plasma can be devastating in a fraction of a second. The intense thermal energy released can cause severe burns or ignite flammable clothing. Molten metal, when blown out from the circuit, can burn skin or

ignite flammable clothing, resulting in serious burns over much of the body. The worker might inhale hot air and vaporized metal, sustaining severe injury to the respiratory system. The tremendous pressure blast from the vaporization of conducting materials and superheating of air can fracture ribs, collapse lungs, and knock a worker down or throw him or her some distance.

It is important to realize that the time in which the arcing fault event runs its course might be only a fraction of a second. In a few thousands of a second, a single-phase arcing fault can begin to escalate to a 3-phase arcing fault. Tremendous energy can be released in a few hundredths of a second. Humans cannot detect, comprehend, or react to events in these time frames.

Sometimes a greater respect for arcing fault and electric shock hazards is afforded to medium- and high-voltage systems. However, injury reports reveal that serious accidents occur on systems of 600 volts or less, in part because of the high fault currents that are possible. Also, some designers, managers, and workers may not take the same necessary precautions when designing or working on low-voltage systems.

Staged Arc Flash Tests

An ad-hoc electrical safety working group within the IEEE Petroleum and Chemical Industry Committee conducted staged arc flash tests to investigate arcing fault hazards. These tests and

Figure 2-5	Skin Temperature and Tolerance	
Skin Temperature	**Duration**	**Damage Caused**
110°F	6.0 hours	Cell breakdown begins
158°F	1.0 second	Total cell destruction
176°F	0.1 second	Curable (second degree) burns
205°F	0.1 second	Incurable (third degree) burns

Source: Bussmann Safety BASICs Handbook, Courtesy of Cooper Bussmann, Inc. 2004.

Figure 2-5. There is a relationship between skin temperature and tolerance.

***Code* Excerpts** are "ripped" from *NFPA 70E* or other sources.

Figures, including photographs, tables, and artwork, clearly illustrate concepts from the text.

Quick Response Codes (QR Codes) create a link between the textbook and the Internet. They can be scanned using Smartphone applications to obtain additional information online. (To access the information without using a Smartphone, visit qr.njatcdb.org and enter the referenced Item #.)

For additional information related to QR Codes, visit qr.njatcdb.org Item #1079

Features

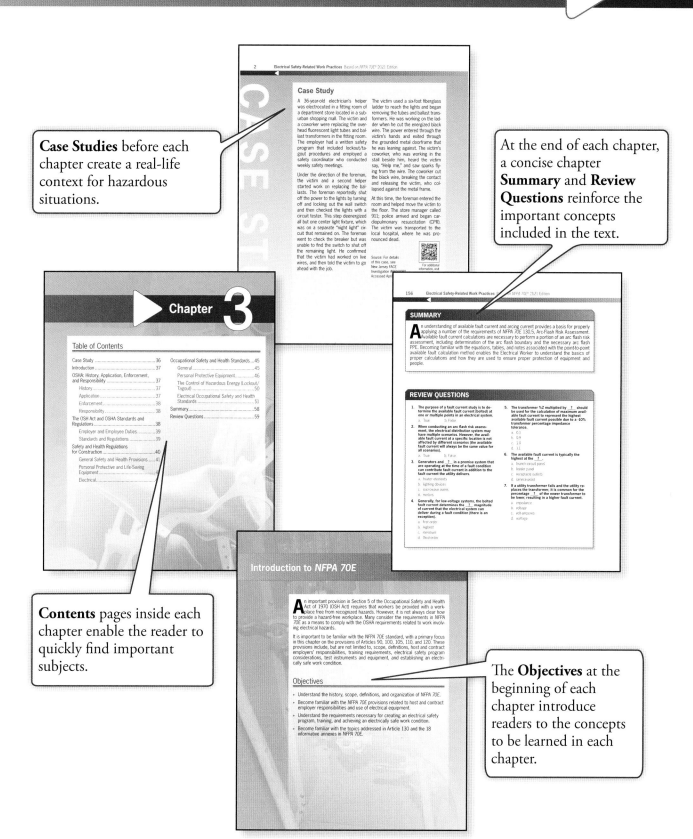

Case Studies before each chapter create a real-life context for hazardous situations.

At the end of each chapter, a concise chapter **Summary** and **Review Questions** reinforce the important concepts included in the text.

Contents pages inside each chapter enable the reader to quickly find important subjects.

The **Objectives** at the beginning of each chapter introduce readers to the concepts to be learned in each chapter.

Electrical Safety Culture

Too often a culture exists in the workplace where workers are routinely allowed and expected to work on or near energized electrical circuits. This practice might be due to ignorance of laws that have been in place for decades, lack of knowledge of the severity of the hazards, or perhaps failure to realize how quickly a task situation might change and cause an energy release.

This tendency to dismiss the risk of an electrical injury is unacceptable and must change. It is less likely that workers, contractors, and facility owners would allow energized work if everyone involved in the decision-making process fully understood the laws, requirements, hazards, true costs, and consequences associated with energized work.

Objectives

» Recognize the important role that a safety culture plays for every person and in every organization, and understand how it affects worker exposure to electrical hazards.

» Understand that a number of decisions are made before and during the time a worker is exposed to electrical hazards, and appreciate how decisions can reduce or eliminate electrical hazards.

» Identify the important role that understanding and complying with requirements plays in reducing and eliminating hazards.

Chapter 1

Table of Contents

CASE STUDY

Case Study

A 36-year-old electrician's helper was electrocuted in a fitting room of a department store located in a suburban shopping mall. The victim and a coworker were replacing the overhead fluorescent light tubes and ballast transformers in the fitting room. The employer had a written safety program that included lockout/tagout procedures and employed a safety coordinator who conducted weekly safety meetings.

Under the direction of the foreman, the victim and a second helper started work on replacing the ballasts. The foreman reportedly shut off the power to the lights by turning off and locking out the wall switch and then checked the lights with a circuit tester. This step deenergized all but one center light fixture, which was on a separate "night light" circuit that remained on. The foreman went to check the breaker but was unable to find the switch to shut off the remaining light. He confirmed that the victim had worked on live wires, and then told the victim to go ahead with the job.

The victim used a six-foot fiberglass ladder to reach the lights and began removing the tubes and ballast transformers. He was working on the ladder when he cut the energized black wire. The power entered through the victim's hands and exited through the grounded metal doorframe that he was leaning against. The victim's coworker, who was working in the stall beside him, heard the victim say, "Help me," and saw sparks flying from the wire. The coworker cut the black wire, breaking the contact and releasing the victim, who collapsed against the metal frame.

At this time, the foreman entered the room and helped move the victim to the floor. The store manager called 911; police arrived and began cardiopulmonary resuscitation (CPR). The victim was transported to the local hospital, where he was pronounced dead.

Source: For details of this case, see New Jersey FACE Investigation #95NJ080. Accessed April 6, 2020.

For additional information, visit qr.njatcdb.org Item #1184

INTRODUCTION

Too often a culture exists in the workplace where workers are routinely allowed and expected to work on or near energized electrical circuits. This tendency to dismiss the risk of an electrical injury is unacceptable and must change.

This practice might be due to ignorance of laws that have been in place for decades, lack of knowledge of the severity of the hazards, or perhaps failure to realize how quickly a task situation might change and cause an energy release. It is less likely that workers, contractors, and facility owners would allow energized work if everyone involved in the decision-making process fully understood the laws, requirements, hazards, true costs, and consequences associated with energized work.

SAFETY CULTURE

A false sense of security devalues safe practice. As a consequence, Electrical Workers may work on energized circuits owing to misperceptions of the risks involved. These paradigms are part of the electrical work culture, and may lead workers to take risks that are not in their best interest. Many do not understand the existing and potential hazards; others, who do understand these risks, do not realize how quickly a situation can change when things go wrong. The following list of statements reflects mindsets and attitudes that can lead to taking unnecessary risks:

- "I don't care what the law says—I'm going to work it energized."
- "I'm an Electrical Worker; working stuff hot is part of my job."
- "That's what the customer expects. If my people won't do it, then they'll get another contractor."
- "It's the office of the president of the company—you can't deenergize the circuit to change that ballast."
- "You can't shut that assembly line down because it will cost too much."
- "There are people out of work looking for a job, so if I won't work it hot, someone else will."

- "I've been doing it this way for 30 years, and nothing has ever happened to me."
- "I know I should be wearing personal protective equipment, but it slows me down."
- "There's no time to shut it down."
- "That protective equipment is too expensive."
- "What's the worst that can happen?"
- "It won't happen to me."

Far too many Electrical Workers believe that working on energized circuits is part of their job or is expected of them; in fact, such tasks are not part of routine electrical work. A tendency to work on or near electrical circuits while energized and dismiss the risk of an electrical injury creates an unacceptable culture. The need to change this mindset must be recognized by all involved in the decision-making process. **See Figure 1-1.**

Contractors have reported feeling pressured by their customers to work on energized equipment when a shutdown is warranted. Likewise, workers have reported feeling pressured by management to perform energized work when it is not justified. Workers who accept this risk expose themselves to injury or death. They also expose the contractors and their clients to undue risks of increased

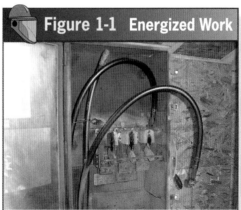

Figure 1-1 Energized Work

Figure 1-1. Energized work is permitted only under limited circumstances as set forth by the Occupational Safety and Health Administration (OSHA) and NFPA 70E®.

NFPA 70E® is a registered trademark of the National Fire Protection Association, Quincy, MA.

insurance premiums and loss of production. In many cases, customers may not understand the total costs and risks associated with energized work.

A well-informed client understands the hazards of energized work and the financial implications associated with an electrical incident. Equipment or circuits that are not permitted to be shut down for a few minutes ultimately might be shut down for days or weeks, or even longer, due to an unplanned event such as a dropped tool or a loose part falling into energized equipment and creating an unscheduled shutdown. A well-informed client is less likely to permit energized work, much less expect it.

HAZARD AWARENESS AND RECOGNITION

A full understanding and recognition of existing and potential hazards is crucial to ensuring that an environment is electrically safe. The following must be done at a minimum:

- Eliminate the hazard.
- Develop and implement appropriate procedures.
- Develop, conduct, and implement training for qualified and unqualified persons.
- Deenergize and follow all of the necessary steps of the lockout/tagout program and establish an electrically safe work condition unless the employer demonstrates

a true need for energized work.
- Develop and implement a risk assessment procedure.
- Engineer out the hazards or reduce them as far as is practicable.
- Provide adequate protection against hazards when the need for energized work is demonstrated.

A comparison can be made between the hazards of driving an automobile and the hazards associated with working on or near energized electrical equipment. Protective systems such as seat belts and air bags were developed to reduce the likelihood of injury or death; likewise, personal protective equipment (PPE) was developed to increase Electrical Worker safety. Such protections have a key limitation, however: they are effective only when they are actually used.

It is much the same with the hazards associated with working while exposed to electricity. Electrical Workers will continue to be exposed to electrical hazards if they do not take appropriate steps. Potential hazards in this environment include fire, falls and falling objects, electrical shock, and the hazards associated with arcing faults, including arc flash and arc blast.

An arcing fault is a fault characterized by an electrical arc through the air. Arc flash is a dangerous condition caused by the release of energy in an electric arc, usually associated with electrical distribution equipment. **See Figure 1-2.** An arcing fault, for example, could be initiated by a dropped tool or by operation of equipment that has not been maintained properly. Electrical Workers may believe that the chance of such a lapse is unlikely; however, it may need to happen only once to result in injury or death. If used, protective systems, work practices, and protective equipment can reduce or eliminate exposure to the hazards. Workers may still suffer injury or death if circuits and equipment are not worked on in an electrically safe work condition. An electrically safe work condition is defined in *NFPA 70E* Article 100 and established through the implementation of the requirements in Article 120.

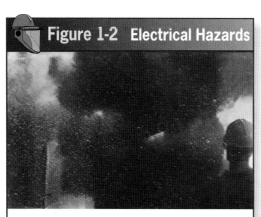

Figure 1-2 Electrical Hazards

Figure 1-2. *Shock, arc flash, and arc blast subject workers to a number of hazards.*

Courtesy of Eaton's Bussmann Division

Background

Historical Methods for Testing Voltage

As late as the mid-1900s, Electrical Workers performed testing for voltage procedures by employing a variety of less desirable techniques when viewed from today's perspective. On lower voltages typically found on bell, signal, and low-voltage control work, the presence of voltage (or pressure, as it commonly was called) could be tested using the "tasting method."

- The worker would strip the ends of the conductors from both sides of the circuit and place the ends of these conductors a short distance apart on the tongue. The "tester" would experience a burning sensation followed by a slight salt taste. Depending on the amount of voltage present, holding one of the conductors in the bare hand and touching the other to the tongue could also be used. In this case, the body was acting as a voltage divider, lessening the burning sensation on the tongue.

Other variations of voltage testing included standing on wet ground when one end of the voltage system was grounded, while touching the tongue with the other terminal of the voltage source. This also was an "approved method." Individuals using this method were known to state that once these test methods were performed, the end result was not easily forgotten.

On higher voltages typically found in building power applications, the "finger method" was employed as an acceptable method of determining the presence of voltage in circuits of 250 volts or less.

- Electrical Workers would test the wires for voltage by touching the conductors to the ends of the fingers on one hand. Often, due to skin thickness, skin dryness, and calluses, the Electrical Worker would have to first lick the fingers to wet them to be able to sense the voltage being measured.

This method was billed as easy and convenient for determining whether live wires were present. The individual Electrical Worker's threshold for pain determined whether or not this was an acceptable method for everyday use. Some Electrical Workers supposedly had the ability, depending on the intensity of the sensation, to determine the actual voltage being tested.

Source: American Electrician's Handbook: A Reference Book for Practical Electrical Workers, 5th edition, by Terrell Croft (revised by Clifford C. Carr). Copyright © 1942 by The McGraw-Hill Companies, Inc. Reprinted by permission of The McGraw-Hill Companies, Inc.

The hazard of electrical shock has been recognized since the dawn of electricity. The industry has evolved and made great strides to protect against electrical shock through the use of ground-fault circuit interrupters (GFCIs) and rubber protective goods such as insulating gloves and blankets.

These products are effective when used and maintained properly. Even with these advances, however, injury and death still occur from electrical shock. **See Figure 1-3.**

A snapshot into this hazard comes from the Bureau of Labor Statistics (BLS) historical data. For electric shocks in nonfatal cases involving days away from work for the period 1992–2001, the data indicate an average of 2,726 cases annually in private industry.

Arc flash and arc blast constitute lesser-known hazards; electrical burns

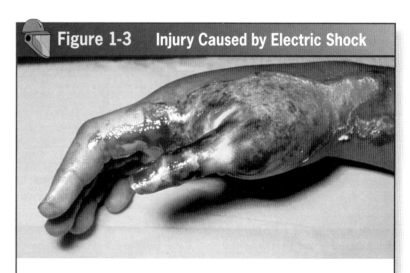

Figure 1-3   Injury Caused by Electric Shock

Figure 1-3. The consequences of exposure to electrical hazards are often traumatic.

Courtesy of Charles Stewart & Associates

Background

Cardiopulmonary Resuscitation: Accepted Practice in the Early 1900s

A review of several techniques used as methods of resuscitation show that medical technology has come a long way since the early 1900s.

The primary method of treating an individual who had experienced heart failure and/or respiratory arrest was simple. This primary method required two rescuers to perform the resuscitation procedure:

- After placing the victim on his or her back, one rescuer would grab and wiggle the victim's tongue, while the other rescuer would work the victim's arms back and forth to help induce breathing.

While this possibly resuscitated some stricken individuals, a secondary approach was to be used should the first method fail:

- In cases where manual inflation of the lungs was attempted with no success, an attempt to cause the victim to gasp for air was performed. To initiate this gasping, the rescuers would insert two fingers into the victim's rectum, pressing them suddenly and forcibly towards the back of the individual.

Needless to say, today's CPR methods provide more favorable results for both the victim and the rescuer.

Source: The Fire Underwriters of the United States, Standard Wiring: Electric Light and Power. H. G. Cushing Jr., New York, NY, 1911.

happen frequently. The historical BLS data for nonfatal cases involving days away from work for the period 1992–2001 indicate an average of 1,710 electrical burns per year (peaking at 2,200 in 1995) in private industry. That averages out to nearly one worker suffering the consequences of electrical burns every hour, based on a 40-hour work week. These data were instrumental in advancing electrical safety in general and *NFPA 70E* in particular during that time period.

OSHA Tip

Occupational Safety and Health Administration (OSHA) 29 CFR 1910.333(a)(1)

Deenergized parts. Live parts to which an employee may be exposed shall be deenergized before the employee works on or near them, unless the employer can demonstrate that deenergizing introduces additional or increased hazards or is infeasible due to equipment design or operational limitations. Live parts that operate at less than 50 volts to ground need not be deenergized if there will be no increased exposure to electrical burns or to explosion due to electric arcs.

Recognizing Limitations of PPE

It is important to recognize that electrical protective equipment provides limited protection against electrical hazards, much like seat belts and air bags provide limited protection from the hazards that could be encountered in an automobile accident. In much the same way that a hard hat could not be expected to protect a worker from a falling steel beam, arc-rated garments should not be expected to always allow a worker to escape an incident unscathed. An arc rating is defined in *NFPA 70E*.

Although arc-rated apparel might provide a level of protection against a thermal event for which it is rated, many other hazards might be associated with an incident. Explosive effects, including shrapnel, could rip through protective clothing; a pressure wave could rupture eardrums; or the differential pressure that results from the wave might collapse lungs and damage other internal organs. Review 130.7(A) Informational Note No. 1 and 130.7(C)(15)(c) Informational Note No. 2. This explanatory material advises of the limitations of PPE requirements.

Understanding Requirements

It is safe to assume that not all energized work performed today falls within what OSHA recognizes as justification to work on an energized circuit. OSHA requires employers to furnish each employee with a place of employment free from recognized hazards that are causing or are likely to cause death or serious physical harm. Live parts to which an employee might be exposed must be deenergized before the employee works on or near them, unless the employer can demonstrate that deenergizing introduces additional or increased hazards or is infeasible due to equipment design or operational limitations.

It is worthwhile to consider why some laws are followed routinely while others, such as refraining from working on exposed energized electrical equipment, are often ignored. One factor that can lead to the performance of energized work is ignorance of the laws in effect. It is critical to recognize the limitations on energized work. Both *NFPA 70E* and OSHA generally stipulate that energized work is permitted only where the employer can demonstrate that deenergizing introduces additional or increased hazards or where the task to be performed is infeasible in a deenergized state due to equipment design or operational limitations. **See Figure 1-4.** Equipment must be locked out and tagged out in accordance with established policy, unless the need to work energized is demonstrated.

Electrical Workers must be intimately familiar with company policies on working while exposed to electrical hazards. While it may be laudable to work on energized equipment only when "we absolutely have to," that may not be entirely possible. For example, voltage testing is among the tasks that are infeasible to perform deenergized. However, as the OSHA and *NFPA 70E* requirements are fully explored, it will become apparent that the vast majority of work performed on energized equipment does not qualify as work allowed by OSHA and *NFPA 70E*.

DECISIONS

Many choices about how to perform a task are made long before a worker is placed before a hazard. Other decisions are made along the way. Many decisions are made just before, and even during, the performance of a task.

Many factors should be considered in creating a safe work environment. The following questions should be among those included in the development and implementation of a safety program, training, and risk assessment procedure:
- Has an electrical safety program been developed and implemented?
- Has appropriate training been provided?

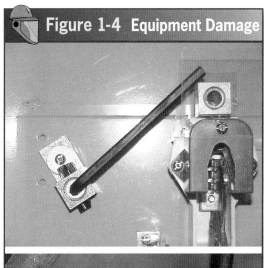
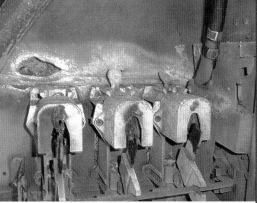

Figure 1-4 Equipment Damage

Figure 1-4. Personnel and equipment could be severely damaged in the event of a mishap during energized work.

- Are safe work practices in place and understood, including lockout/tagout and placing equipment in an electrically safe work condition?
- Has the required protective equipment been provided?
- Has an attempt been made to reduce the potential worker exposure through work practice or design considerations, such as implementation of the hierarchy of risk control methods or arc-resistant switchgear or remote switching?
- Was the overcurrent protection selected solely to protect the equipment or was worker protection considered as well?
- Was a current-limiting overcurrent protective device (OCPD) selected?
- Was the OCPD applied within its rating?
- If the OCPD was replaced, was the appropriate degree of current limitation applied?
- Has the OCPD been maintained properly?
- Has the impedance on the transformer on the supply side of the service changed?

These are among a few of the concerns that must be addressed when a hazard identification and risk assessment procedure is conducted.

Appropriate Priorities

A corporation's management might say that it cannot afford to develop a safety program, provide necessary training, or provide the appropriate PPE and insulated tools. In such a case, corporate priorities should be analyzed. While there may be other important financial priorities, crucial items such as appropriate training and PPE should always be a primary consideration.

70E Highlights

See the Hierarchy of Risk Control Methods in 110.5(H)(3).

70E Highlights

NFPA 70E includes informational notes. Per *NFPA 70E* Section 90.4(C), these materials are considered informational only and are not enforceable as requirements.

Training and Personal Responsibility

Some Electrical Workers who fail to maintain a safety culture might argue that they were never trained or were never provided with the required protective equipment. It is possible that a worker might receive training in safe work practices, but then fail to implement that training. In such a case, there is no lack of training, but the worker makes the conscious decision not to wear protective equipment. Other barriers to working in an electrically safe work condition include a lack of a safety program and, as discussed, a lack of understanding of the hazards.

Costs of Energized Work Versus Shutting Down

The true cost of an electrical injury or fatality must be considered before deciding that work must be performed on energized equipment. Consider the following:

- What is the true cost if something goes wrong?
- As mentioned earlier, a shutdown that "cannot" be scheduled could become an unscheduled shutdown. An unscheduled shutdown may ultimately cost more than a planned shutdown.
- Have the costs associated with human life, equipment, loss of production, insurance premium increases, potential exclusion from bid lists, corporate image, and worker morale been considered in the decision-making process?
- Can the equipment be shut down at night when potentially fewer people will be inconvenienced?
- Can equipment be shut down over the weekend?
- Can a shutdown be scheduled at some other time?

Consider whether supervisors are rewarded for safety shortcuts. Are the costs associated with injuries and citations charged against the job, or are they considered overhead (a cost of doing business)? If such costs are not charged against the job, a job site where injuries occur may appear to be more profitable than it really is. A manager who is rewarded for safety shortcuts may not make decisions that are in the best interest of Electrical Workers or the company.

Time Pressure

Imagine an Electrical Worker operating out of a service truck who responds to a report of a transfer switch that malfunctioned at 3 a.m. at a nursing home. In such a case, the worker will be expected to get the power restored as soon as possible. An Electrical Worker must adjust the customer's understanding of "as soon as possible" to include working safely, and the added time that working safely could require. The Electrical Worker must know how to evaluate the magnitude of the hazards present, and how to make decisions about the job while simultaneously prioritizing electrical safety.

Employee Qualification

Electrical Workers must be qualified to perform the tasks to which they are assigned. An Electrical Worker must receive qualification in advance of responding to an emergency call. In such a case, items to consider include the following: Is the personal and other protective equipment in the truck? Is the protection adequate? Is the Electrical Worker qualified to make those decisions at the job site, or will someone from the engineering department need to be consulted as well? Has the worker been trained to know how to use the equipment properly and understand its limitations?

Background

INTRODUCTION TO THE NIOSH FACE PROGRAM

The National Institute for Occupational Safety and Health's (NIOSH) Fatality Assessment and Control Evaluation (FACE) program is a research program designed to identify and study all fatal occupational injuries, including those of an electrical nature. The goal of the FACE program is to prevent occupational fatalities across the United States by identifying and investigating work situations at high risk for injury and then formulating and disseminating prevention strategies to those who can intervene in the workplace.

FACE Program's Two Components

NIOSH's in-house FACE began in 1982. Participating states voluntarily notify NIOSH of traumatic occupational fatalities resulting from targeted causes of death that have included confined spaces, electrocutions, machine-related fatalities, falls from elevation, and logging incidents. The program is currently focusing on deaths associated with machinery, deaths of youths younger than 18 years of age, and street/highway construction work-zone fatalities.

The FACE program began operating as a state program in 1989. Today, nine state health or labor departments have cooperative agreements with NIOSH for conducting surveillance, targeted investigations, and prevention activities at the state level using the FACE model.

FACE is a research program; investigators do not enforce compliance with state or federal occupational safety and health standards and do not determine fault or blame.

Primary Activities of the FACE Program

The primary activities of the FACE program include the following:
- Conducting surveillance to identify occupational fatalities
- Performing investigations of specific types of events to identify injury risks
- Developing recommendations designed to control or eliminate identified risks
- Making injury prevention information available to workers, employers, and safety and health professionals

Background cont.

On-Site Investigations

On-site investigations are essential for observing sites where fatalities have occurred and for gathering facts and data from company officials, witnesses, and coworkers. Investigators collect facts and data on what was happening just before, at the time of, and right after the fatal injury. These facts become the basis for writing investigative reports.

During the on-site investigations, facts and data are collected on items such as the following:

- Type of industry involved
- Number of employees in the company
- Company safety program
- The victim's age, sex, and occupation
- The working environment
- The tasks the victim was performing
- The tools or equipment the victim was using
- The energy release that resulted in fatal injury
- The role of management in controlling how these factors interact

Each day, on average, 16 workers die as a result of a traumatic injury on the job. Investigations conducted through the FACE program allow the identification of factors that contribute to fatal occupational injuries. This information is used to develop comprehensive recommendations for preventing similar deaths.

FACE Information and Reports

Surveillance and investigative reports are maintained by NIOSH in a database. NIOSH researchers use this information to identify new hazards and case clusters. FACE information may suggest the need for new research or prevention efforts or for new or revised regulations to protect workers. NIOSH publications are developed to highlight high-risk work situations and to provide safety recommendations. These reports are disseminated to targeted audiences and are available on the Internet through the NIOSH homepage or through the NIOSH publications office.

The names of employers, victims, and/or witnesses are not used in written investigative reports or included in the FACE database.

Adapted from: Fatality Assessment and Control Evaluation (FACE) program website. Accessed April 6, 2020.

For additional information, visit qr.njatcdb.org
Item #4271

SUMMARY

The list of workers' perspectives addressing safety culture might seem justified and realistic. It might be true that the worker is pressured to do a job quickly or that PPE seems inconvenient or uncomfortable to wear. Nevertheless, not wearing PPE increases the potential for serious injury and—even worse—death. When a work situation is so inherently dangerous, issues such as time pressure are irrelevant. The need to ensure the worker's safety overrides any other concerns that, though real and pressing, are not nearly as important.

A customer's needs, while important to a business, should not be prioritized over the need of the worker to remain alive and uninjured. Remember the family and friends who will suffer the consequences of these decisions if things go wrong. Whether an incident results in an injury or a fatality, family and friends suffer emotionally and financially. If the worker does survive, he or she often requires months or years of rehabilitation.

A person might get only one chance to make a decision that those left behind will regret for years, or a lifetime. What would a loved one recommend when asked if it is worth the risk of ignoring the rules "just this one time"?

SUMMARY cont.

There are many reasons why risks are taken. Sometimes, it could be calculated risk; at other times, it might be uninformed. Whatever the reason, it is not likely worth the risk.

There is little question that, all too often, a culture is in place where workers are allowed and expected to work on energized equipment. Too often the existing culture supports a tendency to work routinely on or near energized electrical circuits. The most important outcome—that the worker performs the work without becoming injured or killed—happens only when workers, contractors, and customers become educated about the hazards and ways to properly handle them. Workers, contractors, and their customers must be made aware of the requirements that are in place, the hazards that exist, the decisions that can and should be made, and the true costs associated with an incident when things go wrong. It is a multifaceted challenge that requires a multifaceted education process and a multifaceted change in culture.

REVIEW QUESTIONS

1. Often, a culture exists in the workplace where workers are routinely expected or allowed to work on or near energized electrical circuits. This practice might be due to ignorance of laws that have been in place for decades, lack of knowledge of the severity of the hazards, or perhaps failure to realize how   ?   a task situation might change and cause an energy release.

    a. inexplicably
    b. quickly
    c. rarely
    d. slowly

2. It is less likely that workers, contractors, and facility owners would allow energized work if   ?   involved in the decision-making process fully understood the laws and requirements, hazards, true costs, and consequences associated with energized work.

    a. builders
    b. employees
    c. employers
    d. everyone

3. To ensure that an environment is electrically safe, the following must be done at a minimum: develop, conduct, and implement   ?   for qualified and unqualified persons, develop and implement risk assessment procedures, and engineer out the hazards or reduce them as far as is practicable.

    a. guidelines
    b. quizzes
    c. study skills
    d. training

4. The industry has evolved and made great strides to protect personnel against electrical shock through the use of   ?   and rubber protective goods such as insulating gloves and blankets.

    a. arc-fault circuit interrupters (AFCIs)
    b. circuit breakers
    c. fuses
    d. ground-fault circuit interrupters (GFCIs)

5. Electrical protective equipment generally does not provide protection from   ? .

    a. arc blast
    b. arc flash
    c. shock
    d. all of the above

6. An Electrical Worker must adjust the customer's understanding of "as soon as possible" while on a troubleshooting call to include the added time that could be required to work safely, evaluate the magnitude of the hazards present, and make decisions about the job.

    a. True   b. False

Electrical Hazard Awareness

Working on or near energized electrical equipment can be hazardous for Electrical Workers. Recognizing electrical hazards and understanding the severe consequences of that exposure are important steps to providing a workplace free from recognized hazards and implementing electrically safe work practices.

When a person works on or near electrical equipment and systems that are not in an electrically safe work condition, the electrical hazards are:

- Electric shock
- Arc flash burn
- Thermal burn
- Arc blast injury

To help workers recognize these electrical hazards, any discussion on electrical safety should examine the electric shock and arcing fault phenomena and the effects they can have on the human body if not properly protected. Also significant is the role overcurrent protective devices (OCPDs) play in the level of incident energy released during an arcing fault event.

Objectives

- » Identify electrical hazards.
- » Explain the effects of current on the human body.
- » Describe an arcing fault event and the effects it can have on the human body.
- » Relate the thermal energy released to the arcing fault current magnitude and time duration as well as the working distance from the arc source.
- » Understand the role of overcurrent protective devices in arcing fault energy release.

Chapter 2

Table of Contents

Case Study

A 19-year-old electrician's apprentice and a Journeyman Electrical Worker were installing two new switch boxes during an office building renovation project. The circuits in the room where the new switch boxes were being installed were deenergized, with the exception of the circuit to an existing metal switch box suspended by conduit from the ceiling. The circuit feeding the suspended switch box was energized by a 277-volt circuit from the adjacent room. A metal-sheathed cable fed this box and entered it through the box's side.

The Journeyman momentarily left the room and told the apprentice that "they would figure out how to wire the boxes" when he returned. Apparently, the apprentice thought the circuit feeding the suspended box was deenergized because it was in the same room as the new boxes being installed. While the apprentice was alone, he elected to disassemble the switch box suspended from the ceiling. He reached into the suspended box and cut the conductors from each of the four terminal connections in the box. Then, with his left hand, the apprentice pulled the metal sheathed conductor out of the switch box that he was holding in his right hand. The bare conductors must have contacted the box and/or his left hand. In turn, he provided a path to ground and was electrocuted. Burn marks found on the victim's right hand were consistent with the shape of the box.

The victim was found 14 feet from the switch box. Emergency medical services personnel responded and administered advanced cardiac life-support procedures. Attempts to resuscitate the victim were unsuccessful. He was pronounced dead on arrival at a nearby hospital.

Source: For details of this case, see FACE Program Case 87-34. Accessed April 9, 2020.

For additional information, visit qr.njatcdb.org Item #1186

INTRODUCTION

Electricity is pervasive in modern infrastructure. Electrical Workers continuously install, maintain, and troubleshoot circuits, and both they and their customers often take electricity for granted. Electricity, however, remains a very dangerous hazard for people working on or near it. Even when electrical circuits do not directly pose serious shock or burn hazards by themselves, these circuits are found adjacent to circuits with potentially lethal levels of energy. A minor electric shock from a low energy circuit can cause a worker to drop a tool onto another circuit, resulting in a lethal arcing fault. Involuntary reaction to an electric shock can result in bruises, bone fractures, and even death from collisions or falls.

NFPA 70E recognizes the following as electrical hazards, by definition. Electrical Workers can be exposed to these hazards by contact or equipment failure:

- Electric shock
- Arc flash burn
- Thermal burn
- Arc blast injury

A qualified person must be able to "identify the hazards and reduce the associated risk." See the *NFPA 70E* Article 100 definition for *qualified person*.

WORKPLACE HAZARDS

Electrical Workers face health and safety challenges on a daily basis. Potential dangers abound. As discussed in the chapter, "Electrical Safety Culture," potential reasons for the decision to expose oneself to dangers may include an incomplete understanding of the applicable safe work practices and requirements, such as a lack of understanding of the lockout/tagout program or poor retention of hazardous communication training. Workers may lack knowledge regarding how to read a Safety Data Sheet (SDS) or be unable to recall the location and availability of the written hazardous communication program and the required list of hazardous chemicals. Potential hazards include laser equipment, paints and solvents, improperly built scaffolding, and an improperly designed excavation. Unfortunately, not all Electrical Workers exposed to these and other hazards fully appreciate the exposures they face, nor do they always know how best to avoid the many potential dangers that can cause injury and death.

Though the workplace must be evaluated to identify and eliminate all hazards, the initial focus will primarily be on the electrical hazards of electric shock, arc flash, and arc blast.

ELECTRIC SHOCK

Most Electrical Workers are aware of the danger of electric shock, including electrocution. Historically, an electric shock is the electrical hazard most prominently mentioned in the majority of electrical safety standards. In reality, few Electrical Workers truly understand that only a minimal amount of current is required to cause injury or death. The current drawn by a 7.5-watt, 120-volt lamp, passing across the chest from hand to hand or from hand to foot, is enough to cause electrocution.

The effects of electric current on the human body depend on the following factors:

- Circuit characteristics (current, resistance, frequency, and voltage)
- Contact resistance and internal resistance of the body

OSHA Tip

Lockout is one of the main protective measures that can be taken to prevent workers from working on an energized circuit. This specific procedure involves placing a lockout device on an energy isolating device, making it physically impossible to operate the equipment until the lockout device is removed.

OSHA defines *lockout* in 1910.147(b) as follows:

Lockout. The placement of a lockout device on an energy-isolating device, in accordance with an established procedure, ensuring that the energy-isolating device and the equipment being controlled cannot be operated until the lockout device is removed.

OSHA Tip

Tagout is a protective measure in which a prominent warning device, such as a tag, is placed on the energy-isolating device, indicating that the equipment must not be operated. The tagout device warns that a worker might be injured if he or she operates the energy-isolating device.

OSHA defines *tagout* in 1910.147(b) as follows:

Tagout. The placement of a tagout device on an energy-isolating device, in accordance with an established procedure, to indicate that the energy-isolating device and the equipment being controlled may not be operated until the tagout device is removed.

- The current's pathway through the body, which is determined by the contact locations and internal body chemistry
- Duration of the contact
- Environmental conditions that affect the body's contact resistance

Skin and Internal Body Resistance

An integral concept for understanding the magnitude of a current flowing through the human body is skin-contact resistance. **See Figure 2-1.** The skin's resistance can change as a function of the moisture present in its external and internal layers, which can be altered by such factors as ambient temperatures, humidity, fear, and anxiety.

Body tissue, vital organs, blood vessels, and nerve (nonfat) tissue in the human body contain water and electrolytes, which are highly conductive and offer only limited resistance to electrical current. As the skin is broken down by electrical current, resistance drops and current levels increase.

Consider a person with hand-to-hand resistance of 1,000 ohms. The voltage determines the amount of current passing through the body. While 1,000 ohms might appear to be low, even lower levels can occur. For example, an Electrical Worker wearing sweat-soaked non-insulating gloves on both hands while maintaining a full-hand grasp of an energized bare conductor and a grounded pipe or conduit would approach lower levels. Moreover, cuts, abrasions, or blisters on hands can negate skin resistance, leaving only internal body resistance to oppose current flow. A circuit in the range of 50 volts could be dangerous in this instance.

Figure 2-1	Human Resistance Values	
	Resistance (ohms)	
Condition	**Dry**	**Wet**
Finger touch	40,000 to 1,000,000	4,000 to 15,000
Hand holding wire	15,000 to 50,000	3,000 to 6,000
Finger-thumb grasp	10,000 to 30,000	2,000 to 5,000
Hand holding pliers	5,000 to 10,000	1,000 to 3,000
Palm touch	3,000 to 8,000	1,000 to 2,000
Hand around 1 1/2-inch pipe	1,000 to 3,000	500 to 1,500
Two hands around 1 1/2-inch pipe	500 to 1,500	250 to 750
Hand immersed	N/A	200 to 500
Foot immersed	N/A	100 to 300
Human body, internal, excluding skin	200 to 1,000	
N/A: Not applicable		
Data source: Kouwenhoven, W. B., and Milnor, W. R., Field Treatment of Electric Shock Cases—1, AIEE Trans. Power Apparatus and Systems, Volume 76, pp. 82–84, April 1957; discussion pp. 84–87.		

Figure 2-1. *Human resistance values range for a variety of skin-contact conditions.*

Using Ohm's Law, the current (*I*, in amperes) in a circuit can be calculated based on the circuit voltage (*V*) and the resistance (*R*). *Ohm's Law* is the mathematical relationship between voltage, current, and resistance in an electrical circuit; it states that current flowing in a circuit is proportional to electromotive force (voltage) and inversely proportional to resistance: $I = E \div R$. Current (amperes) equals voltage (volts) divided by resistance (ohms), a relationship that may be expressed in equation form:

$$I \text{ (amperes)} = \frac{V \text{ (volts)}}{R \text{ (ohms)}}$$

$$\text{Example 1: } I = \frac{480}{1,000}$$

$$= 0.480 \text{ amp (480 mA)}$$

$$\text{Example 2: } I = \frac{120}{1,000}$$

$$= 0.120 \text{ amp (120 mA)}$$

Electrical currents flowing through the body can cause muscles to lock up, resulting in the inability of a person to release their grip from the current source. The lowest current at which muscle lockup occurs is known as the let-go threshold current. The *let-go threshold* is the electrical current level at which the brain's electrical signals to muscles can no longer overcome the signals introduced by an external electrical system. Because these external signals lock muscles in the contracted position, the body may not be able to let go when the brain tells it to do so. At 60 hertz, most people have a let-go threshold of 10 to 40 milliamperes. **See Figure 2-2.**

Potential injury (current flow) also increases with time. A victim who cannot "let go" of a current source is much more likely to be electrocuted than someone whose reaction removes him or her from the circuit more quickly. A victim who is exposed for only a fraction of a second is less likely to sustain an injury.

Data addressing the levels where DC current starts flowing through the body are not identical to the information

Figure 2-2   Electric Shock Effects

Response	60 Hz AC Current (mA)
Tingling sensation	0.5 to 3
Muscle contraction and pain	3 to 10
Let-go threshold	10 to 40
Respiratory paralysis	30 to 75
Heart fibrillation; might clamp tight	100 to 200
Tissue and organ burns	More than 1,500

Data source: Kouwenhoven, W. B., and Milnor, W. R., Field Treatment of Electric Shock Cases—1, AIEE Trans. Power Apparatus and Systems, Volume 76, pp. 82–84, April 1957; discussion pp. 84–87.

Figure 2-2. *The effects of electric shock vary according to current level (60 Hz AC).*

presented. However, the nature of DC is that the current remains at the same magnitude, whereas AC approaches and goes through zero 120 times a second for a 60-hertz system. Consequently, a DC system can represent a more severe electric shock hazard than an equivalent magnitude AC system.

Extent of Injury

The most damaging paths for electrical current are through the chest cavity or head. **See Figure 2-3.** Any prolonged exposure to 60-hertz current of 10 milliamperes or more might be fatal. Fatal

Figure 2-3   Current Pathways

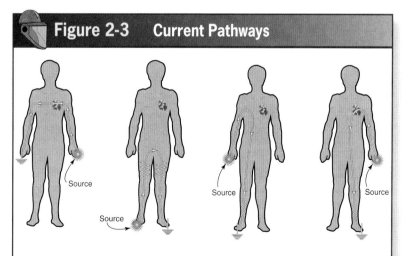

Figure 2-3. *Current pathways through the body include hand to hand, foot to foot, right hand to right foot, and left hand to left foot.*

ventricular fibrillation of the heart (a state in which the heart begins twitching, stopping its rhythmic pumping action) can be initiated by a current flow of 100 to 200 milliamperes. These injuries can cause fatalities resulting from direct paralysis of the respiratory system, failure of the rhythmic heart-pumping action, or immediate heart stoppage.

During fibrillation, the victim might become unconscious. Alternatively, the individual may remain conscious, deny needing help, walk a few feet, and then collapse. Either situation can result in death within a few minutes or hours. Prompt medical attention is needed for anyone receiving an electric shock. Many people involved in electrical incidents can be saved, provided that they receive proper medical treatment, including cardiopulmonary resuscitation (CPR), quickly.

Typically, the extent of injury resulting from electric shock may not immediately be visible because the current flows through muscle tissue and organs and not through the skin, except at the entrance and exit points. Entrance and exit wounds are usually coagulated areas and may exhibit charring. Or, these areas might be missing, having "exploded" away from the body due to the level of energy present. The smaller the area of contact, the greater the heat produced. For a given current, damage in the limbs might be the greatest due to the higher current flux per unit of cross-sectional area.

Within the body, the current can burn internal body parts in its path, yet leave the skin unaffected. This type of injury might be difficult to diagnose, as the only initial signs of injury are the entry and exit wounds. Damage to the internal tissues along the current path, while not apparent immediately, might cause delayed internal tissue swelling and irritation. Prompt medical attention can minimize possible loss of blood circulation. However, for some surviving electric shock victims, so much internal tissue is permanently damaged that amputation of an extremity is necessary to prevent death.

Prevention

All electrocutions are preventable. A significant number of OSHA requirements are dedicated to electrical safety. Current OSHA regulations were promulgated many years ago; OSHA compliance is considered a minimum requirement for improving the safety of the workplace.

Several standards offer insight regarding safe approach distances to minimize the possibility of electric shock from exposed electrical conductors of different voltage levels. Some of the most recent, and perhaps the most authoritative, requirements are presented in *NFPA 70E*: *Standard for Electrical Safety in the Workplace*®, in Section 130.4, Shock Risk Assessment. The requirements related to Shock Protection Approach Boundaries will be covered separately.

ARCING FAULTS: ARC FLASH AND ARC BLAST

The unique aspect of an arcing fault is that the fault current flows through the air between conductors or a conductor and a grounded part. The arc has an associated arc voltage because of arc impedance. The product of the arcing fault current and arc voltage in a concentrated area for a time duration may result in a tremendous amount of energy that is released in several forms. A simple image can represent the basics of various types of energies released during an arcing fault. **See Figure 2-4.** High energy release single-phase arcing faults can readily self-sustain on medium- and high-voltage systems. Single-phase arcing faults on systems of 600 volts AC or less are more difficult to self-sustain. The lower the system voltage, the lower the probability that a single-phase arcing fault will self-sustain.

70E Highlights

Refer to *NFPA 70E* Section 130.7(A) Informational Note, which provides guidance as to which hazards the PPE requirements of 130.7 are to protect against. Note that even with PPE, a person could sustain burns, but they should be survivable.

The most prevalent high energy release arcing fault scenario for systems of 600 volts or less is a 3-phase arcing fault. However, a single-phase arcing fault initiated on a 600-volt AC or less 3-phase circuit can rapidly escalate to a 3-phase arcing fault due to the resulting explosive metal vapor "cloud." DC arcing faults have a greater propensity to self-sustain than an arcing fault initiated on a single-phase AC circuit, since DC voltage does not approach and go to zero 120 times per second in a 60-hertz system. Therefore a DC arcing fault creates metal vapor more continuously, which increases its ability to self-sustain.

The resulting energies can take the form of intense heat, brilliant light, and tremendous pressures. The temperature of the arc terminals can reach approximately 35,000°F, which is about four times as hot as the surface of the sun. (Note: This value is taken from Annex K of the 2004 and 2009 editions of *NFPA 70E* and Informative Annex K in the 2012 and 2015 editions of *NFPA 70E.*) The high arc temperature changes the state of conductors from solid to both hot molten metal and metal vapor. The immediate vaporization of the conductors can be an explosive change in state. Copper vapor expands to 67,000 times the volume of solid copper; thus a copper conductive component the size of a penny could expand as it vaporizes to the size of a refrigerator. Because of the expansive vaporization of conductive metal, a line-to-line or line-to-ground arcing fault can escalate into a 3-phase arcing fault in a few thousandths of a second.

The release of intense thermal energy superheats the immediate surrounding air, which can also expand in an explosive manner. The rapid vaporization of conductors and superheating of air result in a pressure wave of air and gases and a conductive plasma cloud that can engulf a person. In addition, the pressure and thermal energy can violently destroy circuit components. Pressure waves can hurl destroyed, fragmented components like shrapnel in excess of 700 miles per hour, or about the speed at which shotgun pellets leave a gun barrel. Molten

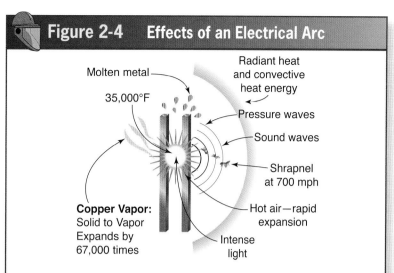

Figure 2-4   Effects of an Electrical Arc

Molten metal
35,000°F
Radiant heat and convective heat energy
Pressure waves
Sound waves
Shrapnel at 700 mph
Hot air—rapid expansion
Intense light

Copper Vapor: Solid to Vapor Expands by 67,000 times

Figure 2-4. *Current flows through the air between two copper conductors (represented by rods) during an electric arc.*

metal droplets at high temperatures are also typically blown out from the event due to the pressure waves.

Testing has proved that the arcing fault current magnitude and time duration are among the most critical variables in determining the amount of energy released. Notably, the predictability of arcing faults and the energy released by an arcing fault are subject to significant variance. Among the variables that affect the outcome are the following:
- Available fault current (bolted): arcing fault current is proportional to the available fault current (bolted). The greater the available fault current, the greater the available arcing fault current; however, it is a nonlinear relationship
- The time the fault is permitted to flow, typically determined by the speed of the overcurrent protective device or other means to sense and interrupt arcing fault currents
- Arc-gap spacing
- Size of the enclosure (or lack of an enclosure)
- System voltage
- Whether the arcing fault can sustain itself

Another important variable for an Electrical Worker exposed to an arcing fault event is the distance between the

Caution

It is not necessary to be in contact with the circuit to incur a serious burn. Serious or fatal burns can occur at distances of more than 10 feet from energized conductors.

worker's body parts and the arcing fault source. The farther an Electrical Worker is from the arc source, the less thermal energy is impressed on the Electrical Worker.

Arc Flash

Arc flash is the hazard associated with the release of energy caused by an electrical arc. See *NFPA 70E* Article 100 for the definitions of *arc flash hazard* and *electrical hazard*. In recent years, awareness of arc flash hazards has been increasing.

Electrical burns are considered extremely hazardous for a number of reasons. Direct contact with the circuit is not necessary to incur a serious, even deadly, burn. In fact, serious or fatal burns can occur at distances of more than 10 feet from the source of an arc flash.

Ignition of flammable clothing worn by a worker is a cause of some of the most severe burns and fatalities. Molten metal splatter or thermal energy emitted from an arcing fault can ignite flammable clothing, and severe burns can result before the burning clothes can be removed.

When having to work in other than an electrically safe work condition, implement a hierarchy of risk control methods such as those in *NFPA 70E* 110.5(H)(3), where PPE is listed as the sixth of six preventative and protective risk control methods:

1. Elimination
2. Substitution
3. Engineering controls
4. Awareness
5. Administrative controls
6. PPE

Arc Flash Test Flammable Clothing

In this test, a flammable shirt made of a blend of polyester and cotton was exposed to an arcing fault approximately 18 inches from the arc source. If this were an actual incident, the person likely would have sustained second and third-degree burns over a large percentage of the body. These types of incidents can be avoided by working in an electrically safe work condition.

For additional information, visit qr.njatcdb.org
Item #4339

Three important terms related to Electrical Worker safety in regards to arc flash are defined in *NFPA 70E* Article 100:

Incident energy. The amount of thermal energy impressed on a surface, a certain distance from the source, generated during an electrical arc event. Incident energy is typically expressed in calories per square centimeter (cal/cm²).

Working Distance. The distance between a person's face and chest area and a prospective arc source.

Informational Note. Incident energy increases as the distance from the arc source decreases. See 130.5(C)(1) for further information.

Boundary, Arc Flash. When an arc flash hazard exists, an approach limit from an arc source at which incident energy equals 1.2 cal/cm² (5 J/cm²).

Informational Note: According to the Stoll skin burn injury model, the onset of a second degree burn on unprotected skin is likely to occur at an exporsure of 1.2 cal/cm² (5 J/cm²) for one second.

Arc Blast Injury

Arc blast injury is associated with the release of tremendous pressure that can occur during an arcing fault event. The worst arc blast hazards typically result from arcing faults that release high energy in a short-time duration. Various individuals and organizations in the industry have researched and continue to research ways to quantify the risks associated with arc blast injury. There is little or no information at this time on arc-blast hazard risk assessment or on ways to protect workers from an arc blast hazard. Arc flash suits and other arc-rated clothing used to protect Electrical Workers from arc flash burns might not protect them from arc blast.

How Arcing Faults Can Affect Humans

The physical effects of an arcing fault can be devastating to anyone exposed to one.

Burns are the most prevalent consequence of electrical incidents. These injuries can be due to either contact (electric shock hazard) or arc flash. Three basic types of such burns are distinguished:

- **Electrical burns due to current flow** – Tissue damage (whether skin-level or deeper) occurs because the body is unable to dissipate the heat from the current flow through the body. The damage to tissue can be internal and initially not obvious from external examination. Typically, electrical burns are slow to heal and frequently result in amputation.
- **Arc burns by radiant or convective heat** – Temperatures generated by electrical arcs can burn flesh and ignite clothing at a distance of 10 feet or more.
- **Thermal contact burns (conductive heat)** – These injuries are normally experienced from skin contact with the hot surfaces of overheated electrical conductors or a person's clothing that ignites due to an arc flash.

Studies show that when skin temperature is as low as 110°F, the body's temperature equilibrium begins to break down in about six hours. At 158°F, a one-second duration is sufficient to cause total cell destruction. Skin at temperatures of 205°F for more than 0.1 second can cause incurable third-degree burns. **See Figure 2-5.**

In addition to burn injuries, victims of arcing faults can experience damage to their sight, hearing, and lungs, as well as skeletal, respiratory, muscular, and nervous systems. The speed of an arcing fault event can be so rapid that the human system cannot react quickly enough for a worker to take corrective measures. The release of thermal energy and high-pressure waves, spewing of hot molten metal, intense light, hurling shrapnel, and the hot conductive plasma can be devastating in a fraction of a second. The intense thermal energy released can cause severe burns or ignite flammable clothing. Molten metal, when blown out from the circuit, can burn skin or ignite flammable clothing, resulting in serious burns over much of the body. The worker might inhale hot air and vaporized metal, sustaining severe injury to the respiratory system. The tremendous pressure blast from the vaporization of conducting materials and superheating of air can fracture ribs, collapse lungs, and knock a worker down or throw him or her some distance.

It is important to realize that the time in which the arcing fault event runs its course might be only a fraction of a second. In a few thousands of a second, a single-phase arcing fault can begin to escalate to a 3-phase arcing fault. Tremendous energy can be released in a few hundredths of a second. Humans cannot detect, comprehend, or react to events in these time frames.

Sometimes a greater respect for arcing fault and electric shock hazards is afforded to medium- and high-voltage systems. However, injury reports reveal that serious accidents occur on systems of 600 volts or less, in part because of the high fault currents that are possible. Also, some designers, managers, and workers may not take the same necessary precautions when designing or working on low-voltage systems.

Staged Arc Flash Tests

An ad-hoc electrical safety working group within the IEEE Petroleum and Chemical Industry Committee conducted staged arc flash tests to investigate arcing fault hazards. These tests and

Figure 2-5	Skin Temperature and Tolerance	
Skin Temperature	**Duration**	**Damage Caused**
110°F	6.0 hours	Cell breakdown begins
158°F	1.0 second	Total cell destruction
176°F	0.1 second	Curable (second degree) burns
205°F	0.1 second	Incurable (third degree) burns
Source: Bussmann Safety BASICs Handbook, 2004, Courtesy of Eaton's Bussmann Division		

Figure 2-5. *There is a relationship between skin temperature and tolerance.*

Figure 2-6 — Thresholds for Injury

Threshold for Injury	Measurement
Curable burn threshold	80°C / 176°F for 0.1 second
Incurable burn threshold	96°C / 205°F (just under the temperature where water will boil) for 0.1 second
Eardrum rupture threshold	720 lb/ft²
Lung damage threshold	1,728–2,160 lb/ft² (approximately the equivalent of a compact car resting its weight on one's chest)
OSHA-required ear protection threshold	85 decibel (db) for a sustained time period (Note: An increase of 3 db is equivalent to doubling the sound level.)

Source: Eaton's Bussmann Division 2014 SPD Electrical Protection Handbook.

Figure 2-6. There are several key thresholds for injury from an arcing fault.

Figure 2-7 — Results of Tests 4, 3, and 1

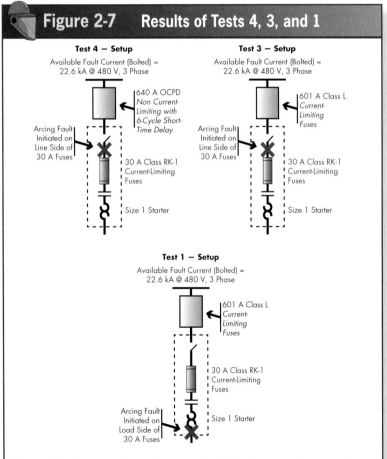

Figure 2-7. The one-line diagrams for Tests 4, 3, and 1 show the same available bolted fault current for all three tests, but the OCPDs differ and the physical point of initiation of the arcing fault differs.

Courtesy of Eaton's Bussmann Division

others are detailed in "Staged Tests Increase Awareness of Arc-Fault Hazards in Electrical Equipment" (*IEEE Petroleum and Chemical Industry Conference Record*, September 1997, pp. 313–322). To better assess the lessons learned from these tests, it is important to note some key thresholds of injury for humans. **See Figure 2-6.** Results of the staged arc flash tests were recorded by sensors on a mannequin and can be compared to these thresholds.

The results of three of the electrical safety working group's tests are identified as Test 4, Test 3, and Test 1. All three of these tests were conducted on the same electrical source 3-phase circuit, which was calibrated at an available bolted fault current of 22,600 symmetrical root mean square (RMS) amperes at 480 volts. Reviewing these test videos and test results illustrates that the thermal energy released during an arcing fault event is related to the magnitude and time duration of the arcing fault current. **See Figure 2-7.**

In each case, an arcing fault was initiated in a size 1 combination motor controller enclosure with the door open, as if an Electrical Worker were performing work on the unit while energized or before it was placed in an electrically safe work condition. The tests were filmed via high-speed camera, and still photos were extracted. The results of the tests were recorded from the various sensors on the mannequin closest to the arcing fault. T1 and T2 recorded the temperature on the bare hand and neck, respectively. The hand with the T1 sensor was very close to the arcing fault. T3 recorded the temperature on the chest under the shirt. P1 recorded the pressure on the chest. The sound level was measured at the ear. Some results "pegged the meter"—that is, the specific measurements were unable to be recorded because the actual level exceeded the range of the sensor/recorder setting. These values are shown as >, which indicates that the actual value exceeded the value given, but it is unknown how high the actual value was. These tests did not have sensing

Figure 2-8   Test 4

For additional information, visit qr.njatcdb.org Item #1223

Figure 2-8. Test 4 was a staged test in which the OCPD (not a current-limiting overcurrent protective device) interrupted the fault current in six cycles (0.1 second). Unexpectedly, there was an additional fault in the wireway, and the blast caused the cover to hit the mannequin in the head.

Courtesy of Eaton's Bussmann Division

equipment to measure the incident energy (IE), nor to determine the arc flash boundary (AFB). When incident energy and arc flash boundary values are calculated, the 2018 publication of *IEEE 1584, IEEE Guide for Performing Arc Flash Hazard Calculations*, is the source for the calculation method.

The 2018 version of *IEEE 1584* realizes that the size of the enclosure influences the amount of incident energy that the Electrical Worker will experience. For this example, the dimensions of 11.66 inches wide by 25.99 inches high and 8.03 inches deep are assumed for the size 1 combination motor controller enclosure taken from manufacturer catalogs relating to this solution. Additional parameters that will impact the calculations of incident energy and arc flash boundary include the configuration of the vertical conductors/electrodes inside the enclosure (VCB bus configuration), a 25-millimeter gap between electrodes, and a working distance of 18 inches.

Test 4 and Test 3 were identical except for the OCPD protecting the circuit. As used in this publication, the protecting-OCPD is the OCPD used to determine the incident energy and is upstream and often in a different location from the equipment upon which work is being conducted. In Test 4, the 640-ampere OCPD protecting the circuit cleared the test arcing fault current in six cycles. **See Figure 2-8, Figure 2-9, and Figure 2-10.**

Figure 2-9   Test 4 Results

Results: Test No. 4

Sound
141.5 db @ 2 ft

T2
> 225°C / 437°F

T3
50°C / 122°F

P1
> 2160 lbs/sq ft

T1
> 225°C / 437°F

> Indicates Meter Pegged

Figure 2-9. Monitoring sensors on the mannequin recorded these temperatures, pressures and sound levels.

Figure 2-10 Test 4 I.E. and Arc Flash Boundary

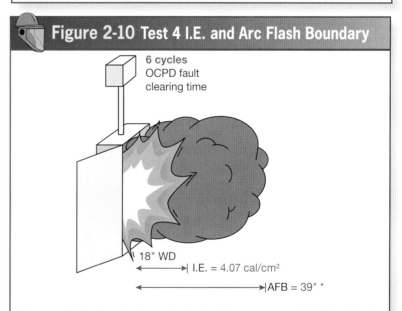

6 cycles
OCPD fault clearing time

18" WD
I.E. = 4.07 cal/cm²
AFB = 39" *

Figure 2-10. Analysis results in incident energy of 4.07 cal/cm² at 18-inch working distance and arc flash boundary of 39 inches. (Incident energy and arc flash boundary calculated using 2018 IEEE 1584.)

Figure 2-11   Test 3

For additional information, visit qr.njatcdb.org Item #1224

Figure 2-11. Test 3 was a staged test protected by KRP-C-601SP Low-Peak™ current-limiting fuses (Class L). These fuses were in their current-limiting range and cleared in less than ½ cycle (0.008 second).

Courtesy of Eaton's Bussmann Division

Figure 2-12   Test 3 Results

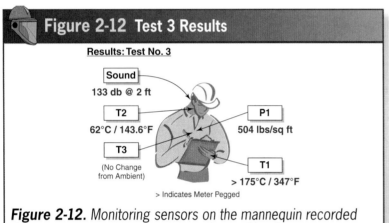

Results: Test No. 3

Sound
133 db @ 2 ft

T2
62°C / 143.6°F

T3
(No Change from Ambient)

P1
504 lbs/sq ft

T1
> 175°C / 347°F

> Indicates Meter Pegged

Figure 2-12. Monitoring sensors on the mannequin recorded these temperatures, pressures, and sound levels.

In Test 3, 601-ampere (KRP-C-601SP) current-limiting fuses (Class L) were protecting the circuit; these fuses opened the test arcing fault current in less than one half-cycle and limited the current. In addition, the arcing fault was initiated on the line side of the branch-circuit device in both Test 4 and Test 3 (the fault is on the feeder circuit, but within the controller enclosure). **See Figure 2-11, Figure 2-12, and Figure 2-13.**

Figure 2-13 Test 3 Incident Energy and Arc Flash Boundary

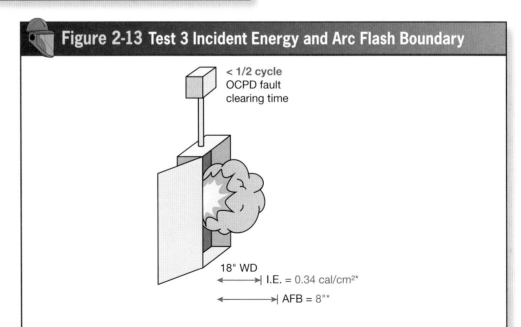

< 1/2 cycle
OCPD fault
clearing time

18" WD

I.E. = 0.34 cal/cm²*

AFB = 8"*

Figure 2-13. Analysis results in incident energy of 0.34 cal/cm² at 18 inches working distance and an arc flash boundary of 8 inches. (Incident energy and arc flash boundary calculated using 2018 IEEE 1584.)

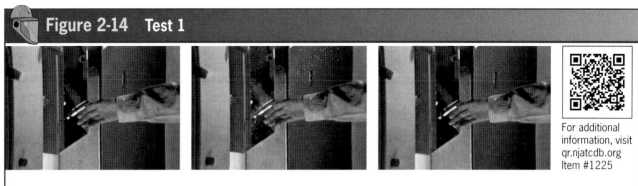

Figure 2-14   Test 1

For additional information, visit qr.njatcdb.org Item #1225

Figure 2-14. Test 1 was a staged test protected by LPS-RK-30SP, Low-Peak™ current-limiting fuses (Class RK1). These fuses were in current-limiting range and cleared in approximately 1/4 cycle (0.004 second).

Courtesy of Eaton's Bussmann Division

In Test 1, the arcing fault was initiated on the load side of the 30-ampere branch-circuit OCPD (LPS-RK 30SP) current-limiting fuses (Class RK1). **See Figure 2-14, Figure 2-15, and Figure 2-16.** These fuses limited this arcing fault current to a much lower level and cleared the circuit in approximately 1/4 cycle or less.

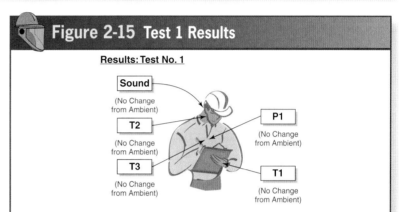

Figure 2-15   Test 1 Results

Results: Test No. 1

Sound (No Change from Ambient)

T2 (No Change from Ambient)

T3 (No Change from Ambient)

P1 (No Change from Ambient)

T1 (No Change from Ambient)

Figure 2-15. Monitoring sensors on the mannequin recorded these temperatures, pressures, and sound levels.

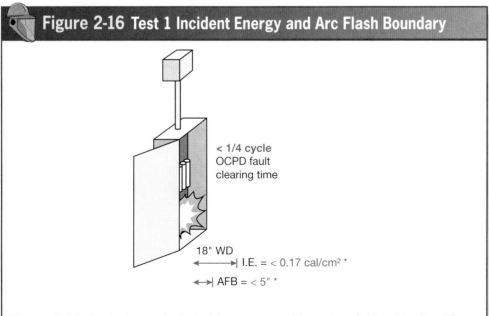

Figure 2-16   Test 1 Incident Energy and Arc Flash Boundary

< 1/4 cycle OCPD fault clearing time

18" WD

I.E. = < 0.17 cal/cm² *

AFB = < 5" *

Figure 2-16. Analysis results in incident energy of less than 0.17 cal/cm² at 18 inches working distance and an arc flash boundary of 5 inches. (Incident energy and arc flash boundary calculated using 2018 IEEE 1584.)

The Role of Overcurrent Protective Devices (OCPDs) in Electrical Safety

There are various means to mitigate arcing fault energy releases, but OCPDs are the most commonly used. The selection and performance of OCPDs can play a significant role in electrical safety. Extensive tests and analysis by industry members have shown that the energy released during an arcing fault is related primarily to two characteristics of the OCPD protecting the affected circuit:

- The time it takes the OCPD to open – The faster the fault is cleared by the OCPD, the lower the amount of energy released.
- The amount of fault current the OCPD lets through – Current-limiting OPCDs have the ability to reduce the arcing fault energy released if the arcing fault current is within the OCPD's current-limiting range.

The photos and recording sensor readings from Tests 4, 3, and 1 illustrate that the lower the amount of energy released, the better for both worker safety and equipment protection.

The following conclusions can be drawn from the staged tests:

1. Arcing faults can release tremendous amounts of energy in many forms in a very short period of time, as indicated by the measured values compared to key thresholds of injury for humans. Although the circuit in Test 4 was protected by a 640-ampere OCPD, it was a non–current-limiting device and took six cycles (0.1 second) to open.

Test	Overcurrent Protective Device	OCPD Clearing Time	Oscillograph of Arcing Fault Current	Incident Energy at 18" Working Distance *	Arc Flash Boundary *
4	640 ampere, non-current-limiting	Six cycles	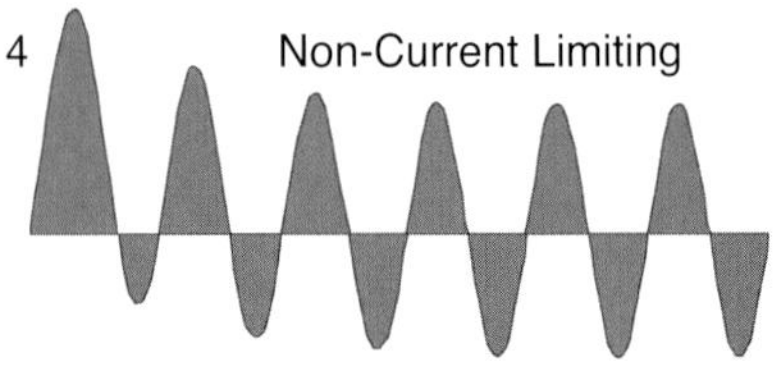 Test 4 — Non-Current Limiting	4.07 cal/cm²	39"
3	KRP-C601SP fuse, 601 ampere current-limiting (Class L fuse)	Less than ½ cycle	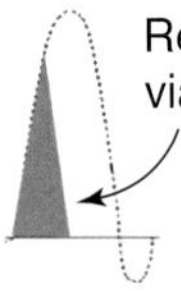 Reduce Fault Current via Current-Limitation	0.34 cal/cm²	8"
1	LPS-RK30SP fuse, 30 ampere current-limiting (Class RK1 fuse)	Less than ¼ cycle	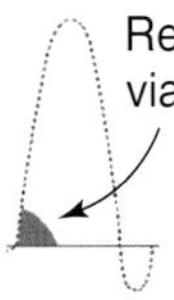 Reduce Fault Current via Current-Limitation	0.17 cal/cm²	5"

Figure 2-17   Comparison of Tests

* Incident energy and arc flash boundary calculated using 2018 IEEE 1584.

Figure 2-17. The three staged arc flash tests can be compared to determine the effects of the OCPDs used. Review the results of each test to compare the temperature, pressure, and sound values for each.

2. The OCPD's characteristic can have a significant impact on the outcome. A 601-ampere, current-limiting OCPD protected the circuit in Test 3. The current that flowed was reduced (limited), and the clearing time was one half-cycle or less. This was a significant reduction compared to Test 4. **See Figure 2-17.** Compare the Test 3 and Test 4 results to the threshold for injury values, and note the difference in exposure. In addition, note that the results of Test 1 are significantly less than those in Test 4, and even those in Test 3. The reason is that Test 1 utilized a much smaller (30-ampere) current-limiting device.

Test 3 and Test 1 both show that there are benefits of using current-limiting OCPDs. Test 1 proves the point that the greater the current limitation, the more the arcing fault energy may be reduced. Both Test 3 and Test 1 utilized current-limiting fuses, but the lower ampere-rated fuses limited the current more than the larger ampere-rated fuses. Note that the fault current must be in the current-limiting range of the OCPD to receive the benefit of the lower current let-through.

3. The shirt reduced the thermal energy exposure on the chest (the T3 sensor measured temperature under the shirt).

Emphasis on Increasing Distance and Reducing Arcing Fault Time and Current

Incident energy decreases as distance from the arc source increases. The farther a worker is from an arcing fault source of a specific energy release magnitude, the less thermal energy will be impressed on the worker. If an arcing fault occurs in open air and not in an enclosure, the thermal energy impressed on the object is inversely proportional to the square of the distance. **See Figure 2-18.** As an example, assume the incident energy at an 18-inch working distance is 36.05 cal/cm². The

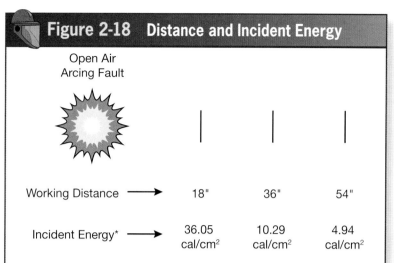

Figure 2-18 Distance and Incident Energy

Open Air Arcing Fault

Working Distance → 18" 36" 54"

Incident Energy* → 36.05 cal/cm² 10.29 cal/cm² 4.94 cal/cm²

Figure 2-18. The thermal energy impressed on an object is inversely proportional to the square of the distance from the arcing fault in open air.
* Incident energy and arc flash boundary calculated using 2018 IEEE 1584.

incident energy at a 36-inch working distance, twice the 18-inch working distance, would be 10.29 cal/cm² (36.05 ÷ 2² = 10.29). At a 54-inch working distance, which is three times the 18-inch working distance, the incident energy would be 4.94 cal/cm² (36.05 ÷ 3² = 4.94). (Incident energy and arc flash boundary calculations calculated using 2018 *IEEE 1584.*)

When an arcing fault occurs in an enclosure with the door open, the dynamics of the thermal energy impressed on an object at various distances do not exactly adhere to being inversely proportional to the square of the distance. However, a greater distance from an arcing fault source in an enclosure will still significantly reduce the incident energy in a similar exponential manner.

Time matters in the severity of energy released by an arcing fault. The thermal energy released is directly proportional to the time it takes to interrupt the fault current. In an example with a 20,000-ampere arcing fault current at 480 volts, 3-phase, if the OCPD clears in 0.01 second, the incident energy is calculated as 0.42 cal/cm² at a working distance of 18 inches. If the OCPD clearing time is 0.1 second, which is ten times longer, the incident energy is ten times greater, which is 4.2 cal/cm² at an 18-inch working distance. (Incident energy and arc flash boundary calculations calculated using 2018 *IEEE 1584*.)

The magnitude of the arcing fault current is the third variable that has a significant effect on the energy released during an arcing fault. For a given OCPD clearing time, comparing the incident energies and arc flash boundaries for a 20,000-ampere arcing fault current to those of a 10,000-ampere

---

Figure 2-19   Comparison of Arcing Fault Currents

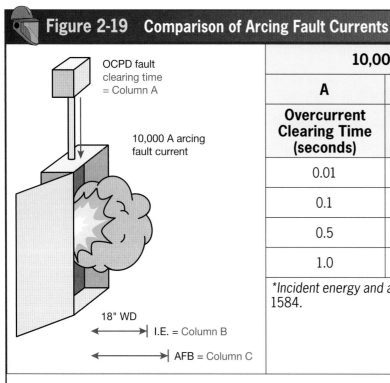

10,000 A Arcing Fault Current

A	B	C
Overcurrent Clearing Time (seconds)	Incident Energy * at 18" Working Distance (cal/cm²)	Arc Flash * Boundary (inches)
0.01	0.23	6
0.1	2.28	27
0.5	11.4	74
1.0	22.8	114

*Incident energy and arc flash boundary calculated using 2018 IEEE 1584.

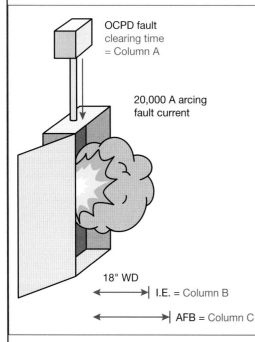

20,000 A Arcing Fault Current

A	B	C
Overcurrent Clearing Time (seconds)	Incident Energy * at 18" Working Distance (cal/cm²)	Arc Flash * Boundary (inches)
0.01	0.48	10
0.1	4.23	40
0.5	22.2	112
1.0	48.0	181

*Incident energy and arc flash boundary calculated using 2018 IEEE 1584.

Figure 2-19. *Compare the incident energy and arc flash boundary for various OCPD clearing times for two different arcing fault currents: 10,000 and 20,000 amperes. The system voltage is 480 volts, 3-phase.*

arcing fault current shows that the higher the arcing fault current, the higher the incident energy and arc flash boundary. **See Figure 2-19.**

Actual applications can result in different outcomes. When using OCPDs that have a fixed opening time and that are not current-limiting, the higher the available arcing current, the greater the resulting arc flash energies released.

However, high arcing fault currents do not necessarily result in high incident energies in all situations. For instance, if the protecting OCPD is current-limiting and in its current-limiting range for the available arcing fault current, the OCPD will reduce the magnitude of the arcing current that actually flows and clear the arcing current in less than one half-cycle. This results in lower incident energy levels for high available arcing fault currents, as illustrated by comparing Tests 4, 3, and 1.

Electrode Configuration

Additional study occurred in the area of arc flash calculations in the development of *IEEE 1584-2018* - an update to the prior version of the document released in 2002. The additional research resulted in a deeper understanding of the

arc flash phenomenon, revealing that other physical parameters of the equipment have an impact on the amount of incident energy that an Electrical Worker could experience. It was found that the electrode configuration and size of the enclosure plays an important role in the calculation of incident energy.

Electrode configuration is defined in *IEEE 1584-2018* as follows:

Electrode configuration: The orientation and arrangement of the electrodes used in the testing performed for the model development.

There are five general electrode configurations within electrical enclosures:
- Vertical conductors/electrodes inside a metal box/enclosure (VCB)
- Vertical conductors/electrodes terminated in an insulating barrier inside a metal box/enclosure (VCBB)
- Horizontal conductors/electrodes inside a metal box/enclosure (HCB)
- Vertical conductors/electrodes in open air (VOA)
- Horizontal conductors/electrodes in open air (HOA)

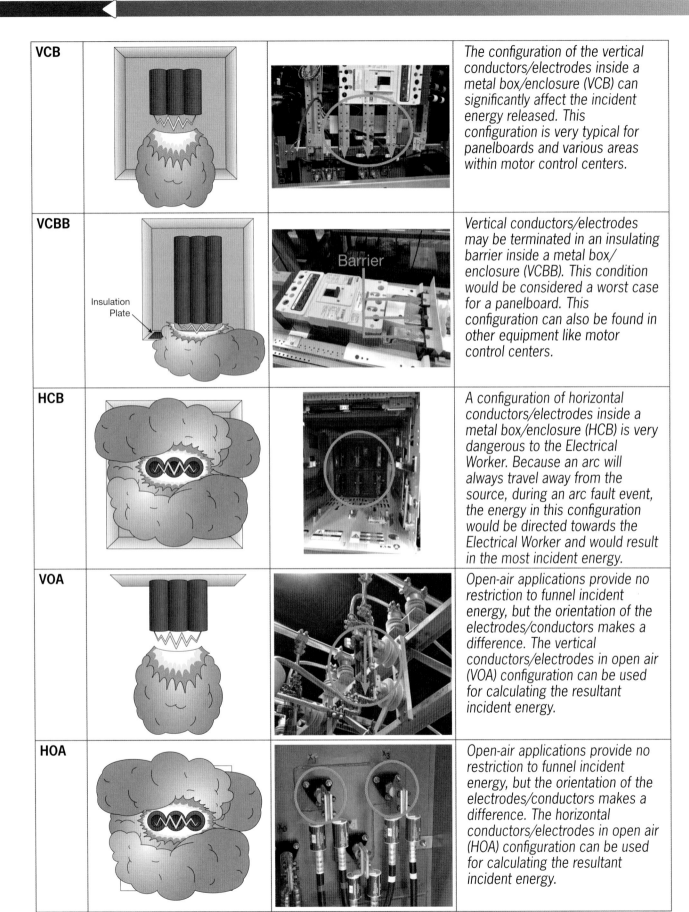

VCB			The configuration of the vertical conductors/electrodes inside a metal box/enclosure (VCB) can significantly affect the incident energy released. This configuration is very typical for panelboards and various areas within motor control centers.
VCBB			Vertical conductors/electrodes may be terminated in an insulating barrier inside a metal box/ enclosure (VCBB). This condition would be considered a worst case for a panelboard. This configuration can also be found in other equipment like motor control centers.
HCB			A configuration of horizontal conductors/electrodes inside a metal box/enclosure (HCB) is very dangerous to the Electrical Worker. Because an arc will always travel away from the source, during an arc fault event, the energy in this configuration would be directed towards the Electrical Worker and would result in the most incident energy.
VOA			Open-air applications provide no restriction to funnel incident energy, but the orientation of the electrodes/conductors makes a difference. The vertical conductors/electrodes in open air (VOA) configuration can be used for calculating the resultant incident energy.
HOA			Open-air applications provide no restriction to funnel incident energy, but the orientation of the electrodes/conductors makes a difference. The horizontal conductors/electrodes in open air (HOA) configuration can be used for calculating the resultant incident energy.

Insulation Plate

Barrier

In addition to the configuration of the bus/electrodes, the size of the enclosure makes a difference. Smaller enclosures can help force the energy in the direction of the Electrical Worker. Generally, everything else being equal, the larger the enclosure, the lower the calculated incident energy.

The impact of this new understanding of arc flash can be demonstrated through some sample calculations. **See Figure 2-20.**

Figure 2-20   Enclosure Size and Incident Energy

Voltage = 480 volts   Clearing time = 0.01 second
I_{sc} = 25,000 amperes   Working distance = 18 inches

	Base enclosure 457 in. × 254 in. × 146.1 in.	2x Size 914 in. × 508 in. × 146.1 in.	3x Size 1,828 in. × 1,016 in. × 146.1 in.
VCB	0.53 cal/cm²	0.39 cal/cm²	0.34 cal/cm²
VCBB	0.73 cal/cm²	0.54 cal/cm²	0.47 cal/cm²
HCB	1.06 cal/cm²	0.78 cal/cm²	0.67 cal/cm²
VOA	N/A	N/A	N/A
HOA	N/A	N/A	N/A

Figure 2-20. Incident energy varies depending on the size of an enclosure and the configuration of the electrodes within that enclosure.

SUMMARY

Recognizing the many hazards to which a worker might be exposed and understanding the severe consequences of that exposure are important steps in convincing everyone involved of the importance of providing a workplace free from recognized hazards. The electrical hazards associated with working on or near exposed energized electrical conductors include the following:

- Electric shock
- Arc flash burn
- Thermal burn
- Arc blast injury

Electric shock hazard is related to the magnitude of current and the path through the human body. Arc flash hazard is related to the arcing-current magnitude, the time duration, and the working distance from the arcing source. Overcurrent protection can have a significant role in the level of arc flash hazard present. Currently, there is insufficient information available to quantify arc blast hazards and recommend appropriate PPE.

REVIEW QUESTIONS

1. **Which of the following electrical hazards can potentially cause injury and even death to a person working on or near electrical equipment and systems?**
   a. Arc blast
   b. Arc flash
   c. Electric shock
   d. All of the above

2. **What is the approximate range of current needed to cause the onset of heart fibrillation?**
   a. 5 to 10 mA
   b. 10 to 20 mA
   c. 30 to 50 mA
   d. 100 to 200 mA

3. **Electrical currents flowing through the body can cause muscles to lock up, resulting in the inability of a person to release their grip from the current source.**
   a. True   b. False

4. **The effects of electrical current flowing through the human body depend on __?__ .**
   a. the amount of current through the body
   b. the current's pathway through the body
   c. the time duration of the contact
   d. all of the above
   e. none of the above

5. The most damaging path for electrical current is through the chest cavity or head. Ventricular fibrillation of the heart can cause fatalities resulting from __?__ .

   a. contractions of the digestive system

   b. indirect contact

   c. stopping the rhythmic heart-pumping action

   d. tingling sensations

6. Which standard offers requirements regarding safe approach distances for different voltage levels to minimize the possibility of electric shock from exposed electrical conductors?

   a. NFPA 70

   b. NFPA 70E

   c. NFPA 72

   d. NFPA 99

7. In an arcing fault, the resulting energies can be in the form of intense heat, brilliant light, and tremendous pressures. The temperature of the arc terminals can reach approximately __?__ , or about four times as hot as the surface of the sun.

   a. 650°F

   b. 800°F

   c. 1,900°F

   d. 35,000°F

8. Incident energy is the amount of energy impressed on a surface a certain distance from the source generated during an electrical arc event. One of the units used to measure incident energy is __?__ .

   a. amperes per square yard (A/yd²)

   b. calories per centimeter squared (cal/cm²)

   c. pounds per square foot (lb/ft²)

   d. watts per cubic foot (W/ft³)

9. Bare skin exposed to an arc flash event can result in injury due to thermal conditions. Skin exposed to temperatures of __?__ for more than 0.1 second can cause incurable third-degree burns.

   a. 110°F

   b. 158°F

   c. 176°F

   d. 205°F

10. The unique aspect of a(n) __?__ is that the fault current flows through the air between conductors or a conductor and a grounded part.

    a. arcing fault

    b. bolted fault

    c. electric shock hazard

    d. overload

11. Extensive tests and analysis by industry members have shown that the energy released during an arcing fault is related primarily to two characteristics of the OCPD protecting the affected circuit: OCPD interrupting rating and the amount of fault current the OCPD lets through.

    a. True   b. False

12. Incident energy __?__ as distance from the arc source increases.

    a. decreases

    b. increases

    c. stays the same

13. The thermal energy released by an arcing fault is __?__ proportional to the time it takes to interrupt the fault current.

    a. directly

    b. exponentially

    c. inversely

    d. not

14. When using OCPDs that have a fixed opening time and that are not current-limiting, the lower the available arcing current, the greater the resulting arc flash energies released.

    a. True   b. False

15. If the protecting OCPD is current-limiting and in its current-limiting range for the available arcing fault current, the OCPD will reduce the magnitude of the arcing current that actually flows and clear the arcing current in less than one half-cycle. The result is lower incident energy levels for high available arcing fault currents.

    a. True   b. False

OSHA Considerations

The Occupational Safety and Health Administration (OSHA) was established over 50 years ago when the U.S. Congress passed the Occupational Safety and Health Act (OSH Act) of 1970. Requirements were put in place that, when complied with, go a long way toward avoiding the hazards encountered in the workplace.

Electrical Workers are exposed to a number of hazards, and the work that they perform may be covered by any number of OSHA regulations. The primary focus is on the regulations in Part 1926, Safety and Health Regulations for Construction, and Part 1910, Occupational Safety and Health Standards.

The information discussed here is not intended to be all-inclusive. It is important to review the OSHA standards themselves to gain a full understanding of the regulations and safety measures required.

Objectives

» Demonstrate an understanding of OSHA's history, application, enforcement, and responsibility.

» Demonstrate an understanding of the OSH Act, the General Duty Clause, and OSHA Standards and Regulations.

» Understand the regulations presented in Part 1926, Safety and Health Regulations for Construction.

» Understand the regulations presented in Part 1910, Occupational Safety and Health Standards.

Chapter 3

Table of Contents

Case Study

A crew of electricians was working at a facility that was shut down for the July 4 holiday. The crew members had approximately one hour of work left to finish before they could go home and enjoy the holiday. The workers were pulling three sets of wiring from a source in the main plant to new electrical equipment in an addition to the facility. Two sets were for air conditioning and one set was for a new lighting panel. Each set of wiring had its own breaker, which the foreman—but not the lead electrician—had locked out, modifying the normally followed lockout/tagout procedure. Normally, the employee performing the work would place his or her lockout/tagout equipment on the breakers and then remove the lockout/tagout equipment after the work was completed.

After completing connections for the new lighting panel, the lead electrician was getting ready to connect the wires for the air conditioning. As he pulled the wires into a junction box, he tapped the ends of the wires on his right hand to make them even. He was not wearing insulated gloves as he handled the wires and made the connections. At the same time, the lead electrician was ready for the breaker to the lighting panel to be turned on and instructed the foreman to throw the breaker to the "on" position. The foreman, thinking he should throw all three breakers to the "on" position, walked over to the breaker panel and removed his lockout/tagout on all three breakers. He then proceeded to throw all three to the "on" position. This action sent electricity through the wires into the lead electrician's hand.

Reportedly, the victim looked at his coworker, said "Help me," and then collapsed. Nearby workers called out to the foreman to contact emergency services, which he did immediately. While emergency services were enroute, cardiopulmonary resuscitation was performed until paramedics arrived. Paramedics took the victim to a nearby hospital, where a physician notified the coroner, who declared the victim dead. The cause of death was electrocution.

Source: For details of this case, see FACE Investigation #03KY115. Accessed April 6, 2020.

For additional information, visit qr.njatcdb.org
Item #1187

INTRODUCTION

The Occupational Safety and Health Administration (OSHA) was established more than five decades ago when the U.S. Congress passed the Occupational Safety and Health Act (OSH Act) of 1970. Its purpose, in part, is "to assure so far as possible every working man and woman in the nation safe and healthful working conditions and preserve our human resources." Requirements were put in place that, when complied with, go a long way toward avoiding the hazards encountered in the workplace.

Electrical Workers are exposed to a number of hazards, and the work that they perform may be covered by any number of OSHA regulations. The primary focus of this chapter is on the regulations in Part 1926, Safety and Health Regulations for Construction, and Part 1910, Occupational Safety and Health Standards. The discussion here provides an overview of a number of performance-based OSHA regulations that may apply.

The information discussed in this chapter is not intended to be all-inclusive or the basis for an electrical safety program. Instead, the intent is to point out a number of regulations that may apply. Part 1926 and Part 1910 regulations must be studied in their entirety for a full and complete look at these provisions and their application.

OSHA: HISTORY, APPLICATION, ENFORCEMENT, AND RESPONSIBILITY

OSHA publication OSHA 3302-01R 2020, titled *All About OSHA*, includes the following general overview of basic topics related to OSHA's mission, what it covers, and how it operates.

In 1970, the United States Congress and President Richard Nixon created the Occupational Safety and Health Administration (OSHA), a national public health agency dedicated to the basic proposition that no worker should have to choose between their life and their job.

History

According to OSHA, in 1970, an estimated 14,000 workers were killed on the job—about 38 every day. For 2016, the Bureau of Labor Statistics reports this number fell to about 5,190 or about 14 workers per day. At the same time, U.S. employment has more than doubled to over 145 million workers at more than 8 million worksites. The rate of reported serious workplace injuries and illnesses has also dropped markedly, from 10.9 per 100 workers in 1972 to 2.9 per 100 workers in 2016.

OSHA's safety and health standards have prevented countless work-related injuries, illnesses, and deaths. Nevertheless, far too many preventable injuries and fatalities continue to occur. Significant hazards and unsafe conditions still exist in U.S. workplaces; each year more than 3.3 million men and women suffer a serious job-related injury or illness. Millions more are exposed to toxic chemicals that may cause illnesses years from now.

In addition to the direct impact on individual workers, the negative consequences for America's economy are substantial. Occupational injuries and illnesses cost American employers more than $59.9 billion a year—over $1 billion a week—in worker's compensation costs alone. Indirect costs to employers, including lost productivity, employee training and replacement costs, and time for investigations following injuries, can more than double these costs. Workers and their families suffer great emotional and psychological costs, in addition to the loss of wages and the expense of caring for the injured, which further weakens the economy.

Application

Under the OSH law, employers are responsible for providing a safe and healthful workplace for their workers. OSHA covers most private sector employers and workers in all 50 states, the District of Columbia, and other U.S. jurisdictions either directly through Federal OSHA or through an OSHA-approved state plan. State plans are

For additional information, visit qr.njatcdb.org Item #1188

For additional information, visit qr.njatcdb.org Item #1189

For additional
information, visit
qr.njatcdb.org
Item #1190

OSHA-approved job safety and health programs operated by individual states instead of Federal OSHA. State-run safety and health programs must be at least as effective as the Federal OSHA program.

Enforcement

Enforcement plays an important part in OSHA's efforts to reduce workplace injuries, illnesses, and fatalities. When OSHA finds employers who fail to uphold their safety and health responsibilities, the agency takes strong, decisive actions. Inspections are initiated without advance notice, conducted using on-site or telephone and facsimile investigations, performed by highly-trained compliance officers, and scheduled based on the following priorities:

For additional
information, visit
qr.njatcdb.org
Item #1191

- Imminent danger
- Catastrophes—fatalities or hospitalizations
- Worker complaints or referrals
- Targeted inspections—particular hazards, high injury rates
- Follow-up inspections

Responsibility

Employers have the responsibility to provide a safe workplace. Employers must provide their workers with a workplace that does not have serious hazards and must follow all OSHA safety and health standards. Employers must find and correct safety and health problems. OSHA further requires that employers must first try to eliminate or reduce hazards by making feasible changes in working conditions rather than relying on personal protective equipment such as masks, gloves, or earplugs. Switching to safer chemicals, enclosing processes to trap harmful fumes, and using ventilation systems to clean the air are examples of effective ways to eliminate or reduce risks.

THE OSH ACT AND OSHA STANDARDS AND REGULATIONS

OSHA requirements are not recommendations; rather, the requirements set forth in the OSHA standards are law. By passing the Occupational Safety and Health Act of 1970, Congress authorized enforcement of the standards developed under the Act. **See Figure 3-1.**

The OSH Act is comprised of 35 sections:

Section 1:	Introduction
Section 2:	Congressional Findings and Purpose
Section 3:	Definitions
Section 4:	Applicability of This Act
Section 5:	Duties
Section 6:	Occupational Safety and Health Standards
Section 7:	Advisory Committees; Administration
Section 8:	Inspections, Investigations, and Recordkeeping
Section 9:	Citations
Section 10:	Procedure for Enforcement
Section 11:	Judicial Review
Section 12:	The Occupational Safety and Health Review Commission

---

Figure 3-1   Occupational Safety and Health Act

Occupational Safety and Health Administration
U S Department of Labor

Occupational Safety and Health Act of 1970

To assure safe and healthful working conditions for working men and women; by authorizing enforcement of the standards developed under the Act; by assisting and encouraging the States in their efforts to assure safe and healthful working conditions; by providing for research, information, education, and training in the field of occupational safety and health; and for other purposes.

Figure 3-1. The Occupational Safety and Health Act of 1970 (OSH Act) was signed into law on December 29, 1970, establishing OSHA.

Section 13: Procedures to Counteract Imminent Dangers

Section 14: Representation in Civil Litigation

Section 15: Confidentiality of Trade Secrets

Section 16: Variations, Tolerances, and Exemptions

Section 17: Penalties

Section 18: State Jurisdiction and State Plans

Section 19: Federal Agency Safety Programs and Responsibilities

Section 20: Research and Related Activities

Section 21: Training and Employee Education

Section 22: National Institute for Occupational Safety and Health

Section 23: Grants to the States

Section 24: Statistics

Section 25: Audits

Section 26: Annual Report

Section 27: National Commission on State Workmen's Compensation Laws

Section 28: Economic Assistance to Small Businesses

Section 29: Additional Assistant Secretary of Labor

Section 30: Additional Positions

Section 31: Emergency Locator Beacons

Section 32: Separability

Section 33: Appropriations

Section 34: Effective Date

Section 35: Historical Notes

The publication *All About OSHA* also discusses standards that may be applicable in the workplace. OSHA's Construction, General Industry, Maritime, and Agriculture standards protect workers from a wide range of serious hazards. Examples of OSHA standards include requirements for employers to take the following steps:

- Provide fall protection
- Prevent trenching cave-ins
- Prevent exposure to some infectious diseases
- Ensure the safety of workers who enter confined spaces
- Prevent exposure to harmful chemicals
- Put guards on dangerous machines
- Provide respirators or other safety equipment
- Provide training for certain dangerous jobs in a language and vocabulary that workers can understand

Employer and Employee Duties

Employers must comply with the General Duty Clause of the OSH Act, which is found in Section 5, Duties. This clause requires employers to keep their workplaces free of serious recognized hazards and is generally cited when no specific OSHA standard applies to the hazard. Note also Section 5(b), which outlines employee responsibility.

Section 5, Duties

(a) Each employer—

　(1) shall furnish to each of his employees employment and a place of employment which are free from recognized hazards that are causing or are likely to cause death or serious physical harm to his employees;

　(2) shall comply with occupational safety and health standards promulgated under this Act.

(b) Each employee shall comply with occupational safety and health standards and all rules, regulations, and orders issued pursuant to this Act which are applicable to his own actions and conduct.

Standards and Regulations

OSHA's Construction, General Industry, Maritime, and Agriculture standards are parts under Title 29 of the Code of Federal Regulations (29 CFR). The subparts are generally categorized by a topic, hazard, or exposure. For example, personal protective equipment (PPE) is primarily addressed in Subpart E of the Safety and Health Regulations for Construction (Part 1926). Many of these regulations are performance-based; that is, they require a result without necessarily spelling out how compliance is to be accomplished.

The two standards applicable to the majority of the work performed by Electrical Workers are found in Part 1926, Safety and Health Regulations for Construction, and in Part 1910, Occupational Safety and Health Standards. Part 1926 applies to Construction, and Part 1910 applies to General Industry.

1910.12(a)

"Standards." The standards prescribed in part 1926 of this chapter are adopted as occupational safety and health standards under section 6 of the Act and shall apply, according to the provisions thereof, to every employment and place of employment of every employee engaged in construction work. Each employer shall protect the employment and places of employment of each of his employees engaged in construction work by complying with the appropriate standards prescribed in this paragraph.

1910.12(d)

For the purposes of this part, to the extent that it may not already be included in paragraph (b) of this section, "construction work" includes the erection of new electric transmission and distribution lines and equipment, and the alteration, conversion, and improvement of the existing transmission and distribution lines and equipment.

SAFETY AND HEALTH REGULATIONS FOR CONSTRUCTION

The 29 CFR Part 1926 Construction regulations are divided into subparts. The scope is contained in Subpart A and advises that Part 1926 sets forth the safety and health standards promulgated by the Secretary of Labor under Section 107 of the Contract Work Hours and Safety Standards Act.

Currently, Part 1926 is divided into the following subparts:

1926 Subpart A: General
1926 Subpart B: General Interpretations
1926 Subpart C: General Safety and Health Provisions
1926 Subpart D: Occupational Health and Environmental Controls
1926 Subpart E: Personal Protective and Life Saving Equipment
1926 Subpart F: Fire Protection and Prevention
1926 Subpart G: Signs, Signals, and Barricades
1926 Subpart H: Materials Handling, Storage, Use, and Disposal
1926 Subpart I: Tools—Hand and Power
1926 Subpart J: Welding and Cutting
1926 Subpart K: Electrical
1926 Subpart L: Scaffolds
1926 Subpart M: Fall Protection
1926 Subpart N: Helicopters, Hoists, Elevators, and Conveyors
1926 Subpart O: Motor Vehicles, Mechanized Equipment, and Marine Operations
1926 Subpart P: Excavations
1926 Subpart Q: Concrete and Masonry Construction
1926 Subpart R: Steel Erection
1926 Subpart S: Underground Construction, Caissons, Cofferdams, and Compressed Air
1926 Subpart T: Demolition
1926 Subpart U: Blasting and the Use of Explosives
1926 Subpart V: Electric Power Transmission and Distribution
1926 Subpart W: Rollover Protective Structures; Overhead Protection
1926 Subpart X: Ladders

1926 Subpart Y: Commercial Diving Operations

1926 Subpart Z: Toxic and Hazardous Substances

1926 Subpart AA: Confined Spaces in Construction

1926 Subpart BB: [Reserved]

1926 Subpart CC: Cranes and Derricks in Construction

Note that the construction regulations are broken down into numerous subparts, each addressing a particular topic as indicated in its title and within its scope. Some subparts cover a particular topic within its scope, such as excavations, ladders, scaffolds, and welding, whereas other subparts apply more broadly, such as the general safety and health provisions of Subpart C.

Some of the Part 1926 Construction regulations will be explored as examples of the types of provisions that could apply and require compliance.

General Safety and Health Provisions

Subpart C provides general safety and health provisions, as indicated by its title. Subpart C begins by providing regulations in 1926.20(a)(1) that state, in part, "no contractor or subcontractor for any part of the contract work shall require any laborer or mechanic employed in the performance of the contract to work in surroundings or under working conditions which are unsanitary, hazardous, or dangerous to his health or safety." Subpart C includes additional general employer provisions.

Personal Protective and Life-Saving Equipment

In 1926.28 in Subpart C, it states that the employer is responsible for requiring employees to wear appropriate personal protective equipment (PPE) in all operations where there is an exposure to hazardous conditions or where this part indicates the need for using such equipment to reduce the hazards to the employees; the employer must provide the necessary PPE to each employee

1926.20(b)

Accident prevention responsibilities.

1926.20(b)(1)

It shall be the responsibility of the employer to initiate and maintain such programs as may be necessary to comply with this part.

1926.20(b)(2)

Such programs shall provide for frequent and regular inspections of the job sites, materials, and equipment to be made by competent persons designated by the employers.

1926.20(f)(1)

Personal protective equipment. Standards in this part requiring the employer to provide personal protective equipment (PPE), including respirators and other types of PPE, because of hazards to employees impose a separate compliance duty with respect to each employee covered by the requirement. The employer must provide PPE to each employee required to use the PPE, and each failure to provide PPE to an employee may be considered a separate violation.

1926.20(f)(2)

Training. Standards in this part requiring training on hazards and related matters, such as standards requiring that employees receive training or that the employer train employees, provide training to employees, or institute or implement a training program, impose a separate compliance duty with respect to each employee covered by the requirement. The employer must train each affected employee in the manner required by the standard, and each failure to train an employee may be considered a separate violation.

1926.21(b)

Employer responsibility.

1926.21(b)(2)

The employer shall instruct each employee in the recognition and avoidance of unsafe conditions and the regulations applicable to his work environment to control or eliminate any hazards or other exposure to illness or injury.

1926.28(a)

The employer is responsible for requiring the wearing of appropriate personal protective equipment in all operations where there is an exposure to hazardous conditions or where this part indicates the need for using such equipment to reduce the hazards to the employees.

Employers must provide for frequent and regular inspections of job sites by competent persons as part of their accident prevention responsibilities.

who is required to use PPE. Regulations from Subpart E include:

1926.95(a)

"Application." Protective equipment, including personal protective equipment for eyes, face, head, and extremities, protective clothing, respiratory devices, and protective shields and barriers, shall be provided, used, and maintained in a sanitary and reliable condition wherever it is necessary by reason of hazards of processes or environment, chemical hazards, radiological hazards, or mechanical irritants encountered in a manner capable of causing injury or impairment in the function of any part of the body through absorption, inhalation, or physical contact.

1926.95(b)

"Employee-owned equipment." Where employees provide their own protective equipment, the employer shall be responsible to assure its adequacy, including proper maintenance and sanitation of such equipment.

1926.100(b)(2)

The employer must ensure that the head protection provided for each employee exposed to high-voltage electric shock and burns also meets the specifications contained in Section 9.7 ("Electrical Insulation") of any of the consensus standards identified in paragraph (b)(1) of this section.

1926.102 Eye and face protection.

1926.102(a)

General requirements.

1926.102(a)(1)

The employer shall ensure that each affected employee uses appropriate eye or face protection when exposed to eye or face hazards from flying particles, molten metal, liquid chemicals, acids or caustic liquids, chemical gases or vapors, or potentially injurious light radiation.

1926.102(b)(1)

Protective eye and face protection devices must comply with any of the following consensus standards:

1926.102(b)(1)(i)

ANSI/ISEA Z87.1-2010, Occupational and Educational Personal Eye and Face Protection Devices, incorporated by reference in § 1926.6;

1926.102(b)(1)(ii)

ANSI Z87.1-2003, Occupational and Educational Personal Eye and Face Protection Devices, incorporated by reference in § 1926.6; or

1926.102(b)(1)(iii)

ANSI Z87.1-1989 (R-1998), Practice for Occupational and Educational Eye and Face Protection, incorporated by reference in § 1926.6;

1926.102(b)(2)

Protective eye and face protection devices that the employer demonstrates are at least as effective as protective eye and face protection devices that are constructed in accordance with one of the above consensus standards will be deemed to be in compliance with the requirements of this section.

Protective equipment must be provided and used as necessary.

Courtesy of Salisbury by Honeywell

OSHA Tip

Design requirements for specific types of electrical protective equipment for construction are located in 1926.97. These include rubber insulating blankets, rubber insulating matting, rubber insulating covers, rubber insulating line hose, rubber insulating gloves, and rubber insulating sleeves.

Protective helmets must be used to protect employees where there is a potential for head injury.
Courtesy of Salisbury by Honeywell

Eye and face protection must be provided as necessary.
Courtesy of Salisbury by Honeywell

Electrical

Subpart K addresses electrical safety requirements that are necessary for practical safeguarding of employees involved in construction work. This part is divided into four major divisions and applicable definitions:

1926.400(a)
Installation safety requirements. Installation safety requirements are contained in 1926.402 through 1926.408. Included in this category are electric equipment and installations used to provide electric power and light on jobsites.

1926.400(b)
Safety-related work practices. Safety-related work practices are contained in 1926.416 and 1926.417. In addition to covering the hazards arising from the use of electricity at jobsites, these regulations also cover the hazards arising from the accidental contact, direct or indirect, by employees with all energized lines, above or below ground, passing through or near the jobsite.

1926.400(c)
Safety-related maintenance and environmental considerations. Safety-related maintenance and environmental considerations are contained in 1926.431 and 1926.432.

1926.400(d)
Safety requirements for special equipment. Safety requirements for special equipment are contained in 1926.441.

1926.400(e)
Definitions. Definitions applicable to this subpart are contained in 1926.449.

OSHA Tip

Subpart V generally covers the construction of electric power transmission and distribution lines and equipment. Line-clearance tree trimming operations and work involving electric power generation installations must generally comply with 1910.269.

An overview of a number of these requirements follows:

1926.404 Wiring design and protection.

1926.404(b)

Branch circuits—

1926.404(b)(1)

Ground-fault protection—

1926.404(b)(1)(i)

General. The employer shall use either ground fault circuit interrupters as specified in paragraph (b)(1)(ii) of this section or an assured equipment grounding conductor program as specified in paragraph (b)(1)(iii) of this section to protect employees on construction sites. These requirements are in addition to any other requirements for equipment grounding conductors.

1926.416 General requirements.

1926.416(a)

Protection of employees—

1926.416(a)(1)

No employer shall permit an employee to work in such proximity to any part of an electric power circuit that the employee could contact the electric power circuit in the course of work, unless the employee is protected against electric shock by deenergizing the circuit and grounding it or by guarding it effectively by insulation or other means.

1926.416(a)(2)

In work areas where the exact location of underground electric powerlines is unknown, employees using jack-hammers, bars, or other hand tools which may contact a line shall be provided with insulated protective gloves.

1926.416(a)(3)

Before work is begun the employer shall ascertain by inquiry or direct observation, or by instruments, whether any part of an energized electric power circuit, exposed or concealed, is so located that the performance of the work may bring any person, tool, or machine into physical or electrical contact with the electric power circuit. The employer shall post and maintain proper warning signs where such a circuit exists. The employer shall advise employees of the location of such lines, the hazards involved, and the protective measures to be taken.

1926.416(b)

Passageways and open spaces—

1926.416(b)(1)

Barriers or other means of guarding shall be provided to ensure that workspace for electrical equipment will not be used as a passageway during periods when energized parts of electrical equipment are exposed.

1926.416(b)(2)

Working spaces, walkways, and similar locations shall be kept clear of cords so as not to create a hazard to employees.

1926.417 Lockout and tagging of circuits.

1926.417(a)

Controls. Controls that are to be deactivated during the course of work on energized or deenergized equipment or circuits shall be tagged.

1926.417(b)

Equipment and circuits. Equipment or circuits that are deenergized shall be rendered inoperative and shall have tags attached at all points where such equipment or circuits can be energized.

1926.417(c)

Tags. Tags shall be placed to identify plainly the equipment or circuits being worked on.

Deenergizing and grounding the circuit is one OSHA-recognized method of employee protection in Subpart K.
Courtesy of National Electrical Contractors Association (NECA)

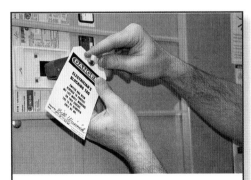

Circuits that are deenergized must be rendered inoperative and have tags attached in accordance with 1926.417(b).
Courtesy of National Electrical Contractors Association (NECA)

OCCUPATIONAL SAFETY AND HEALTH STANDARDS

Currently, 29 CFR Part 1910 General Industry regulations are divided into 26 subparts. Note that, while a number of the subpart titles in Part 1910 are similar to those in Part 1926, they are located in a different subpart letter in each standard. For example, Fire Protection is located in Subpart F in Part 1926 and in Subpart L in Part 1910.

1910 Subpart A: General
1910 Subpart B: Adoption and Extension of Established Federal Standards
1910 Subpart C: Adoption and Extension of Established Federal Standards
1910 Subpart D: Walking–Working Surfaces
1910 Subpart E: Means of Egress
1910 Subpart F: Powered Platforms, Manlifts, and Vehicle-Mounted Work Platforms
1910 Subpart G: Occupational Health and Environmental Control
1910 Subpart H: Hazardous Materials
1910 Subpart I: Personal Protective Equipment
1910 Subpart J: General Environmental Controls
1910 Subpart K: Medical and First Aid
1910 Subpart L: Fire Protection
1910 Subpart M: Compressed Gas and Compressed Air Equipment
1910 Subpart N: Materials Handling and Storage
1910 Subpart O: Machinery and Machine Guarding
1910 Subpart P: Hand and Portable Powered Tools and Other Hand-Held Equipment
1910 Subpart Q: Welding, Cutting, and Brazing

1910 Subpart R: Special Industries
1910 Subpart S: Electrical
1910 Subpart T: Commercial Diving Operations
1910 Subpart U: [Reserved]
1910 Subpart V: [Reserved]
1910 Subpart W: Program Standard
1910 Subpart X: [Reserved]
1910 Subpart Y: [Reserved]
1910 Subpart Z: Toxic and Hazardous Substances

For additional information, visit qr.njatcdb.org Item #1193

The requirements are generally not identical in each standard (Part 1926 and Part 1910). The electrical requirements are a good example: Compare the Subpart K electrical requirements from Part 1926 with the Subpart S electrical requirements from Part 1910.

General

Subpart A of Part 1910 contains the general provisions of the Occupational Safety and Health Standards. A number of these general provisions follow. Section 1910.1 addresses the purpose and scope, Section 1910.2 contains definitions, Section 1910.6 covers incorporation by reference, and Section 1910.9 addresses compliance duties owed to each employee.

1910.1 Purpose and Scope

1910.1(a)

Section 6(a) of the Williams-Steiger Occupational Safety and Health Act of 1970 (84 Stat. 1593) provides that "without regard to chapter 5 of title 5, United States Code, or to the other subsections of this section, the Secretary shall, as soon as practicable during the period beginning with the effective date of this Act and ending 2 years after such date, by rule promulgate as an occupational safety or health standard any national consensus standard, and any established Federal standard, unless he determines that the promulgation of such a standard would not result in improved safety or health for specifically designated employees." The legislative purpose of this provision is to establish, as rapidly as possible and without regard to the rule-making provisions of the Administrative Procedure Act, standards with which industries are generally familiar, and on whose adoption interested and affected persons have already had an opportunity to express their views. Such standards are either (1) national consensus standards on whose adoption affected persons have reached substantial agreement, or (2) Federal standards already established by Federal statutes or regulations.

1910.1(b)

This part carries out the directive to the Secretary of Labor under section 6(a) of the Act. It contains occupational safety and health standards which have been found to be national consensus standards or established Federal standards.

1910.6(a)(1)

The standards of agencies of the U.S. Government, and organizations which are not agencies of the U.S. Government which are incorporated by reference in this part, have the same force and effect as other standards in this part. Only the mandatory provisions (i.e., provisions containing the word "shall" or other mandatory language) of standards incorporated by reference are adopted as standards under the Occupational Safety and Health Act.

1910.9(a)

Personal protective equipment. Standards in this part requiring the employer to provide personal protective equipment (PPE), including respirators and other types of PPE, because of hazards to employees impose a separate compliance duty with respect to each employee covered by the requirement. The employer must provide PPE to each employee required to use the PPE, and each failure to provide PPE to an employee may be considered a separate violation.

1910.9(b)

Training. Standards in this part requiring training on hazards and related matters, such as standards requiring that employees receive training or that the employer train employees, provide training to employees, or institute or implement a training program, impose a separate compliance duty with respect to each employee covered by the requirement. The employer must train each affected employee in the manner required by the standard, and each failure to train an employee may be considered a separate violation.

The employer is required to train each affected employee in the manner required by the OSHA standard.

Courtesy of Service Electric Company

Subpart I requires that necessary protective equipment be provided, used, and maintained in a sanitary and reliable condition.

Courtesy of Salisbury by Honeywell

Personal Protective Equipment

Personal protective equipment is covered in Subpart I of Part 1910. A number of the PPE provisions from the Occupational Safety and Health Standards are covered in this section of the text, including those related to application, design, hazard assessment and selection, training, payment, and electrical protective devices. Many of these regulations are performance-based; that is, they require compliance without necessarily spelling out how to comply.

Note that the employer is required to assess the workplace to determine the need for the use of PPE. This assessment, which must be in writing, must identify the workplace evaluated, the person who performed the assessment, and the date of the assessment. PPE is also required to be provided, used, and maintained properly.

The employer is also responsible for training and retraining related to PPE and for the adequacy of PPE, including any employee-provided PPE. Each affected employee must demonstrate an understanding of the training and the ability to use PPE properly before being allowed to perform work requiring the use of that PPE. Notice the application notes in 1910.132(g). The employer is generally required to provide PPE at no cost to employees.

1910.132(a)

Application. Protective equipment, including personal protective equipment for eyes, face, head, and extremities, protective clothing, respiratory devices, and protective shields and barriers, shall be provided, used, and maintained in a sanitary and reliable condition wherever it is necessary by reason of hazards of processes or environment, chemical hazards, radiological hazards, or mechanical irritants encountered in a manner capable of causing injury or impairment in the function of any part of the body through absorption, inhalation, or physical contact.

1910.132(b)

Employee-owned equipment. Where employees provide their own protective equipment, the employer shall be responsible to assure its adequacy, including proper maintenance and sanitation of such equipment.

1910.132(d)

Hazard assessment and equipment selection.

1910.132(d)(1)

The employer shall assess the workplace to determine if hazards are present, or are likely to be present, which necessitate the use of personal protective equipment (PPE). If such hazards are present, or likely to be present, the employer shall:

1910.132(d)(1)(i)

Select, and have each affected employee use, the types of PPE that will protect the affected employee from the hazards identified in the hazard assessment;

1910.132(d)(1)(ii)

Communicate selection decisions to each affected employee; and,

1910.132(d)(1)(iii)

Select PPE that properly fits each affected employee.

1910.132(d)(2)

The employer shall verify that the required workplace hazard assessment has been performed through a written certification that identifies the workplace evaluated; the person certifying that the evaluation has been performed; the date(s) of the hazard assessment; and, which identifies the document as a certification of hazard assessment.

1910.132(e)

Defective and damaged equipment. Defective or damaged personal protective equipment shall not be used.

1910.132(f)

Training.

1910.132(f)(1)

The employer shall provide training to each employee who is required by this section to use PPE. Each such employee shall be trained to know at least the following:

1910.132(f)(1)(i)

When PPE is necessary;

1910.132(f)(1)(ii)

What PPE is necessary;

1910.132(f)(1)(iii)

How to properly don, doff, adjust, and wear PPE;

1910.132(f)(1)(iv)

The limitations of the PPE; and,

1910.132(f)(1)(v)

The proper care, maintenance, useful life, and disposal of the PPE.

1910.132(f)(2)

Each affected employee shall demonstrate an understanding of the training specified in paragraph (f)(1) of this section, and the ability to use PPE properly, before being allowed to perform work requiring the use of PPE.

1910.132(f)(3)

When the employer has reason to believe that any affected employee who has already been trained does not have the understanding and skill required by paragraph (f)(2) of this section, the employer shall retrain each such employee. Circumstances where retraining is required include, but are not limited to, situations where:

1910.132(f)(3)(i)

Changes in the workplace render previous training obsolete; or

1910.132(f)(3)(ii)

Changes in the types of PPE to be used render previous training obsolete; or

1910.132(f)(3)(iii)

Inadequacies in an affected employee's knowledge or use of assigned PPE indicate that the employee has not retained the requisite understanding or skill.

1910.132(g)

Paragraphs (d) and (f) of this section apply only to §§ 1910.133, 1910.135, 1910.136, 1910.138, and 1910.140. Paragraphs (d) and (f) of this section do not apply to §§ 1910.134 and 1910.137.

Protector gloves are generally required to be worn over insulating gloves. Insulating gloves used without protector gloves may not be reused until they have been retested.

Courtesy of Salisbury by Honeywell

Markings on gloves, such as type, class, size, and manufacturer information, must be nonconductive and be confined to the cuff portion of the glove.

Courtesy of Salisbury by Honeywell

Section 1910.137 addresses electrical protective equipment. These regulations cover topics such as design requirements and in-service care and use, including daily inspection and periodic electrical tests.

1910.137(a)(1)(ii)

Each item shall be clearly marked as follows:

1910.137(a)(1)(ii)(A)

Class 00 equipment shall be marked Class 00.

1910.137(a)(1)(ii)(B)

Class 0 equipment shall be marked Class 0.

1910.137(a)(1)(ii)(C)

Class 1 equipment shall be marked Class 1.

1910.137(a)(1)(ii)(D)

Class 2 equipment shall be marked Class 2.

1910.137(a)(1)(ii)(E)

Class 3 equipment shall be marked Class 3.

1910.137(a)(1)(ii)(F)

Class 4 equipment shall be marked Class 4.

1910.137(a)(1)(ii)(G)

Nonozone-resistant equipment shall be marked Type I.

1910.137(a)(1)(ii)(H)

Ozone-resistant equipment shall be marked Type II.

1910.137(a)(1)(iii)

Markings shall be nonconducting and shall be applied in such a manner as not to impair the insulating qualities of the equipment.

1910.137(a)(1)(iv)

Markings on gloves shall be confined to the cuff portion of the glove.

1910.137(c)

In-service care and use of electrical protective equipment.

1910.137(c)(1)

General. Electrical protective equipment shall be maintained in a safe, reliable condition.

1910.137(c)(2)

Specific requirements. The following specific requirements apply to rubber insulating blankets, rubber insulating covers, rubber insulating line hose, rubber insulating gloves, and rubber insulating sleeves:

1910.137(c)(2)(i)

Maximum use voltages shall conform to those listed in Table I-4.

1910.137(c)(2)(ii)

Insulating equipment shall be inspected for damage before each day's use and immediately following any incident that can reasonably be suspected of causing damage. Insulating gloves shall be given an air test, along with the inspection.

1910.137(c)(2)(iii)

Insulating equipment with any of the following defects may not be used:

1910.137(c)(2)(iii)(A)

A hole, tear, puncture, or cut;

1910.137(c)(2)(iii)(B)

Ozone cutting or ozone checking (that is, a series of interlacing cracks produced by ozone on rubber under mechanical stress);

1910.137(c)(2)(iii)(C)

An embedded foreign object;

1910.137(c)(2)(iii)(D)

Any of the following texture changes: swelling, softening, hardening, or becoming sticky or inelastic.

1910.137(c)(2)(iii)(E)

Any other defect that damages the insulating properties.

Table I-4 Rubber Insulating Equipment, Voltage Requirements			
Class of Equipment	Maximum Use Voltage[1] AC rms	Retest Voltage[2] AC rms	Retest Voltage[2] DC avg
00	500	2,500	10,000
0	1,000	5,000	20,000
1	7,500	10,000	40,000
2	17,000	20,000	50,000
3	26,500	30,000	60,000
4	36,000	40,000	70,000

[1] The maximum use voltage is the ac voltage (rms) classification of the protective equipment that designates the maximum nominal design voltage of the energized system that may be safely worked. The nominal design voltage is equal to the phase-to-phase voltage on multiphase circuits. However, the phase-to-ground potential is considered to be the nominal design voltage if:
(1) There is no multiphase exposure in a system area and the voltage exposure is limited to the phase-to-ground potential, or
(2) The electric equipment and devices are insulated or isolated or both so that the multiphase exposure on a grounded wye circuit is removed.
[2] The proof-test voltage shall be applied continuously for at least 1 minute, but no more than 3 minutes.

Table I-4 provides the requirements for rubber insulation equipment voltage.

1910.137(c)(2)(iv)

Insulating equipment found to have other defects that might affect its insulating properties shall be removed from service and returned for testing under paragraphs (c)(2)(viii) and (c)(2)(ix) of this section.

1910.137(c)(2)(v)

Insulating equipment shall be cleaned as needed to remove foreign substances

1910.137(c)(2)(vi)

Insulating equipment shall be stored in such a location and in such a manner as to protect it from light, temperature extremes, excessive humidity, ozone, and other damaging substances and conditions.

1910.137(c)(2)(vii)

Protector gloves shall be worn over insulating gloves, except as follows:

1910.137(c)(2)(vii)(A)

Protector gloves need not be used with Class 0 gloves, under limited-use conditions, when small equipment and parts manipulation necessitate unusually high finger dexterity.

Note to paragraph (c)(2)(vii)(A): Persons inspecting rubber insulating gloves used under these conditions need to take extra care in visually examining them. Employees using rubber insulating gloves under these conditions need to take extra care to avoid handling sharp objects.

1910.137(c)(2)(vii)(B)

If the voltage does not exceed 250 volts, ac, or 375 volts, dc, protector gloves need not be used with Class 00 gloves, under limited-use conditions, when small equipment and parts manipulation necessitate unusually high finger dexterity.

Note to paragraph (c)(2)(vii)(B): Persons inspecting rubber insulating gloves used under these conditions need to take extra care in visually examining them. Employees using rubber insulating gloves under these conditions need to take extra care to avoid handling sharp objects.

1910.137(c)(2)(vii)(C)

Any other class of glove may be used without protector gloves, under limited-use conditions, when small equipment and parts manipulation necessitate unusually high finger dexterity but only if the employer can demonstrate that the possibility of physical damage to the gloves is small and if the class of glove is one class higher than that required for the voltage involved.

1910.137(c)(2)(vii)(D)

Insulating gloves that have been used without protector gloves may not be reused until they have been tested under the provisions of paragraphs (c)(2)(viii) and (c)(2)(ix) of this section.

1910.137(c)(2)(viii)

Electrical protective equipment shall be subjected to periodic electrical tests. Test voltages and the maximum intervals between tests shall be in accordance with Table I-4 and Table I-5.

OSHA Tip

Section 1910.269 covers the operation and maintenance of electric power generation, control, transformation, transmission, and distribution lines and equipment.

The Control of Hazardous Energy (Lockout/Tagout)

Lockout/tagout regulations are primarily addressed in two subparts in Part 1910, Occupational Safety and Health Standards: Subpart J, General Environmental Controls; and Subpart S, Electrical.

The Subpart J regulations are located in 1910.147, The Control of Hazardous Energy (lockout/tagout). Section 1910.147 is organized into the following subdivisions:

- Scope, application, and purpose
- Definitions
- General
- Application of control
- Release from lockout or tagout
- Additional requirements

The Subpart S lockout and tagging regulations are located in 1910.333(b)(2), Lockout and Tagging. One section and an accompanying note from these Subpart S requirements are included for reference. These lockout and tagging regulations must be reviewed in their entirety for a complete look at what is required. The provisions of 1910.333(b)(2) are covered in greater detail in the chapter, "Introduction to Lockout, Tagging, and the Control of Hazardous Energy."

Table I-5 Rubber Insulating Equipment, Test Intervals	
Type of Equipment	**When to Test**
Rubber insulating line hose	Upon indication that insulating value is suspect and after repair.
Rubber insulating covers	Upon indication that insulating value is suspect and after repair.
Rubber insulating blankets	Before first issue and every 12 months thereafter;[1] upon indication that insulating value is suspect; and after repair.
Rubber insulating gloves	Before first issue and every 6 months thereafter;[1] upon indication that insulating value is suspect; after repair; and after use without protectors.
Rubber insulating sleeves	Before first issue and every 12 months thereafter;[1] upon indication that insulating value is suspect; and after repair.
[1] If the insulating equipment has been electrically tested but not issued for service, the insulating equipment may not be placed into service unless it has been electrically tested within the previous 12 months.	
Table I-5 details the rubber insulation equipment test intervals.	

1910.333(b)(2)

"Lockout and Tagging." While any employee is exposed to contact with parts of fixed electric equipment or circuits which have been deenergized, the circuits energizing the parts shall be locked out or tagged or both in accordance with the requirements of this paragraph. The requirements shall be followed in the order in which they are presented.

Note 2: Lockout and tagging procedures that comply with paragraphs (c) through (f) of 1910.147 will also be deemed to comply with paragraph (b)(2) of this section provided that:

[1] The procedures address the electrical safety hazards covered by this Subpart; and

[2] The procedures also incorporate the requirements of paragraphs (b)(2)(iii)(D) and (b)(2)(iv)(B) of this section.

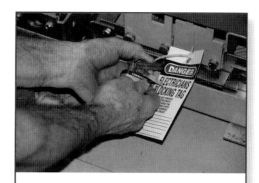

Both a lock and a tag are generally required to comply with lockout/tagout requirements while any employee is exposed to contact with parts of fixed electric equipment or circuits that have been deenergized.
Courtesy of National Electrical Contractors Association (NECA)

Electrical Occupational Safety and Health Standards

Subpart S details the electrical regulations of Part 1910, Occupational Safety and Health Standards. This subpart addresses electrical safety requirements that are necessary for the practical safeguarding of employees in their workplaces and is divided into four major divisions:

- Design safety standards for electrical systems
- Safety-related work practices
- Safety-related maintenance requirements
- Safety requirements for special equipment

The primary focus is a review of a number of the safety-related work practice regulations of Subpart S, including some from 1910.332, Training; 1910.333, Selection and Use of Work Practices; 1910.334, Use of Equipment; and 1910.335, Safeguards for Personnel Protection. A number of the definitions applicable to Subpart S located in 1910.399 are included as well.

1910.332(b)

Content of training.

1910.332(b)(1)

Practices addressed in this standard. Employees shall be trained in and familiar with the safety-related work practices required by 1910.331 through 1910.335 that pertain to their respective job assignments.

1910.333(a)

"General." Safety-related work practices shall be employed to prevent electric shock or other injuries resulting from either direct or indirect electrical contacts, when work is performed near or on equipment or circuits which are or may be energized. The specific safety-related work practices shall be consistent with the nature and extent of the associated electrical hazards.

1910.333(a)(1)

"Deenergized parts." Live parts to which an employee may be exposed shall be deenergized before the employee works on or near them, unless the employer can demonstrate that deenergizing introduces additional or increased hazards or is infeasible due to equipment design or operational limitations. Live parts that operate at less than 50 volts to ground need not be deenergized if there will be no increased exposure to electrical burns or to explosion due to electric arcs.

Note 1: Examples of increased or additional hazards include interruption of life support equipment, deactivation of emergency alarm systems, shutdown of hazardous location ventilation equipment, or removal of illumination for an area.

Note 2: Examples of work that may be performed on or near energized circuit parts because of infeasibility due to equipment design or operational limitations include testing of electric circuits that can only be performed with the circuit energized and work on circuits that form an integral part of a continuous industrial process in a chemical plant that would otherwise need to be completely shut down in order to permit work on one circuit or piece of equipment.

Note 3: Work on or near deenergized parts is covered by paragraph (b) of this section.

1910.333(a)(2)

"Energized parts." If the exposed live parts are not deenergized (i.e., for reasons of increased or additional hazards or infeasibility), other safety-related work practices shall be used to protect employees who may be exposed to the electrical hazards involved. Such work practices shall protect employees against contact with energized circuit parts directly with any part of their body or indirectly through some other conductive object. The work practices that are used shall be suitable for the conditions under which the work is to be performed and for the voltage level of the exposed electric conductors or circuit parts. Specific work practice requirements are detailed in paragraph (c) of this section.

1910.333(b)

"Working on or near exposed deenergized parts."

1910.333(b)(1)

"Application." This paragraph applies to work on exposed deenergized parts or near enough to them to expose the employee to any electrical hazard they present. Conductors and parts of electric equipment that have been deenergized but have not been locked out or tagged in accordance with paragraph (b) of this section shall be treated as energized parts, and paragraph (c) of this section applies to work on or near them.

1910.333(c)

"Working on or near exposed energized parts."

1910.333(c)(1)

"Application." This paragraph applies to work performed on exposed live parts (involving either direct contact or by means of tools or materials) or near enough to them for employees to be exposed to any hazard they present.

1910.333(c)(2)

"Work on energized equipment." Only qualified persons may work on electric circuit parts or equipment that have not been deenergized under the procedures of paragraph (b) of this section. Such persons shall be capable of working safely on energized circuits and shall be familiar

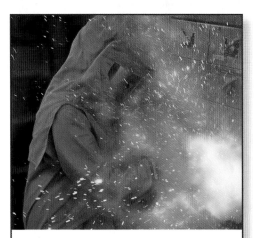

Other safety-related work practices must be used to protect employees who may be exposed to the electrical hazards involved if the exposed live parts are not deenergized.
Courtesy of Salisbury by Honeywell

with the proper use of special precautionary techniques, personal protective equipment, insulating and shielding materials, and insulated tools.

1910.333(c)(3)

"Overhead lines." If work is to be performed near overhead lines, the lines shall be deenergized and grounded, or other protective measures shall be provided before work is started. If the lines are to be deenergized, arrangements shall be made with the person or organization that operates or controls the electric circuits involved to deenergize and ground them. If protective measures, such as guarding, isolating, or insulating, are provided, these precautions shall prevent employees from contacting such lines directly with any part of their body or indirectly through conductive materials, tools, or equipment.

Note: The work practices used by qualified persons installing insulating devices on overhead power transmission or distribution lines are covered by 1910.269 of this Part, not by 1910.332 through 1910.335 of this Part. Under paragraph (c)(2) of this section, unqualified persons are prohibited from performing this type of work.

1910.333(c)(3)(i)

"Unqualified persons."

1910.333(c)(3)(i)(A)

When an unqualified person is working in an elevated position near overhead lines, the location shall be such that the person and the longest conductive object he or she may contact cannot come closer to any unguarded, energized overhead line than the following distances:

1910.333(c)(3)(i)(A)(1)

For voltages to ground 50kV or below— 10 feet (305 cm);

1910.333(c)(3)(i)(A)(2)

For voltages to ground over 50kV— 10 feet (305 cm) plus 4 inches (10 cm) for every 10kV over 50kV.

1910.333(c)(3)(i)(B)

When an unqualified person is working on the ground in the vicinity of overhead lines, the person may not bring any conductive object closer to unguarded, energized overhead lines than the distances given in paragraph (c)(3)(i)(A) of this section.

Other protective measures must be provided before work is started if that work is to be performed near overhead lines and the lines are not deenergized and grounded.

Courtesy of Salisbury by Honeywell

1910.333(c)(3)(ii)

"Qualified persons." When a qualified person is working in the vicinity of overhead lines, whether in an elevated position or on the ground, the person may not approach or take any conductive object without an approved insulating handle closer to exposed energized parts than shown in Table S-5 unless:

1910.333(c)(3)(ii)(A)

The person is insulated from the energized part (gloves, with sleeves if necessary, rated for the voltage involved are considered to be insulation of the person from the energized part on which work is performed), or

1910.333(c)(3)(ii)(B)

The energized part is insulated both from all other conductive objects at a different potential and from the person, or

1910.333(c)(3)(ii)(C)

The person is insulated from all conductive objects at a potential different from that of the energized part.

1910.333(c)(3)(iii)

"Vehicular and mechanical equipment."

1910.333(c)(3)(iii)(A)

Any vehicle or mechanical equipment capable of having parts of its structure elevated near energized overhead lines shall be operated so that a clearance of 10 ft. (305 cm) is maintained. If the voltage is higher than 50kV, the clearance shall be increased 4 in. (10 cm) for every 10kV over that voltage. However, under any of the following conditions, the clearance may be reduced:

1910.333(c)(3)(iii)(A)(1)

If the vehicle is in transit with its structure lowered, the clearance may be reduced to 4 ft. (122 cm). If the voltage is higher than 50kV, the clearance shall be increased 4 in. (10 cm) for every 10 kV over that voltage.

OSHA 1910.333 Table S-5 Approach Distances for Qualified Employees: Alternating Current	
Voltage Range (Phase to Phase)	**Minimum Approach Distance**
300 V and less	Avoid Contact
Over 300 V, not over 750 V	1 ft. 0 in. (30.5 cm)
Over 750 V, not over 2 kV	1 ft. 6 in. (46 cm)
Over 2 kV, not over 15 kV	2 ft. 0 in. (61 cm)
Over 15 kV, not over 37 kV	3 ft. 0 in. (91 cm)
Over 37kV, not over 87.5 kV	3 ft. 6 in. (107 cm)
Over 87.5 kV, not over 121 kV	4 ft. 0 in. (122 cm)
Over 121 kV, not over 140 kV	4 ft. 6 in. (137 cm)

The minimum approach distances for alternating current for qualified employees are set forth in Table S-5 in Subpart S of Part 1910.

1910.333(c)(3)(iii)(A)(2)

If insulating barriers are installed to prevent contact with the lines, and if the barriers are rated for the voltage of the line being guarded and are not a part of or an attachment to the vehicle or its raised structure, the clearance may be reduced to a distance within the designed working dimensions of the insulating barrier.

1910.333(c)(3)(iii)(A)(3)

If the equipment is an aerial lift insulated for the voltage involved, and if the work is performed by a qualified person, the clearance (between the uninsulated portion of the aerial lift and the power line) may be reduced to the distance given in Table S-5.

1910.333(c)(3)(iii)(B)

Employees standing on the ground may not contact the vehicle or mechanical equipment or any of its attachments, unless:

1910.333(c)(3)(iii)(B)(1)

The employee is using protective equipment rated for the voltage; or

1910.333(c)(3)(iii)(B)(2)

The equipment is located so that no uninsulated part of its structure (that portion of the structure that provides a conductive path to employees on the ground) can come closer to the line than permitted in paragraph (c)(3)(iii) of this section.

1910.333(c)(3)(iii)(C)

If any vehicle or mechanical equipment capable of having parts of its structure elevated near energized overhead lines is intentionally grounded, employees working on the ground near the point of grounding may not stand at the grounding location whenever there is a possibility of overhead line contact. Additional precautions, such as the use of barricades or insulation, shall be taken to protect employees from hazardous ground potentials, depending on earth resistivity and fault currents, which can develop within the first few feet or more outward from the grounding point.

1910.333(c)(4)

"Illumination."

1910.333(c)(4)(i)

Employees may not enter spaces containing exposed energized parts, unless illumination is provided that enables the employees to perform the work safely.

1910.333(c)(4)(ii)

Where lack of illumination or an obstruction precludes observation of the work to be performed, employees may not perform tasks near exposed energized parts. Employees may not reach blindly into areas which may contain energized parts.

1910.333(c)(5)

"Confined or enclosed work spaces." When an employee works in a confined or enclosed space (such as a manhole or vault) that contains exposed energized parts, the employer shall provide, and the employee shall use, protective shields, protective barriers, or insulating materials as necessary to avoid inadvertent contact with these parts. Doors, hinged panels, and the like shall be secured to prevent their swinging into an employee and causing the employee to contact exposed energized parts.

1910.333(c)(6)

"Conductive materials and equipment." Conductive materials and equipment that are in contact with any part of an employee's body shall be handled in a manner that will prevent them from contacting exposed energized conductors or circuit parts. If an employee must handle long dimensional conductive objects (such as ducts and pipes) in areas with exposed live parts, the employer shall institute work practices (such as the use of insulation, guarding, and material handling techniques) which will minimize the hazard.

1910.333(c)(7)

"Portable ladders." Portable ladders shall have nonconductive siderails if they are used where the employee or the ladder could contact exposed energized parts.

1910.333(c)(8)

"Conductive apparel." Conductive articles of jewelry and clothing (such as watch bands, bracelets, rings, key chains, necklaces, metalized aprons, cloth with conductive thread, or metal headgear) may not be worn if they might contact exposed energized parts. However, such articles may be worn if they are rendered nonconductive by covering, wrapping, or other insulating means.

1910.333(c)(9)

"Housekeeping duties." Where live parts present an electrical contact hazard, employees may not perform housekeeping duties at such close distances to the parts that there is a possibility of contact, unless adequate safeguards (such as insulating equipment or barriers) are provided. Electrically conductive cleaning materials (including conductive solids such as steel wool, metalized cloth, and silicon carbide, as well as conductive liquid solutions) may not be used in proximity to energized parts unless procedures are followed which will prevent electrical contact.

1910.333(c)(10)

"Interlocks." Only a qualified person following the requirements of paragraph (c) of this section may defeat an electrical safety interlock, and then only temporarily while he or she is working on the equipment. The interlock system shall be returned to its operable condition when this work is completed.

1910.334(b)(2)

Reclosing circuits after protective device operation. After a circuit is deenergized by a circuit protective device, the circuit may not be manually reenergized until it has been determined that the equipment and circuit can be safely energized. The repetitive manual reclosing of circuit breakers or reenergizing circuits through replaced fuses is prohibited.

Note: When it can be determined from the design of the circuit and the overcurrent devices involved that the automatic operation of a device was caused by an overload rather than a fault condition, no examination of the circuit or connected equipment is needed before the circuit is reenergized.

1910.335(a)

Use of protective equipment.

1910.335(a)(1)

Personal protective equipment.

1910.335(a)(1)(i)

Employees working in areas where there are potential electrical hazards shall be provided with, and shall use, electrical protective equipment that is appropriate for the specific parts of the body to be protected and for the work to be performed.

Note: Personal protective equipment requirements are contained in subpart I of this part.

1910.335(a)(1)(ii)

Protective equipment shall be maintained in a safe, reliable condition and shall be periodically inspected or tested, as required by 1910.137.

1910.335(a)(1)(iii)

If the insulating capability of protective equipment may be subject to damage during use, the insulating material shall be protected. (For example, an outer covering of leather is sometimes used for the protection of rubber insulating material.)

1910.335(a)(1)(iv)

Employees shall wear nonconductive head protection wherever there is a danger of head injury from electric shock or burns due to contact with exposed energized parts.

1910.335(a)(1)(v)

Employees shall wear protective equipment for the eyes or face wherever there is danger of injury to the eyes or face from electric arcs or flashes or from flying objects resulting from electrical explosion.

1910.335(a)(2)

General protective equipment and tools.

1910.335(a)(2)(i)

When working near exposed energized conductors or circuit parts, each employee shall use insulated tools or handling equipment if the tools or handling equipment might make contact with such conductors or parts. If the insulating capability of insulated tools or handling equipment is subject to damage, the insulating material shall be protected.

1910.335(a)(2)(i)(A)

Fuse handling equipment, insulated for the circuit voltage, shall be used to remove or install fuses when the fuse terminals are energized.

1910.335(a)(2)(i)(B)

Ropes and handlines used near exposed energized parts shall be nonconductive.

1910.335(a)(2)(ii)

Protective shields, protective barriers, or insulating materials shall be used to protect each employee from shock, burns, or other electrically related injuries while that employee is working near exposed energized parts which might be accidentally contacted or where dangerous electric heating or arcing might occur. When normally enclosed live parts are exposed for maintenance or repair, they shall be guarded to protect unqualified persons from contact with the live parts.

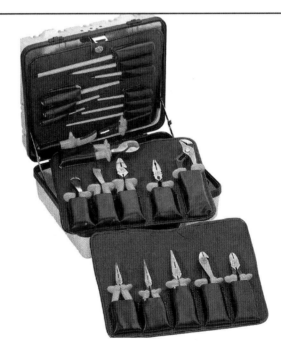

OSHA requires that insulated tools be used if the tool could contact exposed energized conductors or circuit parts when employees are working on or near such conductors or parts.

Courtesy of Klein Tools

1910.335(b)

Alerting techniques. The following alerting techniques shall be used to warn and protect employees from hazards which could cause injury due to electric shock, burns, or failure of electric equipment parts:

1910.335(b)(1)

Safety signs and tags. Safety signs, safety symbols, or accident prevention tags shall be used where necessary to warn employees about electrical hazards which may endanger them, as required by 1910.145.

1910.335(b)(2)

Barricades. Barricades shall be used in conjunction with safety signs where it is necessary to prevent or limit employee access to work areas exposing employees to uninsulated energized conductors or circuit parts. Conductive barricades may not be used where they might cause an electrical contact hazard.

1910.335(b)(3)

Attendants. If signs and barricades do not provide sufficient warning and protection from electrical hazards, an attendant shall be stationed to warn and protect employees.

1910.399, Definitions, in part.

Deenergized. Free from any electrical connection to a source of potential difference and from electrical charge; not having a potential different from that of the earth.

Energized. Electrically connected to a source of potential difference.

Overcurrent. Any current in excess of the rated current of equipment or the ampacity of a conductor. It may result from overload, short circuit, or ground fault.

Overload. Operation of equipment in excess of normal, full-load rating, or of a conductor in excess of rated ampacity that, when it persists for a sufficient length of time, would cause damage or dangerous overheating. A fault, such as a short circuit or ground fault, is not an overload. (See Overcurrent.)

Qualified person. One who has received training in and has demonstrated skills and knowledge in the construction and operation of electric equipment and installations and the hazards involved.

Note 1 to the definition of "qualified person:" Whether an employee is considered to be a "qualified person" will depend upon various circumstances in the workplace. For example, it is possible and, in fact, likely for an individual to be considered "qualified" with regard to certain equipment in the workplace, but "unqualified" as to other equipment. (See 1910.332(b)(3) for training requirements that specifically apply to qualified persons.)

Note 2 to the definition of "qualified person:" An employee who is undergoing on-the-job training and who, in the course of such training, has demonstrated an ability to perform duties safely at his or her level of training and who is under the direct supervision of a qualified person is considered to be a qualified person for the performance of those duties.

An arc suppression blanket is not designed for electrical insulating protection.

Courtesy of Salisbury by Honeywell

SUMMARY

Every day, workers are exposed to hazards associated with working on energized parts, or hazards associated with working close enough to energized parts to allow potential exposure to electrical hazards. When requirements are adhered to and appropriate procedures are in place and implemented, the likelihood of adverse incidents, injuries, and fatalities can be reduced. Many of these requirements have been discussed; however, the requirements covered are only a few of the full set that must be considered when assessing workplace hazards and developing an effective safety program.

An understanding of the General Duty Clause; Part 1926, Safety and Health Regulations for Construction; and Part 1910, Occupational Safety and Health Standards, is important. Implementing and following the requirements, such as those for training, selection and use of work practices, use of equipment, and safeguards for personnel protection will help ensure that the workplace is free of recognized hazards.

This knowledge will also provide a foundation for what is required by OSHA and for how the requirements of *NFPA 70E: Standard for Electrical Safety in the Workplace*® may be an aid in accomplishing what OSHA requires. Consider this analogy: "OSHA is the *shall*, and *NFPA 70E* is the *how*." It can be useful to determine whether the provisions of *NFPA 70E* can be a compliance solution and what, if anything, *NFPA 70E* requires that OSHA does not already require.

REVIEW QUESTIONS

1. The Occupational Safety and Health Act (OSH Act) of 1970 states that its purpose is to assure so far as possible every working man and woman in the nation safe and __?__ working conditions and to preserve our human resources.
   a. convenient
   b. healthful
   c. legal
   d. reliable

2. The primary focus of this chapter are the regulations in Part __?__, Safety and Health Regulations for Construction, and Part __?__, General Industry Occupational Safety and Health Standards.
   a. 1910 / 1926
   b. 1926 / 1910
   c. 1970 / 1972
   d. 1992 / 2022

3. OSHA's safety and health standards have prevented countless work-related injuries, illnesses, and deaths. Unfortunately, far too many __?__ injuries and fatalities continue to occur.
   a. obvious
   b. preventable
   c. unavoidable
   d. unpreventable

4. Under the OSHA __?__, employers are responsible for providing a safe and healthful workplace for their workers.
   a. guidelines
   b. law
   c. recommendations
   d. wishes

5. OSHA's rules and regulations are __?__; they are not recommendations.
   a. guidelines
   b. non-mandatory
   c. requirements
   d. wishes

6. Many of the OSHA regulations are __?__-based, which means that they require a result without necessarily spelling out how compliance is to be accomplished.
   a. common sense
   b. fact
   c. performance
   d. prescriptive

7. The employer must provide for frequent and regular inspections of job sites by __?__ persons as part of their accident prevention responsibilities.
   a. competent
   b. independent
   c. qualified
   d. recognized

8. Subpart C of Part 1926 requires that the __?__ is responsible for employees wearing appropriate personal protective equipment in all operations where there is an exposure to hazardous conditions.
   a. employee
   b. employer
   c. union
   d. warehouse supervisor

9. OSHA calls for personal protective equipment (PPE) to be provided by the __?__, which is required to assess the workplace to determine the need for the use of PPE.
   a. employee
   b. employer
   c. union
   d. warehouse supervisor

10. Live parts to which an employee may be exposed shall be deenergized before the employee works on or near them, unless the __?__ can demonstrate that deenergizing introduces additional or increased hazards or is infeasible due to equipment design or operational limitations.
    a. employee
    b. employer
    c. job steward
    d. JATC Training Director

Introduction to Lockout, Tagging, and the Control of Hazardous Energy

The Occupational Safety and Health Administration's (OSHA's) requirements are performance-oriented in many cases; that is, protection of workers is required, although the requirements do not necessarily spell out precisely how worker protection is to be accomplished. This includes requirements related to protecting workers from electrical hazards. Employers are increasingly looking to *NFPA 70E* for guidance in an effort to understand how to comply with OSHA's performance-oriented requirements. However, OSHA's requirements related to lockout/tagout and working on or near exposed deenergized parts are examples where OSHA may offer specific details, including the steps that must be followed to comply with their requirements.

In addition to developing lockout/tagout programs based on requirements from OSHA, the requirements from *NFPA 70E* Article 120 should be considered as part of electrical safety-related work practices. The provisions of *NFPA 70E* Article 120 generally meet or exceed OSHA's lockout/tagout requirements and should be examined carefully for any other considerations that might lead to a more comprehensive lockout/tagout program.

Objectives

» Demonstrate an understanding of the reasons why the Occupational Safety and Health Act of 1970 was enacted, the Congressional finding and purpose of the act, and the employer and employee responsibilities established in the General Duty Clause.

» Become familiar with Safety and Health Regulations for Construction, including Subpart C, General Safety and Health Provisions, and the Subpart K provisions for lockout and tagging of circuits.

» Demonstrate an understanding of the Occupational Safety and Health Standards, including the Subpart S provisions related to lockout and tagging, and the six major headings of the control of hazardous energy (lockout/tagout) in Subpart J.

» Discuss the structure of Article 120 and the eight-step process required to establish and verify an electrically safe work condition.

Chapter 4

Table of Contents

CASE STUDY

Case Study

A 48-year-old machine operator was killed when he was crushed inside a machine. The employer had been in business for more than 80 years and had approximately 175 employees. There were 55 employees at the facility where the incident occurred. The victim had been employed with the company for 19 years.

The employer had a written safety program with task-specific safe work procedures for all positions in the shop. Employees held informal weekly tailgate safety meetings with the supervisors, as well as formal monthly safety meetings. The company's training program was usually accomplished through on-the-job training monitored by the supervisors.

The machine involved in the incident was completely automated. The operating portion of the machine was enclosed for safety. Whenever any regular access panel or door to the machine was opened, the machine was supposed to shut off automatically. The pedestal on which the machine sat was also enclosed, with the exception of the area where the conveyor belt exited from underneath the machine. The guarding around the pedestal had to be mechanically removed to gain access to the pedestal.

On the day of the incident, the machine stopped working, and its warning lights came on. The victim was not at his workstation. His coworkers contacted the supervisor, who discovered the victim inside the machine with his head trapped between the pedestal frame and the mobile plate frame. Coworkers called 911, and the responding firefighters had to unbolt the guarding around the pedestal frame to gain access to the victim and extricate him. Paramedics pronounced the victim dead after they removed him from the machine.

Investigation of the incident site revealed the victim's tools lying next to the opening in the pedestal where the conveyor belt was located; in addition, several pieces of the machine product were scattered about the conveyor belt. The guard or shield on the side of the conveyor belt was unbolted on one side. These factors suggested that the victim crawled into the machine from the opening for the conveyor belt.

The cause of death, according to the death certificate, was blunt head trauma.

Source: For details of this case, see FACE Investigation #03CA006. Accessed April 7, 2020.

For additional information, visit qr.njatcdb.org
Item #1194

INTRODUCTION

OSHA's requirements are performance-oriented in many cases; that is, protection of workers is required, although the requirements do not necessarily spell out precisely how worker protection is to be accomplished. This includes requirements related to protecting workers from electrical hazards. While increasingly more employers are looking to *NFPA 70E* for guidance in an effort to understand how to comply with OSHA's performance-oriented requirements, OSHA's requirements related to lockout/tagout and working on or near exposed deenergized parts are examples where OSHA may offer more specific details, including the steps that must be followed to comply with these requirements.

Electrical Workers should be familiar with OSHA's requirements for lockout and tagging of circuits located in 1926.417, control of hazardous energy (lockout/tagout) located in 1910.147, the lockout and tagging provisions of 1910.333(b)(2), and the ways that provisions in *NFPA 70E* Article 120 can meet or supplement OSHA's provisions, including those in the Occupational Safety and Health Act (OSH Act) of 1970.

Many lockout/tagout programs are based on OSHA 1910.147. OSHA notes that lockout and tagging procedures complying with 1910.147 are also deemed to comply with 1910.333(b)(2), provided that the procedures address the electrical safety hazards covered by Subpart S of 29 CFR 1910, and that those procedures incorporate the requirements of two additional paragraphs not contained in 1910.147.

In addition to developing lockout/tagout programs based on requirements from OSHA, the requirements from *NFPA 70E* Article 120, Establishing an Electrically Safe Work Condition, should be considered as part of electrical safety practices. The provisions of *NFPA 70E* Article 120 generally meet or exceed OSHA's lockout/tagout requirements and should be examined carefully for any other considerations that might lead to a more comprehensive lockout/tagout program. This includes, but is not limited to, the eight-step process outlined in Section 120.5 to establish and verify that an electrically safe work condition exists after the applicable provisions contained in *NFPA 70E* Article 120 have been taken into account. The provisions of Article 120 need to be reviewed in their entirety for a full understanding of their use and application.

THE OCCUPATIONAL SAFETY AND HEALTH ACT OF 1970

The Occupational Safety and Health Act of 1970 was enacted "to assure safe and healthful working conditions for working men and women; by authorizing enforcement of the standards developed under the Act; by assisting and encouraging the States in their efforts to assure safe and healthful working conditions; by providing for research, information, education, and training in the field of occupational safety and health; and for other purposes." This Act consists of 35 sections. Part of the content of two of those sections follows:

Section 2, Congressional Findings and Purpose

(a) The Congress finds that personal injuries and illnesses arising out of work situations impose a substantial burden upon, and are a hindrance to, interstate commerce in terms of lost production, wage loss, medical expenses, and disability compensation payments.

(b) The Congress declares it to be its purpose and policy, through the exercise of its powers to regulate commerce among the several States and with foreign nations and to provide for the general welfare, to assure so far as possible every working man and woman in the Nation safe and healthful working conditions and to preserve our human resources.

Section 2(b) includes 13 points that detail how to accomplish the purpose and satisfy the policy of assuring, so far as possible, that every working man and woman in the nation has safe and healthful working conditions and of preserving human resources.

Section 5, Duties, is commonly known as "the General Duty Clause." It identifies responsibilities for both employers and employees:

> (a) Each employer—
>> (1) shall furnish to each of his employees employment and a place of employment which are free from recognized hazards that are causing or are likely to cause death or serious physical harm to his employees;
>> (2) shall comply with occupational safety and health standards promulgated under this Act.
>
> (b) Each employee shall comply with occupational safety and health standards and all rules, regulations, and orders issued pursuant to this Act which are applicable to his own actions and conduct.

A fundamental understanding of the reason why the Occupational Safety and Health Act of 1970 was enacted, the Congressional finding and purpose in enacting this legislation, and employer and employee responsibilities is necessary as a foundation for understanding why safe work practices are essential "to assure safe and healthful working conditions for working men and women." Lockout and tagging of circuits, control of hazardous energy, and achieving an electrically safe work condition are among the safe work practices intended to accomplish this goal.

SAFETY AND HEALTH REGULATIONS FOR CONSTRUCTION

Part 1926, Safety and Health Regulations for Construction, sets forth the safety and health standards promulgated by the Secretary of Labor under Section 107 of the Contract Work Hours and Safety Standards Act. Subpart C sets forth the general safety and health regulations of Part 1926, while Subpart K addresses electrical safety requirements within the scope of that subpart.

General Safety and Health Provisions

Subpart C provides general safety and health provisions for Part 1926, Safety and Health Regulations for Construction. The following definition and general provisions help clarify the application of Part 1926. Subpart C is to be referred to in its entirety for a complete understanding of these regulations.

1926.21(b)(2)

> The employer shall instruct each employee in the recognition and avoidance of unsafe conditions and the regulations applicable to his work environment to control or eliminate any hazards or other exposure to illness or injury.

1926.20(f)(2)

> *Training.* Standards in this part requiring training on hazards and related matters, such as standards requiring that employees receive training or that the employer train employees, provide training to employees, or institute or implement a training program, impose a separate compliance duty with respect to each employee covered by the requirement. The employer must train each affected employee in the manner required by the standard, and each failure to train an employee may be considered a separate violation.

1926.32(g)

> "Construction work." For purposes of this section, "Construction work" means work for construction, alteration, and/or repair, including painting and decorating.

Electrical Safety Requirements

Subpart K, Electrical, addresses electrical safety requirements that are necessary for the practical safeguarding of

OSHA's general safety and health provisions require that employees be instructed in any regulations applicable to their work and be able to recognize and avoid unsafe conditions.

Courtesy of Ideal Industries, Inc.

Deenergized equipment or circuits shall be rendered inoperative and have tags attached at all points where such equipment or circuits can be energized. The tags must be placed so as to clearly identify the equipment or circuits being worked on.

Courtesy of Ideal Industries, Inc.

employees involved in construction work. Subpart K is divided into four major divisions plus an applicable definitions section. Safety-related work practices—one of those four major divisions—are contained in Sections 1926.416 and 1926.417, with Section 1926.417 addressing lockout and tagging of circuits.

1926.417 - Lockout and tagging of circuits.

1926.417(a)

Controls. Controls that are to be deactivated during the course of work on energized or deenergized equipment or circuits shall be tagged.

1926.417(b)

Equipment and circuits. Equipment or circuits that are deenergized shall be rendered inoperative and shall have tags attached at all points where such equipment or circuits can be energized.

1926.417(c)

Tags. Tags shall be placed to identify plainly the equipment or circuits being worked on.

OCCUPATIONAL SAFETY AND HEALTH STANDARDS

The title of Part 1910 is the Occupational Safety and Health Standards. Per 1910.1(b), Part 1910 carries out the directive of the Secretary of Labor under section 6(a) of the Occupational Safety and Health Act of 1970. It contains occupational safety and health standards that have been found to be national consensus standards or established federal standards. A number of provisions from Subparts J and S are examined here. Subpart S, Electrical, includes 1910.333(b)(2), Lockout and Tagging. Subpart J, General Environmental Controls, includes 1910.147, The Control of Hazardous Energy (Lockout/Tagout).

Lockout and Tagging

Part 1910, Subpart S, addresses electrical safety requirements that are necessary for the practical safeguarding of employees in their workplaces. It is divided into four major divisions, one of which contains safety-related work practice regulations, in Sections 1910.331 through 1910.360. Lockout and tagging within the scope of Subpart S is covered within 1910.333(b), which deals with working on or near exposed deenergized parts. **See Figure 4-1.**

Figure 4-1   Locks and Tags

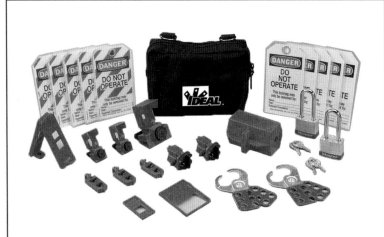

Figure 4-1. *Both locks and tags are generally required when working on or near exposed deenergized parts.*

Courtesy of Ideal Industries, Inc.

Appropriate lockout and tagout devices must be used in compliance with any applicable requirements while any employee is exposed to contact with equipment or circuits that have been deenergized.

Courtesy of Ideal Industries, Inc.

Application

1910.333(b)(1)

"Application." This paragraph applies to work on exposed deenergized parts or near enough to them to expose the employee to any electrical hazard they present. Conductors and parts of electric equipment that have been deenergized but have not been locked out or tagged in accordance with paragraph (b) of this section shall be treated as energized parts, and paragraph (c) of this section applies to work on or near them.

1910.333(b)(2)

"Lockout and Tagging." While any employee is exposed to contact with parts of fixed electric equipment or circuits which have been deenergized, the circuits energizing the parts shall be locked out or tagged or both in accordance with the requirements of this paragraph. The requirements shall be followed in the order in which they are presented (i.e., paragraph (b)(2)(i) first, then paragraph (b)(2)(ii), etc.).

Note 1: As used in this section, fixed equipment refers to equipment fastened in place or connected by permanent wiring methods.

Note 2: Lockout and tagging procedures that comply with paragraphs (c) through (f) of 1910.147 will also be deemed to comply with paragraph (b)(2) of this section provided that:

[1] The procedures address the electrical safety hazards covered by this Subpart; and

[2] The procedures also incorporate the requirements of paragraphs (b)(2)(iii)(D) and (b)(2)(iv)(B) of this section.

Procedures

1910.333(b)(2)(i)

"Procedures." The employer shall maintain a written copy of the procedures outlined in paragraph (b)(2) and shall make it available for inspection by employees and by the Assistant Secretary of Labor and his or her authorized representatives.

Note: The written procedures may be in the form of a copy of paragraph (b) of this section.

Deenergizing Equipment

1910.333(b)(2)(ii)

"Deenergizing equipment."

1910.333(b)(2)(ii)(A)

Safe procedures for deenergizing circuits and equipment shall be determined before circuits or equipment are deenergized.

1910.333(b)(2)(ii)(B)

The circuits and equipment to be worked on shall be disconnected from all electric energy sources. Control circuit devices, such as push buttons, selector switches, and interlocks, may not be used as the sole means for deenergizing circuits or equipment. Interlocks for electric equipment may not be used as a substitute for lockout and tagging procedures.

1910.333(b)(2)(ii)(C)

Stored electric energy which might endanger personnel shall be released. Capacitors shall be discharged and high capacitance elements shall be short-circuited and grounded, if the stored electric energy might endanger personnel.

Note: If the capacitors or associated equipment are handled in meeting this requirement, they shall be treated as energized.

1910.333(b)(2)(ii)(D)

Stored non-electrical energy in devices that could reenergize electric circuit parts shall be blocked or relieved to the extent that the circuit parts could not be accidentally energized by the device.

All electrical energy sources must be accounted for.

Courtesy of Ideal Industries, Inc.

The lockout and tagging procedures must be in writing and made available for inspection.

Photo courtesy of National Electrical Contractors Association (NECA)

Stored nonelectrical energy must be blocked or relieved as necessary.

Courtesy of Ideal Industries, Inc.

Application of Locks and Tags

1910.333(b)(2)(iii)

"Application of Locks and Tags."

1910.333(b)(2)(iii)(A)

A lock and a tag shall be placed on each disconnecting means used to deenergize circuits and equipment on which work is to be performed, except as provided in paragraphs (b)(2)(iii)(C) and (b)(2)(iii)(E) of this section. The lock shall be attached so as to prevent persons from operating the disconnecting means unless they resort to undue force or the use of tools.

1910.333(b)(2)(iii)(B)

Each tag shall contain a statement prohibiting unauthorized operation of the disconnecting means and removal of the tag.

1910.333(b)(2)(iii)(C)

If a lock cannot be applied, or if the employer can demonstrate that tagging procedures will provide a level of safety equivalent to that obtained by the use of a lock, a tag may be used without a lock.

1910.333(b)(2)(iii)(D)

A tag used without a lock, as permitted by paragraph (b)(2)(iii)(C) of this section, shall be supplemented by at least one additional safety measure that provides a level of safety equivalent to that obtained by use of a lock. Examples of additional safety measures include the removal of an isolating circuit element, blocking of a controlling switch, or opening of an extra disconnecting device.

1910.333(b)(2)(iii)(E)

A lock may be placed without a tag only under the following conditions:

1910.333(b)(2)(iii)(E)(1)

Only one circuit or piece of equipment is deenergized, and

1910.333(b)(2)(iii)(E)(2)

The lockout period does not extend beyond the work shift, and

1910.333(b)(2)(iii)(E)(3)

Employees exposed to the hazards associated with reenergizing the circuit or equipment are familiar with this procedure.

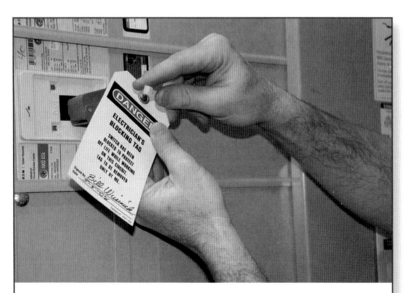

Both a lock and a tag are generally required to be placed on a disconnecting means for circuits and equipment before work begins.

Courtesy of National Electrical Contractors Association (NECA)

A tag must warn against both unauthorized disconnecting means of operation and unauthorized removal of the tag.

Courtesy of Ideal Industries, Inc.

Verification of Deenergized Condition

1910.333(b)(2)(iv)

Verification of deenergized condition. The requirements of this paragraph shall be met before any circuits or equipment can be considered and worked as deenergized.

1910.333(b)(2)(iv)(A)

A qualified person shall operate the equipment operating controls or otherwise verify that the equipment cannot be restarted.

1910.333(b)(2)(iv)(B)

A qualified person shall use test equipment to test the circuit elements and electrical parts of equipment to which employees will be exposed and shall verify that the circuit elements and equipment parts are deenergized. The test shall also determine if any energized condition exists as a result of inadvertently induced voltage or unrelated voltage backfeed even though specific parts of the circuit have been deenergized and presumed to be safe. If the circuit to be tested is over 600 volts, nominal, the test equipment shall be checked for proper operation immediately after this test.

Tags are permitted to be used without a lock under limited circumstances, but only where at least one additional safety measure is employed and safety equal to a lock is assured.

Courtesy of Ideal Industries, Inc.

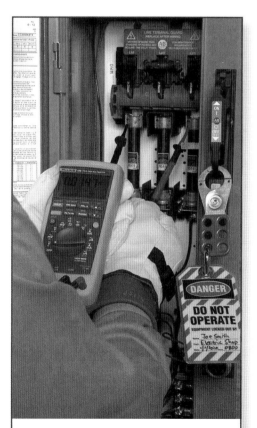

A qualified person must test all circuit elements and electrical parts of equipment to verify that they are in a deenergized state.

Reenergizing Equipment

1910.333(b)(2)(v)

"Reenergizing Equipment." These requirements shall be met, in the order given, before circuits or equipment are reenergized, even temporarily.

1910.333(b)(2)(v)(A)

A qualified person shall conduct tests and visual inspections, as necessary, to verify that all tools, electrical jumpers, shorts, grounds, and other such devices have been removed, so that the circuits and equipment can be safely energized.

1910.333(b)(2)(v)(B)

Employees exposed to the hazards associated with reenergizing the circuit or equipment shall be warned to stay clear of circuits and equipment.

1910.333(b)(2)(v)(C)

Each lock and tag shall be removed by the employee who applied it or under his or her direct supervision. However, if this employee is absent from the workplace, then the lock or tag may be removed by a qualified person designated to perform this task provided that:

1910.333(b)(2)(v)(C)(1)

The employer ensures that the employee who applied the lock or tag is not available at the workplace, and

1910.333(b)(2)(v)(C)(2)

The employer ensures that the employee is aware that the lock or tag has been removed before he or she resumes work at that workplace.

1910.333(b)(2)(v)(D)

There shall be a visual determination that all employees are clear of the circuits and equipment.

The Control of Hazardous Energy (Lockout/Tagout)

Many lockout/tagout programs incorporate OSHA 29 CFR 1910.147. This standard is found in Subpart J, General Environmental Controls, of Part 1910, Occupational Safety and Health Standards, and is entitled "The control of hazardous energy (lockout/tagout)."

Recall that Note 2 to 1910.333(b)(2) clarifies that lockout and tagging procedures that comply with paragraphs (c) through (f) of 1910.147 will also be deemed to comply with paragraph (b)(2) of this section provided that two criteria are satisfied:

- The procedures address the electrical safety hazards covered by Subpart S.
- The procedures incorporate the requirements of paragraphs 1910.333(b)(2)(iii)(D) and 1910.333(b)(2)(iv)(B).

Section 1910.147 is broken down into six different major headings, each of which is indicated by a different lowercase letter:
- a. Scope, application, and purpose
- b. Definitions
- c. General

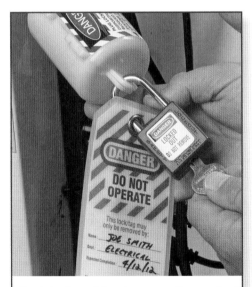

Each lock and tag is generally required to be removed by the employee who applied it.

Courtesy of Ideal Industries, Inc.

- d. Application of control
- e. Release from lockout or tagout
- f. Additional requirements

See 1910.147 for OSHA's requirements for "The control of hazardous energy (lockout/tagout)."

OSHA Tip

Per Note 1 to 1910.269(d)(1), Hazardous energy control (lockout/tagout) procedures, installations in electric power generation facilities that are not an integral part of, or inextricably commingled with, power generation processes or equipment are covered under § 1910.147 and Subpart S of Part 1910.

Typical Minimal Lockout Procedures

Appendix A to OSHA 29 CFR 1910.147 serves as a nonmandatory guideline to assist employers and employees in complying with the requirements of 1910.147 and to provide other helpful information. **See Figure 4-2.** Nothing in the appendix adds to or detracts from any of the requirements of 1910.147. Rather, a simple lockout procedure is described to assist employers in developing their own procedures so they meet the requirements of this standard. For more complex systems, more comprehensive procedures may need to be developed, documented, and utilized.

Definitions

OSHA defines the terms *lockout, energy-isolating device, tagout, lockout device*, and *tagout device* in 1910.147(b). These definitions are applicable within 1910.147:

The terms *deenergized* and *energized* are defined as follows in OSHA 1910.399 and apply to 1910 Subpart S.

Deenergized. Free from any electrical connection to a source of potential difference and from electrical charge; not having a potential different from that of the earth.

Energized. Electrically connected to a source of potential difference.

For additional information, visit qr.njatcdb.org Item #1561

ESTABLISHING AN ELECTRICALLY SAFE WORK CONDITION

OSHA's lockout/tagout requirements are federal law. However, in addition to developing lockout/tagout programs and procedures for working on or near exposed deenergized parts that fulfill

Lockout. The placement of a lockout device on an energy isolating device, in accordance with an established procedure, ensuring that the energy isolating device and the equipment being controlled cannot be operated until the lockout device is removed.

Energy isolating device. A mechanical device that physically prevents the transmission or release of energy, including but not limited to the following: A manually operated electrical circuit breaker; a disconnect switch; a manually operated switch by which the conductors of a circuit can be disconnected from all ungrounded supply conductors, and, in addition, no pole can be operated independently; a line valve; a block; and any similar device used to block or isolate energy. Push buttons, selector switches and other control circuit type devices are not energy isolating devices.

Tagout. The placement of a tagout device on an energy isolating device, in accordance with an established procedure, to indicate that the energy isolating device and the equipment being controlled may not be operated until the tagout device is removed.

Lockout device. A device that utilizes a positive means such as a lock, either key or combination type, to hold an energy isolating device in the safe position and prevent the energizing of a machine or equipment. Included are blank flanges and bolted slip blinds.

Tagout device. A prominent warning device, such as a tag and a means of attachment, which can be securely fastened to an energy isolating device in accordance with established procedure, to indicate that the energy isolating device and the equipment being controlled may not be operated until the tagout device is removed.

Affected employee. An employee whose job requires him/her to operate or use a machine or equipment on which servicing or maintenance is being performed under lockout or tagout, or whose job requires him/her to work in an area in which such servicing or maintenance is being performed.

Figure 4-2   Example Lockout Procedure

General

The following simple lockout procedure is provided to assist employers in developing their procedures so they meet the requirements of this standard. When the energy isolating devices are not lockable, tagout may be used, provided the employer complies with the provisions of the standard which require additional training and more rigorous periodic inspections. When tagout is used and the energy isolating devices are lockable, the employer must provide full employee protection (see paragraph (c) (3)) and additional training and more rigorous periodic inspections are required. For more complex systems, more comprehensive procedures may need to be developed, documented, and utilized.

Lockout Procedure

Lockout Procedure for

_____

(Name of Company for single procedure or identification of equipment if multiple procedures are used).

Purpose

This procedure establishes the minimum requirements for the lockout of energy isolating devices whenever maintenance or servicing is done on machines or equipment. It shall be used to ensure that the machine or equipment is stopped, isolated from all potentially hazardous energy sources and locked out before employees perform any servicing or maintenance where the unexpected energization or start-up of the machine or equipment or release of stored energy could cause injury.

Compliance With This Program

All employees are required to comply with the restrictions and limitations imposed upon them during the use of lockout. The authorized employees are required to perform the lockout in accordance with this procedure. All employees, upon observing a machine or piece of equipment which is locked out to perform servicing or maintenance shall not attempt to start, energize, or use that machine or equipment.

_____

(Type of compliance enforcement to be taken for violation of the above.)

Sequence of Lockout

(1) Notify all affected employees that servicing or maintenance is required on a machine or equipment and that the machine or equipment must be shut down and locked out to perform the servicing or maintenance.

_____

(Name(s)/Job Title(s) of affected employees and how to notify.)

(2) The authorized employee shall refer to the company procedure to identify the type and magnitude of the energy that the machine or equipment utilizes, shall understand the hazards of the energy, and shall know the methods to control the energy.

_____

(Type(s) and magnitude(s) of energy, its hazards and the methods to control the energy.)

(3) If the machine or equipment is operating, shut it down by the normal stopping procedure (depress the stop button, open switch, close valve, etc.).

_____

(Type(s) and location(s) of machine or equipment operating controls.)

(4) De-activate the energy isolating device(s) so that the machine or equipment is isolated from the energy source(s).

_____

(Type(s) and location(s) of energy isolating devices.)

(5) Lock out the energy isolating device(s) with assigned individual lock(s).

(6) Stored or residual energy (such as that in capacitors, springs, elevated machine members, rotating flywheels, hydraulic systems, and air, gas, steam, or water pressure, etc.) must be dissipated or restrained by methods such as grounding, repositioning, blocking, bleeding down, etc.

_____

(Type(s) of stored energy—methods to dissipate or restrain.)

(7) Ensure that the equipment is disconnected from the energy source(s) by first checking that no personnel are exposed, then verify the isolation of the equipment by operating the push button or other normal operating control(s) or by testing to make certain the equipment will not operate.

Caution: Return operating control(s) to neutral or "off" position after verifying the isolation of the equipment.

_____

(Method of verifying the isolation of the equipment.)

(8) The machine or equipment is now locked out.

"Restoring Equipment to Service." When the servicing or maintenance is completed and the machine or equipment is ready to return to normal operating condition, the following steps shall be taken.

(1) Check the machine or equipment and the immediate area around the machine to ensure that nonessential items have been removed and that the machine or equipment components are operationally intact.

(2) Check the work area to ensure that all employees have been safely positioned or removed from the area.

(3) Verify that the controls are in neutral.

(4) Remove the lockout devices and reenergize the machine or equipment. Note: The removal of some forms of blocking may require reenergization of the machine before safe removal.

(5) Notify affected employees that the servicing or maintenance is completed and the machine or equipment is ready for used.

[54 FR 36687, Sept. 1, 1989 as amended at 54 FR 42498, Oct. 17, 1989; 55 FR 38685, Sept. 20, 1990; 61 FR 5507, Feb. 13, 1996]

Figure 4-2. *An example of a simple lockout procedure, found in OSHA 29 CFR 1910.147 Appendix A, describes how employers may create their own procedures.*

the requirements of 29 CFR 1910.147, 1910.333(b), and 1926.417, establishing an electrically safe work condition based on the requirements of *NFPA 70E* Article 120 should be considered. An electrically safe work condition is defined in Article 100 in *NFPA 70E*. Note that, per 110.2, electrical conductors and circuit parts shall not be considered to be in an electrically safe work condition until all of the requirements of Article 120 have been met.

Note that Article 120 is divided into five sections that provide the requirements for establishing an electrically safe work condition:

- Lockout/Tagout Program
- Lockout/Tagout Principles
- Lockout/Tagout Equipment
- Lockout/Tagout Procedures
- Process for Establishing and Verifying an Electrically Safe Work Condition

Articles 100, 110, and 120 need to be referenced for these requirements in their entirety.

Lockout/Tagout Program, Principles, Equipment, and Procedures

Article 120 consists of the requirements outlined in *NFPA 70E* Sections 120.1, 120.2, 120.3, and 120.4, which are established and verified by the eight-step process outlined in Section 120.5. Establishing an electrically safe work condition is one example of how *NFPA 70E* can supplement and enhance OSHA's requirements for lockout and tagging of circuits (1926.417), control of

hazardous energy (lockout/tagout; 1910.147), and the lockout and tagging provisions of 1910.333(b)(2), among others.

Sections 120.1, 120.2, 120.3, and 120.4 set forth the requirements for the lockout/tagout program, principles, equipment, and procedures, respectively. These requirements are to be referenced in their entirety for a complete understanding of their content and application.

The Process for Establishing and Verifying an Electrically Safe Work Condition

The provisions of *NFPA 70E* Article 120 generally meet or exceed OSHA's lockout/tagout requirements and should be examined carefully for considerations related to developing a more comprehensive and complete lockout/tagout program. This includes, but is not limited to, all of Article 120, including the eight steps of the process outlined in Section 120.5. Per 120.5, the eight steps are to be performed in the order presented, if feasible.

Informative Annex G

NFPA 70E Informative Annex G, Sample Lockout/Tagout Program, should also be considered. It is provided for informational purposes only and is not a part of the requirements of *NFPA 70E*. This annex offers a sample program and procedures to assist employers in developing a program and procedures that meet the requirements of *NFPA 70E* Article 120.

SUMMARY

OSHA's steps for lockout/tagout and detailed requirements for working on or near exposed deenergized parts must be followed. Training, planning, and preparation are critical to avoid incidents and injury.

The Occupational Safety and Health Act of 1970 was enacted "to assure safe and healthful working conditions for working men and women." The provisions of OSHA 29 CFR 1926.417 provide performance requirements for lockout and tagging of circuits within the scope of Subpart K. OSHA 29 CFR 1910.333(b)(2) and OSHA 29 CFR 1910.147 cover minimum steps for lockout/tagout, as well as procedures to follow when lockout or tagout devices are removed and energy is restored within the scope of their respective subparts.

Finally, consider *NFPA 70E* Article 120 as a supplement to OSHA's requirements and procedures. Following the process in *NFPA 70E* Section 120.5 for establishment and verification that an electrically safe work condition has been achieved, along with all of Article 120, will allow for a more comprehensive lockout/tagout program.

REVIEW QUESTIONS

1. OSHA defines a __?__ as a device that utilizes a positive means such as a lock, either key or combination type, to hold an energy isolating device in the safe position and prevent the energizing of a machine or equipment.
   a. lockout device
   b. lockout/tagout device
   c. tagout device
   d. tie wrap

2. OSHA defines a __?__ as a prominent warning device, such as a tag and a means of attachment, which can be securely fastened to an energy isolating device in accordance with established procedure, to indicate that the energy isolating device and the equipment being controlled may not be operated until the device is removed.
   a. labeling device
   b. lockout device
   c. lockout/tagout device
   d. tagout device

3. Per OSHA, each __?__ shall furnish to each employee employment and a place of employment which are free from recognized hazards that are causing or are likely to cause death or serious physical harm to employees.
   a. business manager
   b. employer
   c. trade
   d. training director

4. Each __?__ shall comply with occupational safety and health standards and all rules, regulations, and orders issued pursuant to the OSH Act which are applicable to his or her own actions and conduct.
   a. craft
   b. employee
   c. employer
   d. trade

5. Lockout and tagging of circuits, control of hazardous energy, and achieving an electrically safe work condition are among the safe __?__ intended to assure worker safety and health.
   a. habits
   b. happenings
   c. ideas
   d. work practices

6. Per OSHA Part 1926, Subpart C, the employer shall instruct each employee in the recognition and avoidance of __?__ conditions and the regulations applicable to his or her work environment to control or eliminate any hazards or other exposure to illness or injury.
   a. abnormal
   b. normal
   c. safe
   d. unsafe

7. OSHA Part 1910 states that the lock shall be attached so as to __?__ operation of the disconnecting means unless one would resort to undue force or the use of tools.
   a. allow
   b. discourage
   c. encourage
   d. prevent

8. OSHA Part 1910 states that if a lock __?__ be applied, or if the employer can demonstrate that tagging procedures will provide a level of safety equivalent to that obtained by the use of a lock, a tag may be used without a lock.
   a. can
   b. cannot
   c. should not
   d. will not

9. OSHA Part 1910 states that a tag used without a lock shall be __?__ by at least one additional safety measure that provides a level of safety equivalent to that obtained by use of a lock.
   a. complemented
   b. implemented
   c. prevented
   d. supplemented

Introduction to *NFPA 70E*

An important provision in Section 5 of the Occupational Safety and Health Act of 1970 (OSH Act) requires that workers be provided with a workplace free from recognized hazards. However, it is not always clear how to provide a hazard-free workplace. Many consider the requirements in *NFPA 70E* as a means to comply with the OSHA requirements related to work involving electrical hazards.

It is important to be familiar with the *NFPA 70E* standard, with a primary focus in this chapter on the provisions of Articles 90, 100, 105, 110, and 120. These provisions include, but are not limited to, scope, definitions, host and contract employers' responsibilities, training requirements, electrical safety program considerations, test instruments and equipment, and establishing an electrically safe work condition.

Objectives

» Understand the history, scope, definitions, and organization of *NFPA 70E*.

» Become familiar with the *NFPA 70E* provisions related to host and contract employer responsibilities and use of electrical equipment.

» Understand the requirements necessary for creating an electrical safety program, training, and achieving an electrically safe work condition.

» Become familiar with the topics addressed in Article 130 and the 18 informative annexes in *NFPA 70E*.

Chapter 5

Table of Contents

CASE STUDY

Case Study

A 46-year-old electrical project supervisor died when he contacted an energized conductor inside a control panel. The employer was an industrial electrical contracting company that had been in operation for 10 years. It employed 20 workers, including three electrical project supervisors. The company's written safety program, which was administered by the president/CEO and the electrical project supervisors, included disciplinary procedures. The president/CEO served as the safety officer on a collateral duty basis, and the supervisors held monthly safety meetings with all crew members.

The victim had worked for the company for five years and three months as an electrical project supervisor and had approximately 27 years of electrical experience. The company and victim had been working at the packaging plant for six months before the incident; the incident was the company's first fatality.

The company had been contracted to install control cabinets, conduit, wiring, and solid-state compressor motor starters for two 400-horsepower air compressors. On the day of the incident, the victim and three coworkers (one Electrical Worker and two helpers) arrived at the plant at 7 a.m. They were scheduled to install the last starter and to complete the wiring from the compressor motor to the starter in the control panel, and from the starter control panel to the main distribution panel. Once installation was completed, they were to check the operation of the unit.

At approximately 3:15 p.m., the starter had been installed, and all associated wiring had been completed. The victim directed a helper to turn the switch to the "on" position at the main distribution panel, approximately six feet away, to check the starter's operation. The helper turned the switch to the "on" position, energizing the components inside the starter control panel. The victim pushed the "start" button, and the starter indicator light activated, but the compressor motor did not start. When the compressor motor did not engage, the victim concluded that a problem existed inside the starter control panel. The victim directed the helper to retrieve a voltmeter so that he could check the continuity of the wiring inside the starter control panel. In the interim, the victim opened the starter control panel door without deenergizing the unit and reached inside to trace the wiring and check the integrity of the electrical leads. In doing so, he contacted the 480-volt primary lead for the motor starter with his left hand.

Current passed through the victim's left hand and body and exited through his feet to the ground. The victim yelled, and the helper immediately turned the main distribution switch to the "off" position as the victim collapsed to the floor. Emergency medical services (EMS) was called, and the helper checked the victim and immediately administered cardiopulmonary resuscitation (CPR). EMS personnel arrived in 10 to 15 minutes, continued CPR, and transported the victim to the local hospital, where he was pronounced dead one hour and 20 minutes after the incident occurred.

Source: For details of this case, see FACE Investigation #03CA006. Accessed April 7, 2020.

For additional information, visit qr.njatcdb.org Item #1195

INTRODUCTION

An important provision in Section 5 of the Occupational Safety and Health Act of 1970 (OSH Act) requires that workers be provided with a workplace free from recognized hazards. However, it is not always clear how to provide a hazard-free workplace. OSHA requirements addressing electrical hazards are often written in performance language; that is, the rules define a result without providing details of how to accomplish it. Many people consider the requirements defined in *NFPA 70E* as a means to comply with the OSHA requirements related to work involving electrical hazards.

Any Electrical Worker can benefit from an overview of the *NFPA 70E* standard, with a primary focus in this chapter on the provisions of Articles 90, 100, 105, 110, and 120. These provisions include, but are not limited to, scope, definitions, host and contract employers' responsibilities, training requirements, electrical safety program considerations, test instruments and equipment, and establishing an electrically safe work condition.

NFPA 70E HISTORY, INTRODUCTION, AND APPLICATION OF SAFETY-RELATED WORK PRACTICES

NFPA 70E: Standard for Electrical Safety in the Workplace consists of three chapters and 18 informative annexes, as well as the Foreword to *NFPA 70E* and Article 90, Introduction. Chapter 1 is divided into five articles: 100, 105, 110, 120, and 130. Article 100 provides definitions essential to the application of *NFPA 70E*. Article 105 addresses the *application of* safety-related work practices and procedures. Article 110 contains the general requirements for electrical safety-related work practices. Article 120 provides the requirements for establishing an electrically safe work condition. Article 130 contains the provisions related to work involving electrical hazards.

History and Evolution of *NFPA 70E*

The Foreword to *NFPA 70E* offers a look at the history and evolution of this NFPA standard. The appointment of the *NFPA 70E* Committee was announced on January 7, 1976. This committee was formed to assist OSHA in preparing electrical safety standards that would serve its requirements and that could be expeditiously promulgated through the provisions of Section 6(b) of the Occupational Safety and Health Act. A primary concern was OSHA's need for electrical regulations that addressed electrical safety-related work practices and maintenance of the electrical system considered critical to safety for employers and employees in their workplaces.

The committee found it feasible to develop a standard for electrical installations that would be compatible with OSHA requirements for the safety of the employee in locations covered by the *National Electrical Code®* (*NEC*). The new standard was named *NFPA 70E: Standard for Electrical Safety Requirements for Employee Workplaces*. The first edition was published in 1979.

The fifth edition, published in 1995, included the concepts of "limits of approach" and the establishment of an "arc." In 2000, the sixth edition continued to focus on the establishment of flash protection boundaries, the use of personal protective equipment, and charts to assist the user in applying appropriate protective clothing and personal protective equipment for common tasks.

The seventh edition, published in 2004, reflected a name change of the document to *NFPA 70E: Standard for Electrical Safety in the Workplace*, as well as the addition of the energized electrical work permit and related requirements.

The 2021 edition of *NFPA 70E: Standard for Electrical Safety in the Workplace* had an effective date of June 21, 2020, and supersedes all previous editions.

NFPA 70E Introductory Information

Article 90 contains the introductory information for *NFPA 70E: Standard for Electrical Safety in the Workplace*. It spells out the purpose, scope, and arrangement of the *70E* standard. Also covered here are the requirements related to formal interpretations as well as those related to mandatory rules, permissive rules, and explanatory material. Refer to Article 90 for these requirements in their entirety.

Purpose and Scope

The purpose of *NFPA 70E* is covered in the first section of Article 90, Introduction. It is to provide a practical safe working area for employees relative to the hazards arising from the use of electricity. The scope of Article 90 outlines what is covered and not covered by this standard.

Arrangement

The *NFPA 70E* standard is divided into Article 90, Introduction; 3 chapters; and 18 informative annexes. Informative Annex B is reserved for future use.

Application of the three chapters of the *NFPA 70E* standard are described in 90.3, Standard Arrangement. The informative annexes are not part of the requirements of the *NFPA 70E* standard but are included for informational purposes only.

Rules, Explanatory Material, and Formal Interpretations

Section 90.4 spells out the provisions in *NFPA 70E* related to mandatory rules, permissive rules, and explanatory material. Mandatory rules of the *NFPA 70E* standard identify actions that are specifically required or prohibited. Permissive rules, in contrast, identify actions that are allowed but not required.

Explanatory material is included in the form of informational notes, which are not enforceable as requirements. Brackets containing section references to another NFPA document are for informational purposes only and are

provided as a guide to indicate the source of the extracted text.

Section 90.5 states that formal interpretation procedures have been established and are found in the Regulations Governing the Development of NFPA Standards.

Review and apply these and all of the requirements from Article 90 and *NFPA 70E* in their entirety. Recall from Section 90.3 that Chapter 1 of *NFPA 70E* applies generally, for example. Accordingly, the requirements of Article 90 apply beyond Article 90.

NFPA 70E Definitions

The scope of Article 100 indicates that only those definitions deemed essential to the proper application of *NFPA 70E* are provided there. The definitions apply wherever the terms are used throughout *NFPA 70E*.

Refer to Article 100 for these definitions. Become familiar with each defined term, including any informational notes, and apply its defined meaning each time it is used throughout *NFPA 70E*. While there are a number of definitions that are seldom if ever applied, there are a number of definitions that are used frequently and their meaning is essential to understanding and properly applying *NFPA 70E*. Examples include:

- arc flash hazard
- arc rating
- available fault current (fault current, available)
- balaclava
- arc flash boundary (boundary, arc flash)
- condition of maintenance (maintenance, condition of)
- de-energized
- electrical hazard
- electrical safety
- electrically safe work condition
- energized
- incident energy
- incident energy analysis
- limited approach boundary (boundary, limited approach)
- qualified person

- restricted approach boundary (boundary, restricted approach)
- risk
- risk assessment
- shock hazard
- unqualified person
- working distance
- working on (energized electrical conductors or circuit parts)

Review and apply these and all of the definitions from Article 100 and *NFPA 70E* in their entirety. Recall from Section 90.3 that Chapter 1 of *NFPA 70E* applies generally. Accordingly, the definitions in Article 100 apply beyond Article 100.

Application of Safety-Related Work Practices and Procedures

The title of Chapter 1 of *NFPA 70E* is Safety-Related Work Practices. Not only are definitions contained in this chapter, but so too are the rules for the *application of* Chapter 1. These provisions are housed in Article 105, Application of Safety-Related Work Practices and Procedures. Refer to Article 105 for the application of provisions related to the scope, responsibility (employer and employee), priority, and organization in their entirety.

GENERAL REQUIREMENTS FOR ELECTRICAL SAFETY-RELATED WORK PRACTICES

NFPA 70E Chapter 1 also contains general requirements for electrical safety-related work practices. These general requirements are located in Article 110. The following are the first four topics addressed in Article 110:

- Priority
- General
- Electrically safe work condition
- Energized work

A brief overview of these four topic headings in the Article 110 general requirements for electrical safety-related work practices will serve as an introduction to these topics, but Article 110 must be referenced for these requirements in their entirety.

Priority and General

Section 110.1 sets forth the priority of *NFPA 70E*. Here it states that "hazard elimination shall be the first priority in the implementation of safety-related work practices." The two informational notes to this section provide examples of how this first priority may be put into practice. Both informational notes also refer to Informative Annex F for information related to both hierarchy of risk control and hazard elimination.

Section 110.2 addresses two topics. The first paragraph discusses the first topic: the application of Article 120. This Article 110 general requirement states that "electrical conductors and circuit parts shall not be considered to be in an electrically safe work condition until all of the requirements of Article 120 have been met." It is critical to remember and apply this general requirement whenever Article 120 is applied, especially Section 120.5. Although the title of 120.5 is "Process for Establishing and Verifying an Electrically Safe Work Condition," remember that 110.2 stipulates that all of the requirements of Article 120 must be met before electrical conductors and circuit parts are considered to be in an electrically safe work condition.

The second topic addressed in 110.2 is in its second paragraph. Here it states, in part, that "safe work practices . . . shall be used in accordance with Article 110 and Article 130 until such time that electrical conductors and circuit parts are in an electrically safe work condition." This *70E* requirement is somewhat similar to OSHA requirements regarding deenergized electrical equipment. Per 1910.333(b)(1), conductors and parts of electrical equipment that have been deenergized but have not been locked out or tagged in accordance with paragraph (b) of this section shall be treated as energized parts, and paragraph (c) of this section applies to work on or near them.

Electrically Safe Work Condition

Section 110.3 addresses the two conditions where energized electrical

conductors and circuit parts operating at voltages equal to or greater than 50 volts must be put into an electrically safe work condition. These are:
- If the employee is within the limited approach boundary.
- If the employee interacts with equipment where conductors or circuit parts are not exposed but an increased likelihood of injury from an exposure to an arc flash hazard exists.

Review the definitions of "shock hazard" and "arc flash hazard" and their respective informational notes in Article 100 to gain a better understanding of the two conditions above. This includes, in part, the factors that influence the type and severity of injury and damage to health resulting from shock, when the likelihood of occurrence of an arc flash incident increases, and examples of tasks that increase the likelihood of an arc flash incident occurring.

Energized Work

Section 110.4 is divided in four subdivisions that establish the requirements related to energized versus deenergized work. These include:
- Additional Hazards or Increased Risk
- Infeasibility
- Equipment Operating at Less Than 50 Volts
- Normal Operating Condition

Carefully review these requirements in 110.4(A), (B), (C), and (D) related to energized work as well as the related informational notes that provide additional insight into the energized work requirements of 110.4. **See Figure 5-1.**

Review and determine the similarities and differences between the requirements in 110.4 compared to the OSHA requirements in 1910.333(a)(1). Also review the three notes accompanying this OSHA requirement regarding examples of increased or additional hazards, examples of work that may be performed on or near energized circuit parts because of infeasibility, and work on or near deenergized parts.

The next four sections in Chapter 1 address the following four topics:
- Electrical safety program
- Training requirements
- Host and contract employers' responsibilities
- Test instruments and equipment

A brief overview of these four topic headings in the Article 110 general requirements for electrical safety-related work practices follows. As always, Article 110 needs to be referenced for these requirements in their entirety.

Electrical Safety Program

Based on the title of this section, one who opens the pages of *NFPA 70E* might expect to find a comprehensive, ready-to-go electrical safety program. What *NFPA 70E* actually provides is not a complete electrical safety program, but rather a number of minimum considerations that must be evaluated and integrated into the framework of an existing electrical safety

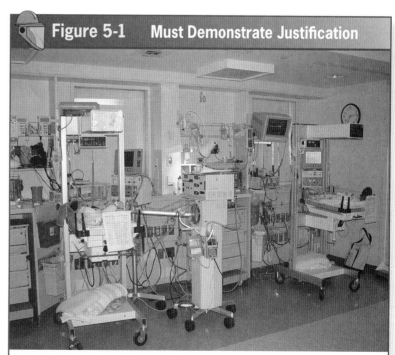

Figure 5-1   Must Demonstrate Justification

Figure 5-1. *Energized work is permitted where the employer can demonstrate that deenergizing introduces additional hazards or increased risk or that the task to be performed is infeasible in a deenergized state due to equipment design or operational limitations.*

Courtesy of Michael J. Johnston-NECA

program to make it more comprehensive. Specific requirements are provided in 110.5 as to what must be included in an *NFPA 70E*-compliant electrical safety program. These are divided into thirteen major categories that begin with the general requirements in 110.5(A) and conclude with the auditing requirements in 110.5(M). Nonmandatory information is also provided in *NFPA 70E* Informative Annex E, Electrical Safety Program.

General, Inspection, Condition of Maintenance, and Awareness and Self-Discipline Requirements

The first of thirteen considerations for an electrical safety program is the general requirements. Here it is required, in part, that the employer must "implement and document an electrical safety program that directs activity appropriate to the risk associated with electrical hazards." There are also four informational notes offering insight into these requirements, including a reference to Informative Annex P.

The second and third of these thirteen considerations are those addressing electrical equipment and system inspection and condition of maintenance. Section 110.5(B), Inspection, stipulates, in part, that the electrical safety program must include elements to verify that newly installed or modified electrical equipment or systems have been inspected as required prior to placing these into service. Section 110.5(C), Condition of Maintenance, requires that the electrical safety program "include elements that consider the condition of maintenance of electrical equipment and systems." This is just one of a number of locations in *NFPA 70E* where electrical equipment maintenance must be considered. Also see 130.5(B)(2), 130.5(G), Informational Note No. 2 to Table 130.5(C), and 205.3, for example.

The fourth of the thirteen factors that *NFPA 70E* requires to be included in the electrical safety program is awareness and self-discipline. These requirements are located in 110.5(D).

Electrical Safety Program Principles, Controls, and Procedures

The fifth, sixth, and seventh of the thirteen factors that *NFPA 70E* requires to be included in the electrical safety program are program principles, controls, and procedures. The electrical safety program must identify the principles upon which it is based, the controls by which it is measured and monitored, and the procedures that are to be utilized before work is started by employees exposed to an electrical hazard. Note that no specific requirements indicate what those program principles, controls, and procedures must be. While reference is made to the information in Informative Annex E through three informational notes, these notes and the informative annex information are nonmandatory. Sections E.1, E.2, and E.3 of Informative Annex E include examples of considerations that could be considered as part of the principles, controls, and procedures required by 110.5(E), (F), and (G), respectively.

Risk Assessment Procedure

The eighth element required by *NFPA 70E* to be included in an electrical safety program is a risk assessment procedure. Here it requires that the electrical safety program both include a risk assessment procedure and that it complies with 110.5(H)(1) through 110.5(H)(3). Three topics are addressed in 110.5(H):

(1) Elements of a Risk Assessment Procedure
(2) Human Error
(3) Hierarchy of Risk Control Methods

Per 110.5(H)(1), the risk assessment procedure must both address employee exposure to electrical hazards and identify the process to be used before work is started to identify hazards, assess risks, and implement risk control according to the hierarchy of risk control methods.

Note that, per 110.6(A)(1)(c)(4)d., qualified persons permitted to work within the limited approach boundary must be trained in the decision-making process necessary to be able to select the appropriate risk control methods from the hierarchy of controls identified in 110.5(H)(3), including personal protective equipment. Note also that this is among the training that must be documented when the employee demonstrates proficiency per 110.6(A)(5).

Additional guidance is offered in five informational notes to these requirements. One of these five informational notes discusses ". . . identifying when a second person might be required and the training and equipment that second person should have." Two of these five informational notes to 110.5(H) mention Informative Annex F and the hierarchy of risk control methods.

Also see 110.5(H)(1)(3), 110.5(H)(3), 110.6(A)(1)(c)(4)d., 130.4(C), 130.5(C), and superscript note b (^b) to Table 130.5(C) for additional requirements related to hierarchy of risk control. These, like all of the requirements in *NFPA 70E*, need to be reviewed and applied in their entirety.

Job Safety Planning and Job Briefing

The ninth of the thirteen topics that *NFPA 70E* requires to be addressed in an electrical safety program is job safety planning and job briefing. All of the requirements of 110.5(I) must be accomplished before any job is started that involves exposure to electrical hazards.

The provisions of 110.5(I)(1) require the job safety plan to be completed by a qualified person, be documented, and include the following information:

- A description of the job and the individual tasks
- Identification of the electrical hazards associated with each task
- A shock risk assessment in accordance with 130.4 for tasks involving a shock hazard
- An arc flash risk assessment in accordance with 130.5 for tasks involving an arc flash hazard
- Work procedures involved, special precautions, and energy source controls

Note that the requirements in 110.5(I)(2) mention examples of the subjects that must be covered during a job briefing. One of these subjects is the information on the energized electrical work permit, if a permit is required.

An informational note alerts that Figure I.1 in Informative Annex I offers an example of a job briefing form and planning checklist. Keep in mind that Informative Annex I is non-mandatory in both format and content.

The job safety planning, job briefing, and change in scope requirements of 110.5(I)(1), (2), and (3) must be reviewed and implemented in their entirety, as applicable.

Incident Investigations

The tenth of the thirteen topics that *NFPA 70E* requires to be included in an electrical safety program is incident investigations. The electrical safety program must include elements to investigate electrical incidents per 110.5(J). An informational note to this section provides additional insight into what might be considered an electrical incident, "close call" or "near miss."

Electrically Safe Work Condition Policy

The eleventh of the thirteen topics that *NFPA 70E* requires to be included in an electrical safety program is an electrically safe work condition policy. Review the requirements of 110.3 since the provisions of 110.5(K) require an electrical safety program to include an electrically safe work condition policy that complies with 110.3.

Lockout/Tagout Program

The twelfth of the thirteen topics that *NFPA 70E* requires to be included in an electrical safety program relates to lockout/tagout program requirements. Locate and review the requirements of 120.1(A) since the provisions of 110.5(L) require an electrical safety program to include the information required by one of the following:

- A lockout/tagout program in accordance with 120.1(A)
- A reference to the employer's lockout/tagout program established in accordance with 120.1(A)

Auditing

The last of the thirteen topics that *NFPA 70E* requires to be included in an electrical safety program is auditing. Section 110.5(M), Auditing, is divided into four topics:

(1) Electrical Safety Program Audit
(2) Field Work Audit
(3) Lockout/Tagout Program and Procedure Audit
(4) Documentation

Per 110.5(M)(1), the electrical safety program must be audited to verify that the principles and procedures of the electrical safety program are in compliance with the 2021 edition of *NFPA 70E* with audits performed at a frequency of not more than three years. Field work audits are addressed in 110.5(M)(2). Among the provisions here is a requirement that field audits be performed at intervals not to exceed one year. Lockout/tagout program and procedure audits are addressed in 110.5(M)(3) and require, in part, that the lockout/tagout program and procedures required by *NFPA 70E* Article 120 be audited by a qualified person at intervals not to exceed one year. Finally, in accordance with 110.5(M)(4), audits required by 110.5(M) must be documented. As always, it is essential to review and apply all of these and other requirements in *NFPA 70E* in their entirety.

Training Requirements

Training requirements are located in 110.6. These requirements are divided into three major headings:

- Electrical safety training
- Lockout/tagout procedure training
- Emergency response training

Electrical Safety Training

The first of three headings for training requirements addresses "electrical safety training." The training addressed in 110.6(A) covers, in part, employee training "to understand the specific hazards associated with electrical energy," training "in safety-related and procedural requirements, as necessary, to provide protection against electrical hazards," and training "to identify and understand the relationship between electrical hazards and possible injury." *NFPA 70E* 110.6(A) is subdivided into the required training for:

(1) Qualified persons
(2) Unqualified persons
(3) Additional training and retraining
(4) Type of training
(5) Electrical safety training documentation

These requirements are quite comprehensive. A brief introduction to a number of the qualified person, unqualified person, additional training and retraining, type of training, and electrical safety training documentation requirements follows. Keep in mind that 110.6(A)(5) requires, in part, that all of the training in 110.6(A) must be documented by the employer when the employee demonstrates proficiency and must be kept on file for the duration of the employee's employment. This includes the training covered in 110.6(A), including qualified person training in (A)(1), unqualified person training in (A)(2), and additional training and retraining in (A)(3).

Note that the *decision-making process* training necessary for a qualified person to work within the limited approach boundary specified in 110.6(A)(1)(c)(4)d. requires, in part, the ability to "select the appropriate risk control methods from the hierarchy of controls identified in 110.5(H)(3), including personal protective equipment."

Section 110.6(A)(1)(e) requires, in part, that employees "be trained to select an appropriate test instrument and shall demonstrate how to use a device to verify the absence of voltage" and that the training must "include information that enables the employee to understand all limitations of each test instrument that might be used."

Training that unqualified persons must receive is also addressed in 110.6(A). Recall that an unqualified person is defined in Article 100 as "a person who is not a qualified person." Accordingly, 110.6(A)(2) addresses the training required for a person who is not a qualified person. Recall that 110.6(A)(5) includes unqualified person training as electrical safety training that must be documented.

Additional training and retraining is covered in 110.6(A)(3) and requires, in part, that "additional training and retraining in safety-related work practices and applicable changes in this standard shall be performed at intervals not to exceed 3 years." In addition, note the five conditions whereby additional training (or retraining) is required as prescribed in this section.

Section 110.6(A)(4), Type of Training, requires that the training specified in 110.6(A), such as training for qualified persons, unqualified persons, and additional training and retraining, "must be classroom, on-the-job, or a combination of the two." Further, "the type and extent of the training shall be determined by the risk to the employee."

Electrical safety training documentation, as mentioned earlier, is addressed in 110.6(A)(5) and requires, in part, that the employer must "document that each employee has received the training required by 110.6(A)." This section further spells out, in part, that the documentation must (1) "be made when the employee demonstrates proficiency," (2) "be retained for the duration of the employee's employment," and (3) "contain the content of the training, each employee's name, and dates of training."

Lockout/Tagout Procedure Training
The subject of the second of the three training requirement headings is "lockout/tagout procedure training." The provisions of 110.6(B) are broken down in three categories. Section 110.6(B)(1) addresses initial training requirements, 110.6(B)(2) addresses retraining requirements, and 110.6(B)(3) covers the requirements related to lockout/tagout training documentation. These require, in part, that required retraining occur at intervals not to exceed three years, that this training be documented when an employee has received the training and when he or she has demonstrated

proficiency, and that the documentation "contain the content of the training, each employee's name, and the dates of the training."

Emergency Response Training
The third of the three headings for training requirements addresses what is categorized as "emergency response training."

This third category of training is subdivided into four subdivisions:
- Contact release
- First aid, emergency response, and resuscitation
- Training verification
- Documentation

The various training requirements under these four subdivisions are located in 110.6(C) in *NFPA 70E*. The training requirements related to contact release, including training in methods of "safe release of victims from contact with energized electrical conductors or circuit parts" and a requirement for annual contact release refresher training are addressed in 110.6(C)(1). Those for first aid, emergency response, and resuscitation, including the provision that such training "shall occur at a frequency that satisfies the requirements of the certifying body" are in 110.6(C)(2). An informational note provides examples of employees that might or might not be those responsible for responding to medical emergencies. The provisions requiring the employer to verify that the first aid, emergency response, and resuscitation training is current at least annually are in 110.6(C)(3), and those that require that all emergency response training be documented are in 110.6(C)(4).

As always, all of the electrical safety training provisions in 110.6(A), (B), and (C), like all of the requirements in *NFPA 70E*, need to be reviewed and applied in their entirety.

Host and Contract Employers' Responsibilities

The Article 110 general requirements that address both host and contractor employers' responsibilities are located in

110.7(A) and (B), respectively. Meeting documentation requirements are located in 110.7(C). A documented meeting between the host employer and the contract employer may be required as part of these joint responsibilities.

Among the host employer responsibilities in 110.7(A) is a requirement to provide the contract employer with the information about the installation necessary to make the assessments required by Chapter 1 of *NFPA 70E*. Among the contract employer responsibilities in 110.7(B) is a requirement that the contract employer ensure that each employee follows the work practices required by *NFPA 70E* in addition to any safety-related work rules of the host employer.

Consult 110.7 to understand and apply all of the host employer, contract employer, and related documentation requirements, as applicable.

Test Instruments and Equipment

Familiarity with the *NFPA 70E* requirements related to test instruments and equipment is also important because tasks where these requirements might apply are performed with some frequency. *NFPA 70E* 110.8 addresses five major topics:

- Testing
- Rating
- Design
- Visual inspection and repair
- Operation verification

Testing

The first of these five categories is covered in 110.8(A). This category covering testing requires that "only qualified persons shall perform tasks such as testing, troubleshooting, and voltage measuring on electrical equipment where an electrical hazard exists." Consider how the definition of *qualified person* from Article 100, the qualified person electrical safety training requirements in 110.6(A)(1), and the documentation of electrical safety training requirements in 110.6(A)(5) apply to the use of the term *qualified person* in 110.8(A).

Rating and Design

The second and third of these five categories are covered in 110.8(B), Rating, and 110.8(C), Design. The provisions in (B) addressing rating require that the rating of test instruments, equipment, and their accessories be (1) rated for the circuits and equipment where they are utilized, (2) approved for the purpose, and (3) used in accordance with any instructions provided by the manufacturer. An informational note here refers to two UL safety requirements. The provisions in (C) address design and require that "test instruments, equipment, and their accessories shall be designed for the environment to which they will be exposed and for the manner in which they will be utilized."

Visual Inspection and Repair

The fourth of the five subdivisions is addressed in 110.8(D). These provisions require, in part, a visual inspection for external defects and damage prior to each use and that anything found to be defective or damaged be removed from

---

OSHA Tip

Qualified person. One who has received training in and has demonstrated skills and knowledge in the construction and operation of electric equipment and installations and the hazards involved.

Note 1 to the definition of "qualified person:" Whether an employee is considered to be a "qualified person" will depend upon various circumstances in the workplace. For example, it is possible and, in fact, likely for an individual to be considered "qualified" with regard to certain equipment in the workplace, but "unqualified" as to other equipment. (See 1910.332(b)(3) for training requirements that specifically apply to qualified persons.)

Note 2 to the definition of "qualified person:" An employee who is undergoing on-the-job training and who, in the course of such training, has demonstrated an ability to perform duties safely at his or her level of training and who is under the direct supervision of a qualified person is considered to be a qualified person for the performance of those duties.

[1910.399, definitions applicable to OSHA 29 CFR Part 1910 Subpart S]

service and not be used until a qualified person performs the repairs and tests necessary to render the equipment safe.

Operation Verification

The fifth of the five subdivisions related to test instruments and equipment is set forth in 110.8(E). It addresses operation verification and requires, in part, that "when test instruments are used for the testing for the absence of voltage . . . greater than 50 volts, the operation of the test instrument shall be verified on any known voltage source before and after an absence of voltage test is performed."

Remember that all of the test instruments and equipment provisions in 110.8(A), (B), (C), (D), and (E), like all of the requirements in *NFPA 70E*, must be reviewed and applied in their entirety.

Compare what is required by 110.8(A), (B), (C), and (D) with what OSHA requires in 1910.334(c) for test instruments and equipment. For example, similar to 110.8(A), 1910.334(c)(1) states that only qualified persons may perform testing work on electric circuits or equipment.

Portable Cord- and Plug-Connected Electric Equipment

Section 110.9 covers the use of cord- and plug-connected equipment, including cord- and plug-connected test instruments and cord sets (extension cords). This section covers six main topics:
- Handling and storage
- Grounding-type equipment

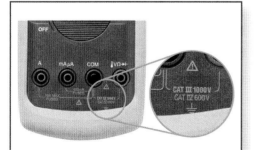

The Overvoltage Installation Category is one of the ratings to be considered for test equipment.

Courtesy of Fluke Corporation

1910.334(c)

Test instruments and equipment.

1910.334(c)(1)

Use. Only qualified persons may perform testing work on electric circuits or equipment.

1910.334(c)(2)

Visual inspection. Test instruments and equipment and all associated test leads, cables, power cords, probes, and connectors shall be visually inspected for external defects and damage before the equipment is used. If there is a defect or evidence of damage that might expose an employee to injury, the defective or damaged item shall be removed from service, and no employee may use it until repairs and tests necessary to render the equipment safe have been made.

1910.334(c)(3)

Rating of equipment. Test instruments and equipment and their accessories shall be rated for the circuits and equipment to which they will be connected and shall be designed for the environment in which they will be used.

For additional information, visit qr.njatcdb.org Item #1562

- Visual inspection and repair of portable cord- and plug-connected equipment and flexible cord sets
- Conductive or wet work locations
- Connecting attachment plugs
- Manufacturer's instructions

Be sure to review and apply the requirements from 110.9(A) through (F) in their entirety. Also consider how these important requirements differ from or can supplement any applicable OSHA requirements and company safety rules.

Ground-Fault Circuit-Interrupter (GFCI) Protection, Overcurrent Protection Modification, and Equipment Use

Sections 110.10, 110.11, and 110.12 cover GFCI protection, overcurrent protection modification, and equipment use, respectively.

The rules in 110.10 covering GFCI protection are divided into four subdivisions: (1) general, (2) maintenance and construction, (3) outdoors, and (4) testing GFCI devices. Be sure to review and apply the important requirements from 110.10(A), (B), (C), and (D) in their entirety. Consider how they differ from or can supplement any applicable *NEC* or OSHA requirements and company safety rules. For example, the provisions in 110.10(D) require GFCI protection devices to be tested in accordance with the manufacturer's instructions.

The *NFPA 70E* Article 110 general requirements for electrical safety-related work practices next address modification of overcurrent protection. Per section 110.11, "overcurrent protection of circuits and conductors is not permitted to be modified, even on a temporary basis, beyond that permitted by applicable portions of electrical codes and standards dealing with overcurrent protection."

The last section in Article 110 is 110.12, Equipment Use. This section requires that equipment must be used in accordance with the manufacturer's instructions. This requirement applies generally because this is a general requirement in Article 110. Review 90.3 and the definition of "equipment" in Article 100 for insight into the application of this requirement.

Review and apply these and all of the requirements from Article 110 and *NFPA 70E* in their entirety. Recall from Section 90.3 that Chapter 1 of *NFPA 70E* applies generally. Accordingly, the requirements of Article 110 apply beyond Article 110.

ESTABLISHING AN ELECTRICALLY SAFE WORK CONDITION

An *electrically safe work condition* is defined in Article 100 of *NFPA 70E*. The requirements for establishing an electrically safe work condition are located in Article 120. This article is divided into five sections:

- Lockout/tagout program
- Lockout/tagout principles
- Lockout/tagout equipment

- Lockout/tagout procedures
- Process for establishing and verifying an electrically safe work condition

Lockout/Tagout Program

Article 120 begins with lockout/tagout program requirements. These lockout/tagout program requirements are divided into two headings: (A) General, and (B) Employer Responsibilities.

The general requirements of 120.1(A) require, in part, that:

- Each employer must establish, document, and implement a lockout/tagout program
- The lockout/tagout program must specify lockout/tagout procedures to safeguard workers from exposure to electrical hazards
- The lockout/tagout program and procedures must also (1) be applicable to the experience and training of the workers and conditions in the workplace, (2) meet the requirements of Article 120, and (3) apply to fixed, permanently installed, temporarily installed, and portable equipment

The employer responsibility requirements of 120.1(B) require, in part, that the employer shall be responsible for:

- Providing the equipment necessary to execute lockout/tagout procedures
- Providing lockout/tagout training to workers per 110.6(B)
- Auditing the lockout/tagout program per 110.5(M)(3)
- Auditing execution of lockout/tagout procedures per 110.5(M)(3)

Remember to review and apply all of the requirements from Section 120.1 and *NFPA 70E* in their entirety and that Chapter 1 of *NFPA 70E* applies generally per 90.3. For example, a number of requirements in 110.5 and 110.6 apply to Article 120, including to 120.1(A) and 120.1(B) noted above.

Lockout/Tagout Principles

The requirements of 120.2 address lockout/tagout principles and are divided into the following eight subdivisions:

- Employee involvement

- Lockout/tagout procedure
- Control of energy
- Electrical circuit interlocks
- Control devices
- Identification
- Coordination
- Forms of control of hazardous electrical energy

Employee Involvement, Lockout/Tagout Procedure, and Control of Energy
Employee involvement is covered in 120.2(A) and requires, in part, that each person who could be exposed to a source of electrical energy shall be involved in the lockout/tagout procedure. The lockout/tagout procedure requirements covered in 120.2(B) require, in part, that procedures be developed based on existing electrical equipment and systems and include suitable documentation including up-to-date drawings. In addition, the procedure must meet the requirements of applicable codes, standards, and regulations for lockout and tagging of electrical sources. Control of energy is covered in 120.2(C) and requires that "all sources of electrical energy shall be controlled in such a way as to minimize employee exposure to electrical hazards."

Electrical Circuit Interlocks, Control Devices, and Identification
Electrical circuit interlocks are covered in 120.2(D), which requires, in part, that documentation shall be reviewed to ensure that no interlock operation can result in reenergizing the circuit being worked on. Control devices are addressed in 120.2(E), which states, in part, that control devices shall not be used as the primary isolating device. The requirements for identification in 120.2(F) require lockout/tagout devices to be unique and readily identifiable as a lockout/tagout device.

Coordination and Forms of Control of Hazardous Electrical Energy
The coordination requirements in 120.2(G) require compliance with three items for coordinating the lockout/tagout procedure. These are set forth in 120.2(G)(1), (2), and (3). Forms of control of hazardous electrical energy requirements are addressed in 120.2(H). These requirements state, in part, that the two forms of hazardous electrical control that shall be permitted include simple lockout/tagout and complex lockout/tagout.

Be sure to review and apply all of these lockout/tagout requirements located in 120.2 in their entirety. Compare them to those required in OSHA-based lockout, tagging, and control of hazardous energy requirements. Remember that, per 120.2(B), the procedure must meet the requirements of applicable codes, standards, and regulations for lockout and tagging of electrical sources. OSHA Parts 1910 and 1926 are examples of such standards and regulations.

Lockout/Tagout Equipment
The third of the five sections in Article 120 is located in 120.3, Lockout/Tagout Equipment. **See Figure 5-2.** These requirements are divided into the following four subdivisions:
1. Lock application
2. Lockout/tagout device
3. Lockout device
4. Tagout device

Figure 5-2 **Lockout/Tagout Equipment**

Figure 5-2. *Lockout/tagout equipment, such as locks and tags, play an important role in achieving an electrically safe work condition.*

Courtesy of Ideal Industries, Inc.

These four subdivisions need to be reviewed thoroughly to understand the comprehensive rules in 120.3, Lockout/Tagout Equipment, and their application within Article 120.

Lockout/Tagout Procedures

The fourth of the five sections in Article 120 addresses lockout/tagout procedures. Note that this section is comprised of a comprehensive set of lockout/tagout procedures and takes up approximately 1.5 pages of the approximately 3.5 pages of Article 120. These lockout/tagout procedures are addressed in 120.4 and require the employer to maintain a copy of these procedures and make them available to all employees. The additional requirements for lockout/tagout procedures are subdivided into those for (A) planning and (B) elements of control.

The *planning* requirements in 120.4(A) are further subdivided into five categories:

- Locating sources
- Exposed persons
- Person in charge
- Simple lockout/tagout procedure
- Complex lockout/tagout

The *elements of control* provisions in 120.4(B) require that "the procedure shall identify elements of control." These are further subdivided into fourteen categories:

- De-energizing equipment (shutdown)
- Stored energy
- Disconnecting means
- Responsibility
- Verification
- Testing
- Grounding
- Shift change
- Coordination
- Accountability for personnel
- Lockout/tagout application
- Removal of lockout/tagout devices
- Release for return to service
- Temporary release for testing/ positioning

Note that the requirements for planning in 120.4(A) not only require the lockout/tagout procedure for planning

For additional information, visit qr.njatcdb.org Item #1561

For additional information, visit qr.njatcdb.org Item #1563

to include everything addressed in the five headings in 120.4(A), Planning, but to also include everything in the fourteen headings in 120.4(B), Elements of Control, as well. See 120.4(A), which states that the procedure shall require planning, including the requirements of 120.4(A)(1) through 120.4(B)(14).

Carefully review and apply all of the requirements from Section 120.4 and *NFPA 70E* in their entirety. Note that many of these provisions are similar to what OSHA sets forth in 1910.147 and 1910.333(b)(2). Compare these procedures with what OSHA requires in its related requirements.

Process for Establishing and Verifying an Electrically Safe Work Condition

Article 120 concludes with the requirements in 120.5, Process for Establishing and Verifying an Electrically Safe Work Condition. Per 120.5, establishing and verifying an electrically safe work condition shall include following all of the eight steps set forth in the order they are presented, if feasible. Note that compliance with 120.5 alone does not establish and verify an electrically safe work condition. See 110.2, which states that electrical conductors and circuit parts shall not be considered to be in an electrically safe work condition until all of the requirements of Article 120 have been met.

Accordingly, establishing an electrically safe work condition includes meeting all of the requirements of Article 120, including those found in 120.1, 120.2, 120.3, 120.4, and 120.5. Carefully review and apply all of the previously covered requirements as well as those in 120.5, including the eight steps that are to be followed in the order presented, if feasible. Note that Temporary Protective Grounding is covered in 120.5(8). **See Figure 5-3.** Also review and consider the exceptions and the informational notes that are included in 120.5 that provide exceptions to requirements and nonmandatory explanatory material, respectively.

Review and apply all the requirements from Section 120.5, Article 120, and *NFPA 70E* in their entirety. Keep in mind that electrical conductors and circuit parts shall not be considered to be in an electrically safe work condition until all of the requirements of Article 120 have been met as stated in 110.2, for example. Recall from Section 90.3 that Chapter 1 of *NFPA 70E* applies generally. Accordingly, the requirements of Article 120 apply beyond Article 120. So too do the requirements in Articles 100, 105, 110, and 130. See the requirements in 110.3, for example. This Article 110 general requirement sets forth the conditions where energized electrical conductors and circuit parts must be put into an electrically safe work condition.

WORK INVOLVING ELECTRICAL HAZARDS

Article 130 contains the requirements related to work involving electrical hazards. In fact, "Work Involving Electrical Hazards" is the title of Article 130. Review the definition of *electrical hazard* in Article 100 of *NFPA 70E*. Per this definition, it is clear that Article 130 covers work involving four hazards caused by either contact or equipment failure.

Article 130 is among the most widely-used articles in *NFPA 70E*. Note that Article 130 is divided into the following ten sections, which provide the framework for the requirements for work involving electrical hazards:
- General
- Energized Electrical Work Permit
- Shock Risk Assessment
- Arc Flash Risk Assessment
- Personal and Other Protective Equipment
- Other Precautions for Personnel Activities
- Work Within the Limited Approach Boundary or Arc Flash Boundary of Overhead Lines
- Underground Electrical Lines and Equipment
- Cutting or Drilling
- Cutting, Removing, or Rerouting of Conductors

Figure 5-3   Temporary Protective Grounding

Figure 5-3. Per 120.5(8)a., the location, sizing, and application of temporary protective grounding shall be identified as part of the employer's job planning.

NFPA 70E needs to be referenced for the Article 130 provisions in their entirety. Article 130 will be covered in-depth in a later chapter.

ADDITIONAL CONSIDERATIONS

It is important to remember that Figure 90.3 provides the following information relative to arrangement of the *NFPA 70E* standard:
- Chapter 1 applies generally to electrical safety in the workplace
- Chapter 2 addresses safety-related maintenance requirements
- Chapter 3 modifies the general requirements of Chapter 1

As an overview, the following is a list of the three chapters, their articles, and the topics addressed in each:

Chapter 1: Safety-Related Work Practices
Article 100: Definitions
Article 105: Application of Safety-Related Work Practices and Procedures
Article 110: General Requirements for Electrical Safety-Related Work Practices
Article 120: Establishing an Electrically Safe Work Condition
Article 130: Work Involving Electrical Hazards

Chapter 2: Safety-Related Maintenance Requirements
Article 200: Introduction
Article 205: General Maintenance Requirements
Article 210: Substations, Switchgear Assemblies, Switchboards, Panelboards, Motor Control Centers, and Disconnect Switches
Article 215: Premises Wiring
Article 220: Controller Equipment
Article 225: Fuses and Circuit Breakers
Article 230: Rotating Equipment
Article 235: Hazardous (Classified) Locations
Article 240: Batteries and Battery Rooms
Article 245: Portable Electric Tools and Equipment
Article 250: Personal Safety and Protective Equipment

Chapter 3: Safety Requirements for Special Equipment
Article 300: Introduction
Article 310: Safety-Related Work Practices for Electrolytic Cells
Article 320: Safety Requirements Related to Batteries and Battery Rooms
Article 330: Safety-Related Work Practices: Lasers
Article 340: Safety-Related Work Practices: Power Electronic Equipment
Article 350: Safety-Related Work Requirements: Research and Development Laboratories
Article 360: Safety-Related Requirements for Capacitors

While *NFPA 70E* contains 18 informative annexes, these are not part of the requirements of the standard but rather are included for informational purposes only. The following list identifies the 18 informative annexes and their topics:

Informative Annex A: Informative Publications
Informative Annex B: Reserved
Informative Annex C: Limits of Approach
Informative Annex D: Incident Energy and Arc Flash Boundary Calculation Methods
Informative Annex E: Electrical Safety Program
Informative Annex F: Risk Assessment and Risk Control
Informative Annex G: Sample Lockout/Tagout Program
Informative Annex H: Guidance on Selection of Protective Clothing and Other Personal Protective Equipment (PPE)
Informative Annex I: Job Briefing and Job Safety Planning Checklist
Informative Annex J: Energized Electrical Work Permit
Informative Annex K: General Categories of Electrical Hazards
Informative Annex L: Typical Application of Safeguards in the Cell Line Working Zone
Informative Annex M: Layering of Protective Clothing and Total System Arc Rating
Informative Annex N: Example Industrial Procedures and Policies for Working Near Overhead Electrical Lines and Equipment
Informative Annex O: Safety-Related Design Requirements
Informative Annex P: Aligning Implementation of This Standard with Occupational Health and Safety Management Standards
Informative Annex Q: Human Performance and Workplace Electrical Safety
Informative Annex R: Working with Capacitors

SUMMARY

Electrical Workers should be familiar with the *NFPA 70E* standard, with a primary focus in this chapter on the provisions of Articles 90, 100, 105, 110, and 120. These provisions include, but are not limited to, definitions, host and contract employers' responsibilities, training requirements, electrical safety program implementation and documentation requirements, test instruments and equipment, and establishing an electrically safe work condition. Understanding the definitions from Article 100 and the requirements of Articles 105, 110, 120, and 130 is essential in any effort to comply with these requirements.

Recognize that Chapters 2 and 3 of *NFPA 70E* also contain numerous additional electrical safety requirements. The entire *NFPA 70E* standard, including the information within the 18 informative annexes, and all applicable OSHA requirements need to be reviewed and considered. Effective electrical safety programs, training, and work practices will adopt and implement appropriate requirements from all sources of information.

SUMMARY cont.

Electrical safety programs and effective training provide a foundation for a workplace free from recognized hazards. Achieving an electrically safe work condition is the primary safety-related work practice and must be honored unless the employer demonstrates otherwise, such as in accordance with applicable OSHA and *NFPA 70E* requirements.

The importance of implementing and documenting an electrical safety program and appropriate training cannot be overstated. An electrical safety program is essential as part of an effort to train and protect workers from electrical hazards and a fundamental component of providing an effective overall safety and health program for worker safety. It is important to review and understand the thirteen sections that *NFPA 70E* requires to be included in an electrical safety program as minimum considerations for making improvements to a new or existing electrical safety program.

REVIEW QUESTIONS

1. *NFPA 70E* requires the employer to implement and document a(n) __?__ program.
   a. cost-benefit analysis
   b. electrical safety
   c. loss prevention
   d. research and development

2. Article __?__ covers safety-related maintenance requirements for fuses and circuit breakers.
   a. 205
   b. 225
   c. 340
   d. 350

3. Article __?__ outlines what is covered and not covered by *NFPA 70E*.
   a. 90
   b. 100
   c. 110
   d. 120

4. *NFPA 70E* requires that emergency response training be documented.
   a. True
   b. False

5. The scope of Article 100 indicates that each term or phrase used within *NFPA 70E* is defined in Article 100 when its meaning is not likely to be well understood.
   a. True
   b. False

6. Unqualified persons must be trained in any safety-related work practices necessary for their safety, and this training must be documented and on file for the duration of their employment.
   a. True
   b. False

7. The host employer is required to provide the contract employer with the information about the installation necessary to make the assessments required by Chapter 1 of *NFPA 70E*.
   a. True
   b. False

8. The title of *UL 61010-1* is "Safety Requirements for Electrical Equipment for Measurement, Control, and Laboratory Use, Part 1: General Requirements, for rating, overvoltage category, and design requirements for voltage measurement and test instruments intended for use on electrical systems 1000 volts and below."
   a. True
   b. False

9. Article __?__ contains the provisions related to work involving electrical hazards.
   a. 100
   b. 130
   c. 200
   d. 330

10. The title of Informative Annex J is __?__.
    a. Electrical Safety Program
    b. Energized Electrical Work Permit
    c. General Categories of Electrical Hazards
    d. Guidance on Selection of Protective Clothing and Other Personal Protective Equipment (PPE)

Work Involving Electrical Hazards

The title to Article 130 of *NFPA 70E* is "Work Involving Electrical Hazards." Accordingly, it contains the requirements related to work involving electrical hazards. Recall that the term *electrical hazard* is defined in Article 100 in *NFPA 70E*. Review that definition and note that Article 130 covers work involving four hazards caused by either contact or equipment failure.

Article 130 is divided into ten sections that provide the requirements for work involving electrical hazards. An overview, excerpts, and abbreviated content from Article 130 will be included in this chapter. This article needs to be referenced in its entirety for a complete understanding of these requirements. In addition, per 90.3, the requirements in Article 100, 105, 110, and 120 also need to be consulted and applied, as applicable.

Objectives

- » Understand the general requirements of Article 130 and the requirements related to an energized electrical work permit.
- » Understand the requirements related to shock risk assessment and arc flash risk assessment.
- » Know the requirements for personal and other protective equipment.
- » Know the requirements related to other precautions for personnel activities, work within the limited approach or arc flash boundary of overhead lines, underground electrical lines and equipment, cutting and drilling, and cutting, removing, or rerouting of conductors.

Chapter 6

Table of Contents

Case Study

A 60-year-old Electrical Worker was electrocuted when he contacted an energized 277-volt circuit. The incident occurred in an office building that was being renovated.

The employer had no electrical training or safety program, explaining that the workers were hired from the union hall and were certified by the union as trained Journeyman or apprentices. As part of the contract with the site owner, the employer was required to follow all of the site owner's safety rules, including the enforcement of a lockout/tagout procedure.

Three employees of the electrical contractor were at the site on the morning of the incident: the foreman, a Journeyman electrician (the victim), and an apprentice. At 7:15 a.m., the foreman gave the victim a set of blueprints and explained the job to him. He was told to install new two-by-two-foot fluorescent lighting fixtures in two offices that were being expanded. He was instructed to install a fixture tail to one fixture and then to connect it to the existing lights. The Journeyman electrician was also told to reconnect the power on a second bank of lights in an adjacent area that had been disconnected a week earlier. The foreman did not instruct the victim to deenergize the circuit breakers.

The Journeyman and the apprentice went to the site. At some point, the victim asked the apprentice, "What's up there?" The apprentice replied, "There are a hot switch leg and another fixture tail to be tied into the new fixtures," to which the victim said, "Okay." The switch leg was an energized 277-volt electrical cable that had been previously connected to a wall switch in a partition wall. The fixture tail was an electrical cable from another fixture that had not yet been connected and was deenergized.

At approximately 9:30 a.m., after a coffee break, the victim resumed work on wiring the fixtures. He contacted the 277 volts apparently while stripping the insulation from the switch leg. The electric shock burned the victim's left hand and knocked him from the ladder. The apprentice heard the Journeyman fall and went to his aid. He checked the victim for a pulse and found none. An office employee then started cardiopulmonary resuscitation (CPR). The paramedics arrived soon after, and the victim was transported to the local hospital, where he was pronounced dead at 10:36 a.m.

It is not known why the victim was working on the energized switch leg. The apprentice thought that the victim grabbed the wrong cable and failed to test both the black and white wires. The foreman later stated that there was no reason for the circuits to be energized and that the crew always tested every circuit beforehand. Although the contractor had access to the breaker, no one had deenergized the circuits in that area. The Occupational Safety and Health Administration (OSHA) noted that the second bank of lights adjacent to the accident site was deenergized by taping off the wall switch.

The county medical examiner attributed the cause of death to electrocution.

Source: For details of this case, see New Jersey Case Report 92NJ007. Accessed April 15, 2020.

For additional information, visit qr.njatcdb.org Item #1196

INTRODUCTION

Article 130 contains the provisions related to work involving electrical hazards. An electrical hazard is defined in *NFPA 70E*.

Therefore, by definition, Article 130 covers work involving four hazards caused by either contact or equipment failure. **See Figure 6-1.**

Article 130 is divided into ten sections that provide the requirements for work involving electrical hazards:

- General
- Energized Electrical Work Permit
- Shock Risk Assessment
- Arc Flash Risk Assessment
- Personal and Other Protective Equipment
- Other Precautions for Personnel Activities
- Work Within the Limited Approach Boundary or Arc Flash Boundary of Overhead Lines
- Underground Electrical Lines and Equipment
- Cutting or Drilling
- Cutting, Removing, or Rerouting of Conductors

An overview, excerpts, and abbreviated content from the requirements for work involving electrical hazards follow.

Figure 6-1 **Electrical Hazard**

Figure 6-1. An electrical hazard is a dangerous condition that may be caused by contact or equipment failure.

Courtesy of Westex

Article 130, along with all of *NFPA 70E*, needs to be referenced in its entirety for a complete understanding of these requirements.

GENERAL AND ENERGIZED ELECTRICAL WORK PERMIT REQUIREMENTS

The first two sections of Article 130 address the general requirements and the energized electrical work permit requirements.

General

Article 130 begins its general requirements in 130.1, which states both what Article 130 covers as well as what safety-related work practices shall be used to safeguard employees.

These Article 130 general requirements also list the requirements that apply when energized electrical conductors and circuit parts operating at voltages equal to or greater than 50 volts are not put into an electrically safe work condition and work is performed as permitted in accordance with 110.4. These are:

- Only qualified persons shall be permitted to work on electrical conductors or circuit parts that have not been put into an electrically safe work condition.
- An energized electrical work permit shall be completed as required by 130.2.
- A shock risk assessment shall be performed as required by 130.4.
- An arc flash risk assessment shall be performed as required by 130.5.

These general requirements in 130.1 also stipulate that all of the requirements of Article 130 apply regardless of whether an incident energy analysis is completed or if the arc flash PPE method is used for the selection of arc flash PPE in lieu of an incident energy analysis. See 130.5(F), 130.7(C)(15), Table 130.7(C)(15)(a), Table 130.7(C)(15)(b), and Table 130.7(C)(15)(c). Review the definition of incident energy analysis from Article 100 to aid in the understanding and application of this rule.

Note that it is a component of an arc flash risk assessment. Refer to 130.5 for all of what is required as part of an arc flash risk assessment, such as the documentation requirements in (D), the arc flash boundary requirements in (E), the arc flash PPE requirements in (F), and the equipment labeling requirements in (H).

Be sure to review and apply all of the requirements in 130.1 in their entirety. When studying and applying Article 130, also keep in mind that the definitions in Article 100, the application of safety-related work practices and procedures in Article 105, the general requirements for electrical safety-related work practices in Article 110, and the rules for establishing an electrically safe work condition in Article 120 apply to Article 130 as well.

Energized Electrical Work Permit

The second of the ten sections in Article 130 covers rules for an energized electrical work permit. The provisions for an energized electrical work permit are set forth in 130.2. Only after satisfying one of the four conditions for energized work in 110.4 may energized work take place. The provisions in 130.2(A) then provide the two conditions when an energized electrical work permit is required. These two conditions are set forth in 130.2(A)(1) and (A)(2).

As the requirements of 130.2(A) are reviewed in detail, be sure to also note the conditions where a permit would be required even when the conductors or circuit parts are "not exposed" as provided for in 130.2(A)(2). Note also that the energized electrical work permit must be documented, per 130.2(A).

Now that it has been determined when an energized electrical work permit is required per 130.2(A), explore the nine headings of the minimum elements that must be included in an energized electrical work permit per 130.2(B)(1) through (9).

The first required element requires that the equipment being worked on and its location be documented. The second element required to be included on the permit is a description of the work to be performed. The third element asks that the justification for energized work from 110.4 be provided. The fourth element points to 130.1 and asks for a description of the safe work practices that will be employed.

Note that there are a number of OSHA and *NFPA 70E* rules that require hazard documentation. The next two required permit elements require the results of the shock risk assessment and the arc flash risk assessment. See 130.2(B)(5) and 130.2(B)(6) for what is required to be included on an energized electrical work permit related to the results of the shock risk assessment and arc flash risk assessment, respectively. **See Figure 6-2.**

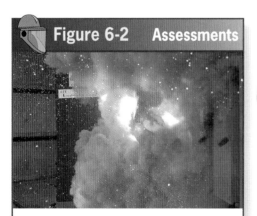

Figure 6-2. Assessments

Figure 6-2. Appropriate safety-related work practices must be determined using a shock risk assessment and an arc flash risk assessment.

OSHA Tip

The regulations for electrical protective equipment in 1926.97 are nearly identical to those for electrical protective equipment in 1910.137. Part 1926 provides Safety and Health Regulations for Construction. Those in part 1910 are Occupational Safety and Health Standards.

Also, recall OSHA's provisions of 1910.132(d)(1) and (d)(2):

1910.132(d)(1)

The employer shall assess the workplace to determine if hazards are present, or are likely to be present, which necessitate the use of personal protective equipment (PPE)...

1910.132(d)(2)

The employer shall verify that the required workplace hazard assessment has been performed through a written certification that identifies the workplace evaluated; the person certifying that the evaluation has been performed; the date(s) of the hazard assessment; and, which identifies the document as a certification of hazard assessment.

The seventh element required to be among the minimum requirements in an energized electrical work permit requires that the means employed to restrict access of unqualified persons be included.

This provision points to 130.7(E), Alerting Techniques, as a means to comply.

The eighth element, in part, requires "evidence of completion of a job briefing." Review the job briefing rules in

Figure 6-3   Job Briefing

Figure 6-3. *The information on the energized electrical work permit is required to be covered during a job briefing.*

Courtesy of Service Electric Company

110.5(I) and (I)(2), which require, in part, that the information on any energized electrical work permit be covered by the employee in charge before starting each job that involves exposure to electrical hazards. These two rules work hand in hand. **See Figure 6-3.**

The ninth and final required element is the requirement of signature(s) for energized work approval. It is recognition that energized work is justified with all required information in items (1) through (8) known, accounted for, and documented.

The energized electrical work permit and the equipment labeling requirement in 130.5(H) are among the provisions requiring documentation of shock and arc flash risk assessment.

Thoroughly review all of the requirements in 130.2 for a full and complete understanding of what is required. Also review the informational note pointing to an example energized work permit in Figure J.1 in Informative Annex J, as well as exemptions to the work permit detailed in 130.2(C). Note that the exemptions to the work permit are *not* exemptions from "appropriate safe work practices and PPE in accordance with Chapter 1" of *NFPA 70E*.

SHOCK RISK ASSESSMENT

The title to Section 130.4 is "Shock Risk Assessment." These requirements are divided into seven subdivisions:

- General
- Estimate of likelihood and severity
- Additional protective measures
- Documentation
- Shock protection boundaries
- Limited approach boundary
- Restricted approach boundary

General Shock Risk Assessment Requirements

The general requirements in 130.4(A) state why the shock risk assessment required by 130.1(3) must be performed. **See Figure 6-4.** Review these requirements in their entirety. In part, a shock risk assessment shall be performed to:

- Identify shock hazards

Figure 6-4 Shock Risk Assessment

ALWAYS
WEAR
YOUR
GLOVES

Figure 6-4. *Determination of whether additional protective measures are required, including PPE, is one reason why a shock risk assessment must be performed.*

Courtesy of Salisbury by Honeywell

- Estimate the likelihood of occurrence and potential severity of injury or damage to health
- Determine if additional protective measures are required, including PPE

The result of a shock risk assessment is among the information required to be included on an energized electrical work permit, included on an equipment label, and covered during a job briefing. See 130.2(B)(5)a., b., c., and d.; 130.5(H); and 110.5(I)(2). Also review 110.5(H)(3), Hierarchy of Risk Control Methods, and 110.6(A)(1)(c)(4)d., which must be documented per 110.6(A)(5).

Estimate of Likelihood and Severity

The second subdivision in 130.4 is in 130.4(B) and addresses the need to "estimate . . . likelihood of occurrence of injury or damage to health and the potential severity of injury or damage to health." It requires that the following be taken into consideration:

- The design of the electrical equipment
- The electrical equipment operating condition and the condition of maintenance

Note that both 110.4 and 110.5 require an "estimate of likelihood and severity." However, while Table 130.5(C) shall be permitted to be used to estimate the likelihood of occurrence of an *arc flash* event to determine if additional protective measures are required, there is no such table to estimate the likelihood of occurrence for the *shock* risk assessment.

Additional Protective Measures and Documentation

The third subdivision in 130.4 addresses additional protective measures within a shock risk assessment. The requirements in 130.4(C) state, in part, that additional protective measures must be selected and implemented per 110.5(H)(3). In addition, when additional measures are required and include the use of PPE, the following must be determined:

- The voltage to which personnel will be exposed
- The boundary requirements (limited approach and restricted approach boundaries)
- The personal and other protective equipment required by *NFPA 70E* to protect against the shock hazard

The shock risk assessment documentation requirements are in 130.4(D). Here it is required that the results of the shock risk assessment be documented. Recall that 130.2(B)(5) requires the results of the shock risk assessment as a necessary element of an energized electrical work permit.

Figure 6-5 **Approach Boundaries for Shock Protection for AC Systems**

NFPA 70E, TABLE 130.4(E)(a) SHOCK PROTECTION APPROACH BOUNDARIES TO EXPOSED ENERGIZED ELECTRICAL CONDUCTIONS OR CIRCUIT PARTS FOR ALTERNATING-CURRENT SYSTEMS

| (1) | (2) | (3) | (4) |
| | Limited Approach Boundary[b] | | Restricted Approach Boundary[b]; |
Nominal System Voltage Range, Phase to Phase[a]	Exposed Movable Conductor[c]	Exposed Fixed Circuit Part	Includes Inadvertent Movement Adder
Less than 50 V	Not specified	Not specified	Not specified
50 V–150 V[d]	3.0 m (10 ft 0 in.)	1.0 m (3 ft 6 in.)	Avoid contact
151 V–750 V	3.0 m (10 ft 0 in.)	1.0 m (3 ft 6 in.)	0.3 m (1 ft 0 in.)
751 V–15 kV	3.0 m (10 ft 0 in.)	1.5 m (5 ft 0 in.)	0.7 m (2 ft 2 in.)
15.1 kV–36 kV	3.0 m (10 ft 0 in.)	1.8 m (6 ft 0 in.)	0.8 m (2 ft 9 in.)
36.1 kV–46 kV	3.0 m (10 ft 0 in.)	2.5 m (8 ft 0 in.)	0.8 m (2 ft 9 in.)
46.1 kV–72.5 kV	3.0 m (10 ft 0 in.)	2.5 m (8 ft 0 in.)	1.0 m (3 ft 6 in.)
72.6 kV–121 kV	3.3 m (10 ft 8 in.)	2.5 m (8 ft 0 in.)	1.0 m (3 ft 6 in.)
138 kV–145 kV	3.4 m (11 ft 0 in.)	3.0 m (10 ft 0 in.)	1.2 m (3 ft 10 in.)
161 kV–169 kV	3.6 m (11 ft 8 in.)	3.6 m (11 ft 8 in.)	1.3 m (4 ft 3 in.)
230 kV–242 kV	4.0 m (13 ft 0 in.)	4.0 m (13 ft 0 in.)	1.7 m (5 ft 8 in.)
345 kV–362 kV	4.7 m (15 ft 4 in.)	4.7 m (15 ft 4 in.)	2.8 m (9 ft 2 in.)
500 kV–550 kV	5.8 m (19 ft 0 in.)	5.8 m (19 ft 0 in.)	3.6 m (11 ft 8 in.)
765 kV–800 kV	7.2 m (23 ft 9 in.)	7.2 m (23 ft 9 in.)	4.9 m (15 ft 11 in.)

Notes:
(1) For arc flash boundary, see 130.5(E).
(2) All dimensions are distance from exposed energized electrical conductors or circuit part to employee.
[a]For single-phase systems above 250 volts, select the range that is equal to the system's maximum phase-to-ground voltage multiplied by 1.732.
[b]See definition in Article 100 and text in 130.4(D)(2) and Informative Annex C for elaboration.
[c]*Exposed movable conductors* describes a condition in which the distance between the conductor and a person is not under the control of the person. The term is normally applied to overhead line conductors supported by poles.
[d]This includes circuits where the exposure does not exceed 120 volts nominal.

Figure 6-5. *The shock protection boundaries for AC systems are determined from Table 130.4(E)(a).*

Courtesy of NECA

Shock Protection Boundaries

The title to 130.4(E) is "Shock Protection Boundaries." These rules identify the two shock protection boundaries (limited approach and restricted approach) where they are applicable. They also indicate that Table 130.4(E)(a) establishes distances for various AC system voltages. **See Figure 6-5.** Table 130.4(E)(b) is to be used for the distances associated with various DC system voltages. **See Figure 6-6.** Review and apply the requirements of 130.4(E), Table 130.4(E)(a), and Table 130.4(E)(b) in their entirety. Review the definitions of *limited approach boundary* and *restricted approach boundary* in Article 100. An informational note to 130.4(E) points out that, in certain instances, the arc flash boundary may be a greater distance than the limited approach boundary and that these boundaries are independent of each other. The distance associated with each shock boundary is determined by voltage. Conversely, the arc flash boundary distance is not a fixed distance and is not based solely on voltage. See 130.5(E)(1), for example.

Also, recall that these boundary distances are among the information required to be included on an energized electrical work permit. See 130.2(B)(5) b. and c. Therefore, it is also required to be covered in any job briefing in accordance with 110.5(I)(2).

Limited Approach Boundary

The title to 130.4(F) is "Limited Approach Boundary." These rules are broken down into three subcategories:

1. Approach by unqualified persons
2. Working at or close to the limited approach boundary
3. Entering the limited approach boundary

Review the requirements of 130.4(F) in their entirety. Among other things, these limited approach boundary rules address:

• An unqualified person's approach near the limited approach boundary

- The role of alerting techniques where unqualified persons are working at or close to this boundary
- What must occur if there is a need for an unqualified person to cross the limited approach boundary
- That an unqualified person is not permitted to cross the restricted approach boundary

Pay particular attention to the limited approach boundary and its relevance to unqualified persons. Recall that the requirements of 130.4(E) reference Table 130.4(E)(a) and Table 130.4(E)(b). Table 130.4(E)(a) is intended for use with AC systems, while Table 130.4(E)(b) is intended for use with DC systems. Note that both tables have four columns numbered (1) to (4) from left to right. Column (1) addresses nominal system voltage and nominal potential difference. Columns (2) through (4) address boundary distances. Also pay attention to the notes attached to the tables. For example, Note ᶜ to Table 130.4(E)(a) and the "*" to Table 130.4(E)(b) clarify the application of columns (2) and (3) and indicate which

of these columns would be used to determine the limited approach boundary for a particular application.

Note the limited approach distance associated with a particular voltage after determining if it is the column (2) distance for an "exposed movable conductor" or the column (3) distance for an "exposed fixed circuit part." This limited approach boundary distance is among the information required to be included on an energized electrical work permit. See 130.2(B)(5)b. It is also information required to be covered during any job briefing per 110.5(I)(2). Be sure to review and apply these limited approach boundary requirements in their entirety.

Restricted Approach Boundary

The title to 130.4(G) is "Restricted Approach Boundary." While the requirements in 130.4(F) primarily address the limited approach boundary and its relationship to unqualified persons, note that the requirements in 130.4(G) primarily address the restricted approach boundary and its relationship to qualified persons.

Figure 6-6 Approach Boundaries for Shock Protection for DC Systems

NFPA 70E, TABLE 130.4(E)(b) SHOCK PROTECTION APPROACH BOUNDARIES TO EXPOSED ENERGIZED ELECTRICAL CONDUCTIONS OR CIRCUIT PARTS FOR DIRECT-CURRENT SYSTEMS

(1)	(2)	(3)	(4)
	Limited Approach Boundary		Restricted Approach Boundary; Includes Inadvertent Movement
Nominal Potential Difference	Exposed Movable Conductor*	Exposed Fixed Circuit Part	Adder
Less than 50 V	Not specified	Not specified	Not specified
50 V–300 V	3.0 m (10 ft 0 in.)	1.0 m (3 ft 6 in.)	Avoid contact
301 V–1 kV	3.0 m (10 ft 0 in.)	1.0 m (3 ft 6 in.)	0.3 m (1 ft 0 in.)
1.1 kV–5 kV	3.0 m (10 ft 0 in.)	1.5 m (5 ft 0 in.)	0.5 m (1 ft 5 in.)
5 kV–15 kV	3.0 m (10 ft 0 in.)	1.5 m (5 ft 0 in.)	0.7 m (2 ft 2 in.)
15.1 kV–45 kV	3.0 m (10 ft 0 in.)	2.5 m (8 ft 0 in.)	0.8 m (2 ft 9 in.)
45.1 kV–75 kV	3.0 m (10 ft 0 in.)	2.5 m (8 ft 0 in.)	1.0 m (3 ft 6 in.)
75.1 kV–150 kV	3.3 m (10 ft 8 in.)	3.0 m (10 ft 0 in.)	1.2 m (3 ft 10 in.)
150.1 kV–250 kV	3.6 m (11 ft 8 in.)	3.6 m (11 ft 8 in.)	1.6 m (5 ft 3 in.)
250.1 kV–500 kV	6.0 m (20 ft 0 in.)	6.0 m (20 ft 0 in.)	3.5 m (11 ft 6 in.)
500.1 kV–800 kV	8.0 m (26 ft 0 in.)	8.0 m (26 ft 0 in.)	5.0 m (16 ft 5 in.)

Note: All dimensions are distance from exposed energized electrical conductors or circuit parts to worker.

*Exposed movable conductor describes a condition in which the distance between the conductor and a person is not under the control of the person. The term is normally applied to overhead line conductors supported by poles.

Figure 6-6. *The shock protection boundaries for DC systems are determined from Table 130.4(E)(b).*

Courtesy of NECA

Here it discusses the two circumstances under which a qualified person can approach or take any conductive object closer to exposed energized electrical conductors or circuit parts than the restricted approach boundary.

Review and apply all of these requirements in their entirety for a complete understanding of their application.

Note the restricted approach distance associated with a particular voltage from column (4) in Table 130.4(E)(a) for use with AC systems and Table 130.4(E)(b) for use with DC systems. This restricted approach boundary distance is among the information required to be included on an energized electrical work permit. See 130.2(B)(5)c.

ARC FLASH RISK ASSESSMENT

The title to Section 130.5 is "Arc Flash Risk Assessment." These rules, as well as those in 130.1(4), describe why, how, and when an arc flash risk assessment must be performed. Recall that, per 130.1(4), an arc flash risk assessment shall be performed when energized electrical conductors and circuit parts operating at voltages equal to or greater than 50 volts are not put into an electrically safe work condition and work is performed as permitted in accordance with 110.4. Also recall that, in accordance with 130.1(1), only qualified persons shall be permitted to work on electrical conductors or circuit parts that have not been put into an electrically safe work condition.

Section 130.5 is divided into the following subdivisions:

- General
- Estimate of likelihood and severity
- Additional protective measures
- Documentation
- Arc flash boundary
- Arc flash PPE
- Incident energy analysis method
- Equipment labeling

An introduction to the eight subdivisions of 130.5 follows. Review and apply all of the requirements of 130.5 in their entirety.

General

The general requirements of 130.5(A), the first of the eight subdivisions of 130.5, Arc Flash Risk Assessment, require, in part, that an arc flash risk assessment be performed to:

1) Identify arc flash hazards
2) Estimate the likelihood of occurrence and the potential severity
3) Determine if additional protective measures are required, including the use of PPE

Review and apply the requirements of 130.5(A) in their entirety. Also review the Article 100 definition of "arc flash hazard" and its two informational notes. Closely review the informational note guidance related to the possibility of an arc flash hazard existing when parts are exposed or when they are within equipment in a guarded or enclosed condition.

Estimate of Likelihood and Severity

The second of the eight subdivisions, established in 130.5(B), requires an estimate of likelihood and severity as a part of an arc flash risk assessment. This requirement states, in part, that the estimate of the *likelihood of occurrence* of injury or damage to health and the *potential severity* of injury or damage to health take into account the following two electrical equipment considerations:

- Its design, including its overcurrent protective device and its operating time
- Its operating condition and condition of maintenance

Additional Protective Measures

The third of the eight subdivisions detailing what must be considered as part of an arc flash risk assessment is located in 130.5(C). These requirements state, in part, that if additional protective measures are required, they must be selected and implemented according to the hierarchy of risk control identified in 110.5(H)(3). Recall that PPE is the sixth of six in that hierarchy. In addition, when the additional protective measures include the use of PPE, it is also required that the following things must be determined:

- The appropriate safety-related work practices
- The arc flash boundary
- The PPE to be used within the arc flash boundary

The last paragraph of 130.5(C) states that "Table 130.5(C) shall be permitted to estimate the likelihood of occurrence of an arc flash event to determine if additional protective measures are required." Note that this requirement states that Table 130.5(C) "shall be permitted," but it does not state that Table 130.5(C) must be used.

Table 130.5(C)

Table 130.5(C) is referenced in Section 130.5(C). Carefully study the title, layout, and content of Table 130.5(C). **See Figure 6-7.**

Note that the title of Table 130.5(C) is "Estimate of the Likelihood of Occurrence of an Arc Flash Incident for AC and DC Systems." Accordingly, this table is applicable to both AC and DC systems. Note also that the table is divided into three columns with the following column headings from left to right:

- Task
- Equipment Condition[a]
- Likelihood of Occurrence[b]

The left column heading in Table 130.5(C) is "Task." Note that the column lists numerous tasks vertically within the table.

The center column heading in Table 130.5(C) is "Equipment Condition[a]." "Equipment Condition[a]" is associated with the tasks in the "Task" column and is designated as either "Any," "Normal," or Abnormal." Note the six circumstances that must all be met for equipment condition to be considered "normal," which are detailed in 110.4(D) per the superscript note [a] to Table 130.5(C), which is designated by the superscript [a] in the "Equipment Condition[a]" column heading.

The right column in Table 130.5(C) is "Likelihood of Occurrence[b]." Note how "Likelihood of Occurrence[b]" is associated with the tasks in the "Task" column and the equipment condition

Figure 6-7   Table 130.5(C)

TABLE 130.5(C) ESTIMATE OF THE LIKELIHOOD OF OCCURRENCE OF AN ARC FLASH INCIDENT FOR AC AND DC SYSTEMS, *in part*

Task	Equipment Condition	Likelihood of Occurance
For ac systems, work on energized electrical conductors and circuit parts, including voltage testing.	Any	Yes
For dc systems, working on energized electrical conductors and circuit parts of series connected battery cells, including voltage testing.		
Removal or installation of CBs or switches.		
Opening hinged door(s) or cover(s) or removal of bolted covers (to expose bare, energized electrical conductors and circuit parts). For dc systems, this includes bolted covers, such as battery terminal covers.		
Application of temporary protective grounding equipment, after voltage test.		
Working on control circuits with exposed energized electrical conductors and circuit parts, greater than 120 volts.		
Insertion or removal of individual starter buckets from motor control center (MCC).		

Figure 6-7. *As its title suggests, Table 130.5(C) provides an estimate of the likelihood of occurrence of an arc flash incident for AC and DC systems.*

Courtesy of NECA

in the "Equipment Condition^a" column with either "Yes" or "No" indicated in this column. Also carefully study the note to Table 130.5(C) that provides information related to the superscript [b] designation associated with "Likelihood of Occurrence[b]." While this note, like all of Table 130.5(C), must be reviewed and applied in its entirety, pay attention to what is stated related to "every possible condition or situation" and to "severity of injury or damage to health," to what "No" and "Yes" mean, and to the relationship between Table 130.5(C) and 110.5(H)(3).

Documentation

The heading of 130.5(D) is "documentation." Here it is required that the results of the arc flash risk assessment be documented.

As a review, 130.5, Arc Flash Risk Assessment, is divided into the following subdivisions:

- General
- Estimate of likelihood and severity
- Additional protective measures
- Documentation
- Arc flash boundary
- Arc flash PPE
- Incident energy analysis method
- Equipment labeling

Note that the list of subdivisions above contains documentation requirements both before and after where the documentation requirement is located in 130.5(D). In other words, there are things that need to be documented that come before and after 130.5(D), such as the estimate of likelihood and severity and additional protective measures (before) and the arc flash boundary and arc flash PPE (after). Accordingly, what must be documented as required by the arc flash risk assessment documentation requirements in 130.5(D) requires a full and careful review and application of all of the requirements of 130.5.

Although it is not specifically mentioned where or how arc flash risk assessment documentation is to be made, recall that much of this documentation is among the information required to be included on an energized electrical work permit and therefore covered in any job briefing. See 130.2(B)(6) and 110.5(I)(2), for example. Also see 130.5(H), Equipment Labeling, for other examples of arc flash risk assessment documentation requirements.

Arc Flash Boundary

The heading of 130.5(E), the fifth of the eight subdivisions detailing what is required as part of the arc flash risk assessment requirements of 130.5, is "Arc Flash Boundary." Review the definition of arc flash boundary (*Boundary, Arc Flash*) and its informational note in Article 100. Also review the Article 100 definition of *incident energy*, noting that incident energy "is typically expressed in calories per square centimeter (cal/cm^2)."

Per 130.5(E)(1) and (2), the arc flash boundary can be determined in one of two ways:

- Based on the distance at which the incident energy equals 1.2 cal/cm^2
- According to Table 130.7(C)(15)(a) or Table 130.7(C)(15)(b), when the requirements of these tables apply

Note that the requirements of 130.5(E)(1) offer one of two options for determining the arc flash boundary. In accordance with this requirement, the arc flash boundary is the distance where the incident energy equals 1.2 cal/cm^2. Note that there is not a mandatory method that must be used to calculate the arc flash boundary. An informational note points to Informative Annex D for non-mandatory information on estimating the arc flash boundary. See Table D.1, Limitation of Calculation Methods; Section D.2.1; and Section D.4.2, for example.

The requirements of 130.5(E)(2) offer the second of the two options for determining the arc flash boundary. In accordance with this requirement, the arc flash boundary shall be permitted to be determined by Table 130.7(C)(15)(a) or Table 130.7(C)(15)(b), when the requirements of these tables apply. Note that an arc flash boundary distance is listed in the "Arc-Flash Boundary" column in each of these tables. However, per 130.5(E)(2), this distance is only permitted to be used "when the requirements of these tables apply." See Section 130.7(C)(15)(a), Section 130.7(C)(15)(b), Table 130.7(C)(15)(a), and Table 130.7(C)(15)(b) for examples of the requirements that must be met to use the arc flash boundary listed in those tables. Regardless of which of these two methods is used to determine the arc flash boundary, recall that the arc flash boundary must be documented per 130.5(D) as the arc flash boundary is one of the requirements of 130.5, Arc Flash Risk Assessment. It must be on the energized electrical work permit per 130.2(B)(6)c. It must also be on a label on the equipment per 130.5(H)(2).

Arc Flash PPE

The title of 130.5(F) is "Arc Flash PPE." This subdivision addresses the sixth of the eight components required as part of an arc flash risk assessment. Note that 130.5(F) identifies two methods for the selection of arc flash PPE:
1) The incident energy analysis method per 130.5(G)
2) The arc flash PPE category method per 130.7(C)(15)

Even though either method is permitted to be used for the selection of arc flash PPE, 130.5(F) prohibits both methods from being used on the same piece of equipment. As with all requirements in *NFPA 70E* and 130.5, review 130.5(F) in its entirety, including the text that prohibits using the results of an incident energy analysis to specify an arc flash PPE category in Table 130.7(C)(15)(c).

Incident Energy Analysis Method

The seventh of the eight subdivisions in 130.5, Arc Flash Risk Assessment, is 130.5(G). These requirements address the incident energy analysis method, one of the two methods to be used for the selection of arc flash PPE per 130.5(F)(1). In addition, review the Article 100 definition of *incident energy analysis*. Also thoroughly review all of

> ### OSHA Tip
>
> **1910.335(a)(1)(i)**
> Employees working in areas where there are potential electrical hazards shall be provided with, and shall use, electrical protective equipment that is appropriate for the specific parts of the body to be protected and for the work to be performed.

the requirements of 130.5(G) for specific details on:
- What the incident energy exposure level must be based on
- What arc-rated clothing and other PPE used must be based on
- What shall be used to protect any parts of the body that are closer than the working distance at which incident energy was determined
- Considerations related to the overcurrent protective device, its fault clearing time, and its condition of maintenance
- When the incident energy analysis must be updated and how often it must be reviewed for accuracy

Note that the results of the incident energy analysis must be documented on any energized electrical work permit per 130.2(B)(6)a., and that this information must be covered during any job briefing as required in 110.5(I)(2). This information must also be included on the equipment label, including documentation of the method of calculating and data to support the information on the label in accordance with the provisions of 130.5(H), if applicable.

The requirements of 130.5(G) additionally refer to Table 130.5(G). Note that these requirements state that Table 130.5(G) "shall be permitted to be used" rather than saying it must be used with the incident energy analysis method of selecting arc flash PPE.

Also see the informational note to 130.5(G). Review the referenced information in Informative Annex D for estimating incident energy and the information in Informative Annex H for the selection of arc-rated clothing and other PPE.

Table 130.5(G)

The title of Table 130.5(G) is "Selection of Arc-Rated Clothing and Other PPE When the Incident Energy Analysis Method is Used." Note the two levels of incident energy exposures with corresponding arc-rated clothing and other PPE when the incident energy analysis method is used:

- equal to 1.2 cal/cm^2 up to and including 12 cal/cm^2
- greater than 12 cal/cm^2

In addition, recall that the requirements in 130.5(G) state, in part, that "Table 130.5(G) . . . shall be permitted to be used with the incident energy analysis method of selecting arc flash PPE." Also pay attention to the notes to Table 130.5(G) where an explanation is provided as to what "SR," "AR," and superscript letters such as "^{a}," "^{b}," and "^{c}" indicate within this table.

Figure 6-8   Equipment Labeling

⚠ WARNING

**Arc Flash and Shock Hazard
Appropriate PPE Required**

132"	Arc Flash Hazard Boundary
22.7	Cal/cm2 Incident Energy at 1'-6"
480	Volts Shock Hazard When Cover is Removed
3' - 6"	Limited Approach Boundary
1' - 0"	Restricted Approach Boundary

Device ID:
SMH1-6A

PANEL 1J

STARK SAFETY
CONSULTANTS
(866) 923-7922   Date: 11.14.16

SMH 1.0

Figure 6-8. *Many of the labels installed on equipment provide information beyond the minimum required by 130.5(H). Exception No. 1 states, in part, that labels applied prior to the effective date of this edition of the standard shall be acceptable if they complied with the requirements for equipment labeling in the standard in effect at the time the labels were applied.*

Courtesy of Stark Safety Consultants

Equipment Labeling

The heading of 130.5(H), the eighth of the eight components required as part of an arc flash risk assessment, is "Equipment Labeling." **See Figure 6-8.** Note that 130.5(H) does not require a label on all electrical equipment under all conditions of installation and use. The rule both provides examples of electrical equipment requiring labels and details the conditions under which electrical equipment must be marked with a label. Review these requirements in their entirety. Pay particular to attention to the "likely to require" provisions and the examples of types of electrical equipment requiring a label by the use of "such as" in conjunction with this list of equipment.

The requirements of 130.5(H)(1), (2), and (3) specify what information must be marked on any required equipment label. This includes, in part:

1) The nominal system voltage
2) The arc flash boundary
3) At least one of the following:
   - The available incident energy and the corresponding working distance, or the arc flash PPE category in Table 130.7(C)(15)(a) or Table 130.7(C)(15)(b) for the equipment, but not both
   - The minimum arc rating of clothing
   - Site-specific level of PPE

Review these requirements in their entirety. Also review the Article 100 definitions of incident energy, incident energy analysis, and arc rating, and consider their application in this equipment labeling requirement. "Site-specific level of PPE" is an option in 130.5(H)(3) for those employers or workplaces that specify their level of PPE in ways other than those identified in 130.5(H)(3)a. or b.

Also review the two exceptions to the equipment labeling requirements. Note that, per Exception No. 1, unless changes in electrical distribution system(s) render the label inaccurate, labels applied prior to the effective date of this edition of the standard shall be acceptable if they complied with the requirements for equipment labeling in the standard in effect at the time the labels were applied. Note also the provisions of Exception No. 2 related to "supervised industrial installations" and the permitted manner of documentation.

Also carefully review the last two paragraphs in 130.5 in their entirety. They require, in part:

- Documentation of the method of calculating and the data to support the information for the label
- A review of the data for accuracy at intervals not to exceed five years
- Updating of the label where a review of the data identifies a change that makes the information on the label inaccurate
- Recognition that the owner of the electrical equipment is responsible for the marked label documentation, installation, and maintenance.

PERSONAL AND OTHER PROTECTIVE EQUIPMENT

The requirements related to personal and other protective equipment are broken down into two broad categories: personal protective equipment (PPE) and other protective equipment. PPE, such as arc flash protective equipment, shock protection, and head, face, eye, and hearing protection, is covered in 130.7(C). **See Figure 6-9.** Also see Table 130.7(C)(14) Informational Note: Standards for PPE for examples of personal protective equipment. Other protective equipment, such as insulated tools, protective shields, and rubber insulating equipment used for protection from accidental contact, is covered in 130.7(D). **See Figure 6-10.** Also see Table 130.7(G) Informational Note: Standards on Other Protective Equipment for examples of other protective equipment.

The requirements of 130.7 begin with two topic areas that apply to both the personal protective and other protective equipment requirements. The two topic areas include general requirements and provisions addressing care of equipment. The general requirement in

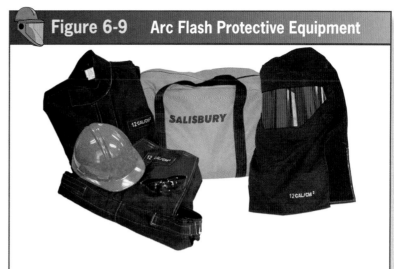

Figure 6-9. *Personal protective equipment includes arc flash protective equipment.*

Courtesy of Salisbury by Honeywell

130.7(A) that PPE be provided and used is similar to what OSHA requires in 1910.335(a)(1)(i). There is an Informational Note associated with the general requirements, and an Informational Note associated with care of equipment. The Informational Note to 130.7(A) advises, in part, that even when protection is selected in accordance with the PPE requirements of 130.7, some situations could still result in burns to the skin, although burn injury should be reduced and survivable.

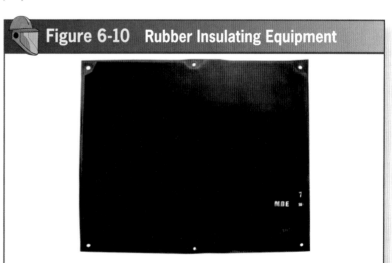

Figure 6-10. *Other protective equipment includes protective equipment such as rubber insulating blankets.*

Courtesy of Salisbury by Honeywell

In part, 130.7(B) addresses the need for protective equipment to be:
- Maintained in a safe, clean, and reliable condition
- Visually inspected before each use
- Stored in a manner to prevent damage

Personal Protective Equipment (PPE)

The Article 130 requirements for PPE are primarily covered in 130.7(C). These PPE requirements must be reviewed and applied in their entirety. They are broken down into the following 15 categories:
- General
- Movement and Visibility
- Head, Face, Neck, and Chin (Head Area) Protection
- Eye Protection
- Hearing Protection
- Body Protection
- Hand and Arm Protection
- Foot Protection
- Factors in Selection of Protective Clothing
- Arc Flash Protective Equipment
- Clothing Material Characteristics

Figure 6-11. *Shock protection must be worn within the restricted approach boundary, and arc flash protection must be worn within the arc flash boundary.*

Courtesy of Salisbury by Honeywell

- Clothing and Other Apparel Not Permitted
- Care and Maintenance of Arc-Rated Clothing and Arc-Rated Arc Flash Suits
- Standards for Personal Protective Equipment (PPE)
- Arc Flash PPE Category Method

In addition to the general requirements of 130.7(A) and the care of equipment requirements of 130.7(B) that cover both personal and other protective equipment, certain PPE general requirements apply specifically to personal protective equipment. Note that the requirements in 130.7(C)(1) address both shock and arc flash protective equipment. **See Figure 6-11.** When an employee is working within the restricted approach boundary, he or she must wear PPE in accordance with 130.4. When an employee is working within the arc flash boundary, he or she is required to wear protective clothing and other personal protective equipment in accordance with 130.5. Further, all parts of the body inside the arc flash boundary must be protected. Review the Informational Note to 130.7(C)(1) as well as the four risk reduction methods listed there.

Movement and visibility are covered in 130.7(C)(2). When arc-rated clothing is worn as protection, it is required to cover all ignitable clothing. The arc-rated clothing worn must also allow for movement and visibility. Also review 130.7(C)(9) and 130.7(C)(9)(d), (e), and (f) for related information.

Protection

The PPE requirements of 130.7(C) provide a number of protection requirements for both general and specific parts of the body. Keep in mind the provisions of 130.1 while exploring the following abbreviated look at protection requirements. Remember that these and other requirements may be applicable even where the "arc flash PPE category method" is used rather than the "incident energy analysis method" per 130.1.

Recall that 130.7(C) is divided into 15 subdivisions. The requirements of

130.7(C)(1) through (14) are used to select PPE to fulfill shock and arc flash PPE needs when the "Arc Flash PPE Method" set forth in 130.7(C)(15) per 130.5(F)(2) is not used. Sections 130.7(C)(1) and (2) have already been covered. Also review 130.1, 130.4, 130.5, Table 130.5(C), Table 130.5(G), and Informative Annex H. Note that the arc flash protective equipment requirements of 130.7(C)(10) may modify or supplement one or more of the requirements of 130.7(C) as indicated by the Informational Note to the head, face, neck, and chin requirements in 130.7(C)(3), for example. **See Figure 6-12.**

A continuation of an overview of the 130.7(C) PPE requirements follows. Again, these, like all requirements in *NFPA 70E*, need to be reviewed and applied in their entirety.

These PPE requirements continue with those related to head, face, neck, and chin (head area) protection in 130.7(C)(3). In addition to the need for nonconductive head protection and protective equipment for the face, neck, and chin, as necessary, hairnets and beard nets, where used, must be arc rated.

Eye protection is addressed in 130.7(C)(4). It is generally required in addition to face protection and must be worn whenever there is danger of injury from electric arcs, from flashes, or from flying objects resulting from electrical explosion.

Hearing protection is addressed in 130.7(C)(5) and is required when working inside the arc flash boundary. Note that hearing protection is required in each of the four arc flash PPE categories in Table 130.7(C)(15)(c).

The "body protection" provisions of 130.7(C)(6) require arc-rated clothing wherever there is possible exposure to an electric arc flash above 1.2 cal/cm². Body protection includes all parts of the body as clarified in the committee statement on Proposal 70E-271 for the 2009 edition of *NFPA 70E*. That proposal sought to replace the word "body" with the word "torso." The *NFPA 70E* Technical Committee rejected that

Figure 6-12   Modify or Supplement

Figure 6-12. Specific arc flash protective equipment requirements may modify or supplement other PPE requirements for specific parts of the body.

Courtesy of Salisbury by Honeywell

recommendation with a unanimous 24-0 vote with the following response:

Committee Statement: "Removing the word 'body' and replacing it with the word 'torso' could mislead the user of the standard by implying that other parts of the body need not be protected. The committee concludes that this section is intended to address all parts of the body."

Hand and arm protection requirements are set forth in 130.7(C)(7). **See Figure 6-13.** These hand and arm pro-

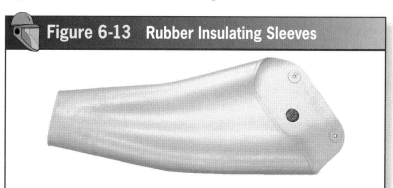

Figure 6-13   Rubber Insulating Sleeves

Figure 6-13. Rubber insulating sleeves must be worn in addition to insulating gloves with leather protectors where there is a danger of electric shock due to contact with energized electrical conductors or circuit parts.

Courtesy of Salisbury by Honeywell

tection provisions are divided into the following subdivisions:

- Shock protection
- Arc flash protection
- Maintenance and use
- Periodic electrical tests

The rules in 130.7(C)(7)(a) for shock protection require that rubber insulating gloves be rated for voltage exposure. Requirements are also provided on when rubber insulating gloves with leather protectors must be worn as well as when they must be worn in conjunction with rubber insulating sleeves. In addition to a complete examination of these rules, review the three conditions addressing when it shall be permitted to wear rubber insulating gloves without leather protectors. Also review 130.7(C)(14) relative to the standards on protective equipment in Table 130.7(C)(14) Informational Note: Standards for PPE. Standards for rubber insulating gloves, insulating sleeves, and leather protector gloves are among the standards listed in this table.

The rules in 130.7(C)(7)(b) for arc flash protection state that hand and arm protection must be worn where there is possible exposure to arc flash burn. Review this requirement in its entirety and note the additional references to 130.7(C)(10)(d) and 130.7(C)(6) for compliance with hand and arm arc flash protection provisions, respectively. This review will reveal that *hand protection* related to arc flash is addressed by the hand protection arc flash protective equipment requirements of 130.7(C)(10)(d). This review will also reveal that the *arm protection* related to arc flash is addressed by the *body protection* PPE requirements of 130.7(C)(6) that were previously covered.

The rules in 130.7(C)(7)(c) address maintenance and use of hand and arm protection. How electrical protective equipment must be maintained, when and how insulating equipment must be tested and inspected for damage, the maximum use voltages, and the required distance between the top of the cuff of the protector glove and the rolled top of the cuff of the insulating glove are among the requirements set forth here. In addition to examining the requirements of 130.7(C)(7)(c), review Table 130.7(C)(7)(a), which is comprised of four columns addressing:

- Class Designation of Glove or Sleeve
- Maximum ac Use Voltage rms, volts
- Maximum dc Use Voltage avg, volts
- Distances Between Gauntlet and Cuff, minimum

The final subdivision in 130.7(C)(7) addresses periodic electrical tests. Here, in 130.7(C)(7)(d), it states, in part, that rubber insulating equipment shall be subjected to periodic electrical tests. Also review the informational note to 130.7(C)(7)(d), which references three related ASTM Standard Specifications and OSHA 29 CFR 1910.137. **See Figure 6-14.**

Also review Table 130.7(C)(7)(b), which prescribes the maximum intervals between these required periodic electrical tests. This table consists of two columns, which address the "rubber insulating equipment" and "when to test" that equipment. Per the requirements of 130.7(C)(7)(d) and the title to Table 130.7(C)(7)(b), the information in the "when to test" column represents maximum intervals between tests.

The title to 130.7(C)(8) is "foot protection." While "foot protection" is covered here in 130.7(C)(8), these

Figure 6-14	Electrical Protective Devices
Part Number	1910
Part Title	Occupational Safety and Health Standards
Subpart	I
Subpart Title	Personal Protective Equipment
Standard Number	1910.137
Title	Electrical protective devices.

Figure 6-14. OSHA's requirements in 1910.137 address electrical protective devices. These provisions are located within Subpart I, Personal Protective Equipment.

requirements also address protection against step and touch potential, the need for dielectric footwear, and limitations of insulated soles. An informational note provides insight into a standard addressing electrical hazard footwear. Review the rules in 130.7(C)(8) in their entirety and note that this requirement does not address foot protection as it relates to protection against arc flash. Also review 130.1, including the last paragraph regarding "all requirements of Article 130 shall apply…," including 130.7(C)(10)(e), 130.7(A), 130.7(C)(1), and Table 130.7(C)(15)(c) as foot protection and foot protection requirements are considered.

Factors in Selection of Protective Clothing

The 130.7(C)(9) requirements address factors in the selection of protective clothing. The rules that apply generally require several things. First, similar to what is required in 130.7(C)(2), flammable clothing, as well as all associated parts of the body, must be covered when arc-rated clothing is required while allowing for movement and visibility. Second, similar to what is required per 130.7(C)(1), clothing and equipment that protect against shock and arc flash hazards must be used. Additional requirements in 130.7(C)(9) clarify whether garments without an arc rating can increase an arc rating and if clothing and equipment can be worn alone or be used with flammable, nonmelting apparel. An informational note discusses examples of protective clothing, including arc-rated rainwear.

Review the general requirements in 130.7(C)(9) in their entirety. Note that the "factors in selection of protective clothing" provisions are further addressed in six additional subdivisions:

- Layering
- Outer layers
- Underlayers
- Coverage
- Fit
- Interference

Requirements in the first three of these six subdivisions address "layers and layering." These are covered in 130.7(C)(9)(a), (b), and (c) and detail the use of nonmelting flammable fiber garments, the need for arc-rated garments worn as outer layers, and the prohibition of meltable fibers used as underlayers next to the skin, respectively. **See Figure 6-15.**

A number of these considerations include:

- If nonmelting, flammable fiber garments are used as underlayers, the system arc rating must be sufficient to prevent breakopen of the innermost arc-rated layer at the expected arc exposure incident energy level to prevent ignition of flammable underlayers.
- Garments that are not arc rated cannot increase the arc rating of a garment or of a clothing system.
- Garments worn as outer layers over arc-rated clothing, such as jackets or rainwear, must also be made from arc-rated material.
- Meltable fibers are generally not permitted in fabric underlayers next to the skin.
- An incidental amount of elastic used on nonmelting fabric underwear or socks shall be permitted.

Finally, coverage, fit, and interference are additional topics that are included

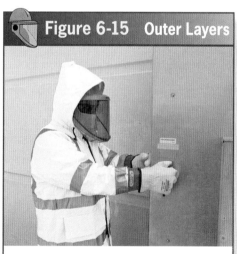

Figure 6-15   Outer Layers

Figure 6-15. Garments worn as outer layers over arc-rated clothing must also be made from arc-rated material.

Courtesy of Salisbury by Honeywell

in the requirements to be considered as factors in the selection of protective clothing. **See Figure 6-16.** A number of these considerations in 130.7(C)(9)(d), (e), and (f) include:

- Tight-fitting clothing must be avoided.
- Arc-rated apparel must fit properly so as not to interfere with the task.
- Clothing must cover potentially exposed areas as completely as possible.
- Shirt and coverall sleeves must be fastened at the wrists, shirts must be tucked into pants, and shirts, coveralls, and jackets must be closed at the neck.
- The garment selected shall result in the least interference with the task but still provide the necessary protection.

Review all of the requirements, exceptions, and informational notes related to these six subdivisions in their entirety as well. Additional requirements that apply to "factors in selection of protective clothing" include those set forth in 130.7(C)(11), (12), and (14) and will therefore be covered next.

Clothing Material Characteristics

NFPA 70E Article 130 also provides requirements addressing the clothing material characteristics; these are

Figure 6-16 Fasten Sleeves

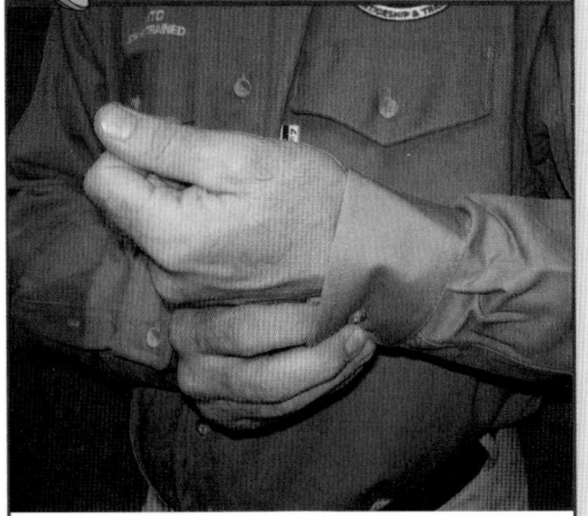

Figure 6-16. Shirt and coverall sleeves must be fastened at the wrist.

primarily located in 130.7(C)(11). If the protective clothing is arc rated, it must meet the requirements of 130.7(C)(12) and 130.7(C)(14). Table 130.7(C)(14) Informational Note: Standards for PPE identifies examples of standards for PPE, such as arc-rated apparel, rubber insulating gloves, leather protectors, and arc-rated face protective products. Three informational notes provide information related to the application of this provision.

Further, 130.7(C)(11) requires that clothing incorporating fabrics, zipper tapes, and findings made from flammable synthetic materials that melt at temperatures below 315°C (600°F), such as acetate, acrylic, nylon, polyester, polyethylene, polypropylene, and spandex, either alone or in blends, must not be used. An informational note to this requirement provides insight into this provision. Also review the exception addressing fiber blends that contain materials that melt as well as the additional informational note that follows this exception.

Review all of these requirements, exceptions, and informational notes in their entirety, including all cross-references and tables for standards for PPE. Also review the requirements of 130.1, as applicable.

Types of Clothing and Other Apparel Not Permitted

The PPE requirements given in 130.7(C)(12) address the types of clothing and other apparel that are not permitted. Note that these requirements reference 130.7(C)(11), which in turn refers back to 130.7(C)(12), as well as to 130.7(C)(14). Table 130.7(C)(14) Informational Note: Standards for PPE identifies examples of standards for PPE.

Clothing and other apparel (such as hard hat liners and hair nets) made from materials that do not meet the requirements of 130.7(C)(11) regarding melting, or made from materials that do not meet the flammability requirements, are generally not be permitted to be worn.

An informational note and two

exceptions to the requirements of 130.7(C)(12) are provided. Exception No. 1 to 130.7(C)(12) conditionally allows nonmelting, flammable clothing to be used as underlayers when it is worn under arc-rated clothing.

As always, review all of these requirements, exceptions, and informational notes in their entirety and consider the application of the requirements of 130.1 regardless of the method used to select arc flash PPE.

Arc Flash Protective Equipment
The arc flash protective equipment requirements are addressed in 130.7(C)(10) and are divided into five subdivisions. In addition to detailing unique and specific arc flash protective equipment requirements, these rules supplement or modify other requirements in 130.7(C), such as in the informational note to 130.7(C)(3). The five subdivisions addressed by 130.7(C)(10) are as follows:
• Arc flash suits
• Head protection
• Face protection
• Hand protection
• Foot protection
An abbreviated look at these requirements follows. As these requirements are reviewed in full, consider their application throughout Article 130, such as to Table 130.7(C)(15)(c), as indicated in 130.1. Recall too how these "arc flash protective equipment" requirements modify or supplement other rules in Article 130. See 130.7(C)(3), (4), (6), (7), and (8), for example.

Arc Flash Suits. The first of the five subdivisions is addressed in 130.7(C)(10)(a), arc flash suits. **See Figure 6-17.** By definition, an arc flash suit must cover the entire body except for the hands and feet. See Article 100 for the defined term *arc flash suit.* A number of arc flash suit considerations, in part, include:
• Design must permit easy and rapid removal.
• The entire arc flash suit must have an arc rating suitable for the arc flash exposure.

Figure 6-17 Arc Flash Suit

Figure 6-17. *The entire arc flash suit, including the hood's face shield, must have an arc rating that is suitable for the arc flash exposure.*

Courtesy of Salisbury by Honeywell

• The air hoses and pump housing must be either covered by arc-rated materials or constructed of nonmelting and nonflammable materials when exterior air is supplied into the hood.

Head Protection. The second of the five major topics addressed in 130.7(C) is head protection. **See Figure 6-18.**

In addition to meeting other head protection requirements, such as those in 130.7(C)(3) and 130.7(C)(14), head

Figure 6-18 Head Protection

Figure 6-18. *An arc-rated hood or an arc-rated balaclava in conjunction with an arc-rated face shield is required when the back of the head is within the arc flash boundary.*

Courtesy of Salisbury by Honeywell

protection must meet head protection requirements for arc flash protective equipment in 130.7(C)(10)(b). In part, these considerations include:

- When an arc-rated balaclava is required to be used with an arc-rated face shield
- When an arc-rated hood must be used instead of an arc-rated face shield and balaclava combination

Again, recall that 130.1 states, in part, that all requirements of Article 130 apply. Apply the head protection requirements for arc flash protective equipment, as applicable, as protective clothing and equipment is determined by Table 130.7(C)(15)(c), for example.

Face Protection. The third of the five major topics addressed in 130.7(C)(10) is face protection. In addition to meeting other face protection requirements, such as those in 130.7(C)(3) and 130.7(C)(14), face protection must

meet the specific face protection requirement for arc flash protective equipment provided in 130.7(C)(10)(c). In particular, face shields with an adequate arc rating must be worn and eye protection must be worn even when face protection is worn. **See Figure 6-19.** Face shields must also incorporate wrap-around guarding that protects the face, chin, forehead, ears, and neck area. An informational note to these requirements provides insight into this provision, including the potential need for additional illumination, as these shields are tinted and can reduce visual acuity and color perception.

Hand Protection. The fourth of the five major topics addressed in 130.7(C)(10) is hand protection. In addition to meeting other hand protection requirements, such as those in 130.7(C)(7) and 130.7(C)(14), hand protection must meet the requirements for arc flash protective equipment, when applicable. Heavy-duty leather gloves or arc-rated gloves must be worn when required for arc flash protection. Arc-rated gloves and heavy-duty leather gloves are required to provide arc flash protection for the hands. Where insulating rubber gloves are used for shock protection, leather protectors must be worn over the rubber gloves. Additional information is provided in the two informational notes. This includes the thickness of leather that would qualify leather gloves as heavy duty and insight into the protection provided by leather protectors worn over rubber insulating gloves for arc flash protection.

Foot Protection. The fifth of these five major "arc flash protective equipment" topics, addressed in 130.7(C)(10)(e), covers foot protection. In addition to meeting other foot protection requirements, such as those in 130.7(C)(8) and 130.7(C)(14), foot protection must be in the form of leather footwear or dielectric footwear, or both, where arc flash exposures exceed 4 cal/cm². This requirement also provides conditional allowance for other than leather footwear

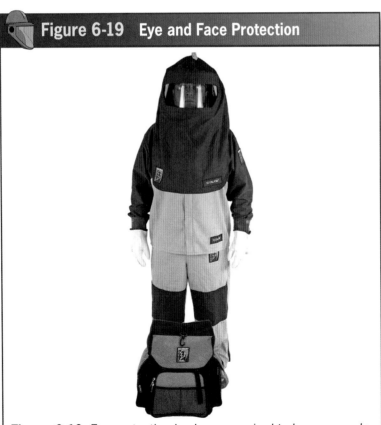

Figure 6-19   Eye and Face Protection

Figure 6-19. Eye protection is always required to be worn under face shields or hoods.

Courtesy of Salisbury by Honeywell

or dielectric footwear. Be sure to review and apply this requirement, like all *NFPA 70E* requirements, in its entirety.

As 130.1 is considered, compare this requirement with the foot protection required by Table 130.7(C)(15)(c), where leather footwear is required for PPE Categories 1, 2, 3, and 4 per this table. Even though there is no method recognized in the requirements of *NFPA 70E* to equate an incident energy calculation with an arc flash PPE category, it is worth noting that Table 130.7(C)(15)(c) mentions "leather footwear" for all arc-flash PPE categories ("AN" for Category 1 and required for Categories 2, 3, and 4), while the provisions of 130.7(C)(10)(e) generally require leather footwear or dielectric footwear or both above 4 cal/cm^2 (recognizing that this requirement also provides conditional allowance for other than leather footwear or dielectric footwear).

Care and Maintenance of Arc-Rated Clothing and Arc-Rated Arc Flash Suits

Several requirements cover the care and maintenance of arc-rated clothing and arc flash suits. **See Figure 6-20.**

These rules are primarily located in 130.7(C)(13) and are divided into four subdivisions:

- Inspection
- Manufacturer's Instructions
- Storage
- Cleaning, Repairing, and Affixing Items

Among the requirements of these rules are compliance with 130.7(C)(14) and the following provisions:

- Apparel must be inspected before each use.
- Garments that are contaminated or damaged to the extent that their protective qualities are impaired cannot be used.
- Manufacturer's instructions for care, maintenance, and cleaning must be followed.
- The same arc-rated materials used to manufacture the clothing must be used for repair.

In addition to reviewing the three informational notes following 130.7(C)(13)(d), review and apply the requirements in 130.7(C)(13). These and all related requirements must be referred to and applied in their entirety for full and complete understanding and application.

Standards for Personal Protective Equipment (PPE)

NFPA 70E requires protective equipment to meet the requirements of 130.7(C)(14)(a), (b), and (c) which cover general, conformity assessment, and marking, respectively. See 130.7(C)(14)(a), where it is required, in part, that PPE shall conform to applicable state, federal, or local codes and standards. Examples of personal protective equipment standards are presented in Table 130.7(C)(14) Informational Note: Standards for PPE.

See also Informational Note No. 1 to 130.7(C)(14)(a), where this nonmandatory table is referenced for examples of standards that contain information on the care, inspection, testing, and manufacturing of PPE. This includes PPE such as arc-rated apparel, eye and face protection, arc-rated face protection, fall protection, leather protectors, rubber insulating gloves, hard hats, and arc-rated rainwear, for example. Also

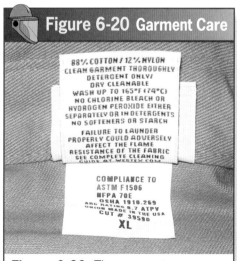

Figure 6-20 Garment Care

88% COTTON / 12% NYLON
CLEAN GARMENT THOROUGHLY
DETERGENT ONLY/
DRY CLEANABLE
WASH UP TO 165°F (74°C)
NO CHLORINE BLEACH OR
HYDROGEN PEROXIDE EITHER
SEPARATELY OR IN DETERGENTS
NO SOFTENERS OR STARCH

FAILURE TO LAUNDER
PROPERLY COULD ADVERSELY
AFFECT THE FLAME
RESISTANCE OF THE FABRIC
SEE COMPLETE CLEANING
GUIDE AT WESTEX.COM

COMPLIANCE TO
ASTM F1506
NFPA 70E
OSHA 1910.269
ARC RATING 8.7 ATPV
MADE IN THE USA
CUT # 3959D
XL

Figure 6-20. *The garment manufacturer's instructions for care and maintenance of arc-rated apparel must be followed.*

note that non–arc-rated or flammable fabrics are not covered by a standard in Table 130.7(C)(14) Informational Note: Standards for PPE, even though such fabrics are permitted to be used in some cases per Informational Note No. 2 to 130.7(C)(14)(a), which points to 130.7(C)(11) and 130.7(C)(12) for reference. Also review the three conformity assessment choices and the two related informational notes in 130.7(C)(14)(b), as well as the list of five marking requirements that all suppliers or manufacturers are required to provide and how they must provide them as detailed in 130.7(C)(14)(c).

Arc Flash PPE Category Method

One of the required outcomes of an arc flash risk assessment in accordance with 130.5(A) is determining if additional protective measures are required, including the personal protective equipment that people within the arc flash boundary must use. **See Figure 6-21.** When the additional protective measures include the use of PPE, 130.5(C)(3) requires that the PPE to be used within the arc flash boundary be determined. There are two methods that shall be used to make this determination: the incident energy analysis method per 130.5(F)(1) and 130.5(G), or the arc flash PPE category method per 130.5(F)(2) and 130.7(C)(15). The requirements for selecting arc flash PPE using the incident energy analysis method were covered previously. The requirements for selecting arc flash PPE using the arc flash PPE category method will be explored here.

The requirements in 130.7(C)(15) apply when the arc flash PPE category method is used for the selection of arc flash PPE. See 130.5(F)(1) and 130.5(F)(2). Review the requirements in 130.1, including, in part, that "all requirements of this article shall apply,"

Figure 6-21   Determining Arc Flash PPE

Figure 6-21. Determination of whether additional protective measures are required, including the use of arc flash PPE to be used within the arc flash boundary, is one reason why an arc flash risk assessment is performed.

Courtesy of Salisbury by Honeywell

Figure 6-22   Arc Flash PPE Categories for AC

DETERMINING ARC FLASH HAZARD PPE CATEGORIES **ALTERNATING CURRENT**
Excerpts from Table 130.7(C)(15)(a)
Requirements for rubber insulating gloves and leather protectors are also included (See 130.4)

Equipment	Arc Flash PPE Category	Arc-Flash Boundary	Rubber-Insualted Gloves (Minimum) 130.4
Panelboards or other equipment rated 240 V and below Parameters: Maximum of 25 kA available fault current; maximum of 0.03 sec (2 cycles) fault clearing time; working distance 455 mm (18 in.)	1	485 mm (19 in.)	Class 00
Panelboards or other equipment rated >240 V and up to 600 V Parameters: Maximum of 25 kA available fault current; maximum of 0.03 sec (2 cycles) fault clearing time; working distance 455 mm (18 in.)	2	900 mm (3 ft.)	Class 00 (<500V) Class 0 (>500V < 1000V)
600-V class motor control centers (MCCs) Parameters: Maximum of 65 kA available fault current; maximum of 0.03 sec (2 cycles) fault clearing time; working distance 455 mm (18 in.)	2	1.5 m (5 ft)	Class 00 (<500V) Class 0 (>500V < 1000V)

Figure 6-22. *Table 130.7(C)(15)(a) provides arc flash PPE categories and arc flash boundaries for AC systems when the arc flash PPE category method is used and arc flash PPE is required. The arc flash PPE categories, arc flash boundaries, equipment, and parameters shown in the excerpt from the "NECA NFPA 70E Personal Protective Equipment (PPE) Selector" are based on Table 130.7(C)(15)(a).*

Courtesy of NECA

which would include all applicable requirements in Article 130.

The requirements and informational notes in 130.7(C)(15) address protective equipment determination where the arc flash PPE category method, rather than an incident energy analysis, constitutes the method used to select protective equipment. Note that 130.7(C)(15) is divided into the following three subdivisions:

- Alternating Current (ac) Equipment
- Direct Current (dc) Equipment
- Protective Clothing and PPE

The requirements for AC equipment are covered in 130.7(C)(15)(a), those for DC equipment in 130.7(C)(15)(b), and those for protective clothing and PPE in 130.7(C)(15)(c). These, like all of the requirements in *NFPA 70E*, must be reviewed and applied in their entirety. Also review the informational notes for explanatory information related to the requirements of 130.7(C)

(15)(a), (b) and (c).

Per 130.7(C)(15)(a), Table 130.7(C)(15)(a) is used to identify the arc flash PPE category for AC systems when arc flash PPE is required by the arc flash risk assessment and the arc flash PPE category method is used. **See Figure 6-22.** In addition, 130.7(C)(15)(a) refers to the estimated maximum available fault current, maximum fault clearing times, and minimum working distances for various equipment types and classifications in Table 130.7(C)(15)(a). Note that this table cannot be used if these conditions are not met. See 130.7(C)(15)(a)(1), (2), and (3). An incident energy analysis shall be required when any three of these conditions cannot be met in accordance with 130.7(C)(15)(a).

Per 130.7(C)(15)(b), Table 130.7(C)(15)(b) is used to identify the arc flash PPE category for DC systems when arc flash PPE is required by the arc flash risk assessment and the arc flash PPE

Figure 6-23   Arc Flash PPE Categories for DC

DETERMINING ARC FLASH PPE CATEGORIES **DIRECT CURRENT**
Excerpts from Table 130.7 (C)(15)(b)
Requirements for rubber insulating gloves and leather protectors are also included (See 130.4)

Equipment	Arc Flash PPE Category	Arc-Flash Boundary	Rubber-Insualted Gloves (Minimum)
Storage batteries, dc switchboards, and other dc supply sources Parameters: Greater than or equal to 100 V and less than or equal to 250 V Maximum arc duration and working distance: 2 sec @ 455 mm (18 in.)			
Available fault current less than 4 kA	2	900mm (3 ft.)	Class 00*
Available fault current greater than or equal to 4 kA and less than 7 kA	2	1.2m (4 ft.)	Class 00*
7Available fault current greater than or equal to 7 kA and less than 15 kA	3	1.8m (6 ft.)	Class 00*
Storage batteries, dc switchboards, and other dc supply sources Parameters: Greater than 250 V and less than or equal to 600 V Maximum arc duration and working distance: 2 sec @ 455 mm (18 in.)			
Available fault current less than 1.5 kA	2	900mm (3 ft.)	Class 00*
Available fault current greater than or equal to 1.5 kA and less than 3 kA	2	1.2m (4 ft.)	Class 00*
MAvailable fault current greater than or equal to 3 kA and less than 7 kA	3	1.8m (6 ft.)	Class 00*
Available fault current greater than or equal to 7 kA and less than 10 kA	4	2.5m (8 ft.)	Class 00*

Figure 6-23. Table 130.7(C)(15)(b) provides arc flash PPE categories and arc flash boundaries for DC systems when the arc flash PPE category method is used and arc flash PPE is required. The arc flash PPE categories, arc flash boundaries, equipment, and parameters shown in the excerpt from the "NECA NFPA 70E Personal Protective Equipment (PPE) Selector" are based on Table 130.7(C)(15)(b).

Courtesy of NECA

category method is used. **See Figure 6-23.** In addition, 130.7(C)(15)(b) lists the estimated maximum available fault current, maximum arc duration, and working distances for DC equipment in Table 130.7(C)(15)(b). Note that this table cannot be used if these conditions are not met. See 130.7(C)(15)(b) (1), (2), and (3). An incident energy analysis shall be required when any of these three conditions cannot be met in accordance with 130.7(C)(15)(b).

Per 130.7(C)(15)(c), Table 130.7(C) (15)(c) is used to determine the required PPE once an arc flash PPE category has been determined from either Table 130.7(C)(15)(a) or Table 130.7(C)(15)(b). **See Figure 6-24.** The clothing and equipment identified in Table 130.7(C)(15)(c) must be used within the arc flash boundary. Note that the arc flash boundary is identified in Table 130.7(C)(15)(a) and Table 130.7(C)(15)(b) for AC and DC,

respectively. In addition, review the three informational notes for explanatory information related to the requirements of 130.7(C)(15)(c).

Arc Flash PPE Category Method Tables

There are three tables associated with the requirements of 130.7(C)(15). These are Table 130.7(C)(15)(a), Table 130.7(C)(15)(b), and Table 130.7(C) (15)(c). These tables are subject to their respective requirements in 130.7(C) (15), 130.7(C)(15)(a), 130.7(C)(15)(b), and 130.7(C)(15)(c).

Table 130.7(C)(15)(a)

Table 130.7(C)(15)(a), Arc-Flash PPE categories for Alternating Current (ac) Systems, has three columns. The column on the left side of the table is titled "Equipment" and, per 130.7(C)(15)(a), sets forth the "various ac equipment types or classifications" to which this table applies. Note that this "Equipment" column also includes the parameters associated with the particular equipment, including maximum available fault current, fault clearing time, and minimum working distance. Recall that per 130.7(C)(15)(a), this table is not permitted to be used, and an incident energy analysis is required, if all of the conditions in 130.7(C)(15)(a)(1), (2), and (3) are not met.

The middle column of Table 130.7(C)(15)(a) specifies an arc-flash PPE category for equipment listed in the left column based on its associated parameters. Also review the "Note" to this table addressing where an arc flash PPE category can be reduced by one number.

The right column of Table 130.7(C)(15)(a) specifies the arc flash boundary for equipment listed in the left column based on its associated parameters. See 130.5(E)(2) stating, in part, that "the arc flash boundary shall be permitted to be determined by . . . Table 130.7(C)(15)(a) . . . when the requirements of these tables apply."

For example, a review of this table shows that the arc flash boundary is 19 inches and the arc flash PPE category is 1 for "panel boards or other equipment rated 240 volts and below" that has a maximum of 25 kA available fault current, a maximum of 2 cycle fault clearing time, and a minimum working distance of 18 inches.

The provisions of 130.7(C)(15)(a) and Table 130.7(C)(15)(a), like all of the requirements in *NFPA 70E*, must be reviewed and applied in their entirety. In addition to reviewing and applying the table note, as applicable, review the informational notes for explanatory information related to the requirements of this table. Additionally, note the six items provided as explanatory material in Informational Note No. 1 to Table 130.7(C)(15)(a)

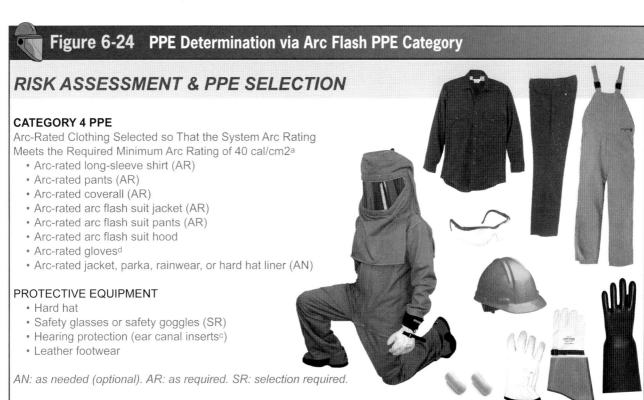

Figure 6-24 PPE Determination via Arc Flash PPE Category

RISK ASSESSMENT & PPE SELECTION

CATEGORY 4 PPE
Arc-Rated Clothing Selected so That the System Arc Rating Meets the Required Minimum Arc Rating of 40 cal/cm2[a]
- Arc-rated long-sleeve shirt (AR)
- Arc-rated pants (AR)
- Arc-rated coverall (AR)
- Arc-rated arc flash suit jacket (AR)
- Arc-rated arc flash suit pants (AR)
- Arc-rated arc flash suit hood
- Arc-rated gloves[d]
- Arc-rated jacket, parka, rainwear, or hard hat liner (AN)

PROTECTIVE EQUIPMENT
- Hard hat
- Safety glasses or safety goggles (SR)
- Hearing protection (ear canal inserts[c])
- Leather footwear

AN: as needed (optional). AR: as required. SR: selection required.

Figure 6-24. *PPE is selected from Table 130.7(C)(15)(c) based on the arc flash PPE category when the arc flash PPE category method is used and arc flash PPE is required. The PPE shown in the excerpt from the "NECA NFPA 70E Personal Protective Equipment (PPE) Selector" is based on Table 130.7(C)(15)(c).*

Courtesy of NECA

related to "typical clearing times of overcurrent protective devices."

Table 130.7(C)(15)(b)

Table 130.7(C)(15)(b), Arc-Flash PPE categories for Direct Current (dc) Systems, has three columns. The column on the left side of the table is titled "Equipment" and, per 130.7(C)(15)(b), sets forth the "dc equipment" to which this table applies. Note that this "Equipment" column also includes the parameters associated with the particular equipment, including voltage, maximum arc duration, and minimum working distance. Note also the various available fault current levels applicable to the equipment listed in this table. Recall that per 130.7(C)(15)(b), this table is not permitted to be used, and an incident energy analysis is required, if all of the conditions in 130.7(C)(15)(b)(1), (2), and (3) are not met.

The middle column of Table 130.7(C)(15)(b) specifies an arc-flash PPE category for the DC equipment listed in the left column based on its associated parameters and the available fault current.

The right column of Table 130.7(C)(15)(b) specifies the arc flash boundary for the DC equipment listed in the left column based on its associated parameters and available fault current. See 130.5(E)(2) stating, in part, that "the arc flash boundary shall be permitted to be determined by . . . Table 130.7(C)(15)(b) . . . when the requirements of these tables apply."

Also note what is covered in the two notes to this table as well as their respective informational notes. Additionally, consider the information provided as explanatory material in Informational Notes No. 1 and 2 that are applicable to this table. These, like all of the requirements in *NFPA 70E*, must be reviewed and applied in their entirety.

Table 130.7(C)(15)(c)

Per 130.7(C)(15)(c), Table 130.7(C)(15)(c) is to be used to determine the required PPE once an arc flash PPE category has been determined from either Table 130.7(C)(15)(a) or Table 130.7(C)(15)(b).

Note that Table 130.7(C)(15)(c), Personal Protective Equipment (PPE), consists of two columns. The column on the left side of this table is the "Arc-Flash PPE Category." The column on the right side of this table establishes the "PPE" that is required for the corresponding arc-flash PPE category. Per 130.7(C)(15)(c), "Table 130.7(C)(15)(c) lists the requirements for PPE based on arc flash PPE categories," and "this clothing and equipment shall be used when working within the arc flash boundary." Note that the last sentence in this section provides alternatives to the PPE that is listed in the table where it states that "the use of PPE other than or in addition to that listed shall be permitted provided it meets 130.7(C)(7)."

Also review and apply the notes to this table that include an explanation as to what "AN," "AR," and "SR" indicate, as well as the application of superscript notes [a], [b], [c], [d], [e], and [f] in this table. Also, review 130.5(F)(2), which permits the PPE category method in accordance with 130.7(C)(15).

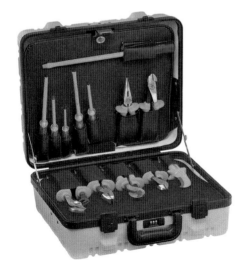

Figure 6-25   Other Protective Equipment

Figure 6-25. Other protective equipment, such as insulated tools, must comply with 130.7(G).

Courtesy of Klein Tools

Other Protective Equipment

Personal protective equipment is covered in 130.7(C) and includes equipment such as arc flash protective equipment, shock protection, and head, face, eye, and hearing protection. Other protective equipment, such as insulated tools, protective shields, and rubber insulating equipment used for protection from accidental contact, is covered in 130.7(D). The other protective equipment required by 130.7(D) must comply with those requirements as well as those in 130.7(G). **See Figure 6-25.**

The requirements and an informational note addressing insulated tools and equipment are located in 130.7(D)(1). The other protective equipment requirements of 130.7(D)(1) begin with requirements that apply to the five categories of insulated tools and equipment. These requirements of 130.7(D)(1), in part, state:

- Employees must use insulated tools when working inside the restricted approach boundary.
- Insulated tools must be protected from damage to the insulating material.

The requirements of 130.7(D)(1) are broken down into five categories of insulated tools and equipment:

- Requirements for Insulated Tools
- Fuse or Fuseholder Handling Equipment
- Ropes and Handlines
- Fiberglass-Reinforced Plastic Rods
- Portable Ladders

The specific requirements for each of the five categories of insulated tools and equipment are contained in 130.7(D)(1)(a) through (e). Be sure to refer to *NFPA 70E* to explore the requirements in the five categories of topics of 130.7(D)(1) that were introduced in the list above. Much of this "other protective equipment" including, but not limited to, insulated tools and portable ladders, is utilized fairly often. These and all related requirements must be referred to in their entirety for a full and complete understanding.

The requirements of 130.7(D)(2) address "Barriers" and are broken down into the following three categories:

- Rubber Insulating Equipment
- Voltage-Rated Plastic Guard Equipment
- Physical or Mechanical Barriers

The specific requirements for each of the three categories of barriers are contained in 130.7(D)(2)(a) through (c). These and all related requirements must be referred to in their entirety for a full and complete understanding.

Standards for Other Protective Equipment

NFPA 70E requires protective equipment, and also mandates that much of this protective equipment meet specific requirements. **See Figure 6-26.** In

Figure 6-26 Standards on Other Protective Equipment

Figure 6-26. Examples of standards on other protective equipment are located in Table 130.7(G) Informational Note: Standards on Other Protective Equipment.

Courtesy of Salisbury by Honeywell

particular, personal protective equipment must conform to the requirements in 130.7(C)(14); other protective equipment required in 130.7(D) must conform to the requirements of 130.7(G).

Examples of other protective equipment standards, such as those for arc protective blankets, insulated hand tools, ladders, line hose, safety signs and tags, and temporary protective grounds, are identified in Table 130.7(G) Informational Note: Standards on Other Protective Equipment.

Alerting Techniques

Alerting techniques are located in a subdivision of 130.7, Personal and Other Protective Equipment, and are therefore, per its title, recognized as a form of protective equipment. These protective equipment requirements are broken down into the following categories in 130.7(E):

- Safety Signs and Tags
- Barricades
- Attendants

Figure 6-27 Employer and Employee Responsibility

Figure 6-27. The requirements for work within the limited approach boundary or arc flash boundary of overhead lines within the scope of NFPA 70E address topics including employer and employee responsibility.

Courtesy of Service Electric Company

Safety signs and tags are an example of one of the standards presented in Table 130.7(G) Informational Note: Standards on Other Protective Equipment. Recall that one of the required elements of the energized work permit per 130.2(B)(7) is "means employed to restrict access of unqualified persons from the work area." The alerting techniques identified in 130.7(E) may be among the ways to meet this requirement. Refer to *NFPA 70E* to explore the requirements in the three categories of alerting techniques of 130.7(E) that were introduced in the list above. These and all related requirements must be referred to and applied in their entirety for a full and complete understanding.

Look-Alike Equipment

The requirements of 130.7(F) address "look-alike equipment" where work performed on equipment that is deenergized and placed in an electrically safe condition exists in a work area with other energized equipment that is similar in size, shape, and construction. In this case, one of the alerting methods in 130.7(E)(1), (2), or (3) shall be employed to prevent the employee from entering look-alike equipment.

OTHER PRECAUTIONS FOR PERSONNEL ACTIVITIES

The next category of requirements related to work involving electrical hazards is located in 130.8 and addresses "other precautions for personnel activities." These provisions are broken down into the following 14 subdivisions:

- Alertness
- Blind Reaching
- Illumination
- Conductive Articles Being Worn
- Conductive Materials, Tools, and Equipment Being Handled
- Confined or Enclosed Work Spaces
- Doors and Hinged Panels
- Clear Spaces
- Housekeeping Duties
- Occasional Use of Flammable Materials
- Anticipating Failure

- Routine Opening and Closing of Circuits
- Reclosing Circuits After Protective Device Operation
- Safety Interlocks

A number of these topics are similar to what OSHA requires in Subpart S of 29 CFR Part 1910. Each of these topics is an important consideration that must be carefully reviewed in its entirety, with most—if not all—of these issues likely to be included in an electrical safety program or procedures based on *NFPA 70E*.

An abbreviated look at a number of these 130.8 provisions includes:

- Instruction must generally be provided to alert employees to be alert at all times where electrical hazards might exist.
- Working where electrical hazards might exist is generally prohibited while alertness is recognizably impaired.
- Illumination must be provided that enables work to be performed safely prior to employee entry into spaces containing electrical hazards.
- Conductive articles cannot be worn within the restricted approach boundary or where they present an electrical contact hazard.
- Conductive materials, tools, and equipment must be handled in a manner that prevents unintentional contact with energized electrical conductors or circuit parts.
- Conductive materials must not approach exposed energized electrical conductors or circuit parts closer than that permitted by 130.4(F).
- Protective shields, protective barriers, or insulating materials must generally be provided and used to avoid the effects of electrical hazards and inadvertent contact with exposed energized parts before entry into a confined or enclosed space.
- Required working space must not be used for storage.

All of the requirements in 130.8 must be reviewed in their entirety for a full and complete understanding and application.

OVERHEAD LINES

Section 130.9 deals with overhead line work—specifically, requirements for work within the limited approach boundary or arc flash boundary of overhead lines. This section is divided into six subdivisions. These and all requirements related to this work must be referred to in their entirety for a full and complete understanding. These six subdivisions are:

- Uninsulated and Energized
- Determination of Insulation Rating
- Employer and Employee Responsibility; **see Figure 6-27**
- Deenergizing or Guarding; see **Figure 6-28**
- Approach Distances for Unqualified Persons
- Vehicular and Mechanical Equipment

Notice that the only mention of where the requirements of 130.9 apply is in the

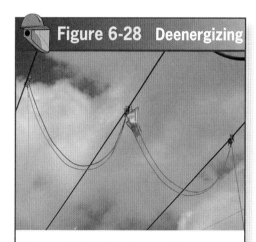

Figure 6-28 Deenergizing

Figure 6-28. *The deenergizing provisions in 130.9 require that arrangements be made with the person or organization that operates or controls the lines to deenergize them and visibly ground them at the point of work if the lines are to be deenergized.*

Courtesy of Service Electric Company

title—that is, Work Within the Limited Approach Boundary or Arc Flash Boundary of Overhead Lines. Review the definition of each of those boundaries in Article 100, their application in 130.4, and associated distances in Table 130.4(E)(a) for AC systems and Table 130.4(E)(b) for DC systems.

The note for superscript C (^{c}) in Table 130.4(E)(a) and the note for the asterisk (*) in Table 130.4(E)(b) advise, in part, that the limited approach boundary for an exposed movable conductor normally applies to overhead line conductors supported by poles. Recall that the arc flash boundary is either the distance where the incident energy equals 1.2 cal/cm^2 per 130.5(E)(1) or determined by Table 130.7(C)(15)(a) for AC systems or Table 130.7(C)(15)(b) for DC systems per 130.5(E)(2).

The requirements of 130.9 reference both qualified persons and unqualified persons. Recall that training requirements for both qualified and unqualified persons are located in 110.6(A) and that both are defined in Article 100.

Be sure to refer to *NFPA 70E* to fully explore the requirements in the six subdivisions of 130.9 that were introduced here.

Recognizing that the 130.9 provisions—like all of Article 130—are not independent of the rest of the requirements of *NFPA 70E*, be sure to reference and apply these in their entirety as well as all applicable *NFPA 70E* rules and definitions, including those in Articles 90, 105, 100, 110, 120, and 130.

UNDERGROUND ELECTRICAL LINES AND EQUIPMENT

NFPA 70E includes provisions that introduce a number of concepts from OSHA's 29 CFR Part 1926 requirements for underground installations.

NFPA 70E addresses this topic in Section 130.10 and requires, in part, that, before excavation starts, and where there exists a reasonable possibility of contacting electrical lines or equipment, the employer must take the necessary steps to contact the appropriate owners or authorities to identify and mark the location of the electrical lines or equipment. Review this requirement in its entirety, including determining when appropriate safe work practices and PPE must be used.

1926.651(b)

Underground installations.

1926.651(b)(1)

The estimated location of utility installations, such as sewer, telephone, fuel, electric, water lines, or any other underground installations that reasonably may be expected to be encountered during excavation work, shall be determined prior to opening an excavation.

1926.651(b)(2)

Utility companies or owners shall be contacted within established or customary local response times, advised of the proposed work, and asked to establish the location of the utility underground installations prior to the start of actual excavation. When utility companies or owners cannot respond to a request to locate underground utility installations within 24 hours (unless a longer period is required by state or local law), or cannot establish the exact location of these installations, the employer may proceed, provided the employer does so with caution, and provided detection equipment or other acceptable means to locate utility installations are used.

1926.651(b)(3)

When excavation operations approach the estimated location of underground installations, the exact location of the installations shall be determined by safe and acceptable means.

1926.651(b)(4)

While the excavation is open, underground installations shall be protected, supported or removed as necessary to safeguard employees.

CUTTING OR DRILLING

Section 130.11 is the next-to-last section in Article 130. It addresses cutting or drilling into equipment, floors, walls, or structural elements where a likelihood of contacting energized electrical lines or parts exists. These are among tasks that Electrical Workers perform with some frequency. Review the provisions of 130.11 in their entirety and consider how the risk assessment required to be performed by the employer will identify and mark locations, create an electrically safe work condition, and identify necessary safe work practices and PPE.

As always, consider all of the requirements of *NFPA 70E* that apply to this requirement.

CUTTING, REMOVING, OR REROUTING OF CONDUCTORS

Although Section 130.12 is the last section in Article 130 and Chapter 1, it is certainly not the least important. This requirement, like many OSHA and *NFPA 70E* requirements, was written in response to a fatality not unlike the case studies at the beginning of every chapter in this publication. The goal of this requirement is to prevent a future injury or fatality.

Carefully review the requirement in 130.12 and its informational note. It addresses where conductors are deenergized in order to cut, remove, or reroute them and the conductor terminations are not within sight from the point of work. It states that additional steps to verify absence of voltage or identify the conductors shall be taken prior to cutting, removing, or rerouting the conductors. The informational note provides examples of additional steps to be taken where conductors are deenergized in order to cut, remove, or reroute them. Be sure to review and apply this requirement and all of *NFPA 70E* in its entirety.

SUMMARY

The Article 130 requirements are broken down into ten sections covering topics including, but not limited to, those related to energized electrical work permits, shock and arc flash risk assessments (including whether additional protective measures are required), personal protective equipment, and other protective equipment.

These requirements, like all *NFPA 70E* requirements, apply within the scope of the standard spelled out in Article 90. Remember to review and apply all pertinent definitions in Article 100, the requirements of Article 105, the general requirements of Article 110, the requirements for establishing an electrically safe work condition in Article 120, and the requirements for work involving electrical hazards in Article 130. In addition, review and apply any relevant *NFPA 70E* Chapter 2 and 3 requirements and any of the related information in the Informative Annexes.

1. Incident energy analysis is defined as a component of an arc flash risk assessment used to predict the incident energy of an arc flash for a __?__ set of conditions.
   a. general
   b. nominal
   c. specified
   d. theoretical

2. An energized electrical work permit is only required when work is performed within the restricted approach boundary.
   a. True   b. False

3. All requirements of Article 130 shall apply whether an incident energy analysis is completed or if Table 130.7(C)(15)(a), Table 130.7(C)(15)(b), and Table 130.7(C)(15)(c) are used in lieu of an incident energy analysis.
   a. True   b. False

4. One reason a shock risk assessment is required is to determine if additional __?__ are required, including the use of personal protective equipment.
   a. corrective actions
   b. protective measures
   c. qualified personnel
   d. remediation strategies

5. Under no circumstance is an unqualified person permitted to cross the __?__ approach boundary.
   a. arc flash
   b. limited
   c. restricted
   d. secured

6. The incident energy analysis must take into consideration the characteristics of the overcurrent protective device and its fault clearing time, __?__ its condition of maintenance.
   a. eliminating
   b. excluding
   c. ignoring
   d. including

7. Which one of the following is not among the category of requirements related to "other precautions for personnel activities" in 130.8?
   a. Alertness, blind reaching, and confined or enclosed work spaces
   b. Conductive articles being worn, clear spaces, and doors and hinged panels
   c. Electrical hazard, arc blast, and cost-benefit analysis
   d. Illumination, housekeeping duties, and anticipating failure

8. Shock protection must be worn within the __?__ approach boundary, and arc flash protection must be worn within the __?__ boundary.
   a. limited / arc blast
   b. limited / arc flash
   c. restricted / arc flash
   d. restricted / limited

9. When using the arc flash PPE category method to select arc flash personal protective equipment where required for work performed on alternating current (AC) equipment, it is important to note the parameters that must be met, such as minimum working distance, estimated maximum available fault current, and __?__ fault clearing times to determine the appropriate protective equipment.
   a. anticipated
   b. approximated
   c. maximum
   d. minimum

10. An arc flash PPE category __?__ be determined through an incident energy analysis.
    a. can
    b. cannot
    c. should
    d. should not

Fault Current Fundamentals

The available fault current (bolted) is identified through a fault current study. The purpose of a fault current study is to determine the available fault current (bolted) at one or multiple points in an electrical system so as to ensure compliance with OSHA, *NEC*, and *NFPA 70E* requirements, as well as for other electrical system analysis purposes. The available fault current is a value that may be necessary to be determined as part of an arc-flash risk assessment.

It is important to understand the variables that affect the available fault current magnitude at various points in an AC electrical system. In addition, Electrical Workers should be familiar with the procedures, including equations and tables, for performing simple available fault current calculations for 3-phase systems, referred to as the point-to-point method.

Objectives

» Understand two types of fault (short-circuit) current—bolted and arcing— and their relationship.

» Recognize key variables and different scenarios that may affect the available fault current.

» Understand the procedures and calculation methods to determine the 3-phase available fault current to a specific point or multiple points in an electrical system.

Chapter 7

Table of Contents

Case Study

A large industrial facility expanded its manufacturing facility. This included adding on to their existing facility as well as a new facility with a new 3,000-ampere, 480/277-volt service. As required for compliance with *NEC* Section 110.9 (overcurrent device interrupting rating) and Section 110.10 (equipment short-circuit current rating), the available fault current was calculated by the design-build contractor at the new equipment. Similarly, existing electrical equipment requires an examination to comply with OSHA 1910.302(b)(1), 1910.303(b)(4), and 1910.303(b)(5) to determine whether the available fault current is now higher than the interrupting rating (IR) of the overcurrent devices or the short-circuit current rating (SCCR) of the existing equipment. Additional considerations may include electrical hazard analysis and work practices, as well as a selection of personal protective equipment (PPE).

The analysis of the existing facility determined the available fault current was relatively low (around 20,000 amperes) and the existing switchboard was fusible with current-limiting fuses, so proper interrupting rating (IR) was not an issue. The new equipment contained circuit breakers with proper interrupting ratings (25,000 amperes). However, the issue that was discovered during the coordination and arc flash study was that the HVAC equipment only had a short-circuit current rating (SCCR) of 5,000 amperes. Due to long conductor runs, only two of the eight units had an available fault current more than 5,000 amperes, and a current-limiting fuse could be applied to reduce the available fault current to provide proper protection of the equipment.

For the new 3,000-ampere, 480/277-volt service, the available fault current was around 50,000 amperes, and the facility included HVAC and industrial control panels. Similar to the existing facility equipment, the HVAC and industrial control panels for the new facility had an SCCR of 5,000 amperes. In this facility, the available fault current exceeded the equipment SCCR for 14 of the 28 units. Current-limiting fuses could be applied to reduce the available fault current at eight of the 14 units. The remaining six units needed to be redesigned to meet the higher available fault current, which typically requires changing circuit breakers to current-limiting fuses to achieve higher interrupting ratings and component short-circuit current ratings.

Uncovering safety hazards of inadequate IR and SCCR of equipment is unwelcome news to the facility owner, but important as part of the effort to protect persons and property. In this case, the design-build contractor who has been educated on the requirement for proper IR and SCCR of equipment was able to identify and correct the issues before equipment was released for manufacturing. All too often, however, it is only after an incident occurs that the extent of the hazard is realized. Recognition, acceptance, and application of *NEC*, *NFPA 70E*, and OSHA requirements are helping to improve the safety levels of today's new and existing electrical systems.

All parties play an important role in ensuring a safe and reliable electrical installation, both today and in the future. Data collection is an essential part of the analysis and must not be overlooked. The calculation and software options available today make it easier than ever to specify, install, and maintain *Code-* and OSHA-compliant installations.

Source: Dan Neeser,
Eaton's Bussmann Division

INTRODUCTION

The available fault current is identified through an available fault current study. The purpose of a fault current study is to determine the available fault current (bolted) at one or multiple points in an electrical system. If either the arc-flash PPE category method or the incident energy analysis method is used to determine arc flash PPE, typically the available fault current must be determined as part of an arc-flash risk assessment.

Electrical Workers will benefit from some insight into the variables that affect the available fault current magnitude at various points in an AC electrical system. These variables, such as switching schemes or magnitude of motor current contribution at the time a fault occurs, result in various scenarios. An analysis typically includes evaluating the potential scenarios for a particular system and choosing the most conservative results.

The arcing fault current that could flow during an arcing fault incident is proportional to the available fault (bolted) current.

It is important to be familiar with the procedures, including equations and tables, for performing simple available fault (bolted) current calculations for 3-phase systems, referred to as the point-to-point method. Two examples of using this calculation method are provided. Access to a free, easy-to-use point-to-point method app is also provided.

FAULT CURRENT

Overcurrent is defined as either an overload current or a fault current.

Overload current is an excessive current relative to normal operating current, and one that is confined to the normal conductive path provided by the conductors, circuit components, and loads of the distribution system. A sustained overload current results in overheating of conductors and other circuit components or adjacent materials, and can cause deterioration of insulation. If the overload current is not interrupted in sufficient time, it may eventually result in severe damage, fires, and faults.

A *fault current*, which often is referred to as a *short-circuit current*, is a current that flows outside the normal conducting path. A fault current flows when a phase or ungrounded conductor comes in contact with, or arcing current commences between, another phase conductor, neutral, or ground.

Whereas overloads are modest multiples of the normal current, a fault can be many hundreds or thousands of times larger than the normal operating current. The magnitude of available bolted fault currents in commercial and industrial facilities varies dramatically, from roughly 1,000 amperes to more than 200,000 amperes.

Two categories of fault currents are distinguished: bolted and arcing. A bolted or arcing fault can occur between various parts of a circuit, such as line-line (L-L), line-line-line (L-L-L), line-neutral (L-N), line-ground (L-G), or any other combination of L, N, and G.

Bolted Fault Currents

A bolted fault condition represents a "solid" (bolted or welded) connection of relatively low (or assumed "zero") impedance. Because of the low-impedance path, a 3-phase bolted fault condition is typically considered to be the highest magnitude fault current. **See Figure 7-1.**

The magnitude of a bolted fault current is a function of the system voltage and the impedance from the electrical source to the point of the fault. In an

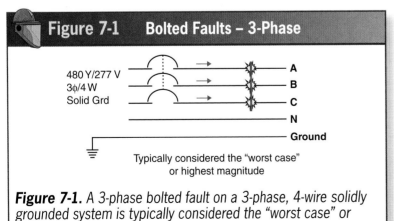

| Figure 7-1 | Bolted Faults – 3-Phase |

480 Y/277 V
3φ/4 W
Solid Grd

A
B
C
N
Ground

Typically considered the "worst case"
or highest magnitude

Figure 7-1. *A 3-phase bolted fault on a 3-phase, 4-wire solidly grounded system is typically considered the "worst case" or highest magnitude of fault current.*

Courtesy of Eaton's Bussmann Division

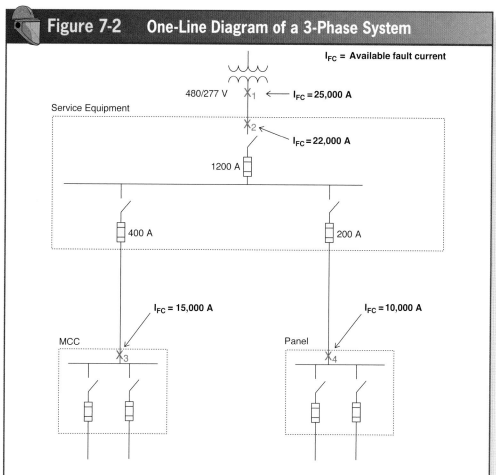

Figure 7-2   One-Line Diagram of a 3-Phase System

I_FC = Available fault current

480/277 V   X₁   ← I_FC = 25,000 A

Service Equipment

X₂   ← I_FC = 22,000 A

1200 A

400 A   200 A

I_FC = 15,000 A   I_FC = 10,000 A

MCC   Panel
X₃   X₄

Figure 7-2. *A system is depicted as a simplified one-line diagram with available 3-phase fault current. The available 3-phase fault currents at various points in the system are shown with "X" symbols, with the value for the symmetrical root mean square (RMS) amperes denoted by "IFC" (such as X₃ with 15,000 amperes available fault current).*

electrical distribution system, the bolted fault current varies depending on the point in the system at which the fault occurs. Calculating the available bolted fault current that could flow if a bolted fault occurred in a system is a well-established procedure that is commonly performed.

A simple 3-phase electrical system is depicted as a one-line diagram. **See Figure 7-2.** The highest available 3-phase fault current is typically found at the service transformer's secondary terminals and service equipment.

Arcing Faults
An arcing fault condition does not have a solid (bolted) connection between conductors or buses; instead, an arcing

current path through the air between conductive parts with an associated arc resistance is present. **See Figure 7-3.** Arcing faults can be 3-phase, phase-to-phase, phase-to-ground, or phase-to-neutral, or

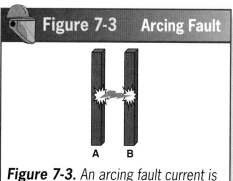

Figure 7-3   Arcing Fault

A   B

Figure 7-3. *An arcing fault current is characterized by current flow via an arc through the air.*

Figure 7-4 **3-Phase Arcing Fault**

A   B   C

Figure 7-4. A 3-phase arcing fault has arcing current from phase A to phase B, from phase B to phase C, and from phase C to phase A (in addition, the arcing current can go from any of the phases to ground or neutral).

can include one or more phases with ground and/or neutral.

Generally, for low-voltage systems that experience high intensity thermal arcing fault events, if an arcing fault is initiated on a single-phase circuit (L-L, L-N, or L-G on a single-phase system) or an L-L, L-N, or L-G circuit (on a 3-phase system without the third phase being present), the arcing current may very well self-extinguish (that is, not sustain itself). By comparison, an arcing fault current that is initiated on a 3-phase circuit as a L-L arcing fault, L-N arcing fault, or L-G arcing fault can quickly (in a few one-thousandths of a second) escalate into a 3-phase arcing fault. **See Figure 7-4.** However, a 3-phase arcing fault current may or may not sustain itself based on the parameters of the electrical circuit and variables of the fault conditions, such as arc-gap spacing, the current's containment within an enclosure, the size of the enclosure, the available bolted fault current, and other factors. *IEEE 1584-2018* notes that sustainable arcs are possible but less likely in 3-phase systems operating at 240 volts, nominal, or less with an available short-circuit current less than 2,000 amperes. For medium- and high-voltage systems, single-phase arcing fault currents are more readily sustainable.

An arcing fault current is always less than the available bolted fault current value at a specific location due to the additional resistance of the arc. As discussed, its magnitude depends on many variables.

While calculating the 3-phase bolted available fault current is rather straightforward, and several methods and industry tools are available to assist with this process, calculating 3-phase arcing fault currents is not as straightforward and the results are not as certain. This uncertainty arises because of the nature of arcing faults as well as the many variables pertaining to the immediate surroundings that can affect an arcing fault event,

Figure 7-5 **Relationship between Fault Current Types at 480 Volts, 3-Phase**

Arcing Fault Current as Percentage of Available Fault Current		
480 Volt 3-Phase MCC or Panelboard (1" arc gap, VCBB)		
3-Phase Available Fault Current (Amperes)	**3-Phase Arcing Fault Current* (Amperes)**	**Arcing Fault Current as Percentage of Available Fault Current**
5,000	3,900	78%
10,000	8,000	80%
30,000	24,000	80%
100,000	47,300	47%

* Arcing fault current calculated using 2018 *IEEE 1584 Guide for Performing Arc Flash Hazard Calculations*. The maximum arcing current value is shown here.

Figure 7-5. The arcing fault current is less than the available fault current. As the available fault current increases so does the arcing fault current, and the arcing fault current as a percentage of the available fault current decreases as the available fault current increases. These values and percentages will differ based on variables such as voltage and arc gap.

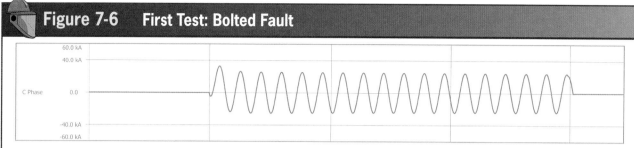

Figure 7-6   First Test: Bolted Fault

Figure 7-6. *The C-phase current oscillograph of the first 480-volt, 3-phase bolted fault calibration test shows 18,000 symmetrical RMS amperes.*

including system voltage, arc gap, amount of copper or aluminum vapor that helps sustain an arcing fault, and whether the arcing fault is in an enclosure or open air.

A direct relationship exists between the magnitude of the available fault (bolted) current and the arcing fault current. For a given point in the electrical system, the arcing fault current is less than the available fault current. The greater the available fault current, the greater the arcing fault current. However, the relationship between the magnitude of the available bolted fault current and the magnitude of the arcing fault is not linear. In other words, the arcing fault current is not a fixed percentage of the available fault current over the range of low to high available fault currents. **See Figure 7-5.** Arcing fault currents on medium- and high-voltage systems may be a high percentage of the available fault current, and in some cases, approaching the available fault current.

Bolted faults typically produce predictable, smooth oscillograph current curves; that is, smooth sine waves, some being asymmetrical and some symmetrical. However, arcing faults tend to be dynamic with variability in the flow of

current, resulting in erratic, unpredictable current flow.

Oscillographs from two tests (with an identical test set-up other than one test being a bolted fault condition and the other being an arcing fault condition) illustrate this phenomena. Recorded were the C phase current oscillographs from these two tests with the horizontal axis being time (moving from left to right) and the vertical axis being instantaneous current. The duration of both tests were approximately 17 1/2 cycles. The test set-up consisted of three one-inch copper anodes spaced approximately one inch apart, representing A, B, and C phases, and installed in a 20-inch by 20-inch by 20-inch stainless steel box with an open front.

First, the test anodes were shorted out via a bolted 480-volt, 3-phase fault condition (near zero impedance). This bolted fault calibration test resulted in 18,000 symmetrical RMS amperes. **See Figure 7-6.**

In the next test, an arcing fault was initiated between the anodes, creating a very different current trace. **See Figure 7-7.** The average RMS amperes of

For additional information, visit qr.njatcdb.org Item #4340

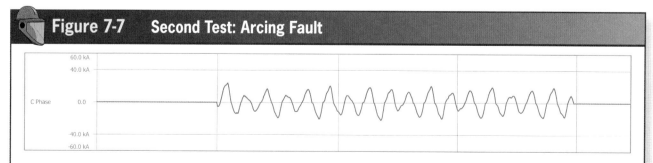

Figure 7-7   Second Test: Arcing Fault

Figure 7-7. *The average RMS current of A, B, and C phases during the arcing fault test resulted in 11,930 RMS amperes. Notice the erratic current traces, which are typical of arcing fault currents.*

A, B, and C phase arcing current is 66% of the bolted fault current, resulting in 11,930 RMS amperes. Notice the irregularity of the current trace; the current is erratic due to the dynamic nature of an arcing fault. This is symptomatic of the metal vapor's instantaneous variability and the arcing current stream dynamics during an arcing fault event. Arcing faults are like snowflakes in that no two are exactly alike, even under controlled test conditions.

RELEVANCE OF AVAILABLE FAULT CURRENT

Knowledge of and the ability to calculate the available fault current at various points in an electrical system is necessary in order to determine the arc flash boundary per *NFPA 70E* 130.5(E)(1), where additional protective measures are required and include the use of arc flash PPE. See 130.5(C), 130.5(F), 130.5(G), and 130.7(C)(15). The available fault current at the prospective arc source is needed as part of the process. Calculating the available fault current for this purpose uses the same calculation methods as used for determining the available fault current to ensure proper application of overcurrent protective device (OCPD) interrupting ratings, equipment short-circuit current

ratings, and OCPD selective coordination requirements.

AVAILABLE FAULT CURRENT CALCULATION BASICS

The magnitude of fault current available at a specific location depends on two key factors:
1. The magnitude of fault current that the electrical energy source(s), such as the utility system, generators, and running motors, can deliver.
2. The impedance (resistance and reactance) of transformers, conductors, and busway from the source(s) to the point of the fault.

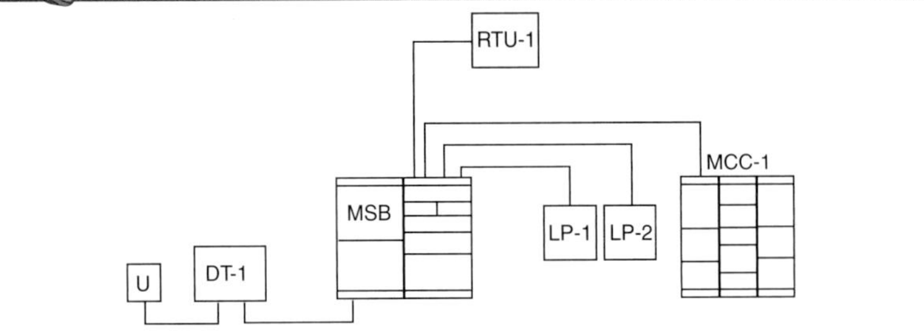

In general, the fault current decreases as the distance from an electrical source increases due to the increased impedance added by circuit components that have impedance, such as transformers, conductors, and busways.

Most often for arc-flash risk assessments on low-voltage systems, fault studies involve calculating a bolted 3-phase available fault current condition. This scenario can be characterized as all three phases "bolted" together to create a near-zero impedance connection.

Generally, for low-voltage systems, the available bolted fault current determines the highest magnitude of current that the electrical system can deliver during a fault condition. There are situations where line-ground fault currents near the transformer secondary can be of a greater magnitude, but this is beyond the scope of available fault current calculation basics.

For a system-wide study, the available fault current calculations should be completed for all critical points in the system. **See Figure 7-8.** These would include, but are not limited to, the following:
- Switchboards
- Panelboards
- Motor control centers (MCC)
- Motor starters
- Disconnect switches
- Transfer switches

| Figure 7-8 | Available Fault Current |

U – Utility
DT – Dry type transformer
MSB – Main switch board
RTU – Roof top unit (HVAC)
LP – Lighting panel
MCC – Motor control center

Figure 7-8. Available fault current should be calculated at all critical points in the system.

Sources of Available Fault Current

Sources of available fault current that are normally taken into consideration include utility generation, local generation, and synchronous and induction motors. In addition, alternative energy sources, such as batteries, energy storage systems, photovoltaic systems, fuel cells, wind turbines, and flywheels, may also feed into an AC fault, in some cases through a DC-to-AC converter.

When electrical systems are supplied from a utility- or customer-owned transformer, the amount of available fault current depends on the size (kVA) and impedance (%Z) of the transformer. The larger the kVA rating and/or the lower the impedance of a transformer, the higher the available fault current.

The available fault current cannot be determined or estimated just by considering the ampere rating of an electrical panel or the type of facility. For instance, one 800-ampere distribution panelboard in a facility may have an available fault current of 15,000 amperes at its line terminals, whereas another 800-ampere distribution panel in the same facility or in another facility may have an available fault current of 80,000 amperes. Calculations must be done to determine the available fault current.

Small residential building systems (100-ampere to 200-ampere service) typically have fault currents of 10,000 amperes to 15,000 amperes or less. Small commercial building systems (400-ampere to 800-ampere service) typically have fault currents of 15,000 amperes to 30,000 amperes. Larger commercial and manufacturing building systems (2,000-ampere to 3,000-ampere service) typically have available fault currents in the range of 50,000 amperes to 65,000 amperes.

These available fault current values can be much higher where low-impedance transformers are used. When commercial buildings are directly connected to a utility "low-voltage grid system," such as in major metropolitan cities (such as New York, Chicago, or Dallas), the fault currents can approach or exceed 200,000 amperes. The busway plug-in drops in auto production plants may have 100,000-ampere available fault currents. Some hospitals with large alternate supply generators that can operate in parallel may have high available fault currents as well.

Available Fault Current Factors

The magnitude of available fault current at a specific point depends on many factors, including the fault current contribution of the utility, local generation, and motors as well as the kVA rating and impedance of transformers, the size and length of the wires, and more. **See Figure 7-9.**

The fault current is typically the highest at the service point. Further in an electrical system, the circuit conductors

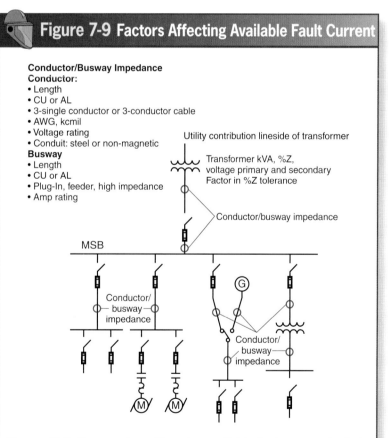

Figure 7-9 Factors Affecting Available Fault Current

Conductor/Busway Impedance
Conductor:
• Length
• CU or AL
• 3-single conductor or 3-conductor cable
• AWG, kcmil
• Voltage rating
• Conduit: steel or non-magnetic
Busway
• Length
• CU or AL
• Plug-In, feeder, high impedance
• Amp rating

Utility contribution lineside of transformer

Transformer kVA, %Z, voltage primary and secondary Factor in %Z tolerance

Conductor/busway impedance

MSB

Conductor/busway impedance

Conductor/busway impedance

Figure 7-9. *Factors that affect the available fault current include the utility, transformer (kVA and %Z), generators, motors, voltage, and conductor size and length.*

Courtesy of Eaton's Bussmann Division

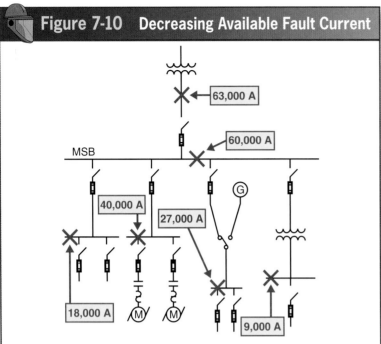

Figure 7-10. *The available fault current typically decreases downstream due to the presence of conductors and transformers.*

Courtesy of Eaton's Bussmann Division

and additional transformers will decrease the available fault current at downstream equipment. **See Figure 7-10.**

Effects of Generators and Motors on Fault Current

Generators and motors in a premise system that are operating at the time of a fault condition can contribute fault current in addition to the fault current the utility delivers. Typically, the range of a fault current from a generator is 7 to 14 times the full-load ampere rating of the generator, with a general rule of thumb being 10 times. If the generator is operated in parallel with the utility during transfer (closed-transition transfer), the fault current of the generator is added to the fault current of the utility.

When a fault occurs, a motor in operation can act like a generator and may contribute to the fault current. **See Figure 7-11.** The motor contribution is usually four to six times the full-load

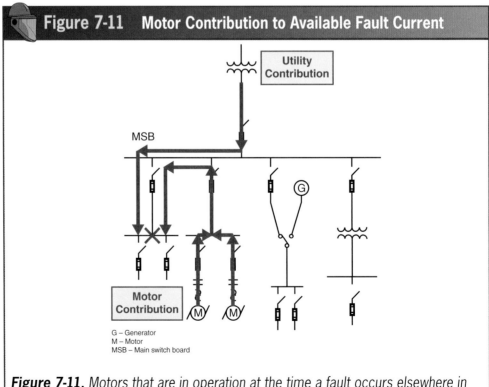

G – Generator
M – Motor
MSB – Main switch board

Figure 7-11. *Motors that are in operation at the time a fault occurs elsewhere in the system can contribute to the fault current magnitude.*

Courtesy of Eaton's Bussmann Division

ampere rating of the motor. The additional motor contribution normally must be added to the utility contribution to determine the available fault current.

Effect of Transformers on Available Fault Current

Generally, for a typical low-voltage electrical distribution system, the transformer has the greatest effect on the available fault currents throughout an electrical system. The fault current at a transformer secondary is based on transformer kVA, % impedance, and secondary voltage. In addition, the available fault current on the primary affects the available fault current on the secondary.

If a utility transformer is replaced by the utility, the percentage impedance can be higher or lower than the original by a significant amount. It is common for the percentage impedance of the newer transformers to be lower, resulting in a higher fault current. Many utilities have a policy that if a

Caution

Fault currents can be very high (65,000 amperes to more than 200,000 amperes). For this reason, it is important to verify available fault current levels when applying overcurrent devices and equipment. It is also often necessary to determine the available fault current as part of an arc-flash risk assessment.

transformer needs to be replaced due to failure, the utility can use a transformer with the next larger kVA rating. This practice is necessary in the event that the utility's inventory of transformers with the same kVA rating is depleted at the time of replacement. Thus, the available fault current could increase due to either a kVA rating increase or a percentage impedance decrease, or both. If the available fault current changes at the service equipment, it will also change further downstream in the system. **See Figure 7-12.** Note that calculated available fault current values can vary slightly depending on the

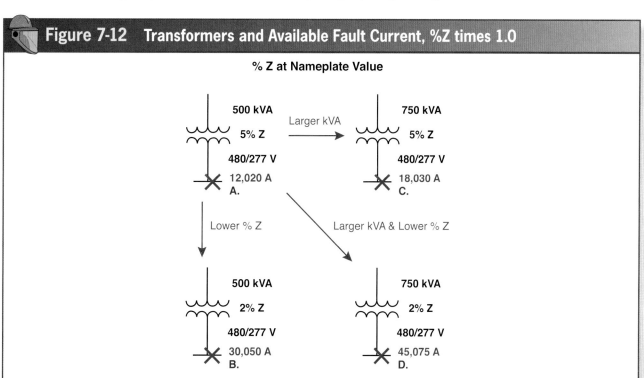

Figure 7-12. Transformers and Available Fault Current, %Z times 1.0

Figure 7-12. Available fault currents shown are on transformer secondary and assume infinite primary available fault current, nominal %Z, and no motor contribution. Consider what happens if a 500 kVA, 480-volt, 3-phase transformer with 5% Z is changed to one of three transformer options.

calculation significant digits and rounding methods used.

Transformer percentage impedance is subject to manufacturing tolerances. The marked (nameplate) transformer impedance value may vary ±10% as per *UL Standard 1561*. As a consequence, under fault conditions, the fault current available on the secondary of a transformer can vary from 90% to 110% of what is calculated using the nameplate percent impedance.

When evaluating OCPD interrupting ratings and equipment short-circuit current ratings, the transformer % Z multiplied by 0.9 should be used for the calculation of maximum available fault current to represent the highest available fault current possible due to a -10% transformer percentage impedance tolerance. The same should be considered when using the arc flash PPE category method (table method) per *NFPA 70E* 130.5(F)(2).

However, when calculating fault current for use with the incident energy analysis method as part of an arc-flash risk assessment per 130.5(F)(1), it is recommended to calculate two different available fault currents on the secondary side of a transformer:

1. Use the -10% transformer percentage impedance tolerance (%Z times 0.9), which will result in a higher available fault current.
2. Use the +10% transformer percentage impedance tolerance (%Z times 1.1), which will result in a lower available fault current.

Informational Note No. 3 after Table 130.5(C) in *NFPA 70E* provides the rationale for using both of these fault values. If calculations of available fault currents are performed for locations further downstream in the system, two sets of values should be calculated for all other downstream points: one set using the transformer highest available fault current, and the other set using the transformer lowest available fault current. **See Figure 7-13.**

Simple Method to Determine "Worst-Case" 3-Phase Transformer Secondary Fault Current

This simple method can help to quickly assess a situation or to roughly double-check calculations. It assumes infinite available fault current on the transformer primary. The easiest way to use this method is as follows:

Transformer Secondary Full-Load Amperes Known

Example transformer: 3-phase, 500 kVA, 480-volt secondary, 2% Z (impedance)

$$I_{SCA} = \frac{\text{Trans FLA} \times 100}{\% Z}$$

$$= 601 \times \frac{100}{2}$$

$$= 601 \times 50$$

$$= 30{,}050 \text{ A available fault current at transformer secondary}$$

Transformer Secondary Full-Load Amperes If Not Known

If the full-load amperes is not known, or remembered, then calculate the full-load amperes using the formula below and use the equation in the previous section. This is Step 1 from the 3-Phase Available Fault Current Calculation Procedure.

$$\text{3-phase transf. } I_{FLA} = \frac{\text{kVA} \times 1{,}000}{E_{L\text{-}L} \times 1.732}$$

Effect of Conductors on Available Fault Current

The conductor size (or busway ampere rating), conductor material (copper or aluminum), conductor length, whether the conduit is magnetic or non-magnetic, and number of conductors per phase may also affect the available fault current. **See Figure 7-14.** Assuming an available fault current at point A of

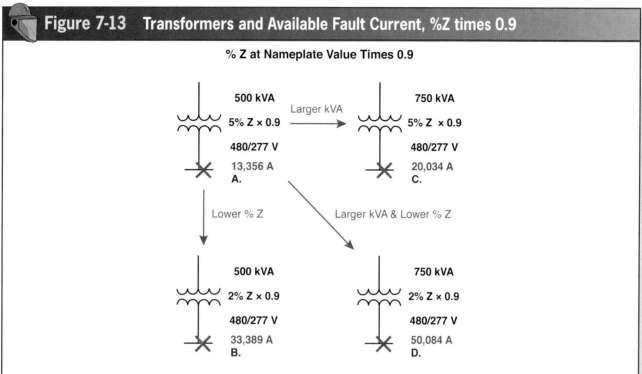

Figure 7-13   Transformers and Available Fault Current, %Z times 0.9

Figure 7-13. Calculations on transformer secondary assuming infinite primary available fault current, %Z times 0.9 representing -10% impedance tolerance, produces the highest value for available fault current when considering only the transformer parameters. Motor contribution was not included, but to get the worst case condition (highest available fault current), it should be.

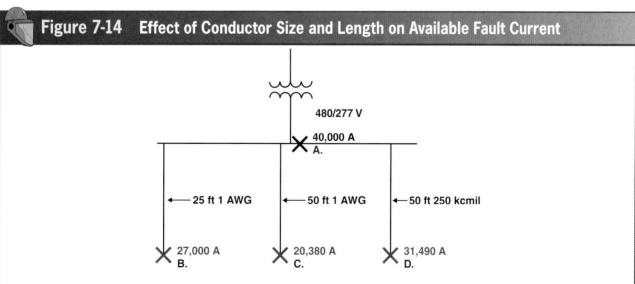

Figure 7-14   Effect of Conductor Size and Length on Available Fault Current

Figure 7-14. The available fault current at the end of a circuit conductor run is affected by the conductor's size and length.

40,000 amperes (at the beginning of the conductor run for each example) at 480/277 volts, the available fault current at the end of the conductor at point B would be 27,000 amperes. If the length of a 1 AWG conductor was increased to 50 feet, as shown from point A to point C, the available fault current at point C would decrease to 20,380 amperes due to the increased impedance of the extra 25 feet of conductor. If the size of the conductor was then increased to 250,000 circular mils (250 kcmil), as shown from point A to point D, the available fault current at point D would be 31,490 amperes, which is higher than the resulting available fault current for the 50 feet of 1 AWG at point C due to the decrease in the impedance per foot of the larger conductor.

EFFECT OF AVAILABLE FAULT CURRENT IN DETERMINING ARC FLASH PPE

The available fault current is a key part of an arc-flash risk assessment when additional protective measures are required and include the use of PPE, per *NFPA 70E* 130.5(C).

In order to use the arc flash PPE category method, the estimated available fault current cannot exceed the value specified in the phrase "*maximum of "X" kA available fault current*" in Table 130.7(C)(15)(a) under the *Equipment* column and specified in *Parameters* for each type of equipment. It is acceptable if the available fault current calculation results in an estimated value that is less than the parameter value. However, for a specific situation where the estimated available fault current exceeds the maximum available fault current parameter value, the arc flash PPE category method is not permitted to be used and an incident energy analysis shall be required. See 130.7(C)(15)(a)(1).

It is permissible to use assumptions that result in a conservatively high available fault current calculation. For instance, assuming infinite available fault current on the primary side of the service transformer will contribute to a conservative result. If this type of estimated calculation results in a value equal to or less than the parameter value, the arc flash PPE category method can be used, assuming the clearing time and working distance parameters are also satisfied.

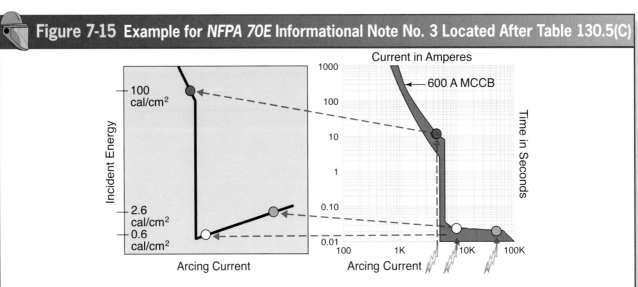

Figure 7-15 Example for *NFPA 70E* Informational Note No. 3 Located After Table 130.5(C)

Figure 7-15. *In some cases, a lower magnitude available fault current results in lower magnitude arcing fault current, which causes significantly longer OCPD opening time and higher incident energy when compared to a higher available fault current driving higher arcing fault current, faster OCPD opening time, and associated incident energy.*

If a conservative calculation results in an estimated value greater than the parameter maximum available fault current, then a more precise estimated calculation can be performed to determine if its results are within the parameter value. It is acceptable if the available fault current calculation is less than the parameter value, but it cannot be greater.

However, it would not be prudent to use assumptions for calculating the available fault current that may result in a low estimated value. For instance, do not use the +10% transformer percentage impedance factor because this results in a lower available fault current.

When calculating the arc flash boundary per 130.5(E)(1) and using the incident energy analysis method per 130.5(G), it is important to calculate the available fault current as accurately as practical. In some cases, a lower value of available fault current means a lower arcing current, which may result in a longer clearing time of the protecting overcurrent device. This longer clearing time may, in turn, cause a higher incident energy and greater arc flash boundary. See Informational Note No. 3 located after Table 130.5(C). Lower arcing fault currents may result in increased OCPD opening time and higher incident energy compared to higher arcing fault currents, which may result in decreased OCPD opening time.

With both circuit breakers and fuses, a low arcing fault current might potentially be in the OCPD's long-time operating region, requiring additional time to interrupt. If this occurs, it may result in the incident energy being greater than the incident energy that was calculated. **See Figure 7-15.**

Scenarios Affect Arc Flash PPE Selection

The electrical distribution system at each specific potential fault location may have several available fault currents due to multiple possible system scenarios. If so, then the arc flash boundary and arc flash PPE for each scenario must be taken into

> **Caution**
>
> Available fault currents can greatly increase when transformer impedance is decreased or when transformer kVA increases. When service transformers are changed, fault studies and arc-flash studies must be updated as well. In addition, the interrupting ratings of OCPDs and short-circuit current ratings for equipment must be verified as sufficient: if these ratings are found to not be adequate, a safety hazard is present. Immediate action to remedy this problem should be taken.

consideration. Example scenarios include the following:
- Available fault current the utility can deliver at the service point
  - As accurate as possible
  - Infinite
  - Maximum
  - Minimum
- Transformer % impedance tolerance
  - Plus 10%
  - Minus 10%
  - Nominal marked value
- Switching scenarios: include multiple sources
  - Normal source
  - Onsite generation
  - Double-ended substation with tie
  - Stored energy systems such as batteries
  - Redundant system designs
- Motor fault current contribution
  - All motors running
  - No motors running

Some facilities' electrical distribution systems can be configured in various ways by opening or closing disconnects. For instance, a double-ended unit substation may include a low-voltage tie disconnect between the switchgear. One scenario might include both transformers energized and the low-voltage tie disconnect open between the switchgear. An alternative scenario might be the same as the first but with the tie disconnect closed. This second scenario might possibly have twice the magnitude of available fault current at the switchgear as compared to the first scenario. **See Figure 7-16.** This variation can have a dramatic effect on determining the arc flash boundary, adhering to the condition of use parameters of the arc flash PPE categories method, or calculating the incident energy.

PROCEDURES AND METHODS

To determine the fault current at any point in the system, first draw a one-line diagram showing all of the sources of fault current. Then include the system components, such as conductors and busway (size or ampere rating, lengths, conductor material (copper or aluminum), number of conductors per phase, conduit type (or no conduit), and transformers (kVA, voltages, and percentage impedances)). Information on the OCPDs (type, part number, ampere rating, voltage rating, interrupting ratings, and settings) is not necessary to perform an available fault current study; however, this information may be needed as part of an arc

flash study or an arc flash risk assessment.

In order to perform an available fault current study, if data must be collected by examining the electrical equipment, it is suggested to record the necessary information to perform an arc flash study or an arc flash risk assessment at the same time, including each OCPD (type, manufacturer, part number, ampere rating, and settings).

Available fault current calculations are performed without OCPDs in the system. These calculations assume that these devices are replaced with copper bars, so as to determine the maximum "available" fault current. After the calculation is completed throughout the system, current-limiting devices can be used to show reduction of the available fault current at a single location only. Current-limiting devices do not operate in series to produce a compounding current-limiting effect.

Various methods have been developed to calculate the available fault current, but all are based on Ohm's Law. These methods include the ohmic method, per-unit method, and point-to-point method, along with computer-based versions of all three methods. Several available fault current calculation software programs are available. Some of these programs not only calculate the available fault current, but also draw one-line diagrams, perform coordination studies, and determine the arc flash boundary and incident energy. These programs are available for purchase, and the price of the software program can vary greatly based on its capabilities.

The application of the point-to-point method permits the quick determination of available fault currents with a reasonable degree of accuracy at various points for either 3-phase or single-phase electrical distribution systems. The procedures and examples that follow focus only on 3-phase systems. The point-to-point calculation methods for 3-phase and single-phase systems are available from sources such as Eaton's Bussmann Division in its *Selecting*

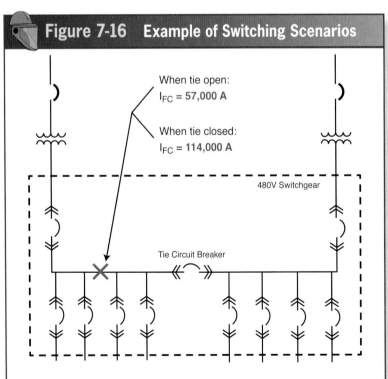

Figure 7-16   Example of Switching Scenarios

When tie open:
I_{FC} = 57,000 A

When tie closed:
I_{FC} = 114,000 A

480V Switchgear

Tie Circuit Breaker

Figure 7-16. *A double-ended unit substation with a tie circuit breaker can result in switching scenarios requiring calculating the available fault current (I_{FC}) for each scenario and possibly affecting the selection of PPE.*

Protective Devices (SPD) publication, which is available online.

POINT-TO-POINT METHOD

The point-to-point method uses equations to calculate the available fault current at:

- the secondary of a transformer assuming infinite primary available fault current available
- the secondary of a transformer with primary available fault current known
- the end of a run of conductor or busway

Following the equations and informative notes shown here are two examples of how the point-to-point method is used.

Several reference tables can be used as resources for using the point-to-point method. **See Appendix.** Review these tables along with their associated notes to become familiar with how this information is applicable in performing available fault current calculations.

3-Phase Available Fault Current Calculation Procedure

Equations to Calculate Available Fault Current on Transformer Secondary with Infinite Primary Available: Steps 1 to 3

Use the following procedure to determine the fault current (I_{FC}) at 3-phase transformer secondary terminals assuming infinite primary available fault current:

Step 1: Determine the transformer full-load amperes (I_{FLA}) from either the nameplate, following equation, or Figure A-1 (**See Appendix**).

3-phase transf. $I_{FLA} = \dfrac{kVA \times 1,000}{E_{L\text{-}L} \times 1.732}$

Where:
$E_{L\text{-}L}$ = line-to-line voltage
kVA = transformer kVA

For additional information, visit qr.njatcdb.org Item #6305

Step 2: Determine the transformer multiplier.

$\text{Multiplier} = \dfrac{100}{\%Z}$

Note 1: The marked (nameplate) transformer impedance (%Z) value may vary ±10% from the actual values determined by *UL Standard 1561*. For the high-fault condition scenario, multiply the transformer %Z by 0.9, and for the low-fault condition scenario, multiply the %Z by 1.1. Use 1.0 times %Z for no impedance tolerance effect.

Step 3: Determine the available fault current (I_{FC}) at 3-phase transformer secondary. (Figure A-6 provides a generalized estimate based on lowest %Z transformer survey. **See Appendix.**)

3-phase transformer (see Note 2 for motor contribution):

$I_{FC\,(L\text{-}L\text{-}L)} = I_{FLA} \times \text{Multiplier}$

Note 2: The motor fault current contribution, if significant, may be determined and added to all fault locations throughout the system. A practical estimate of the motor fault current contribution is to multiply the total motor load current by four or six. A good general rule is to calculate the total motor load current, multiply by 4, and add the result to step 3.

Note 3: The utility voltage may vary ±10% for power, and ±5.8% for 120-volt lighting services. For worst-case conditions, multiply the values calculated in step 3 by 1.1 and/or 1.058, respectively.

Note 4: For 3-phase systems, line-to-line-to-line (L-L-L), line-to-line (L-L), line-to-ground (L-G), and line-to-neutral (L-N) bolted faults are typically a percentage of the 3-phase bolted fault current. *IEEE 1584* uses the 3-phase bolted fault current when determining arcing currents, because studies have shown that other types of fault currents establish a 3-phase fault within two cycles due to the conductive plasma cloud that occurs. Use the equations in

IEEE 1584, Guide for Performing Arc Flash Hazard Calculations, to calculate the 3-phase arcing current when performing an arc flash hazard analysis by incident energy method.

Equations to Calculate Available Fault Current at End of Conductor Run: Steps 4 to 6

Use the following procedure to determine the available fault current (I_{FC}) at the end of a run of conductor or busway:

Step 4: Calculate the "f" factor.
3-phase line-to-line-to-line (L-L-L) fault

$$f = \frac{1.732 \times L \times I_{FC\,(L\text{-}L\text{-}L)}}{C \times n \times E_{LL}}$$

Where:
L = length (feet) of conduit to the fault
C = constant for conductors or busway (See Figure A-2, A-3, or A-4 in Appendix)
n = number of conductors per phase (adjusts the "C" value for parallel runs)
I_{FC} = available fault current in amperes (A) at the beginning of the circuit
$E_{L\text{-}L}$ = line-to-line voltage

Step 5: Determine the "M" (multiplier) from Figure A-5 or the following equation:

$$M = \frac{1}{1 + f}$$

Step 6: Calculate the available fault current (I_{FC}) at the end of the circuit.
3-phase line-to-line-to-line (L-L-L) fault (see Note 2 for motor contribution):

$$I_{FC\,(L\text{-}L\text{-}L)} = I_{FC\,(L\text{-}L\text{-}L)} \times M$$
AT END OF CIRCUIT   AT BEGINNING OF CIRCUIT

Note 5: See Note 4.

Determining Available Fault Current on 3-Phase Transformer Secondary with Primary Available Fault Current Known: Steps A to C

When the primary available fault current at a transformer is known, either through a previous calculation (if it is the second transformer in the system) or if the available fault current of the utility connection is provided, then a more accurate calculation can be performed. Use the following procedure (Steps A to C) to calculate the available fault current at the secondary when the available fault current at the transformer primary is known. **See Figure 7-17.**

Step A: Calculate the "f" factor for the transformer.
3-phase transformer:

$$f = \frac{I_{P(FC)\,L\text{-}L\text{-}L} \times V_P \times 1.732 \times \%Z^*}{100,000 \times kVA}$$

*Transformer Z is multiplied by 0.9 to establish the high-fault condition scenario. See Note 1.
Where:
$I_{P(FC)}$ = primary available fault current
V_P = primary voltage (L-L)
kVA = transformer kVA

Step B: Determine the multiplier "M" for the transformer from Figure A-5 or the following equation:

$$M = \frac{1}{1 + f}$$

Step C: Determine the available fault current at the transformer secondary (see Note 2 for motor contribution):

$$I_{S(FC)} = \frac{V_P}{V_S} \times M \times I_{P(FC)}$$

Where:
$I_{S(FC)}$ = secondary available fault current
V_S = secondary voltage (L-L)
To determine the available fault current at the end of a conductor or busway run connected to the secondary of this transformer, follow Steps 4, 5, and 6.

The point-to-point method is courtesy of Eaton's Bussmann Division.

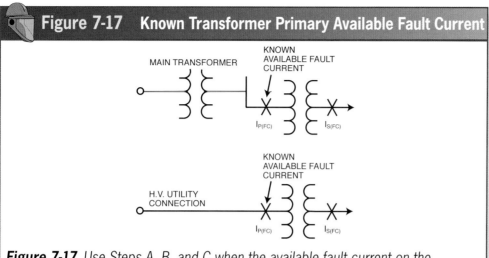

Figure 7-17 Known Transformer Primary Available Fault Current

Figure 7-17. Use Steps A, B, and C when the available fault current on the transformer primary is known.

FC² Available Fault Current Calculator

An electronic application version of the Point-to-Point method is available either as a downloadable app for Apple and Android mobile devices or as a web-based version that can be run from the Eaton's Bussmann Division website. Calculating and documenting available fault currents is simple and quick with the FC² Available Fault Current Calculator. In addition, this app can provide electronic formatted labels that can be used for *NEC* 110.24 compliance or other available fault current marking requirements or needs. Results from doing hand calculations versus this calculator may vary slightly based on the rounding and significant digits used for the calculations.

Courtesy of Eaton's Bussmann Division

For additional information, visit qr.njatcdb.org Item #1215

For additional information, visit qr.njatcdb.org Item #1591

Point-to-Point Method Examples

The following examples show how to use the point-to-point method equations and notes for 3-phase systems. Reference tables are needed for some values, such as the conductor C values. **See Appendix.** For simplicity, the motor contribution and voltage variance are not included. See Notes 2 and 3 in the section on 3-Phase Available Fault Current Calculation Procedure.

Calculations in solving these examples will be shown in two formats side by side:
1. The manual method showing the equations, values inserted, and calculations
2. The FC² results showing one-line, input values, and available fault currents

Example 1
This example has three points in the system to calculate the available fault current. This example assumes the utility available on the transformer primary is infinite.

Calculation Example For Fault #1

Step 1: Determine the transformer full-load amperes (I_{FLA}).

$$I_{FLA} = \frac{kVA \times 1,000}{E_{L\text{-}L} \times 1.732} = \frac{300 \times 1,000}{208 \times 1.732} = 833 \text{ A}$$

Step 2: Find the transformer multiplier.

$$Multiplier = \frac{100}{*0.9 \times Transf. \%Z} = \frac{100}{1.8} = 55.55$$

*Transformer Z is multiplied by 0.9 to establish a high fault condition scenario. See Note 1 in the section on 3-Phase Available Fault Current Calculation Procedure.

Step 3: Determine the available fault current (I_{FC}) **at the transformer secondary.**
**$I_{FC\,(L\text{-}L\text{-}L)} = I_{FLA} \times M = 833 \times 55.55 = 46,273 \text{ A}$
**For simplicity, the motor contribution and voltage variance were not included. See Notes 2 and 3 in the section on 3-Phase Available Fault Current Calculation Procedure.

Calculation Example For Fault #2

(Use $I_{FC\,(L\text{-}L\text{-}L)}$ at Fault #1 in Steps 4 and 6.)

Step 4: Calculate the "f" factor.
$$f = \frac{1.732 \times L \times I_{FC\,(L\text{-}L\text{-}L)}}{C \times E_{LL}}$$
$$= \frac{1.732 \times 20 \times 46,273}{22,185 \times 208} = 0.35$$

Step 5: Determine the "M" (multiplier).
$$M = \frac{1}{1+f} = \frac{1}{1+0.35} = 0.74$$

Step 6: Calculate the available fault current (I_{FC}) **at Fault #2.**

$$I_{FC\,(L\text{-}L\text{-}L)}_{\text{AT END OF CIRCUIT}} = I_{FC\,(L\text{-}L\text{-}L)}_{\text{AT BEGINNING OF CIRCUIT}} \times M$$

$$= 46,273 \times 0.74 = 34,242 \text{ A}$$

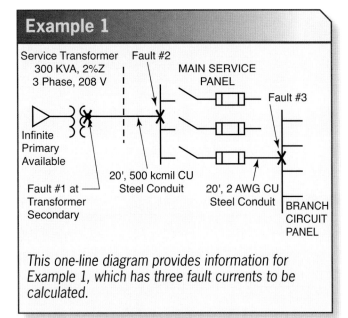

This one-line diagram provides information for Example 1, which has three fault currents to be calculated.

Calculation Example For Fault #3

(Use $I_{FC\,(L\text{-}L\text{-}L)}$ at Fault #2 in steps 4 and 6.)

Step 4: Calculate the "f" factor.
$$f = \frac{1.732 \times 20 \times 34,242}{5,907 \times 208} = 0.97$$

Step 5: Determine the "M" (multiplier).
$$M = \frac{1}{1+0.97} = 0.51$$

Step 6: Calculate the available fault current (I_{FC}) **at Fault #3.**
$$I_{FC\,(L\text{-}L\text{-}L)\,\text{AT FAULT \#3}} = 34,242 \times 0.51 = 17,463 \text{ A}$$

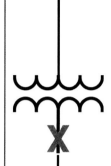

EAT•N
BUSSMANN
SERIES

FC² | available fault current calculator

INFINITE PRIMARY SOURCE

TRANSFORMER - T1

KVA	300
Voltage secondary	208
%Z	2.00
%Z TOL	-10% (Max Fault)

FAULT - X1

$I_{total\ s.c.\ (L-L-L)}$	46,261 AMPS
Voltage (L-L)	208 V

CONDUCTOR RUN - C1

LENGTH	20 FT
SIZE	500
QTY (per phase)	1
TYPE	Three Single Conductors
CONDUIT	Steel
WIRE	Cu, 600 V

FAULT - X2

$I_{total\ s.c.\ (L-L-L)}$	34,335 AMPS
Voltage (L-L)	208 V

CONDUCTOR RUN - C2

LENGTH	20 FT
SIZE	2
QTY (per phase)	1
TYPE	Three Single Conductors
CONDUIT	Steel
WIRE	Cu, 600 V

FAULT - X3

$I_{total\ s.c.\ (L-L-L)}$	17,446 AMPS
Voltage (L-L)	208 V

CONDUCTOR

CONDUCTOR

Example 2

The following is an example of the procedure for the calculation of available fault current on a 3-phase transformer secondary with the primary available fault current known.

Step A: Calculate the "f" factor for the transformer.

$$f = \frac{30,059 \times 480 \times 1.732 \times 0.9^* \times 1.2}{100,00 \times 225} = 1.2$$

*Transformer Z is multiplied by 0.9 to establish a high-fault condition scenario. See Note 1 in the section on 3-Phase Available Fault Current Calculation Procedure.

Step B: Determine the multiplier "M" for the transformer.

$$M = \frac{1}{1 + 1.2} = 0.45$$

Step C: Determine the available fault current at the transformer secondary.

$$I_{S(FC)} = \frac{480}{208} \times 0.45 \times 30,059 = 31,125 \text{ A}$$

Example 2

Fault X_p = 30,059 A

225 KVA Transformer
480V – 208V, 3Ø
1.2%Z

480 V

208 V

Fault X_s

This one-line diagram provides information for Example 2, which has a 3-phase available fault current to be calculated on the secondary of a transformer when the available fault current on the primary is known.

Caution

Available fault currents can change over time due to system changes. To ensure protection of both people and equipment, fault current studies and arc-flash risk assessments must be updated as necessary.

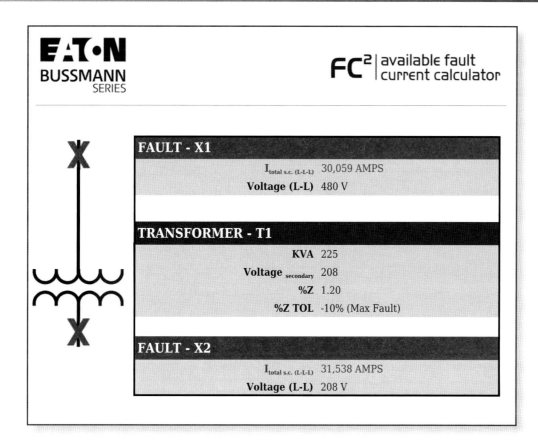

E:T•N
BUSSMANN
SERIES

FC² | available fault
current calculator

FAULT - X1

$I_{total\ s.c.\ (L-L-L)}$	30,059 AMPS
Voltage (L-L)	480 V

TRANSFORMER - T1

KVA	225
Voltage secondary	208
%Z	1.20
%Z TOL	-10% (Max Fault)

FAULT - X2

$I_{total\ s.c.\ (L-L-L)}$	31,538 AMPS
Voltage (L-L)	208 V

SUMMARY

An understanding of available fault current and arcing current provides a basis for properly applying a number of the requirements of *NFPA 70E* 130.5, Arc-Flash Risk Assessment. Available fault current calculations are necessary to perform a portion of an arc flash risk assessment, including determination of the arc flash boundary and the necessary arc flash PPE. Becoming familiar with the equations, tables, and notes associated with the point-to-point available fault calculation method enables the Electrical Worker to understand the basics of proper calculations and how they are used to ensure proper protection of equipment and people.

REVIEW QUESTIONS

1. The purpose of a fault current study is to determine the available fault current (bolted) at one or multiple points in an electrical system.

   a. True   b. False

2. When conducting an arc flash risk assessment, the electrical distribution system may have multiple scenarios. However, the available fault current at a specific location is not affected by different scenarios (the available fault current will always be the same value for all scenarios).

   a. True   b. False

3. Generators and __?__ in a premise system that are operating at the time of a fault condition can contribute fault current in addition to the fault current the utility delivers.

   a. heater elements
   b. lighting devices
   c. microwave ovens
   d. motors

4. Generally, for low-voltage systems, the bolted fault current determines the __?__ magnitude of current that the electrical system can deliver during a fault condition (there is an exception).

   a. first order
   b. highest
   c. minimum
   d. third order

5. The transformer %Z multiplied by __?__ should be used for the calculation of maximum available fault current to represent the highest available fault current possible due to a -10% transformer percentage impedance tolerance.

   a. 0.1
   b. 0.9
   c. 1.0
   d. 1.1

6. The available fault current is typically the highest at the __?__ .

   a. branch-circuit panel
   b. feeder panel
   c. receptacle outlets
   d. service point

7. If a utility transformer fails and the utility replaces the transformer, it is common for the percentage __?__ of the newer transformer to be lower, resulting in a higher fault current.

   a. impedance
   b. voltage
   c. volt-amperes
   d. wattage

8. Generally, for a typical low-voltage electrical distribution system, the __?__ has the greatest effect on the available fault currents throughout an electrical system.

    a. distance from transformer to the service panel

    b. facility square footage

    c. largest motor

    d. transformer

9. Various methods have been developed to calculate the available fault current, but all are based on __?__.

    a. NEC

    b. NFPA 70E

    c. Ohm's Law

    d. OSHA regulations and standards

10. As part of an arc flash risk assessment, typically determining the __?__ is a necessary value in the process for both the arc flash PPE category method (table method) or incident energy method.

    a. arcing current

    b. available fault current

    c. distance to the exit door

    d. square footage of the electrical room

11. Use the simplified method to calculate the available fault current at the secondary of a 500 kVA, 480-volt (secondary), 3-phase, 3.3 %Z transformer. This method assumes infinite available on the primary of the transformer. Use the factor for -10 % impedance tolerance. No motor contribution is to be considered. Choose the answer closest to the correct value. (See *Simple Method to Determine "Worst Case" 3-Phase Transformer Fault Current*.)

    a. 16,556 A

    b. 18,212 A

    c. 20,236 A

    d. 33,389 A

12. Calculate the available fault current at the secondary of a 150 kVA, 480-volt to 208-volt, 3-phase, 3.5% Z transformer. The available fault current at the transformer primary is 20,000 amperes. Use the factor for -10 % impedance tolerance. No motor contribution is to be considered. Choose the answer closest to the correct value.

    a. 7,356 A

    b. 8,762 A

    c. 9,458 A

    d. 10,275 A

    e. 11,500 A

13. The available fault current at the source end of a 500 kcmil conductor run is 15,000 amperes at 480-volt, 3-phase, without motor contribution. Determine the available fault current including motor contribution at the end of the conductor run, which is 75 feet. The conductor is three single copper conductors in metal conduit. This system has 1,000 amperes of motors on the system that can run at the same time.

    a. 12,680 A

    b. 13,680 A

    c. 16,680 A

    d. 19,000 A

Identifying Overcurrent Protective Device (OCPD) Types

Overcurrent protective device (OCPD) time-current characteristics under fault conditions are relevant for determining the arc flash PPE. Different types of OCPDs have different typical fault clearing times. When using the arc flash PPE category method, being able to identify the type of OCPD and associate a typical fault clearing time can facilitate the process of determining the required PPE. The type of electrical assembly can be a clue to the type of OCPDs utilized in the assembly.

Objectives

» Understand the concept of OCPD clearing times.

» Identify OCPD types and their associated typical fault clearing times.

» Understand the value of and the process for identifying an energy reducing maintenance switch (maintenance mode).

» Recognize that the type of assembly may help to determine the type of OCPD that is incorporated within the assembly.

Chapter 8

Table of Contents

Case Study

Within a nine-month timeframe in 2010 and 2011, two 11th grade students enrolled in an Electrical Technology program in the same Chapter 74 approved public regional vocational technical high school education program sustained electrical injuries in two separate incidents. One of the two students was assigned a task of using an existing de-energized wire located in a ceiling as a snake to feed a new higher-voltage wire. While standing on a ladder, the student mistakenly grabbed a wire that was energized, resulting in an electrical shock. The second incident involved a student who was shocked while feeding wire into a piece of metal conduit, a task that reportedly went beyond the assigned scope of work; the wire was live and caused the metal conduit to become electrified, shocking the student. In both cases, the students were being supervised by an instructor, but during the actual time of these incidents the instructor had stepped away to check on other Electrical Technology program students. The school nurse was called for both injuries and performed an evaluation of the students and then called for Emergency Medical Services (EMS). EMS responded to each incident within minutes and transported the students by ambulances to local hospitals. Both students were released from the hospital on the same day they were injured. The Massachusetts Department of Public Health concluded that to prevent similar occurrences in the future, schools with vocational shops should:

- Develop comprehensive safety and health plans, as required by Massachusetts regulations, to protect both students and school personnel by ensuring that schools are providing conditions that, at a minimum, meet occupational safety and health standards set by the Occupational Safety and Health Administration (OSHA);

- Conduct a job safety analysis (JSA) for each assigned task to ensure proper practices and procedures are implemented, enabling the task to be performed safely; and

- Routinely review and enforce lockout/tagout programs and provide relevant training to students and school staff.

Schools with vocational shops that also provide in-house skill-building opportunities for students should:

- Develop guidelines for these opportunities to ensure that:

  a) students have a clear understanding of the tasks they are being asked to perform; and

  b) appropriate levels of supervision are provided.

Source: For details of this case, see FACE Investigation #11MA1NF. Accessed November 3, 2020.

For additional information, visit qr.njatcdb.org Item #4391

INTRODUCTION

Different types of OCPDs are considered to have different typical maximum fault current clearing times. It is important to be familiar with the different types of OCPDs, including keys to identify each type of OCPD in field installations with the objective of determining an estimated typical fault current clearing time for specific arc flash PPE category method situations. In some cases, the type of assembly in which an OCPD is installed is a clue to the OCPD types that may be installed in the assembly. For example, knowing whether the assembly is a panelboard makes the determination of the OCPD type and typical fault clearing time more straightforward.

To use the arc flash PPE category method, the maximum fault current and clearing time specified in Table 130.7(C)(15)(a) under "Parameters" must be met. For example, for a 480-volt panelboard, Table 130.7(C)(15)(a) (under the "Equipment" column) shows that the protecting OCPD must have a fault clearing time not exceeding 0.03 seconds, which is approximately two cycles, and the available fault current cannot exceed 25,000 amperes.

NFPA 70E **Table 130.7(C)(15)(a), in part**

Panelboards or other equipment rated greater than 240 volts and up to 600 volts

Parameters: Maximum of 25 kA available fault current; maximum of 0.03 sec (2 cycles) fault clearing time; minimum working distance 455 mm (18 in.)

The informational note to Table 130.7(C)(15)(a) provides nonmandatory guidance on various OCPD type typical fault current clearing times.

The most straightforward guidance is achieved when working downstream of current-limiting fuses (item 1) and molded case circuit breakers (MCCBs) (item 2). Low-voltage power circuit breakers (LVPCBs) and insulated case

Informational Note to Table 130.7(C)(15)(a): The following are typical fault clearing times of overcurrent protective devices:

(1) 0.5 cycle fault clearing time is typical for current limiting fuses when the fault current is within the current limiting range.

(2) 1.5 cycle fault clearing time is typical for molded case circuit breakers rated less than 1000 volts with an instantaneous integral trip.

(3) 3.0 cycle fault clearing time is typical for insulated case circuit breakers rated less than 1000 volts with an instantaneous integral trip or relay operated trip.

(4) 5.0 cycle fault clearing time is typical for relay operated circuit breakers rated 1 kV to 35 kV when the relay operates in the instantaneous range (i.e., "no intentional delay").

(5) 20 cycle fault clearing time is typical for low-voltage power and insulated case circuit breakers with a short time fault clearing delay for motor inrush.

(6) 30 cycle fault clearing time is typical for low-voltage power and insulated case circuit breakers with a short time fault clearing delay without instantaneous trip.

circuit breakers (ICCBs) present different challenges for the Electrical Worker when determining clearing times. These OCPDs are built to accommodate intentional delays due to their location in the circuit or specific application where they may be applied. These OCPDs are equipped with options or settings that provide the ability to introduce intentional delays for fault clearing times. It can be challenging to differentiate an ICCB from a LVPCB. When it is determined that the upstream OCPD is not an MCCB, the Electrical Worker must then be able to differentiate the ICCB from a power circuit breaker (PCB). This will be accompanied by additional scrutiny, which is required to determine proper clearing times.

CIRCUIT BREAKER TYPES AND TYPICAL CLEARING TIMES

Electrical Workers should be able to easily identify the type of circuit breaker that is protecting the equipment and associate a typical clearing time.

The following material is covered in a broad, general manner. Though the source of much of the information is from one manufacturer, most of the material is applicable across the industry. In practice, there can be circuit breakers that

Figure 8-1   Identifying Circuit Breaker Types

Identifying Circuit Breaker Types Differentiation Summary
Most Important Differentiators Have Rows Highlighted in Gray
(Example Using One Manufacturer)

	MCCB	ICCB	LVPCB
Description	**QUICKLAG®/Series C®/ Series G®**	**Series NRX® w Power Xpert® Trip Unit and Magnum SB®**	**Magnum DS® & Series NRX® w Digitrip)**
Applicable Product Standard	*UL 489*	*UL 489*††	*UL 1066*, ANSI/IEEE C37
Voltage Rating	Many: 120 V, 240 V, 480 V, 600 V, etc.	Up to 635 VAC	Up to 635 VAC
Available Frame Sizes	100–2,500 A	800–6,000 A	800–6,000 A
Ampere Rating Range	15–2,500 A	200–6,000 A	200–6,000 A
Operator Type On-Off	Over center toggle Manually or motor operated	Mechanically operated and electrically operated two-step stored energy	Mechanically operated and electrically operated two-step stored energy
Circuit Breaker Label		May state "Insulated Case Circuit Breaker"	May state "Low Voltage Power Circuit Breaker"
Enclosure Type Used In	Predominantly panelboards, switchboards, MCCs, industrial control panels, & NEMA enclosures	Switchboards, MCCs, & custom	Predominantly switchgear & custom
Mounting	Predominantly fixed, larger ampere ratings available as drawout	Fixed or drawout	Fixed or drawout
Instantaneous Trip	Not required per *UL 489* Instantaneous trip may include an adjustable trip in addition to a fixed instantaneous override. All molded case circuit breakers will have an instantaneous trip.	Not required per *UL 489* Instantaneous trip may include an adjustable trip in addition to a fixed instantaneous override. All insulated case circuit breakers will have an instantaneous trip.	Not required in *UL 1006* May not have instantaneous trip† or may have instantaneous trip.** May permit turning instantaneous trip off by an adjustment setting. Some have instantaneous override
Energy reducing maintenance switch, marked on CB as Maintenance Mode (clearing time may be less than instantaneous trip)	Optional on many CB series for specific range of ampere ratings (such as 400-A frame and above)	Optional	Optional
Relative Cost	Low	Medium	High

† For some circuit breakers, the instantaneous trip current pickup is a multiple of the rating plug (I_n) and not the ampere rating setting (I_r). For a 1,600-ampere rating plug (I_n) set at 1,200 amperes rating (I_r), an instantaneous trip set at 10 times would pick up at $10 \times 1,600$ A = 16,000 A (with ± tolerance).

†† The Magnum SB is listed to *UL 1066* and in addition has an instantaneous trip unit or instantaneous override. As such, it is used in the same applications as an ICCB.

* Some ICCBs have the capability to set the adjustable instantaneous trip setting to "OFF." With this "OFF" setting, a fixed instantaneous override will be active, and if a fault condition occurs, the instantaneous override will operate for fault currents at or above the instantaneous override pickup current. For instance, for the Magnum® SB ICCB, the fixed instantaneous override is typically at 18 times the rating plug (I_n).

** When LVPCBs do not have an instantaneous trip, they will have a short-time delay. LVPCBs without instantaneous trip should only be used for applications where the conductors, components, and assemblies on the circuit to be protected have short-circuit current ratings sufficient for the time duration of fault current the short-time delay setting permits to flow. For instance, switchgear assemblies have short-circuit current ratings with 30 cycle duration. However, panelboard, switchboards, and MCCs do not have short-circuit current ratings for long time durations, and when protected by circuit breakers, the circuit breaker must have an instantaneous trip. Switchboard and MCC bus structures typically have a 3-cycle short-circuit current rating.

Figure 8-1. *Differentiating information for commercially available circuit breaker types is an aid for identifying each type of circuit breaker.*

will have characteristics beyond what is presented, as this material is based on the circuit breakers being marketed today and does not cover the decades of installed legacy circuit breakers. However, the majority of the principles will apply to legacy circuit breakers as well.

Background Information

A solid foundation of knowledge about circuit breakers will help in the overcurrent protective device identification and typical fault clearing time section.

Three Common Circuit Breaker Types

There are three common types of circuit breakers that are used in low-voltage electrical distribution systems for protection of services, feeders, or branch circuits.

- Molded case circuit breaker (MCCB): The MCCB is the most economical and most widely-used in 15- to 2,500-ampere ratings. MCCBs are the only type of circuit breaker used in panelboards. MCCBs can also be used in switchboards and motor control centers (MCCs).
- Insulated case circuit breaker (ICCB): The ICCB is used for larger ampere ratings and is usually used in switchboards and MCCs. They are available in ampere ratings of 200 to 6,000 amperes. An ICCB cannot be used in a panelboard.
- Low-voltage power circuit breaker (LVPCB): The LVPCB is built for durability and features. This device and associated equipment are of the highest cost. LVPCBs are primarily used for larger ampere ratings and primarily in low-voltage switchgear, but they are available in a wide range of ratings, including from 200- to 6,000-ampere ratings. **See Figure 8-1.**

Frame Size, Ampere Rating, and Rating Plug

It is best to illustrate these concepts with examples. **See Figure 8-2.** A manufacturer will offer a circuit breaker series and associated overcurrent trip units for a wide range of ampere ratings. For instance, the range for a

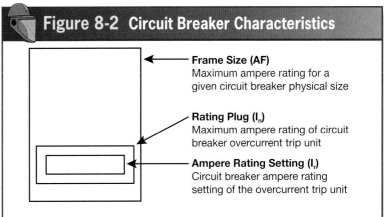

Figure 8-2 Circuit Breaker Characteristics

Frame Size (AF)
Maximum ampere rating for a given circuit breaker physical size

Rating Plug (I_n)
Maximum ampere rating of circuit breaker overcurrent trip unit

Ampere Rating Setting (I_r)
Circuit breaker ampere rating setting of the overcurrent trip unit

Figure 8-2. Important characteristics of a circuit breaker include the frame size (AF), rating plug (I_n) and ampere rating setting (I_r).

typical MCCB series will be 15 to 2,500 amperes. To accommodate this, the circuit breaker series will be offered in various ampere rating frame sizes, such as 150, 225, 400, 600, 800, 1,200, and 2,500 amperes. The acronym AF denotes the maximum ampere rating of a frame size. **See Figure 8-3.**

- Within a given frame size there may be many ampere ratings available. For instance, a J frame may have ampere ratings from 70 to 250 amperes and a K frame may have ampere ratings from 70 to

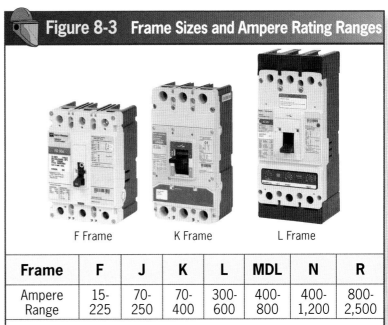

Figure 8-3 Frame Sizes and Ampere Rating Ranges

F Frame   K Frame   L Frame

Frame	F	J	K	L	MDL	N	R
Ampere Range	15-225	70-250	70-400	300-600	400-800	400-1,200	800-2,500

Figure 8-3. Lines of MCCBs are offered with varying frame sizes and ampere ratings. (Circuit breaker images not shown to scale.)

Courtesy of Eaton

400 amperes. In many cases, a rating plug is associated with the overcurrent trip unit. In some cases, there may be two or more rating plug options that can be utilized in a given circuit breaker frame size. For instance, a 1,200-ampere frame (AF) size may have rating plugs of 1,200 and 800 amperes. The 800-ampere rating plug can be set to a maximum of 800 amperes even though it is part of a 1,200 AF circuit breaker. The 1,200-ampere rating plug would have to be installed in the 1,200 AF circuit breaker to have an ampere rating setting greater than 800 to 1,200 amperes. I_n denotes the maximum ampere rating of a rating plug.

- The ampere rating I_r is the ampere rating to which the circuit breaker overcurrent trip unit is set. So, a 1,200-ampere circuit breaker may have an 800-ampere rating plug (I_n) overcurrent trip unit, which has an ampere rating setting (I_r) of 600 amperes. The electronic trip units utilize the terminology I_n and I_r more than the standard thermal magnetic trip units.

In the industry, these terms are not used universally. "AF" for a circuit breaker frame maximum ampere rating is very common. The terms I_n and I_r are used commonly but not universally. Another very common term in the industry is to use "AT" for ampere rating trip setting rather than I_r. "AT/AF" is commonly used to denote a circuit breaker's ampere trip setting (AT) and its frame maximum ampere rating (AF). However, the industry is evolving in response to newer circuit breakers that in some cases include the rating plug (I_n) ampere rating, which in some cases is needed to determine the current pickup for instantaneous trip circuit breakers when the I_n is denoted.

Circuit Breaker Overcurrent Trip Types

Several versions of the three types of circuit breakers (MCCB, ICCB, and LVPCB) are available in the industry, and each may have time-current characteristics that differ in the shape or total clearing times for certain overcurrent values.

Circuit breaker overcurrent trip units are the heart of a circuit breaker's time-current characteristics. For modern circuit breakers, there are primarily three different overcurrent trip technologies that can be used.

1. **Thermal** sensing of current is commonly used for the long-time portion of the time-current characteristics. The intent is for overload protection, but when an instantaneous trip is set at a high multiple of the ampere rating, the long-time portion may be the interrupting means for some low-level fault currents.
   - Can be fixed (non-adjustable) or adjustable
   - Very commonly used in MCCBs, especially for the lower ampere rating and for the least expensive trip unit. Not used for ICCBs or LVPCBs

2. **Magnetic** sensing of current is commonly used for the instantaneous trip of the time-current characteristic. The magnetic trip is intended for fault current protection.
   - Can be fixed (non-adjustable) or adjustable
   - Most commonly used for MCCBs and not used for ICCBs or LVPCBs
   - May be used for an energy-reducing maintenance switching function in ICCBs and LVPCBs

3. **Electronic** sensing of current can provide overcurrent protection for the full range of overcurrents. The simplest circuit breakers with electronic trip provide long-time and instantaneous protection. However, electronic trip units can provide more flexibility and capabilities with additional settings for short-time delay and ground-fault protection of equipment integrated in the trip unit.
   - The various time-current characteristic overcurrent functions can be adjustable or fixed or, in some cases, not included
   - Provides more adjustability to shape the time-current characteristic curve and has tighter

tolerances than thermal or magnetic sensing
- Used in larger-ampere rated MCCBs and for all ICCBs and LVPCBs. Electronic trip unit MCCBs typically cost more than thermal magnetic circuit breakers
- For a given circuit breaker, there may be several different electronic trip unit options, each having different overcurrent protection adjustments

There are five different common overcurrent protection trip types that a circuit breaker may incorporate.

1. **Long-time (L):** Long-time trip types are intended for overcurrents that can persist for many seconds to minutes without damaging the conductors or electrical equipment. It is often considered as overload protection but may include low-level fault protection, too. The long-time trip function provides protection for situations when a fault current is not high enough to cause the instantaneous trip to function or the short-time delay to function, if the circuit breaker is equipped with a short-time delay function.

   The long-time function setting can be:
   a. As simple as the ampere rating marked on a circuit breaker that has no long-time adjustment, such as common 20-ampere circuit breakers
   b. A dial where the ampere rating is dial-selected
   c. Two dial settings: (1) ampere rating and (2) time to interrupt
2. **Short-time delay (S):** Some circuit breakers have a setting that permits a fault to flow for more time than an instantaneous trip unit would permit, but not as long as the long-time trip function would permit. Normally there are two settings for a short-time delay: (1) current pickup and (2) delay time.
3. **Instantaneous trip (I):** Under fault current conditions, the circuit breaker opens as fast as it can; the exact speed depends on the design. This trip can be fixed or adjustable.

If adjustable, there is only one setting: instantaneous pickup current.
4. **Ground-fault protection of equipment trip (G):** Some circuit breakers are equipped with a ground-fault protection function for ground faults that may damage electrical equipment. Normally there are two settings: (1) ground-fault current pickup and (2) ground-fault time-delay.
5. **Energy-reducing maintenance switching trip (A):** This type of trip is a newer feature intended to reduce the incident energy exposure if an arcing fault incident occurs while a worker is working on exposed energized conductors. Some are fixed with no adjustment in time-current characteristics, and others have adjustable current pickup settings.

The industry uses the letters in parentheses to communicate the overcurrent protection trip types a circuit breaker may have, such as "LSI" for long-time, short-time, and instantaneous trip. A specific circuit breaker may have a trip unit that deploys one or multiple of these functions. When a function is used, it may be non-adjustable or it may be adjustable.

Examples of Circuit Breaker Trip Types and Characteristics

Consider a 200-ampere, 3-pole MCCB with a fixed long-time and fixed instantaneous trip unit. **See Figure 8-4.** This style

Figure 8-4 Fixed Long-Time and Instantaneous Trip

Figure 8-4. A very common style of circuit breaker is a 200-ampere, 3-pole MCCB with fixed thermal (long-time) and fixed magnetic (instantaneous) trip unit. There are no adjustment dials. This device is marked only as 200-ampere and does not have designations for I_r or I_n on markings.

Courtesy of Eaton

MCCB is very commonly used in feeder circuits supplying panelboards, mains for panelboards, and branch circuits. The time-current characteristic for this circuit breaker is long-time and instantaneous. **See Figure 8-5.** For a 200-ampere circuit breaker, the thermal trip function protects against overcurrents from 200 to 3,000 amperes and the instantaneous trip function protects against overcurrents from 3,000 to 35,000 amperes (35 kA interrupting rating at 480 volts). In simple terms, depending on the overcurrent magnitude, either the circuit breaker takes a long time to open or it interrupts as fast as it can. If the overcurrent is 4,000 amperes, the instantaneous trip causes the

circuit breaker to interrupt in approximately 0.02 seconds. If the overcurrent is 2,000 amperes, the long-time trip causes the circuit breaker to open in approximately five seconds.

A very common MCCB trip unit is a fixed thermal (long-time) and adjustable magnetic (instantaneous) trip unit. **See Figure 8-6.** The instantaneous trip dial settings provide some flexibility to adjust the instantaneous current pickup setting to overcome inrush currents or to possibly attain a higher degree of coordination.

The instantaneous setting can be adjusted in several increments from a low of five to a high of ten. **See Figure 8-7.** In

Figure 8-5   Time-Current Curve: Fixed Long-Time and Instantaneous Trip Unit

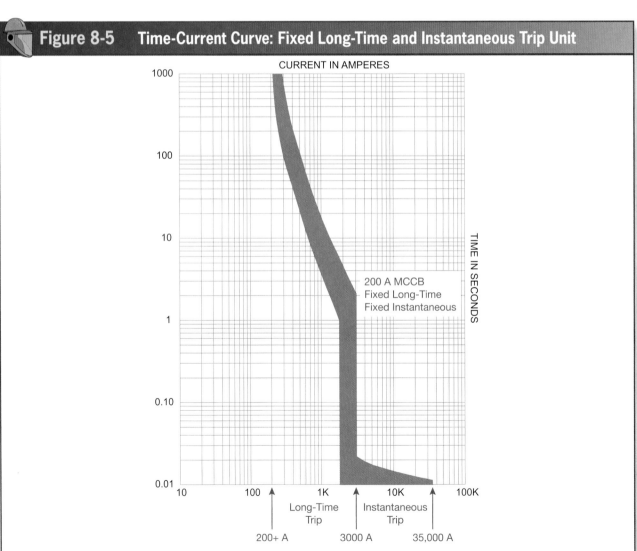

Figure 8-5. The region between the arrows represents the range of overcurrents the thermal trip unit (long-time) and magnetic trip unit (instantaneous) are respectively responsible for protection.

Figure 8-6   Fixed Long-Time and Adjustable Instantaneous Trip Unit

Figure 8-6. *A 400-ampere MCCB with a fixed thermal (long-time) and adjustable magnetic (instantaneous) trip unit allows for some flexibility in instantaneous pickup current settings. Notice the enlarged view of the trip unit faceplate shows that the I_n is 400 amperes and that the text below the left instantaneous dial states "Multiples of I_n."*

Courtesy of Eaton

Figure 8-7   Time-Current Curve: Fixed Long-Time and Adjustable Instantaneous Trip Unit

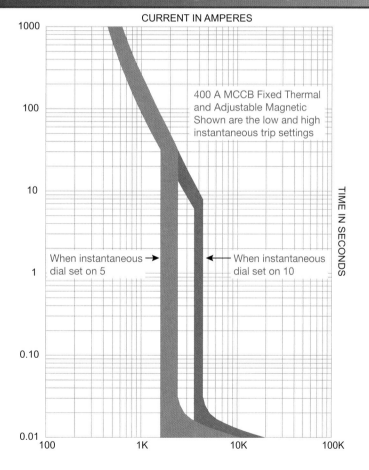

Figure 8-7. *With an adjustable magnetic (instantaneous) trip unit, the instantaneous pickup current setting can be adjusted to increments as a multiple of the 400-ampere rating plug (I_n). The curve on the left labeled "dial set on 5" represents the instantaneous set at 2,000 amperes (400 A × 5) and the curve on the right labeled "dial set on 10" represents the instantaneous set at 4,000 amperes (400 A × 10).*

Figure 8-8   MCCB with Fixed Long-Time and Adjustable Magnetic Instantaneous Trip Unit

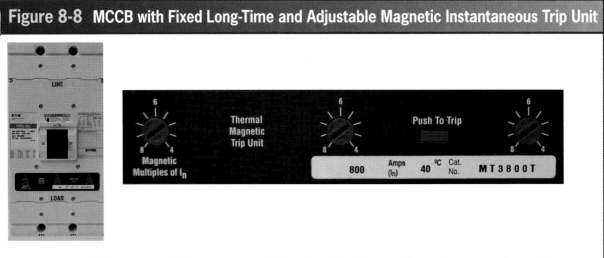

Figure 8-8. *On an 800-ampere MCCB with a trip unit that has fixed thermal long-time protection and adjustable magnetic instantaneous protection, the instantaneous dial setting for each pole is a multiple of I_n, which is 800 amperes, and the dials can be adjusted in increments from a low of four to a high of eight.*

Courtesy of Eaton

application, the dial can only be set on one setting at a given time and the time-current characteristic should only show the curve of one instantaneous dial setting.

The least-expensive MCCBs in the larger ampere ratings typically have a fixed long-time and an adjustable instantaneous trip unit. **See Figure 8-8.**

Electronic trip circuit breakers provide better time-current characteristic tolerances (narrower curves) and more curve shaping options. Consider a circuit breaker with the exact same 800-ampere circuit breaker frame and mechanical mechanism as the circuit breaker shown with fixed long-time and magnetic instantaneous protection, except this circuit breaker has an electronic trip unit. **See Figure 8-9.** The electronic trip unit has adjustments for long-time delay (L), short-time delay (S), and ground-fault protection (G), so it

Figure 8-9   MCCB with Electronic Instantaneous Trip Unit

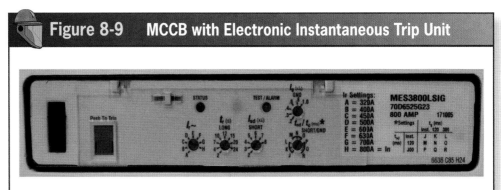

Figure 8-9. *For an LSG electronic trip unit for an 800-ampere MCCB, the rating plug (I_n) is 800 amperes. The ampere rating setting (I_r) is adjustable from 320 to 800 amperes using the dial with settings from A to H. There also are adjustment dials for long-time delay, short-time delay, and ground-fault protection. There is no dial setting for instantaneous trip, which means the MCCB will have an instantaneous override.*

Courtesy of Eaton

may be referred to as an LSG electronic trip unit. An MCCB with this electronic trip unit may have a fixed instantaneous trip capability, which is referred to as an instantaneous override. It means even though it is not obvious by looking at the circuit breaker, there is a fixed instantaneous trip function, which is set at 6,400 amperes in this case.

Electronic trip units have the capability to provide several different adjustable overcurrent protection options, and the time-current characteristics can be shaped by dial settings. **See Figure 8-10.**

For some circuit breaker models with electronic trip units, there can be several different electronic trip unit options available depending on the characteristics desired, such as LI, LSI, LSIG, ALS, etc.

LVPCBs can have time-current characteristics without an instantaneous

---

Figure 8-10   Time-Current Curve: MCCB with Electronic Instantaneous Trip Unit

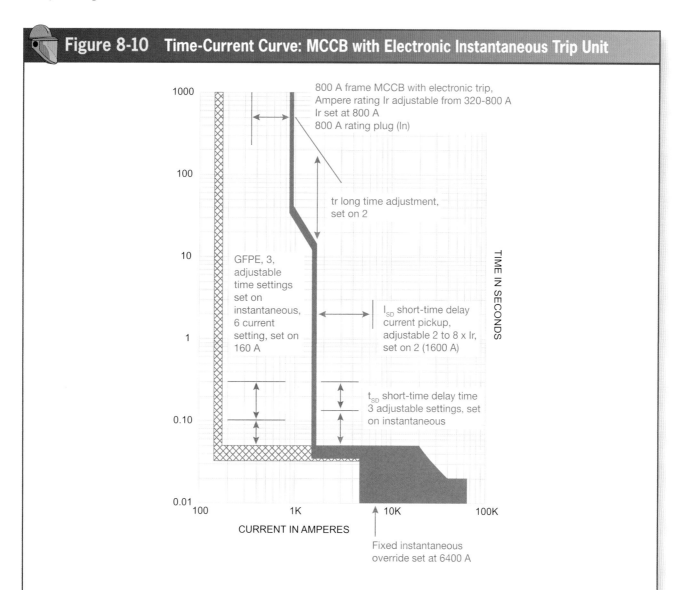

Figure 8-10. The solid blue curve represents the long-time delay (L) and short-time delay (S) settings as shown on the electronic trip unit dials, as well as the instantaneous override. The hashed blue represents the ground-fault protection for equipment (G) shown on the electronic trip unit. The adjustability range of each function is shown by arrows.

Courtesy of Eaton

trip. **See Figure 8-11.** For example, an 800-ampere LVPCB with ALSI electronic trip unit has adjust dials for:

(A) Energy-reducing maintenance switch (ERMS) (The manufacturer of this circuit breaker has trademarked their ERMS as Arc-Flash Reduction Maintenance System™, hence the (A), which is enabled by the maintenance mode.)

(L) Long-time delay

(S) Short-time delay

(I) Instantaneous (The instantaneous dial is set to "off" in this example)

For LVPCBs, typically it is possible to turn "off" the instantaneous function.

This means a fault current is permitted to flow until the short-time delay function initiates the fault current interruption. In this case, a fault of 25,000 amperes will be cleared in 0.3 seconds (18 cycles) per the short-time delay setting. LVPCB short-time delay settings can range from 0.1 second (6 cycles) to 0.5 seconds (30 cycles). The purpose of short-time delay is to allow the downstream OCPD to clear faults before the LVPCB trips, thereby avoiding unnecessary power loss to other loads.

An LVPCB without an instantaneous trip can result in very high incident energy compared to MCCBs and ICCBs, which always must have an

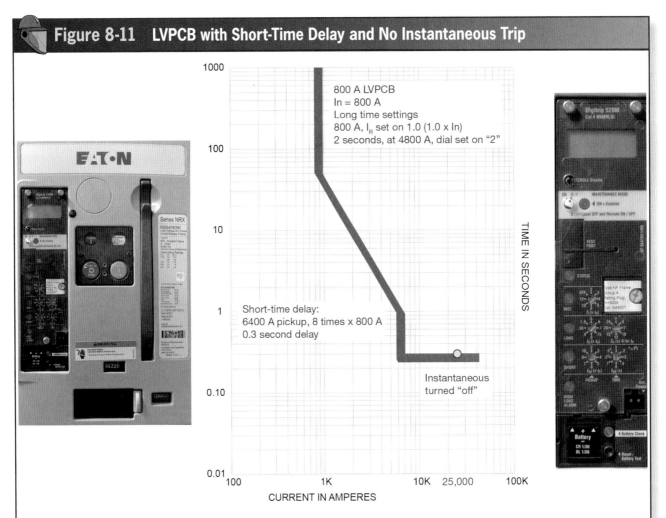

Figure 8-11   LVPCB with Short-Time Delay and No Instantaneous Trip

800 A LVPCB
In = 800 A
Long time settings
800 A, I_R set on 1.0 (1.0 x In)
2 seconds, at 4800 A, dial set on "2"

Short-time delay:
6400 A pickup, 8 times x 800 A
0.3 second delay

Instantaneous turned "off"

CURRENT IN AMPERES

TIME IN SECONDS

Figure 8-11. On an 800-ampere LVPCB with an ALSI electronic trip, the instantaneous dial can be set to "off" so the instantaneous trip is not operational. The short-time delay function is the protection for fault currents above the short-time delay pickup current.

Courtesy of Eaton

instantaneous function. Energy-reducing maintenance switching, or Maintenance Mode, is a solution to reduce the incident energy for this situation.

ENERGY-REDUCING MAINTENANCE SWITCHING

Energy-reducing maintenance switching (ERMS) is an option to include on larger ampere rated circuit breakers and fused switches with the objective of reducing the arcing fault time duration for some range of arcing fault currents. This option is very important for LVPCBs, which do not have an instantaneous trip function. The result can be to mitigate the incident energy when an Electrical Worker is justified to work on electrical equipment that is not in an electrically safe work condition. When the ERMS option is switched "on" or enabled, a state which may be marked as "Maintenance Mode," there is additional enhanced arc flash mitigation protection if an arcing fault event were to occur on the circuit that the ERMS protects.

There are options where the ERMS can be locked in the "on" position. The ERMS option is a good means to comply with *NEC* 240.67 and 240.87, which are arc energy reduction requirements for new installations. ERMS options can be included with many new circuit breakers and retrofitted to many existing installed circuit breakers.

Circuit Breaker ERMS

Consider an 800-ampere LVPCB with Maintenance Mode engaged, meaning that the energy reducing maintenance switch has been turned "on." The electronic trip unit blue light indicates the Maintenance Mode is engaged, and now the time-current characteristic curve includes the hashed blue portion. **See Figure 8-12.** The yellow dots on the time-current curve provide a good example of the benefit. Without the Maintenance Mode engaged (solid blue curve), the 800-ampere LVPCB is set to interrupt a 10,000-ampere arcing fault condition in 0.3 seconds (18 cycles). With the Maintenance Mode engaged

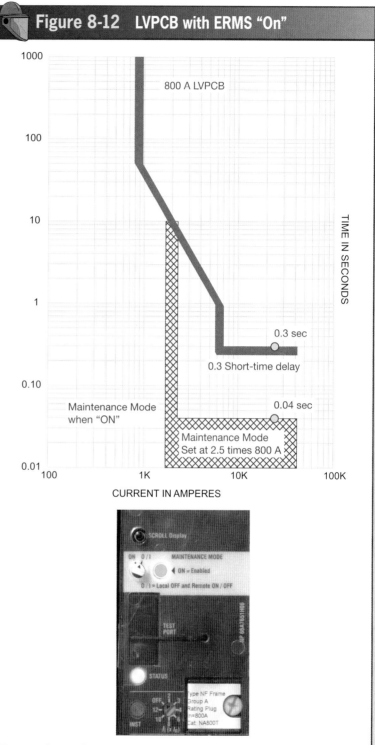

Figure 8-12. Consider the 800-ampere LVPCB time-current characteristics and electronic trip unit portion with the Maintenance Mode engaged. The solid blue curve represents the normal long-time and short-time settings; this circuit breaker does not have an instantaneous trip. The hashed blue represents the Maintenance Mode when enabled (turned "on"), which is an energy-reducing maintenance switch to lower the incident energy.

Courtesy of Eaton

(hashed blue curve), the 800-ampere LVPCB is set to interrupt a 10,000-ampere arcing fault current in 0.04 seconds (2 1/2 cycles). In this example, the Maintenance Mode is estimated to reduce the incident energy by 88%. In addition, the Maintenance Mode can be set at 2.5 times the circuit breaker's 800-ampere plug rating, which means it will react to currents of 1,600 amperes or greater. When the work is completed, the Maintenance Mode is set back to "off" and the overcurrent protection is via the normal circuit breaker settings (solid blue).

ERMS can provide incident energy mitigation benefits for circuit breakers with instantaneous trips, too. Consider a 1,600-ampere MCCB with electronic trip unit and instantaneous override. **See Figure 8-13.** The ALSG represents the adjustability for (A) energy-reducing maintenance switch setting, (L) long-time settings, (S) short-time settings, and (G) ground-fault settings. The (I) instantaneous is via an instantaneous override, so there is not an adjustment dial.

The 1,600-ampere circuit breaker's fixed instantaneous override is 10 times or 16,000 amperes, which was determined from the manufacturer's literature. With the Maintenance Mode engaged, a 6,000-ampere fault will open the circuit breaker in approximately

Figure 8-13 MCCB with Electronic Trip and ERMS

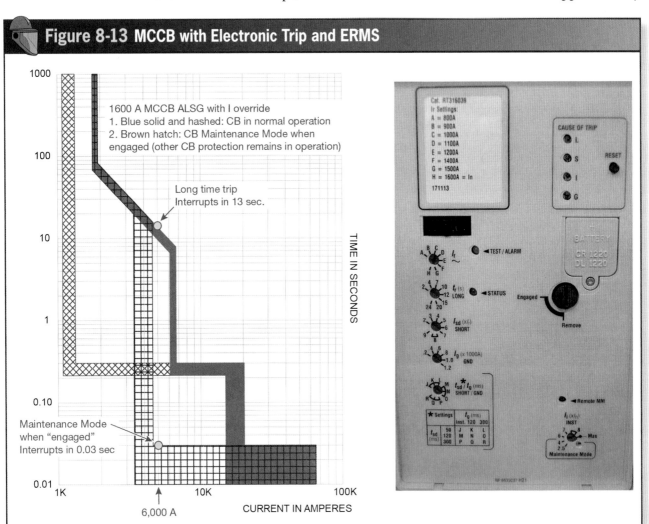

Figure 8-13. *Consider a 1,600-ampere MCCB with ALSG electronic trip and instantaneous override. The time-current characteristic does not represent the same settings as shown on the adjacent electronic trip unit. The brown hashed line represents the Maintenance Mode (ERMS) when engaged.*

Courtesy of Eaton

0.04 seconds rather than approximately 13 seconds without the Maintenance Mode engaged.

Energy-reducing maintenance switch On/Off control can be installed remotely from circuit breakers. In some cases, the ERMS can be controlled by remote electronic devices. **See Figure 8-14.**

Energy-reducing maintenance switches are becoming more prevalent and may visually have various appearances on the face of the circuit breaker trip unit or remote installations. **See Figure 8-15.**

Figure 8-14   LVPCB with Remote ERMS

Figure 8-14. Some LVPCBs have remote but adjacent indicator lights for "Breaker Open" (green), "Breaker Closed" (red), and "Maintenance Mode On" (dark blue). The light blue adjustment dial can turn Maintenance Mode "on" or "off," and there is a provision to apply a lock to retain Maintenance Mode "on" while the Electrical Worker is working on the electrical equipment this circuit breaker protects.

Courtesy of Eaton

Figure 8-15 MCCB with Electronic Trip and ERMS

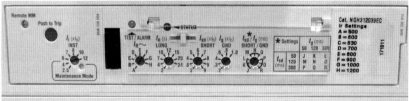

Figure 8-15. A 1,200-ampere MCCB may be installed in a switchboard assembly. The electronic trip unit has an adjustable energy-reducing maintenance switch shown as Maintenance Mode, which can be adjusted from 2.5 to 12 times the rating plug (I_n), which is 1,200 amperes.

Courtesy of Eaton

Fusible Switch ERMS

Energy-reducing maintenance switching can also be integrated with fusible switches. **See Figure 8-16.** When the ERMS option is switched "on," if an arcing fault event were to occur on a circuit protected by a fusible switch, there is additional enhanced arc flash protection for a lower range of arcing fault currents. The ERMS and fuses together can result in significantly lower incident energy levels for a wide range of arcing fault currents from low magnitude to high magnitude. *NEC* 240.67, which in some applications may necessitate using a solution for 1,200-ampere or greater fuse applications, becomes effective in 2020.

DISTINGUISHING CIRCUIT BREAKER TYPES

MCCBs are the most easily identifiable circuit breakers. ICCBs and LVPCBs are very similar to each other in appearance and are not easy to distinguish between by casual observation when installed in assemblies with trim and covers on. Even so, being able to confidentially identify MCCBs is a great benefit to the Electrical Worker, since MCCBs are the most common circuit breaker by quantity and the most often utilized in 15- to 2,500-ampere applications. A circuit breaker above 2,500 amperes will either be an ICCB or an LVPCB.

Distinguishing an MCCB from either an ICCB or LVPCB is relatively

Figure 8-16   1,200-Ampere Fusible Switch with ERMS

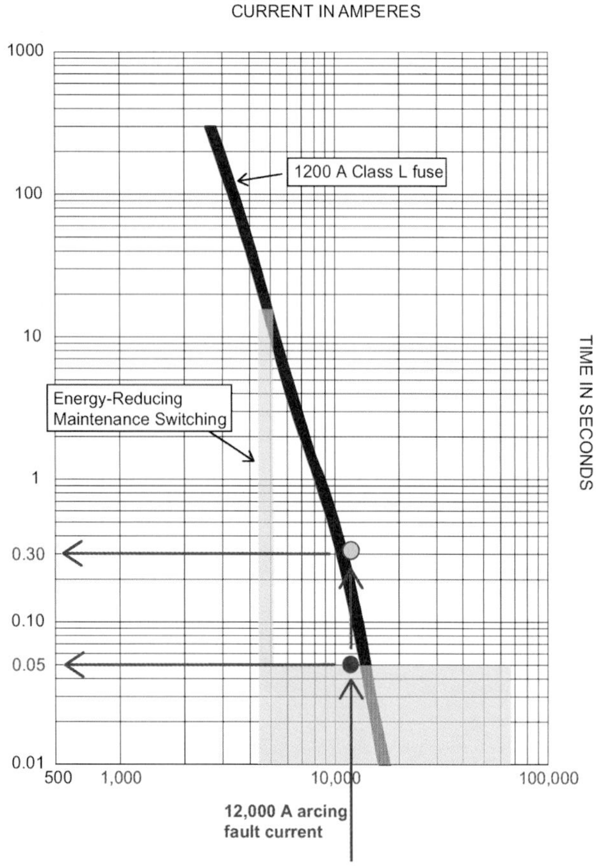

Courtesy of General Electric Corp.

Figure 8-16. *Consider a 1,200-ampere fusible switch equipped with an energy-reducing maintenance switch. The ERMS, when engaged, handles the lower-level fault currents, and the fuses handle higher-level fault currents when the fuses are faster than the ERMS.*

easy. An MCCB has a mechanical on/off toggle handle. Typically, the close and open function for an ICCB or LVPCB is initiated by pushing either a close button or open button, or by remote control. For ICCBs and LVPCBs, the energy to perform the close/open operations comes via a two-step stored energy system using springs built into the circuit breaker. Charging the stored energy springs is accomplished by a handle pumping action or by electrical spring charging process. The two-step stored energy system of opening and closing ICCBs and LVPCBs has been used for over four decades. The mechanism to interrupt overcurrents is independent of the open/close two-step stored energy function.

Visually Identifying MCCBs

The most common circuit breakers by quantity are 1-pole, 20-ampere, non-adjustable thermal magnetic MCCBs, which typically are located in branch-circuit panelboards for lighting and other small ampere loads. The 15-ampere through 400-ampere, 3-pole, non-adjustable thermal magnetic MCCBs are very common as branch circuits in

panelboards, and the 100-ampere, 200-ampere, 225-ampere, and 400-ampere MCCBs are very common as mains for panelboards or lineside feeder protection for main lug only (MLO) panelboards. Notice the on/off handles. The toggle on/off handle is a unique, distinguishing feature for an MCCB. ICCBs and LVPCBs do not have toggle on/off handles.

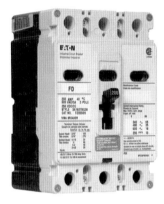

Three-pole, 200-ampere, non-adjustable thermal magnetic molded case circuit breakers are commonly used as the main for panelboards or as the feeder OCPD in upstream distribution panelboards. The on/off toggle handle mechanism uniquely distinguishes this as an MCCB.

Courtesy of Eaton

Plug-On Mounting   Bolt-On Mounting

Thermal-magnetic 1-pole, 20-ampere, 120/240-volt, 10 kA IR circuit breakers have plug-on and bolt-on mounting versions. This type and ampere rating MCCB accounts for a high volume of the MCCBs produced. The on/off toggle handles have 20 amperes marked on the end.

Courtesy of Eaton

MCCBs are distinguished by having an on/off toggle handle mechanism that can be operated manually or by optional motor operator. For both a 3-pole, electronic trip, 225-ampere MCCB (left) and a 3-pole, electronic trip, 600-ampere MCCB (right), the handle is the black object near the center of the circuit breaker front. The handles are in the "ON" or closed position.

Courtesy of Eaton

Figure 8-17 Pumping Handle to Charge

Figure 8-17. Both ICCBs and LVPCBs have a two-step stored energy system for opening and closing. Pumping the handle charges the springs.

Courtesy of Eaton

Visually Identifying ICCBs and LVPCBs

Both ICCBs and LVPCBs are distinguished from MCCBs by having a two-step stored energy system for opening and closing, which can be mechanically or electrically charged. There is a handle mechanism that can be pumped to charge springs, which are the stored energy mechanism. **See Figure 8-17.** They have "Push to Open" and "Push to Close" buttons. **See Figure 8-18.** ICCBs and LVPCBs typically have the option to be remotely opened and closed as well.

The distinguishing features are:
(1) Close and open push buttons and no mechanical toggle on/off handle
(2) The handle to charge the open/close stored energy system

Distinguishing an ICCB from an LVPCB is not as simple as distinguishing ICCBs and LVPCBs from MCCBs. In many cases, the circuit breaker manufacturers use the same basic design platform to offer an ICCB series and an LVPCB series. This results in a very similar look and feel for the ICCB series and LVPCB series from the same manufacturer. However, even though

Figure 8-18 ICCB and LVPCB Status Flags and Push to Open or Close Buttons

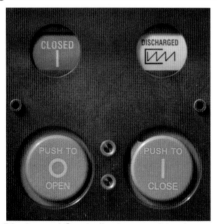

Discharged flag indicates need to charge

Charged flag indicates sufficient charge to close or open

Figure 8-18. ICCBs and LVPCBs display a flag for open or closed status (closed position is red) and a flag indicating whether the springs are charged (yellow) or discharged (white). The "Push to Open" and "Push to Close" buttons are also shown, and the charged springs provide the energy to perform these operations.

Courtesy of Eaton

they are visually similar, there are important performance differences between ICCBs and LVPCBs.

The circuit breaker label may state the words "Insulated Case," which means the circuit breaker is an ICCB. **See Figure 8-19.**

LVPCBs utilizing the on/off push buttons and the handle mechanism that can be pumped to charge springs for the open/close operation have been in use for more than four decades. Prior to the introduction of this style, LVPCBs incorporated a pistol grip rotating handle on/off mechanism.

MCCB Details

There is additional information that may help identify the type of circuit breaker. Molded case circuit breakers have an ampere rating range from 15 to 2,500 amperes with voltage ratings from 120 to 600 volts AC. MCCBs are also available in DC voltage ratings. There are a wide variety of different physical sizes, voltage ratings, interrupting ratings, trip units, and time-current characteristics available. MCCB exterior cases are available in various colors, with gray and black being most prevalent.

Molded case circuit breaker trip units can be thermal magnetic, electronic, or magnetic-only. There are also MCCBs that incorporate fusible elements, which operate on high fault currents and provide MCCBs with high interrupting ratings and current-limiting ability. All MCCBs will have an instantaneous trip which may be adjustable, fixed, or instantaneous override. In essence, a fixed instantaneous and instantaneous override are analogous. The following informational note provides nonmandatory guidance on clearing times for some MCCBs.

Informational Note to Table 130.7(C)(15)(a) for MCCBs:

(2) 1.5 cycle fault clearing time is typical for molded case circuit breakers rated less than 1000 volts with an instantaneous integral trip.

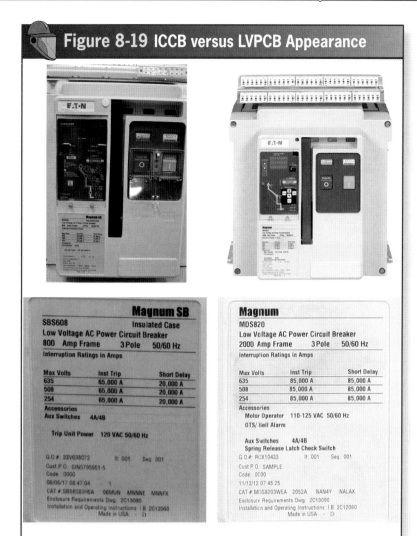

Figure 8-19 ICCB versus LVPCB Appearance

Figure 8-19. On the left is an 800-ampere ICCB and on the right is a 2,000-ampere LVPCB. Their appearances are very similar. Both have the handle for charging the stored energy open/close mechanism, the same flag indicators for open/close and discharged/charged, and buttons for open and close. The electronic trip unit interface is similar. The labels are also very similar; however, only the ICCB label identifies the circuit breaker as "Insulated Case." (Images are not to scale.)

Courtesy of Eaton

Thermal-Magnetic MCCBs

The adjustable magnetic-style trip unit customarily can be set at four or five times for the lowest setting and up to eight, ten, or twelve for the highest setting. There are some MCCB styles that have "high magnetic" characteristics with an instantaneous trip setting (usually fixed) up to 20 times the current rating. These are used to facilitate

Figure 8-20 Thermal-Magnetic MCCBs

Figure 8-20. A 400-ampere K Frame MCCB with a fixed thermal and adjustable magnetic instantaneous trip unit can be adjusted from 5 to 10 times the 400 amperes (I_n).

Courtesy of Eaton

attaining selective coordination. **See Figure 8-20.**

MCCBs are listed to *UL 489* and will contain a marking near the agency symbol. This marking should read "Listed Circuit Breaker" or an abbreviation such as "Cir. Bkr." This marking

Figure 8-21   Listed Circuit Breaker Label

LISTED CIR BKR

Figure 8-21. MCCBs are listed to UL 489 and will contain a marking near the agency symbol. This distinguishes an MCCB from these other molded case devices which are not MCCBs: (1) supplementary protector which is recognized to UL 1077, (2) motor circuit protector (MCP) which is recognized, and (3) a molded case switch listed as a switch.

may or may not be visible when the MCCB is installed in an assembly with the trim on. **See Figure 8-21.**

Electronic Trip MCCBs

The electronic trip MCCBs essentially are the same as thermal-magnetic MCCBs except for the trip unit. In fact, many MCCB models are designed so that either a thermal-magnetic trip unit or an electronic trip unit can be put into the trip unit space. Consider a 1,200-ampere MCCB with an ALSG acronym describing the electronic trip capabilities with adjustable dials for long-time (L), short-time (S), and ground-fault protection (G). **See Figure 8-22.** It incorporates an instantaneous function that is present as an instantaneous override (no adjustment dial). Determining the instantaneous pickup current would require referencing the manufacturer's publications. It also includes an energy-reducing maintenance switch (A) denoted as "Maintenance Mode," which is adjustable from 2.5 to 12 times the rating plug (I_n), which is 1,200 amperes, but not shown. This manufacturer uses a trademarked phrase Arc Flash Reduction Maintenance System™ for their energy-reducing maintenance switching technology, which is the (A) in ALSG.

MCCBs with electronic trip units may have adjustable instantaneous dials or may be an instantaneous override.

- Those that have an adjustable instantaneous trip dial have an instantaneous current pickup setting range from four or five for the low setting and eight, ten, or twelve times for the high setting. The instantaneous current pickup is normally a multiple of the numerical dial setting times the rating plug (I_n) rather than the ampere rating setting (I_r).
- For electronic trip unit MCCBs that do not have a dial for instantaneous adjustment, there is an instantaneous override (no dial setting). In most cases, the pickup current of the instantaneous override is not shown on the circuit

breaker or trip unit. Manufacturer's instructions, time-current curves, or publications must be referenced to determine the instantaneous override pickup current. The instantaneous override will commonly be 10 to 12 times the rating plug (I_n) or sensor rating. There are some cases where the instantaneous override may be up to 18 times or higher of the rating plug (I_n).

Other Molded Case Devices
There are similar looking devices to MCCBs that are not circuit breakers.

1. **Motor circuit protectors** (MCPs) are devices that can only be used for motor branch-circuit short-circuit and ground-fault protection per 430.52(C)(3). Section 430.52(C)(3) uses the term Instantaneous Trip Circuit Breaker, which is commonly called an MCP. In reality, an MCP is an instantaneous only circuit breaker. There is not a long-time trip function, only the instantaneous trip function. **See Figure 8-23.** For

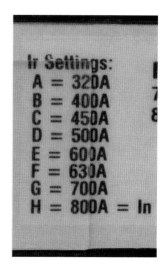

Figure 8-22. *An 800-ampere MCCB with electronic trip unit may have adjustments denoted by ALSG and instantaneous override. The long-time ampere rating (I_r) is adjustable from 320 amperes to 800 amperes by setting one of the adjustment dials per the corresponding alpha legend (right). The rating plug (I_n) is 800 amperes as noted on the expanded view.*

Courtesy of Eaton

 Figure 8-23   Motor Circuit Protector Recognition Mark

Instantaneous-Trip Circuit Breaker

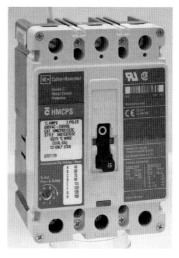

Figure 8-23. *Motor circuit protectors (MCPs), referred to in NEC Section 430.52 as instantaneous trip circuit breakers, are recognized in UL 489 and will contain a recognition or component acceptance marking. This marking typically will not be visible with the assembly trim on or motor control center bucket door closed.*

Courtesy of Eaton

the purposes of OCPD identification and typical clearing time, use the same typical clearing time as an MCCB. MCPs can only be applied in motor branch circuits in combination with a motor starter in which the two are a listed combination. The motor starter provides overload protection. MCPs are most commonly found in motor control center buckets or in combination motor starters.

2. **Molded case switches** look similar to MCCBs, but are switches and not MCCBs. A molded case switch is not an overcurrent protective device. Most often, when a molded case switch is applied, on its load-side will be fuses in a fuse block immediately adjacent (trailing) the molded case switch. For the purposes of OCPD identification and typical clearing time, consider the molded case switch as simply a switch and follow the typical clearing time for fuses. **See Figure 8-24.**

ICCBs and LVPCBs

LVPCBs and ICCBs generally come in frame sizes of 800, 1,200, 1,600, 2,000, 2,500, 3,200, 4,000, 5,000, and 6,000 amperes. The ampere rating range is 200 to 6,000 amperes. The voltage ratings are usually 600 volts or 635 volts. The trip units for ICCBs and LVPCBs sold today are all electronic and have been for several decades.

LVPCBs typically are used in low-voltage switchgear and are more durable and heavy-duty than ICCBs. LVPCBs are rated to be able to have a 30-cycle short-time delay without an instantaneous trip. They have a short-time withstand rating, which is the maximum fault current at a specified voltage they can hold for 30 cycles, and then safely interrupt. This means they can hold the fault current for 30 cycles prior to tripping. They may have an instantaneous trip adjustment, but this instantaneous adjustment can often be set to "off." Low-voltage switchgear most often has a 30-cycle short-circuit current rating, which then allows a LVPCB with a 30-cycle short-time delay and no instantaneous trip to provide protection. However, low-voltage switchboards, panelboards, and motor control centers do not normally have 30-cycle short-circuit current ratings and should not be protected by an LVPCB with a short-time delay and no instantaneous trip. These assemblies may be protected by LVPCBs with an instantaneous trip or protected by ICCBs or MCCBs, which will always have an instantaneous trip.

ICCBs are typically used in switchboards and have lighter durability. They have short-time delay settings up to as high as 30 cycles, but always have an instantaneous function, too. The instantaneous function could be an adjustable setting or a fixed override.

For LVPCBs and ICCBs, the instantaneous trip pickup range, when applicable, may vary and may depend on the manufacturer and model trip unit, but the range typically is two (for the low setting) and 10, 12 or 15 (for the high setting) times the rating plug (I_n). However, the instantaneous trip setting on both LVPCBs may be able to be turned to "off." In that case, the LVPCBs rely on their short-time delay

Figure 8-24   Molded Case Switch Listed Mark

LISTED
Molded Case Switch

Figure 8-24. Molded case switches look similar to MCCBs; however, they are not OCPDs. They should be listed and marked to UL 489 as molded case switches and should state this on the face of the switch. However, this information may not be visible when identifying the device installed in an assembly with the trim or doors closed.

Figure 8-25   ICCBs Have an Instantaneous Trip

Figure 8-25. ICCBs have short-time delay functions as well as instantaneous trips. For the ICCB series shown, the instantaneous override pickup, when applicable, is typically 18 times the rating plug (I_n).

adjustment pickup and time settings; an instantaneous trip is not required because the LVPCBs are rated to withstand up to 30 cycles of fault current for up to their rated short-time withstand rating. However, ICCBs do not have the same fault short-time withstand capability. ICCBs also will rely on a short-time delay adjustment pickup and time setting, but at some value of fault current an instantaneous override will trip an ICCB. **See Figure 8-25.**

As previously stated, ICCBs and LVPCBs can be very similar in appearance. Identifying whether a circuit breaker is an ICCB or LVPCB may require reading the label to determine what is stated, or, in some cases, may require getting the part number on the circuit breaker and investigating which device it may be. Another means is to have someone qualified in identifying circuit breaker types and settings to determine if it is an ICCB or an LVPCB and if it has an active instantaneous trip function. The following informational note provides nonmandatory guidance on clearing times for some ICCBs.

Informational Note to Table 130.7(C)(15)(a) for ICCBs:

(3)   3.0 cycle fault clearing time is typical for insulated case circuit breakers rated less than 1000 volts with an instantaneous integral trip or relay operated trip.

FUSES AND TYPICAL FAULT CLEARING TIMES

For 600-volt and less electrical distribution systems and utilization equipment power circuits, there are two broad categories of fuses: current-limiting fuses and non–current-limiting fuses.

Current-Limiting Fuses

The following informational note provides nonmandatory guidance on clearing times for current-limiting fuses under specific circumstances.

Informational Note to Table 130.7(C)(15)(a) for current-limiting fuses:

(1)   0.5 cycle fault clearing time is typical for current limiting fuses when the fault current is within the current limiting range.

Figure 8-26   Fuse Current-Limiting Threshold

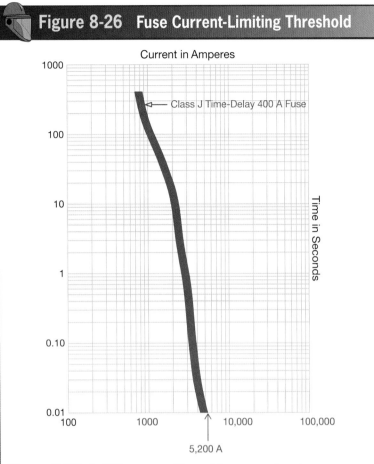

Figure 8-26. A 400-ampere Class J fuse can clear in approximately ¹/₂ cycle or less for fault currents greater than 5,200 amperes.

Current-limiting fuses are the predominant type of fuses used for 600-volt or less electrical distribution systems and the power utilization equipment. The ampere rating range is from a fraction of an ampere to 6,000 amperes, and voltage ratings range from 250 volts or 600 volts. They have high interrupting ratings of 100, 200, or 300 kA. Under fault conditions, these fuses have the ability to limit the current let-through to less than the available fault current and clear the fault current in ¹/₂ cycle or less. **See Figure 8-26.** The combination of decreased clearing times and reduced arcing current can greatly reduce the incident energy when the arcing current is within a fuse's current-limiting range.

There are various UL current-limiting fuse classes with varying current-limiting performance. Class RK5 and Class RK1 fuses are very commonly used. **See Figure 8-27.** Class L and Class J fuses are used commonly in new construction. **See Figure 8-28.** These are some of the most commonly-used time-delay, current-limiting, 600 volt AC fuses. In addition, there can be non–time-delay fuses.

Fuses can have various time-current characteristics. **See Figure 8-29.** These are time-current characteristics for four

Figure 8-27   Class RK5 and RK1 Fuses

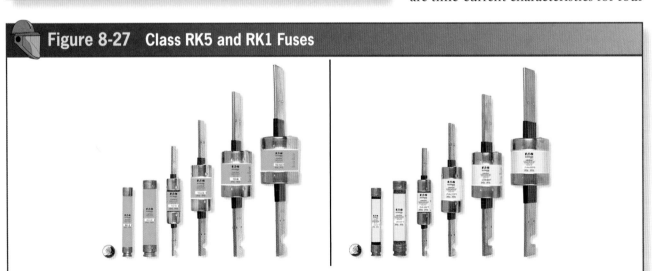

Figure 8-27. On the left are the major case ampere ratings (30, 60, 100, 200, 400, and 600 amperes) for the UL Class RK5 dual-element, time-delay fuses, which are current-limiting. On the right are the same major case ampere ratings for the UL Class RK1 dual-element, time-delay fuses which are even more current-limiting. (The quarters are in the images to indicate scale.)

Courtesy of Eaton's Bussmann Division

Figure 8-28   Class L and J Fuses

Figure 8-28. On the left are two ampere ratings (800 and 2,000) for the UL Class L time-delay fuses, which are current-limiting; these fuses are in ampere ratings from 601 to 6,000 amperes. On the right are the same major case ampere ratings (30, 60, 100, 200, 400, and 600 amperes) for the UL Class J dual-element, time-delay fuses, which are very current-limiting. (The quarters are in the images to indicate scale.)

Courtesy of Eaton's Bussmann Division

Figure 8-29   Various Fuse Time-Current Characteristics

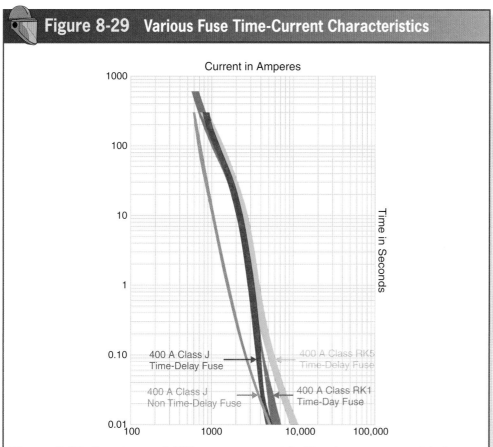

Figure 8-29. Four types of 400-ampere current-limiting fuses may result in four different clearing times for some levels of overcurrent.

different 400-ampere current-limiting fuses. Three of the fuses shown are time-delay fuses and one is a non–time-delay fuse. All three time-delay fuse types have similar time-delay characteristics for times greater than one second. For times less than approximately 0.2 seconds, the 400-ampere Class RK5 fuse has a longer clearing time than the other fuses. For times less than 0.2 seconds, the Class J time-delay fuse has the most advantageous time-current characteristic of all the time-delay fuses. The Class J non–time-delay fuse provides significantly faster clearing times for low-level overcurrents (long-time region) compared to the other fuses.

Non–Current-Limiting Fuses

Non–current-limiting fuses are used much less frequently than the current-limiting type. The ampere rating range is 1 to 600 amperes with voltage ratings of 250 and 600 volts. These fuses only have an interrupting rating of 10 kA and therefore are not permitted on high fault current applications. Because of their lower interrupting rating and non–current-limiting characteristics, they are only suitable for applications with low available fault currents. Class RK1 and RK5 fuses can be installed in the Class H fuse clips and are preferred because of their current-limiting ability.

ASSEMBLIES AND OCPDs

There are many different assemblies that Electrical Workers must be familiar with in regards to safe work practices, including panelboards, switchboards, and low-voltage switchgear. One aspect in identifying the type of OCPD in a system is understanding the type of overcurrent protective devices most often used in these assemblies. This is especially true with panelboards. The OCPDs utilized in panelboards are either MCCBs or fuses.

Enclosed Panelboards

An enclosed panelboard is a wall-mounted electrical distribution assembly for use in commercial and industrial applications. It provides circuit control and overcurrent protection for light, heat, or power circuits. The maximum panelboard rating is 1,200 amperes. The configuration can be main lug only or main disconnect/OCPD.

Note: The OCPDs used in panelboards are either molded case circuit breakers or fuses. ICCBs and LVPCBs are not used in panelboards.

OSHA Tip

Work Hazards and Safety Practices in the Electric Power Industry

Workers in the electric power industry are potentially exposed to a variety of serious hazards, such as arc flashes (which include arc flash burn and blast hazards), electric shock, falls, and thermal burn hazards that can cause injury and death. An eTool seeks to inform employers of their obligations to develop the appropriate hazard prevention and control methodologies designed to prevent workplace injuries and illnesses.

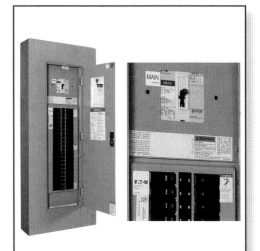

A 240 VAC wall-mounted enclosed panelboard with main MCCB and branch MCCBs is available to 600-ampere main and 100-ampere branches. An enlarged image shows the branch MCCBs.

Courtesy of Eaton

There are two common enclosed panelboard categories:

(1) Lighting and appliance branch-circuit enclosed panelboards typically have ampere ratings of 30, 60, 100, 200, 225, 400, or 600 amperes. There are a variety of enclosed panelboards available based on voltage rating, ampere rating, largest branch-circuit OCPD ampere rating, and MCCB type and interrupting rating, or UL fuse Class.

(2) Power distribution enclosed panelboards are primarily used for power distribution to supply downstream enclosed panelboards and individual branch circuits. Usually this enclosed panelboard type is 400- to 1,200-ampere rated. There are a variety available based on main MCCB or fuse/switches.

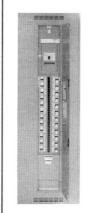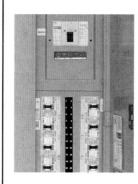

A 480 VAC wall-mounted enclosed panelboard with main MCCB and branch MCCBs is available to 600-ampere main and 125-ampere branches. An enlarged image shows the MCCBs with the handles that, in this case, operate on/off horizontally.

Courtesy of Eaton

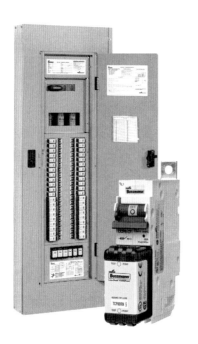

A 600 VAC wall-mounted enclosed panelboard with main fuse/switch and branch fuses/switches is available to 400-ampere main and 100-ampere branches. The enlarged device is the switch with integral finger-safe fuse that plugs into the switch.

Courtesy of Eaton's Bussmann Division

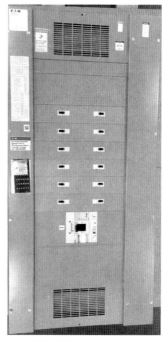

An up to 600 VAC wall-mounted distribution enclosed panelboard is available in ampere ratings up to 1,200-ampere main or main lug only (MLO) and 1,200-ampere branches. This panelboard utilizes MCCBs, evidenced by the MCCB handle mechanisms.

Courtesy of Eaton

Switchboards

A switchboard is a group of sections typically connected with bus structures; however, with a newer style flexible switchboard, the interconnections may be made by insulated conductors. Switchboards are floor mounted, free-standing electrical distribution assemblies for use in commercial and industrial applications. They provide circuit control and overcurrent protection for feeder circuits and occasionally for branch circuits. A switchboard can consist of three section types: incoming, main, and feeder. Not every switchboard utilizes each section type. A variety of devices can be used in switchboards in addition to the OCPDs, including metering, integral panelboard chassis, transformers, automatic transfer switches, lighting control, and uninterruptable power sources (UPS). Access to the interior is usually front only and the structure depth can be from 18 inches minimum to several feet.

Switchboards are available with main OCPDs up to 5,000 amperes and feeder OCPDs up to 4,000 amperes. OCPDs can be MCCBs, ICCBs, fused switches, and occasionally LVPCBs. Most often the circuit breakers are fixed mounted. However, drawout circuit breakers are available for MCCBs, ICCBs, and LVPCBs.

Some switchboard styles have a maximum 4,000-ampere rating and are designed for easy drawout circuit breakers. This switchboard style accommodates drawout MCCBs up to 1,200 amperes and drawout ICCBs up to 2,000 amperes. This particular switchboard is front accessible and has ICCB main in the bottom of the left section and MCCBs in the two feeder sections.

Courtesy of Eaton

Some switchboard sections may have up to four ICCBs.

Courtesy of Eaton

An integrated facility system switchboard can integrate a host of devices into a compact 18-inch deep switchboard. The devices in this switchboard include a transformer, multiple 480/277 volt panelboard chassis, multiple 208/120 volt panelboard chassis (shown enlarged), and individual MCCB feeders and branch circuits. The internal connections are made by insulated conductors rather than busway.

Courtesy of Eaton

Fusible switch switchboards use fuses as OCPDs. Notice the switch handles as the identifying key to being fusible equipment.

Courtesy of Eaton

Low-Voltage Switchgear

Low-voltage (LV) switchgear is also typically a group of sections connected with a bus structure; however, these assemblies differ in several ways. LV switchgear is a floor-mounted, free-standing electrical distribution assembly for use in commercial and industrial applications. It also provides circuit control and overcurrent protection for feeder circuits and occasionally branch circuits.

LV switchgear provides front access and rear access and has a minimum depth of 54 inches unless it has front access, in which case the minimum depth is 40 inches. Compartment barriers are standard. These assemblies have a 30-cycle short-circuit current withstand for the bus structure, and therefore LVPCBs with up to a 30-cycle short-time delay can be utilized to provide protection for this assembly.

LV switchgear is available with main LVPCBs up to 6,000 amperes. Most often, drawout LVPCBs are the OCPDs used for the mains and feeders in LV switchgear, and they can be used with a short-time delay up to 30 cycles and no instantaneous trip. However, LV switchgear can also be constructed with integrated switchboards, which means MCCBs, ICCBs, and fusible switches can be part of these assemblies.

Workers may use racking devices to work on a feeder LVPCB in switchgear.
Courtesy of Eaton

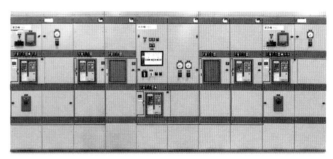

LV switchgear assemblies may include LVPCBs, metering, instrumentation, and controls.
Courtesy of Eaton

Low voltage switchgear assemblies may include a main section containing main LVPCB, metering, and instrumentation, and feeder sections containing feeder LVPCBs.
Courtesy of Eaton

Low voltage 2B arc-resistant switchgear assemblies may include LVPCBs, metering, instrumentation, and controls. If the switchgear incurs an arcing fault condition, the arcing byproducts and pressure are vented via the ductwork at the top of the switchgear.
Courtesy of Eaton

SUMMARY

Identifying OCPDs and associated typical fault current clearing times may be necessary when using the arc flash PPE category method to determine arc flash PPE. MCCBs are distinguished by having an over-the-center, toggle on/off handle. ICCBs and LVPCBs utilize on and off push buttons as well as a pumping handle to charge a stored energy system to power the on/off operation. The assembly may also be a clue as to what type of OCPDs are installed. Panelboards only utilize MCCBs and fuses, while switchgear usually utilizes LVPCBs and switchboards typically use MCCBs, ICCBs, or fuses.

1. The overcurrent protective devices used in panelboards are either __?__ or __?__ .
   a. ICCBs / LVPCBs
   b. MCCBs / fuses
   c. MCCBs / ICCBs
   d. MCCBs / LVPCBs

2. The maximum ampere rating at which panelboards are available is __?__ .
   a. 1,200 A
   b. 2,500 A
   c. 4,000 A
   d. 6,000 A

3. Which is not one of the three common types of circuit breakers that are used in low-voltage electrical distribution systems for protection of services, feeders, or branch circuits?
   a. ICCB
   b. LVPCB
   c. MCCB
   d. Supplementary protector

4. What type of circuit breaker has a mechanical over-the-center on/off toggle handle?
   a. ICCB
   b. LVPCB
   c. MCCB

5. What type(s) of circuit breaker has a mechanically-operated and electrically-operated two-step stored energy process to operate the on/off function via push buttons?
   a. ICCB
   b. ICCB and LVPC
   c. LVPCB
   d. MCCB
   e. MCCB and ICCB

6. The typical fault clearing time for an MCCB in Informational Note to Table 130.7(C)(15)(a) is three cycles.
   a. True   b. False

7. The typical fault clearing time for an ICCB in Informational Note to Table 130.7(C)(15)(a) is 1.5 cycles.
   a. True   b. False

8. The typical fault clearing time for a current-limiting fuse in Informational Note to Table 130.7(C)(15)(a) is $1/2$ cycle.
   a. True   b. False

9. If a circuit breaker has a handle that can be operated in a pumping action and the open/close functions are performed by push buttons on the face of the circuit breaker, the circuit breaker is __?__ .
   a. an ICCB or LVPCB
   b. an MCCB
   c. an MCP
   d. not a circuit breaker, but actually a switch

10. ICCBs are the most common type of circuit breakers used in circuit breaker panelboards.
    a. True   b. False

Methods to Select Arc Flash PPE

Chapter 6, "Work Involving Electrical Hazards," covered the requirements of *NFPA 70E* Section 130.5, Arc Flash Risk Assessment. It is also important to be familiar with the methods to determine the arc flash boundary and arc flash PPE when additional protective measures are required and include the use of PPE.

Previously discussed material should be understood and reviewed as necessary to comprehend and apply these methods, including calculating available fault current, identifying overcurrent protective devices (OCPDs), and determining typical OCPD clearing times.

Objectives

» Understand how to determine if the parameters are satisfied when the arc flash PPE category method is used.

» Explain the requirements, concepts, and steps when the incident energy analysis method is used.

» Know how assessing the "condition of maintenance" applies when determining an arc flash boundary and arc flash PPE.

Chapter 9

Table of Contents

Case Study

An electrician died as a result of burns he received while he was making a connection on a circuit breaker. The victim worked for an electrical contractor that employed 130 people. Safety functions were assigned to the firm's two project managers as an additional duty. The firm had no written safety policy or established safety program, and only on-the-job training was provided. The managers met with the foremen monthly to discuss safety issues.

On the day of the accident, the victim and his helper were to install three new circuit breakers into a panelboard that supplied power to various parts of an industrial complex. Three additional circuit breakers had previously been installed; they supplied power to the occupied portion of the building. The circuit breakers to be installed on the day of the accident were expected to control systems in the unoccupied portion of the building.

Before beginning the job, the victim was instructed by the foreman to install the top breaker first and the bottom breaker last. Although the victim had worked for the firm for only four days, he had approximately 16 years of experience as an Electrical Worker.

The victim did not follow the foreman's instructions. He secured the three breakers in the panelboard, and began to wire the bottom breaker first. The wires to be connected to the breakers were fed through a conduit in the bottom of the panelboard. The wires then had to be fed to the upper portion to make the connections. The line side of the bottom breaker became energized once the connections were completed. The victim then began to make the connections on the middle breaker without replacing the cover on the bottom breaker. He started to feed the wires for the middle breaker through the panelboard. He successfully fed four of the six wires to the upper portion. As the fifth wire was being fed upward, its uninsulated tip contacted one of the exposed energized connection points. The contact caused an arc, and the bottom breaker exploded. The victim was standing immediately in front of the breaker. His clothes caught fire and he received massive burns to the upper portion of his body.

When the helper heard the explosion, he ran away. As he was running, a second explosion occurred. The helper received second- and third-degree burns to his left shoulder and back, and to the back of his left arm.

The foreman was headed towards the room when he heard the explosions. He found the victim lying on the floor with his clothes on fire. He pulled the victim outside the room and extinguished the flames with his hands, receiving second- and third-degree burns in the process. The victim was conscious and talking at this time. The victim received burns to 80% of his body. Emergency rescue transported the victim to the hospital. He was later transferred to a burn center, where he died the following morning. The cause of death was attributed to massive burns to the victim's upper body.

Source: For details of this case, see FACE 8644. Accessed April 30, 2020.

For additional information, visit qr.njatcdb.org Item #1198

PRELIMINARY INFORMATION

"Protecting-OCPD" and "condition of maintenance" will first be discussed.

Protecting-OCPD

The arc flash hazard created during an arc flash event is directly dependent on the OCPD that is protecting the downstream equipment, or the "protecting-OCPD." (The phrase "protecting-OCPD" is not used in *NFPA 70E*.) The protecting-OCPD is in many cases in a separate enclosure from the equipment it is protecting. **See Figure 9-1.**

Condition of Maintenance

Requirements for considering the "condition of maintenance" for electrical equipment and systems are found in both *NFPA 70E* Chapter 1, *Safety-Related Work Practices*, and Chapter 2, *Safety-Related Maintenance Requirements*. See Chapter 10 of this textbook, "Maintenance Considerations," for more information on maintenance and *NFPA 70E* maintenance requirements.

When conducting an arc flash risk assessment in accordance with 130.5, the "condition of maintenance" may affect the assessment results in at least two ways as outlined in 130.5(B).

Protecting-OCPD Condition of Maintenance

Informational Note No. 2 located after Table 130.5(C) provides the rationale: improper or inadequate maintenance may result in the protecting-OCPD taking longer to clear the fault current than its specified published clearing time. As a consequence, an actual arc flash incident may release significantly greater thermal energy than that determined by an incident energy analysis.

Consider, for example, an 800-ampere protecting-OCPD that has a published clearing time of six cycles (0.1 second) for the calculated arcing fault current. **See Figure 9-2.** The arc flash boundary and incident energy values shown were calculated using the published six-cycle clearing time for the protecting-OCPD. However, if the protecting-OCPD has not been properly maintained, it may take longer to interrupt the arcing fault current. If, for example, the OCPD takes 30 cycles to clear the arcing fault current due to poor maintenance, then the actual arc flash boundary and incident energy will be greater than that determined previously. This scenario illustrates one reason why maintenance of OCPDs is so important.

What if the condition of maintenance for a protecting-OCPD is questionable or known to be inadequate? While *NFPA 70E* 130.5(B) directs, in part, to "take into consideration" the condition of maintenance, *NFPA 70E* does not provide specific actions to take if the protecting-OCPD is maintained inadequately or improperly. However, the risk assessment procedure requirements in 110.5(H)(3) that must be part of an electrical safety program and the guidance provided in Informative Annex F, *Risk Assessment Procedure*, are among the *70E* provisions that provide some insight into how to take OCPD maintenance into consideration. See also 110.5(C) and Informational Note No. 1 to 110.5(A) for additional insight.

Figure 9-1 Protecting-OCPD

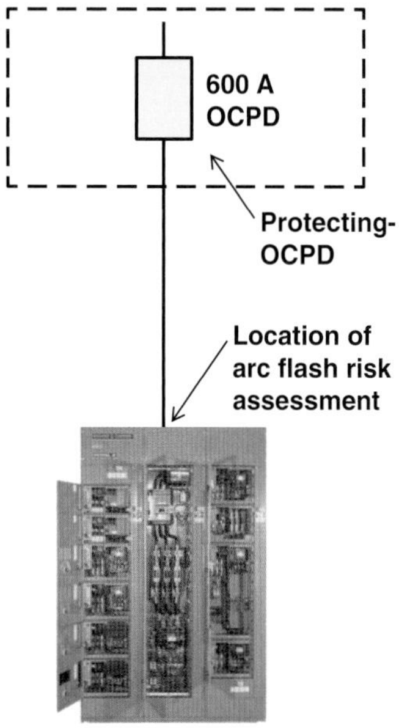

600 A
OCPD

Protecting-OCPD

Location of arc flash risk assessment

Figure 9-1. *The protecting-OCPD may be located in a separate enclosure from the equipment it is protecting.*

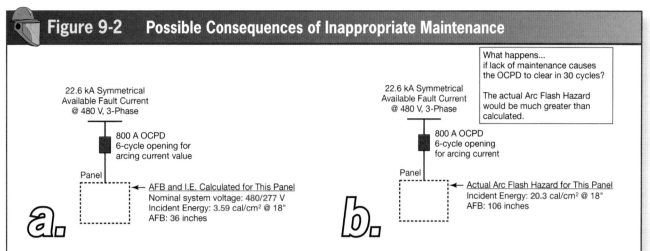

Figure 9-2   Possible Consequences of Inappropriate Maintenance

22.6 kA Symmetrical
Available Fault Current
@ 480 V, 3-Phase

800 A OCPD
6-cycle opening for
arcing current value

Panel

← AFB and I.E. Calculated for This Panel
Nominal system voltage: 480/277 V
Incident Energy: 3.59 cal/cm² @ 18"
AFB: 36 inches

a.

What happens...
if lack of maintenance causes
the OCPD to clear in 30 cycles?

The actual Arc Flash Hazard
would be much greater than
calculated.

22.6 kA Symmetrical
Available Fault Current
@ 480 V, 3-Phase

800 A OCPD
6-cycle opening
for arcing current

Panel

← Actual Arc Flash Hazard for This Panel
Incident Energy: 20.3 cal/cm² @ 18"
AFB: 106 inches

b.

Figure 9-2. (a.) Assuming the OCPD has been maintained and operates as specified by manufacturer's performance data, the incident energy would be 3.59 cal/cm² at 18 inches and the arc flash boundary is 36 inches. (b.) If lack of maintenance causes the OCPD to clear in 30 cycles rather than in six cycles, the actual incident energy is 20.3 cal/cm² at 18 inches, and the arc flash boundary would be 106 inches. (The arc flash boundaries and incident energies were determined using IEEE 1584-2018 equations.) Note that the incident energy values calculated are based on a panelboard enclosure with VCB bus configuration and an enclosure size of 12 inches wide by 14 inches tall by 10 inches deep.

If the original objective was to perform justified energized work, it may be advisable to further investigate the risk assessment procedure per 110.5(H), including the hierarchy of risk control methods in 110.5(H)(3); review the job safety plan per 110.5(I)(1); and establish an electrically safe work condition rather than work on the equipment energized. However, the Electrical Worker still has to interface with the equipment to check for the absence of voltage in the process of putting the equipment in an electrically safe work condition. If the task is to open a large ampere rated disconnect or rackout a circuit breaker, using a remote operator or remote racking device or utilizing an upstream disconnecting means that has been properly maintained may be among the approaches to consider.

When the protecting-OCPD condition of maintenance is unacceptable, other scenarios may need to be explored. For example, a maintenance manager for a large automotive industrial facility may have a policy to investigate upstream OCPDs to locate the next upstream OCPD device which has a suitable condition of maintenance and use that device to determine the arc flash boundary (AFB) and arc rated PPE. However, the values determined further upstream will most likely be greater than those for a properly maintained OCPD further downstream.

Professional service companies that routinely perform incident energy analysis and equipment labeling for facilities generally have disclaimers that the calculation results are based on OCPDs performing to their published time-current characteristics. Some of these professional service companies will not use a particular OCPD in their calculations if it is obvious the OCPD has not been properly maintained or if an old technology is problematic, such as a circuit breaker that utilizes oil dashpot overcurrent sensing technology.

Equipment Condition of Maintenance
In general, maintenance of all electrical equipment that may be worked on when not in an electrically safe work condition is important for electrical safety. Recall that it is required to be considered as part of an electrical safety program per 110.5(C) and taken into consideration in 130.5(B)(2).

Equipment manufacturers' maintenance manuals and industry consensus standards such as *NFPA 70B: Recommended Practice for Electrical Equipment Maintenance* are among the resources available for equipment maintenance guidelines. Note that *NFPA 70B* is currently under revision with the goal of becoming a standard rather than a recommended practice.

METHODS TO DETERMINE AFB AND ARC FLASH PPE

NFPA 70E 130.5(F) has two methods for determining the arc flash PPE:
(1) the arc flash PPE category method in accordance with 130.7(C)(15)
(2) the incident energy analysis method in accordance with 130.5(G)

Arc Flash PPE Category Method

The arc flash PPE category method can be used to determine the AFB and the selection of arc flash PPE if specific conditions and parameters are met. Among the applicable *NFPA 70E* sections and tables are 130.5(C), 130.5(E)(2), 130.5(F)(2), 130.7(C)(15), Table 130.7(C)(15)(a) for AC systems, 130.7(C)(15)(b) for DC systems, and Table 130.7(C)(15)(c).

The requirements in 130.7(C)(15)(a) stipulate when the arc flash PPE category method is permitted to be used for AC systems. The conditions of use are:
1. The estimated available fault current at the equipment to be worked on must be equal to or less than the maximum available fault current value shown in Table 130.7(C)(15)(a) under the parameters for the type of equipment and voltage level.
2. The fault clearing time must be equal to or less than the maximum fault clearing time value in Table 130.7(C)(15)(a) under the "parameters" for the type of equipment and voltage.
3. The working distance must not be less than that shown in Table 130.7(C)(15)(a) under the parameters for the type of equipment and voltage level.

Refer to Section 130.7(C)(15)(a)(1), (2), and (3) for these requirements in their entirety.

Consider the following examples using the arc flash PPE category method and determine whether the situation under consideration complies with the arc flash PPE category parameters in Table 130.7(C)(15)(a).

Example 1
This example goes through the arc flash PPE category method steps in a general manner.

Assume the task is testing for the absence of voltage on a 400-ampere main lug only (MLO), 480-volt AC panelboard during the lockout/tagout process. The protecting-OPCD for this 400-ampere panelboard is a 400-ampere molded case circuit breaker (MCCB) installed in an upstream 1,200-ampere panelboard.

Referencing Table 130.5(C), there is a likelihood of an arc flash incident for the task of voltage testing. Therefore, per the note to this table, "Yes" means, in part, that "additional protective measures are required to be selected and implemented according to the hierarchy of risk control identified in 110.5(H)(3)." Also, see 130.5(C) addressing "when the additional protective measures include the use of PPE." When the additional protective measures include the use of PPE, the AFB and arc flash PPE required within the AFB must be determined.

For a 480-volt panelboard in Table 130.7(C)(15)(a), the parameters that must be satisfied to use this arc flash PPE category method are:
1. Maximum of 25 kA available fault current
2. Maximum of 0.03 second (2 cycles) fault clearing time
3. Working distance of 18 inches

The 400-ampere panelboard application under consideration has:
1. An estimated available fault current of 25 kA or less
2. A protecting-OCPD estimated clearing time of 0.03 second (2 cycles) or less

3. A working distance for this task of 18 inches or more

All three of the parameter conditions for this application in Table 130.7(C)(15)(a) are satisfied, so the arc flash PPE category method can be used. If all three parameters are not met, then the incident energy analysis must be used.

As all three of the parameters are met, the next step is to refer to Table 130.7(C)(15)(a) and note the number "2" in the *Arc Flash PPE Category* column and "3 feet" in the *Arc Flash Boundary* column for this example.

Then proceed to Table 130.7(C)(15)(c) for the selection of personal protective equipment for arc flash PPE category 2 (applicable for this example).

Recall that the AFB and the arc flash PPE category are required to be on the equipment label per 130.5(H)(2) and (3) and on the energized electrical work permit per 130.2(B)(6). In addition, the results of the arc flash risk assessment must be documented per 130.5(D). See also 130.5(H) (second-to-last paragraph), which requires doc-

umenting the calculation method and the data used to support the information that is put on the label.

As discussed earlier, if the Table 130.7(C)(15)(a) parameters are not met for a particular situation, then the arc flash PPE category method cannot be used. Instead, the incident energy analysis method would have to be used.

The following additional examples illustrate how some in the industry determine if a specific application adheres to the parameter values in Table 130.7(C)(15)(a) when using the arc flash PPE category method. There likely are other methods used in the industry to evaluate whether the parameter values are satisfied.

Example 2

Consider a situation where an Electrical Worker must perform diagnostics and testing that can only be performed with the circuit energized on a 400-ampere panelboard. **See Figure 9-3.** In this example, the objective is to determine if the estimated available fault

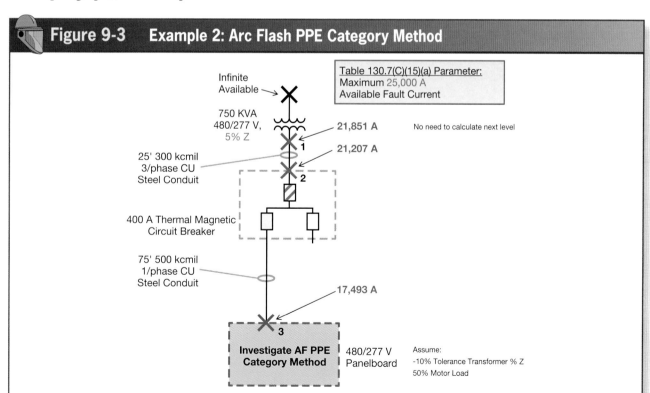

Figure 9-3   Example 2: Arc Flash PPE Category Method

Infinite Available

Table 130.7(C)(15)(a) Parameter:
Maximum 25,000 A
Available Fault Current

750 KVA
480/277 V,
5% Z

21,851 A — No need to calculate next level

1

21,207 A

25' 300 kcmil
3/phase CU
Steel Conduit

2

400 A Thermal Magnetic
Circuit Breaker

75' 500 kcmil
1/phase CU
Steel Conduit

17,493 A

3

Investigate AF PPE Category Method

480/277 V Panelboard

Assume:
-10% Tolerance Transformer % Z
50% Motor Load

Figure 9-3. Use the single-line diagram and given assumptions to determine whether the estimated available fault current parameter is satisfied for the arc flash PPE category method in Example 2.

current X_3 at the panelboard satisfies the parameter value in Table 130.7(C)(15)(a), which is 25,000 amperes or less, for this application.

A means to determine this is to do fault current calculations starting at the secondary of the transformer X_1. Since the panelboard is at the same voltage level as the secondary of this transformer, if X_1 or X_2 is 25,000 amperes or less, no more calculations are necessary; this parameter value is satisfied. The reason is that the further into an electrical system that a fault occurs, the additional length of conductors results in more impedance and less fault current. Therefore, if X_1 is calculated to be 25,000 amperes or less, X_3 will be less than 25,000 amperes.

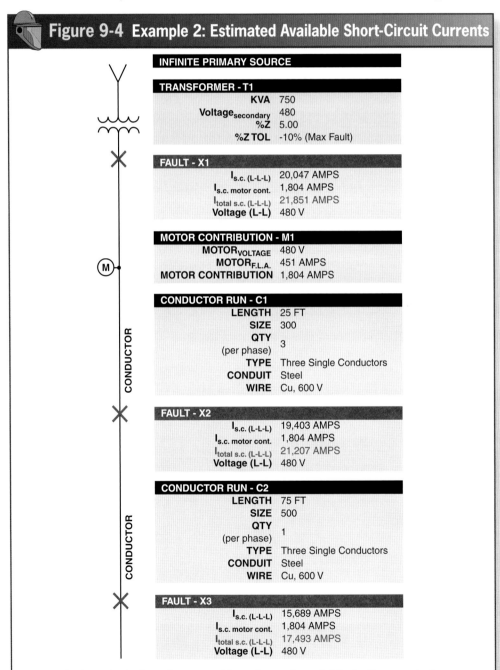

Figure 9-4 Example 2: Estimated Available Short-Circuit Currents

INFINITE PRIMARY SOURCE

TRANSFORMER - T1	
KVA	750
Voltage_{secondary}	480
%Z	5.00
%Z TOL	-10% (Max Fault)

FAULT - X1	
$I_{s.c. (L-L-L)}$	20,047 AMPS
$I_{s.c. motor cont.}$	1,804 AMPS
$I_{total s.c. (L-L-L)}$	21,851 AMPS
Voltage (L-L)	480 V

MOTOR CONTRIBUTION - M1	
MOTOR_{VOLTAGE}	480 V
MOTOR_{F.L.A.}	451 AMPS
MOTOR CONTRIBUTION	1,804 AMPS

CONDUCTOR RUN - C1	
LENGTH	25 FT
SIZE	300
QTY (per phase)	3
TYPE	Three Single Conductors
CONDUIT	Steel
WIRE	Cu, 600 V

FAULT - X2	
$I_{s.c. (L-L-L)}$	19,403 AMPS
$I_{s.c. motor cont.}$	1,804 AMPS
$I_{total s.c. (L-L-L)}$	21,207 AMPS
Voltage (L-L)	480 V

CONDUCTOR RUN - C2	
LENGTH	75 FT
SIZE	500
QTY (per phase)	1
TYPE	Three Single Conductors
CONDUIT	Steel
WIRE	Cu, 600 V

FAULT - X3	
$I_{s.c. (L-L-L)}$	15,689 AMPS
$I_{s.c. motor cont.}$	1,804 AMPS
$I_{total s.c. (L-L-L)}$	17,493 AMPS
Voltage (L-L)	480 V

Figure 9-4. A single-line diagram with estimated available fault currents for Example 2 can be generated by the Bussmann Series FC² Fault Current Calculator.

Courtesy of Eaton's Bussmann Division

Note that the available fault current results were determined using certain assumptions. **See Figure 9-4.** Assumption of -10% tolerance for the transformer percent impedance (%Z) was made, which provides a conservative fault current value. Infinite available fault current was assumed on the transformer primary. This will result in a conservative higher value. Motors are on the 480-volt system and it is assumed approximately 50% of the transformer rating is utilized for motors. When a fault occurs on the 480-volt system, running motors can contribute approximately four times their rated current to the faulted system and therefore need to be added.

To calculate X_3, first X_1 and X_2 must be calculated. The estimated available fault current at X_1 is 21,851 amperes. Since this value is less than the parameter value for this situation, there is no need to calculate X_2 or X_3. The parameter is satisfied for this situation since

any fault current calculation at the same voltage level (e.g. not through a transformer) further into the system, such as at X_2, will be less than at X_1.

Example 3
This example is the same as Example 2 except the transformer has a 3.5% impedance rather than 5%. The objective in this example is to determine if the estimated available fault current at X_3 is equal to or less than the parameter maximum of 25,000 amperes available fault current.

When doing the fault current calculations, it is determined that the estimated available fault currents for X_1 and X_2 exceed the parameter maximum of 25,000 amperes. Therefore, the calculations should not stop at X_1 (or X_2). It is necessary to calculate X_3. In doing so, the calculation for X_3 results in 22,307 amperes estimated available fault current, which is less than the 25,000-ampere parameter value. **See Figure 9-5.**

Figure 9-5   Example 3: Arc Flash PPE Category Method

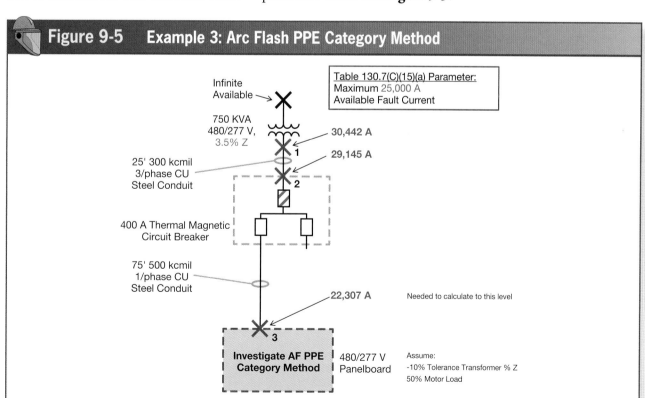

Figure 9-5. *Use the single-line diagram and given assumptions to determine whether the maximum available fault current parameter is satisfied for an arc flash PPE category method in Example 3. The Bussmann Series FC² Fault Current Calculator was used for the calculations.*

Courtesy of Eaton's Bussmann Division

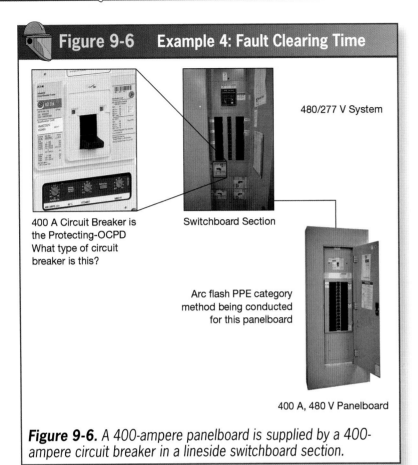

Figure 9-6   Example 4: Fault Clearing Time

400 A Circuit Breaker is the Protecting-OCPD What type of circuit breaker is this?

Switchboard Section

480/277 V System

Arc flash PPE category method being conducted for this panelboard

400 A, 480 V Panelboard

Figure 9-6. A 400-ampere panelboard is supplied by a 400-ampere circuit breaker in a lineside switchboard section.

could be done which results in a value of 25,000 amperes or less. For example, if the available fault current on the primary of the transformer could be determined, the fault current calculations could be done with this value used rather than an infinite available fault current.

Example 4

Consider a situation where an Electrical Worker must perform diagnostics and testing that can only be performed with the circuit energized on a 400-ampere panelboard. **See Figure 9-6.** In this example, the objective is to determine if the 400-ampere protecting-OCPD's estimated clearing time satisfies the maximum fault clearing time parameter value in Table 130.7(C)(15)(a). For this application of a panelboard at 480 volts, this parameter in Table 130.7(C)(15)(a) is a maximum of 0.03 second.

NFPA 70E does not contain requirements on how to determine the protecting-OCPD fault clearing time when conducting an arc flash risk assessment. The chapter titled "Identifying OCPD Types" provides some insight into different types of OCPDs and typical fault clearing times. *NFPA 70E* provides some guidance in an Informational Note to 130.7(C)(15)(a):

However, if the X_3 fault current calculation was greater than 25,000 amperes, the arc flash PPE category method cannot be used for this situation, unless a more accurate calculation

Informational Note No. 1 to Table 130.7(C)(15)(a): The following are typical fault clearing times of overcurrent protective devices:

(1) 0.5 cycle fault clearing time is typical for current limiting fuses and current-limiting molded case circuit breakers when the fault current is within the current limiting range.

(2) 1.5 cycle fault clearing time is typical for molded case circuit breakers rated less than 1000 volts with an instantaneous integral trip.

(3) 3.0 cycle fault clearing time is typical for insulated case circuit breakers rated less than 1000 volts with an instantaneous integral trip or relay operated trip.

(4) 5.0 cycle fault clearing time is typical for relay operated circuit breakers rated 1 kV to 35 kV when the relay operates in the instantaneous range (i.e., "no intentional delay").

(5) 20 cycle fault clearing time is typical for low-voltage power and insulated case circuit breakers with a short time fault clearing delay for motor inrush.

(6) 30 cycle fault clearing time is typical for low-voltage power and insulated case circuit breakers with a short time fault clearing delay without instantaneous trip.

In this example, the type of OCPD used as the protecting-OPCD for the 400-ampere panelboard must be determined. The expanded view of the protecting-OCPD clearly shows that it is a molded case circuit breaker (MCCB), which is shown having a typical clearing time of 1.5 cycles (0.025 second) in the *NFPA 70E* Informational Note No. 1 to Table 130.7(C)(15)(a). (The 400-ampere circuit breaker can be identified as an MCCB by the mechanical on/off toggle handle, used to manually control the open/close operation, that all molded case circuit breakers have, but insulated case circuit breakers (ICCBs) and low-voltage power circuit breakers (LVPCBs) do not have.) This is the method some use to determine if the 400-ampere protecting-OCPD's estimated clearing time satisfies the maximum fault clearing time parameter. Using this method in this example, the parameter value is considered satisfied.

Example 5
An 800-ampere panelboard is supplied by an 800-ampere circuit breaker in the line-side switchgear assembly. **See**

Figure 9-7. Consider an example where an Electrical Worker must work in the 800-ampere panelboard when it is not in an electrically safe work condition. In this example, the objective is to determine if the 800-ampere protecting-OCPD's estimated clearing time satisfies the parameter value. The parameter in Table 130.7(C)(15)(a) for a 480-volt panelboard is a maximum of 0.03-second fault clearing time.

The first thing to do is identify what type of circuit breaker the 800-ampere protecting-OCPD is. The expanded view of the 800-ampere circuit breaker shows that there is not a mechanical on/off toggle handle to control the open/close operations that all molded case circuit breakers have. Instead, this 800-ampere circuit breaker has green and red on/off buttons that electrically operate the circuit breaker's open/close function. These types of circuit breakers have a two-step stored energy system for this open/close system. The other indication that it is not an MCCB is the handle that can be pumped to charge the springs of the two-step stored energy system for the

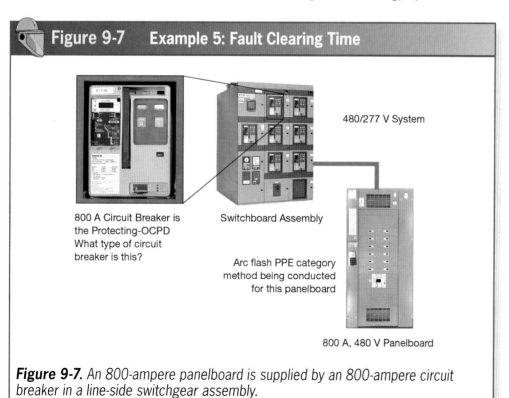

Figure 9-7   Example 5: Fault Clearing Time

480/277 V System

800 A Circuit Breaker is the Protecting-OCPD What type of circuit breaker is this?

Switchboard Assembly

Arc flash PPE category method being conducted for this panelboard

800 A, 480 V Panelboard

Figure 9-7. An 800-ampere panelboard is supplied by an 800-ampere circuit breaker in a line-side switchgear assembly.

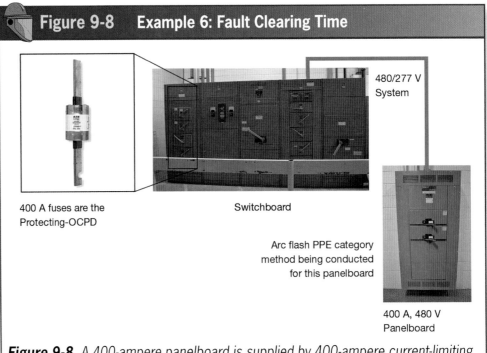

Figure 9-8   Example 6: Fault Clearing Time

400 A fuses are the Protecting-OCPD

Switchboard

480/277 V System

Arc flash PPE category method being conducted for this panelboard

400 A, 480 V Panelboard

Figure 9-8. A 400-ampere panelboard is supplied by 400-ampere current-limiting fuses in a line-side switchboard.

open/close function. This 800-ampere circuit breaker is either an insulated case circuit breaker (ICCB) or a low-voltage power circuit breaker (LVPCB). The label states that it is "Insulated Case."

The typical opening time in Informational Note No. 1 to Table 130.7(C)(15)(a) for an ICCB is 3 cycles or 0.05 second, which is greater than the parameter 0.03-second value. Therefore, based on this informational note, the arc flash PPE category method cannot be used to determine the arc flash PPE required in this case. The incident energy analysis method must be used.

Example 6
A 400-ampere panelboard is supplied by 400-ampere current-limiting fuses in the line-side switchboard. **See Figure 9-8.** Consider an example where Electrical Workers must work in the 400-ampere panelboard when it is not in an electrically safe work condition. In this example, the objective is to determine if the 400-ampere protecting-OCPD's estimated clearing time satisfies the parameter value. The parameter

in Table 130.7(C)(15)(a) for a 480-volt panelboard is a maximum of 0.03-second fault clearing time.

In the *NFPA 70E* Informational Note No. 1 to Table 130.7(C)(15)(a), current-limiting fuses typically have a fault clearing time of 0.5 cycles (0.008 second). This is the method some use to determine if the 400-ampere protecting-OCPD's estimated clearing time satisfies the maximum fault clearing time parameter. Using this method, the parameter value in this example is considered satisfied.

AFB AND INCIDENT ENERGY CALCULATION METHODS

NFPA 70E 130.5(E)(1) and 130.5(G) mandatory text does not provide the AFB or incident energy equations to calculate the AFB or incident energy. Among the most commonly used calculation methods are located in *NFPA 70E* Informative Annex D, *Incident Energy and Arc Flash Boundary Calculation Methods*, which is provided for informational purposes only (non-mandatory). This Informative Annex contains useful

Identifying whether a circuit breaker is an MCCB rather than an ICCB or LVPCB can be straightforward with proper training. Identifying whether a circuit breaker is an ICCB or an LVPCB is more difficult and has potential negative consequences if the circuit breaker is misidentified and overcurrent protection settings are misinterpreted. For example, it may be difficult for an Electrical Worker to distinguish an ICCB from an LVPCB. Other examples include where LVPCBs may be installed without having an instantaneous trip function or where the instantaneous trip may be set to "off." In these cases, the LVPCB may be set to hold off interrupting faults for 30 cycles (0.5 seconds). A person knowledgeable in OCPD identification is always necessary. This is even more challenging for LVPCBs and ICCBs where an additional level of complexity is involved to ensure the time-current characteristics and settings are interpreted correctly.

information and references for these various calculation methods. The limitations/parameters for each of these calculation methods can be reviewed in *NFPA 70E* Informative Annex D, Table D.1 and in the Informative Annex text.

IEEE 1584 Incident Energy and AFB Calculation Methods and Tools

The 2018 *IEEE 1584, Guide for Performing Arc-Flash Hazard Calculations,* is currently the most up-to-date and widely-used industry consensus standard on this topic for systems up to 15 kilovolts, especially for work involving enclosed electrical equipment that requires arc-in-the-box calculations. It is based on extensive arc fault testing and analysis.

The 2018 *IEEE 1584* is based on extensive testing and analysis to develop equations to calculate the AFB, arcing current, and incident energy. Because it is the most up-to-date method with the widest range of system characteristics and variables, it is considered by many to be the preferred calculation method.

Refer to *NFPA 70E* Informative Annex D, D.4.4 for applicable system limitations for the *IEEE 1584* basic equations methods. In summary, *IEEE 1584* is applicable to:
- 3-phase systems
- 208 volts through 15 kV (theoretical equation above 15 kV)

- Available fault currents between 700 and 106,000 amperes
- Conductor gaps 13 millimeters through 152 millimeters
- Arcs-in-open-air or arcs-in-a-box: the 2018 *IEEE 1584* includes three broad methods that can be referred to as basic equations, simplified fuse equations, and simplified circuit breaker equations, respectively. **See Figure 9-9.** In addition, equations for these methods have been incorporated into spreadsheets, programs, and commercial power system analysis packages resulting in simpler and quicker analysis results.

For persons responsible for the calculations and for the workers relying on the calculated results to implement safe work practices and wear proper levels of arc rated PPE, it is important to understand that this is not an exact science. There are many variables involved as well as dynamic, unpredictable behavior with arcing fault current. Even with the *IEEE 1584* testing, which was done under controlled and specific staged conditions, there are variations in the results. The exact same test run a few minutes later may have produced variations in the incident energy results. The equations provided as part of *IEEE 1584* present the worst-case incident energy and AFB based on any given set of parameters. In the process of performing the incident energy analysis, the objective is to model the specific conditions and parameters of the actual circuit and equipment and then use the available *IEEE 1584* equations with the applicable available variables to get the closest match.

Figure 9-9 *IEEE 1584* Arc Flash Boundary and Incident Energy Method Comparison

2018 IEEE 1584 Method	Brief Description (Key Differentiating Points)	Comments

Basic Equations	• Based on testing
	• Ability to change many variables
	• For any overcurrent protective device
	• Process:
	  1. Determine the available (bolted) fault current
	  2. Use the *IEEE 1584* arcing current equations to determine the minimum and maximum arcing currents
	  3. Using OCPD time-current characteristics, determining the OCPD clearing times for both the minimum and maximum arcing current
	  4. Use *IEEE 1584* AFB and incident energy basic equations to calculate AFB and incident energy at specified working distance for both established minimum and maximum arcing fault currents and their associated clearing times; select the worst case of the two results
		• If doing manual calculations, this is the more tedious method. Software applications are almost a necessity to ensure proper calculations.
		• This method is suggested for specific circuit breakers if time-current curves are available.
		• This method is suggested for fuses when the simplified fuse equations are not applicable.

Simplified Fuse Equations	• Equations based on testing
	• For specific types of current-limiting fuses or fuses that open in times equal to or faster than the fuse types used for *IEEE 1584* testing
	• Process:
	  1. Determine the available (bolted) fault current and fuse type/ampere rating
	  2. Use *IEEE 1584* simplified fuse equations for the specific fuse ampere rating to calculate the AFB and incident energy at 18 inches working distance (Tables available)
		• This method is suggested if the fuse type is one that is applicable to this method.
		• Easy method: Eaton's Bussmann Division provides simple published tables.
		• Fuse time-current curve is not needed.
		• No need to determine the arcing current, because the equations are based on actual arcing fault tests.

Simplified Circuit Breaker Equations	• Equations based on testing and analysis
	• For generalized circuit breakers based on type, ampere rating, trip unit type, and maximum settings
	• Process:
	  1. Determine the available (bolted) fault current
	  2. Verify that the available fault current does not exceed the circuit breaker's interrupting rating
	  3. Verify using the *IEEE 1584* simplified circuit breaker equations that the available fault current is high enough to generate an arcing fault current sufficient to cause circuit breaker instantaneous tripping or short-time delay tripping (if the circuit breaker has no instantaneous trip)
	  4. From the *IEEE 1584* simple circuit breaker method table, select and use the appropriate AFB and incident energy (at 18 inches working distance) simplified circuit breaker equations based on circuit breaker ampere rating, type, and trip unit type
		• Easier than the basic equation method.
		• Generalized for all circuit breaker manufacturers – not manufacturer-specific.
		• No need to determine the arcing current.
		• Requires qualifying calculations: available fault current must be within the range of use for circuit breaker settings and interrupting ratings.

Figure 9-9. The IEEE 1584 arc flash boundary and incident energy method comparison table gives a high-level overview of the three methods and the process steps.

IEEE 1584 Basic Equations Method Example

Example 7

Use the *IEEE 1584* basic equation method to calculate the AFB (130.5(E)) and incident energy (130.5(G)) for a potential arcing fault in the panelboard. **See Figure 9-10.** Each step may reference the specific equation(s) used in *NFPA 70E* Informative Annex D and mention the variable values for the equations that are used.

Step 1. Calculate the available (bolted) fault current.

The single-line diagram shows potentially several different scenarios, and calculations are typically made for each scenario to determine worst-case conditions. For illustrative purposes, this discussion assumes only one scenario and assumes that the available fault current X_8, at the panelboard, is 14,500 amperes.

Figure 9-10 Example 7: Single-Line Diagram

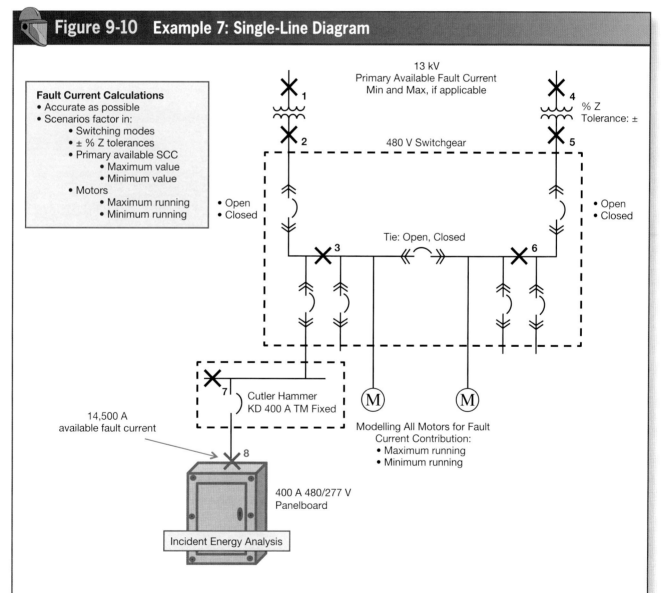

Figure 9-10. The IEEE 1584 equations are used along with the single-line diagram for the electrical system supplying the 400-ampere, 480/277-volt panelboard to determine the AFB and incident energy. This is an analysis that is completed by a software application.

For any of the *IEEE 1584* methods, the thoroughness and accuracy of the data and the fault current calculations are important. This means having an accurate single-line diagram; up-to-date and accurate data of the system components, such as conductor sizes and lengths; full descriptions of each OCPD; and transformer kVA and % impedance. This system has potentially several scenarios in which the available fault current can vary. The process shown here should be performed for each scenario, and then the worst case AFB and incident energy should be chosen for the PPE selection and for the equipment labeling. The chapter "Fundamentals

of 3-Phase Bolted Fault Current" provides information on various scenarios and how to perform a fault current analysis. One professional services company that routinely performs arc flash risk assessment studies for facilities reported running 13 scenarios for a large, complex electrical system.

Step 2. Calculate the minimum and maximum arcing currents.

For a given bolted fault current value, a maximum and minimum arcing current, I_a, can be determined. Parameters that impact the value of arcing current calculations include the

Figure 9-11   Example 7: Determine OCPD Clearing Time

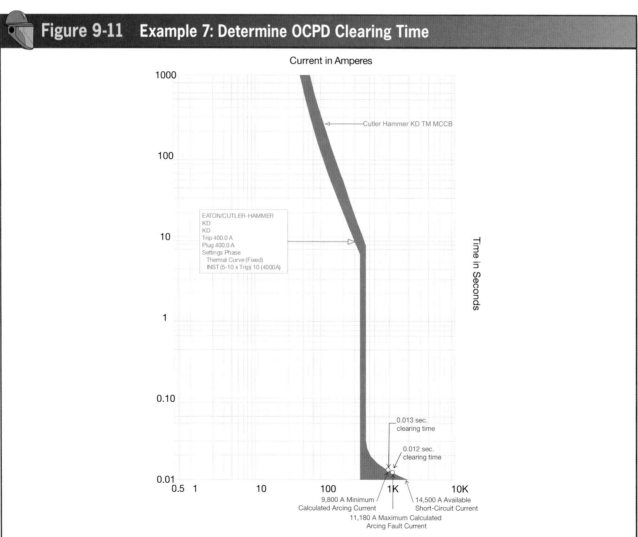

Figure 9-11. *The 400-ampere fixed thermal magnetic molded case circuit breaker clears the 9,800-ampere arcing fault current in 0.013 second and the 11,180 arcing current at 0.012 second.*

voltage, available fault current, conductor gap, and electrode configuration. For this example, the voltage used will be 480 volts, the bolted fault current will be 14,500 amperes, the conductor gap is one inch (25 mm), and the electrode configuration is VCBB. One-inch clearance through the air between phases or phase-to-ground is typical in UL Standards for 600-volt rated panelboards, motor control centers, and similar equipment. 1.5-inch clearance is typical for 600-volt rated switchboards and switchgear.

The minimum and maximum calculated arcing currents are determined as follows:

$$I_{a\,min} = 9,800 \text{ A}$$

$$I_{a\,max} = 11,180 \text{ A}$$

Step 3. Determine the OCPD clearing time at the arcing current value.

Interpreting the time-current curve indicates when this protecting-OCPD clears the arcing fault currents. **See Figure 9-11.**

$I_{a\,min}$ = 9,800 A
  Clearing Time = 0.013 second

$I_{a\,max}$ = 11,180 A
  Clearing Time = 0.012 second

For the IEEE basic equation method, the total or maximum clearing time-current characteristics of the specific protecting-OCPD (manufacturer, type, ampere rating, and setting if applicable) should be used to provide accuracy. The protecting circuit breaker is a 400-ampere, specific type, fixed thermal magnetic molded case circuit breaker. "Fixed" means that its time-current characteristics are non-adjustable.

Step 4. Calculate the incident energy and arc flash boundary (AFB)

The calculated incident energy will be impacted by a few additional parameters, including the size of the enclosure. Width, height, and depth of the enclosure will be considered to properly calculate the energy the Electrical Worker would experience. Testing has shown that smaller enclosures that act to funnel the energy directly out of the enclosure produce higher values of energy than larger enclosures that are less effective at funneling the energy outwards.

For this calculation, the following enclosure size is used: width of 12.0 inches, height of 14 inches, and depth of 10 inches. Any enclosure size larger than this will yield lower incident energy values.

The maximum incident energy based on the above arcing current clearing times will be that of the higher arcing current as both arcing currents have a very close clearing time but a larger difference in current values. The maximum incident energy and arc flash boundary for this example is 0.32 cal/cm^2 and 8 inches, respectively.

Example 8
Lower fault currents can result in higher incident energy. As stated earlier, the *IEEE 1584* basic equation method requires the AFB and incident energy to be calculated at both a maximum and minimum arcing current

value. **See Figure 9-12.**

In this case, the maximum arcing fault current of 4,482 amperes results in the circuit breaker's instantaneous trip to clear in 0.029 second. However, the minimum arcing fault current is below the instantaneous trip region and may take upwards of 11 seconds to clear. The resulting incident energy and AFB is dramatically greater for the minimum arcing current calculation. Assuming a two-second clearing time, the incident energy for this application is 17.2 cal/cm^2 with an arc flash boundary of 95 inches.

Do not assume that higher available short-circuit currents and corresponding higher arcing fault currents mean the AFB and incident energy will be greater. It depends on the protecting-OCPD's time-current characteristics. Some in the electrical industry recommend using high-impedance transformers or installing 1:1 ratio transformers as a means to reduce the available fault current, believing it reduces the arc flash hazard. However, that may not be a good solution in many instances because the fault current may be lower than the circuit breaker's instantaneous pickup current, which results in long interrupting times and higher incident energy for arcing faults. See Informational Note No. 3 located after Table 130.5(C).

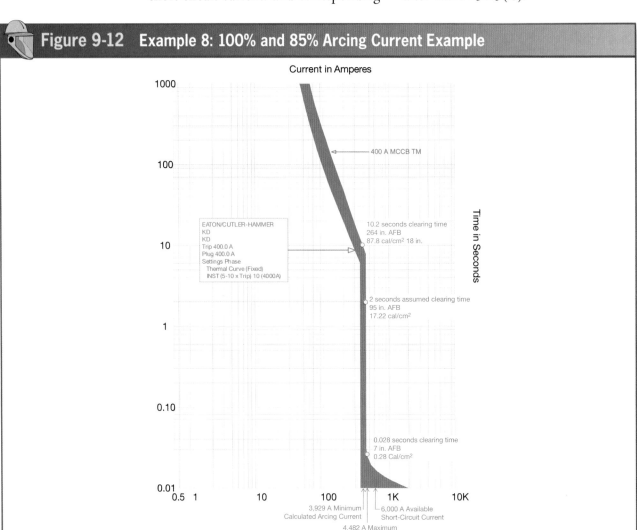

Figure 9-12   Example 8: 100% and 85% Arcing Current Example

Figure 9-12. The IEEE 1584 *basic equation method requires calculation of the AFB and incident energy at both a maximum and a minimum value of arcing fault current. A small change in the arcing fault current near the instantaneous trip pickup setting can result in a dramatic difference in the AFB and the incident energy.*

IEEE 1584 Simplified Equations

The "simplified equations" allow the incident energy and AFB to be calculated directly from the available 3-phase fault current on a low-voltage system if the type and ampere rating of the OCPD are known. These simplified methods do not require the availability of time-current curves for the devices.

IEEE 1584 *Simplified Fuse Equations*

The simplified fuse equations method from *IEEE 1584* is applicable for certain fuse types and for a range of available fault currents. The *IEEE 1584* basic equation method is applicable for the fuses used in the testing to develop these equations or fuses that have equal or faster time-current characteristics. **See Figure 9-13.**

Figure 9-13 Partial Incident Energy Calculator Table

Bussmann Low-Peak™ LPS-RK_SP fuses 1-600 A and Low-Peak KRPC_SP fuse 601-2000 A

Incident Energy (I.E.) values expressed in cal/cm², Arc Flash Boundary (AFB) expressed in inches.

Bolted Fault Current (kA)	1-100 A Fuse		101-200 A Fuse		201-400 A Fuse		401-600 A Fuse		600-800 A Fuse	
	I.E.	AFB	I.E.	AFB	I.E.	AFB	I.E.	AFB	I.E.	AFB
1	2.39	29	>100	>120	>100	>120	>100	>120	>100	>120
2	0.25	6	5.20	49	>100	>120	>100	>120	>100	>120
3	0.25	6	0.93	15	>100	>120	>100	>120	>100	>120
4	0.25	6	0.25	6	20.60	>120	>100	>120	>100	>120
5	0.25	6	0.25	6	1.54	21	>100	>120	>100	>120
6	0.25	6	0.25	6	0.75	13	>100	>120	>100	>120
8	0.25	6	0.25	6	0.69	12	36.85	>120	>100	>120
10	0.25	6	0.25	6	0.63	12	12.82	90	75.44	>120
12	0.25	6	0.25	6	0.57	11	6.71	58	49.66	>120
14	0.25	6	0.25	6	0.51	10	0.60	11	23.87	>120
16	0.25	6	0.25	6	0.45	9	0.59	11	1.94	25
18	0.25	6	0.25	6	0.39	8	0.48	10	1.82	24
20	0.25	6	0.25	6	0.33	7	0.38	8	1.70	23
22	0.25	6	0.25	6	0.27	7	0.28	7	1.58	22
24	0.25	6	0.25	6	0.25	6	0.25	6	1.46	21
26	0.25	6	0.25	6	0.25	6	0.25	6	1.34	19
28	0.25	6	0.25	6	0.25	6	0.25	6	1.22	18
30	0.25	6	0.25	6	0.25	6	0.25	6	1.10	17

Figure 9-13. The Incident Energy Calculator table from the Eaton Bussmann SPD Handbook is based on the IEEE 1584 *Simplified Fuse Equations*. For example, for a 400-ampere LPS-RK-400SP fuse with 14 kA available fault current, the incident energy is 0.51 cal/cm² and the AFB is 10 inches for a working distance of 18 inches, arc-in-box, and switchboard (1.25-inch arc gap). Reference the Eaton's Bussmann Division publication for more important information.

IEEE 1584 *Simplified Circuit Breaker Equations*

The simplified circuit breaker equation method is also included in *IEEE 1584*. If the short-circuit current falls outside the range of use for a circuit breaker setting or interrupting rating, the simplified equations cannot be used. In that case, *IEEE 1584* basic equations should be used. When equations are used for low-voltage power circuit breakers with short-time delay (without an instantaneous trip unit), the maximum setting (30 cycles) is assumed.

Other Incident Energy and Arch Flash Boundary Calculation Methods

NFPA 70E Informative Annex D includes other calculations methods. Some of these predate the release of the 2018 *IEEE 1584*, and they helped in the progression of quantifying arc flash hazards.

Direct-Current Incident Energy Method

NFPA 70E Informative Annex D.5 provides information and an equation method on a direct-current incident energy analysis method. This method is provided in a paper authored by Dan Doan and was presented at the 2010 IEEE Electrical Safety Workshop. Informative Annex D.5.2 provides three reference sources on DC arcing current and energy.

Ralph Lee Method: AFB and Incident Energy

The Ralph Lee AFB and incident energy calculation method, detailed in *NFPA 70E* Informative Annex D, Section D.2, is based on Ralph Lee's seminal paper, "The Other Electrical Hazard: Electrical Arc Blast Burns," which appeared in *IEEE Transactions on Industrial Applications*, vol. 1A-18, no. 3, p. 246, May/June 1982. This important paper represented one of the first efforts focusing on the quantification of arcing fault hazards. The method outlined in Lee's paper is not applicable for most commercial and industrial electrical work, as these premises typically involve enclosed equipment (arc-in-a-box). The incident energy from open-air arcs is less than the energy from arcs-in-a-box.

Owing to this difference, this method would not be suitable to determine the AFB or incident energy for an arc-in-a-box, because these equations would yield results lower than the expected values. The Ralph Lee AFB and incident energy calculation method predates *IEEE 1584*.

Doughty Neal Paper: Incident Energy

The Doughty/Neal method, detailed in *NFPA 70E* Informative Annex D, Section D.3, is based on the paper noted in Informative Annex D, Section D.3.4, by R. L. Doughty, T. E. Neal, and H. L. Floyd II. This paper, which is entitled "Predicting Incident Energy to Better Manage the Electric Arc Hazard on 600-V Power Distribution Systems," is part of the Record of the Conference Papers for the IEEE IAS 45th Annual Petroleum and Chemical Industry Conference held on September 28–30, 1998. The range of short-circuit current values, voltages, and working distances is limited compared to the *IEEE 1584* method. This paper and method predate *IEEE 1584*.

Premise-Wide Equipment Labeling

Some facility owners have an arc flash risk assessment conducted for their entire premises to label the electrical equipment. The typical process may include updating or creating a complete and accurate single-line diagram of the electrical facilities, calculating the available fault currents, calculating the arc flash boundaries and incident energies throughout the premises, and affixing labels on the electrical equipment per 130.5(H).

Updating the Incident Energy Analysis

NFPA 70E 130.5(G) requires the incident energy analysis to be updated (if one was performed) when a major modification or renovation occurs. In addition, the incident energy analysis must be reviewed periodically (in periods not to exceed five years), because changes in the electrical distribution systems could affect the results of the incident energy analysis. Per the last paragraph of 130.5(H), the owner of the electrical equipment is responsible for the documentation, installation, and maintenance of the field-marked labels.

SUMMARY

There are two methods to determine the arc flash boundary and arc flash PPE when an arc flash risk assessment requires additional protective measures that include PPE. See 130.5(E) for the arc flash boundary requirements. Per 130.5(F), one of the following methods shall be used for the selection of arc flash PPE:

(1) the arc flash PPE category method in accordance with 130.7(C)(15)

(2) the incident energy analysis method in accordance with 130.5(G)

When using the arc flash PPE category method, it is important that the circuit parameters for the specific equipment to be worked on adhere to the parameters in Table 130.7(C)(15)(a) for the type of equipment and voltage. The parameter limits include the maximum available fault current, maximum fault clearing time, and the minimum working distance.

IEEE 1584, Guide for Performing Arc-Flash Hazard Calculations, has commonly used incident energy calculation methods. This approach requires more effort and knowledge. *NFPA 70E* Annex D provides some information for these methods and other incident energy analysis methods.

When conducting an arc flash risk assessment in accordance with 130.5, the "condition of maintenance" may affect the assessment results in at least two ways:

1. If the protecting-OCPD has not been properly maintained, it may take longer to interrupt the arcing fault current and result in much greater incident energy than anticipated.

2. In general, maintenance of all electrical equipment that may be worked on when not in an electrically safe work condition is important for electrical safety.

REVIEW QUESTIONS

1. **The term "protecting-OCPD" best describes which one of the following?**
   a. A defined term in Article 100, Definitions, in *NFPA 70E*
   b. A term used numerous times in *NFPA 70E* but not defined
   c. The OCPD located within the equipment being worked on
   d. The OCPD that is protecting the downstream equipment

2. **Which of the following is/are part of the mandatory requirements in *NFPA 70E*?**
   a. The arc flash PPE category method
   b. The means (formula) to determine the arc flash boundary
   c. The means (formula) to determine the available fault current
   d. The means (formula) to determine the incident energy

3. **The arc flash hazard created during an arc flash event is directly dependent on the OCPD that is protecting the downstream equipment where the arcing fault occurs.**
   a. True   b. False

4. **The clearing time of the "protecting-OCPD" can be longer than expected with inadequate maintenance. However, the condition of maintenance does not have to be considered when an arc flash risk assessment is performed.**
   a. True   b. False

5. **Which of the following best describes what must be used to determine arc flash PPE, when required, as part of an arc flash risk assessment in accordance with *NFPA 70E*?**
   a. Both the arc flash PPE category method and the incident energy analysis method
   b. Both the arc flash PPE category method and the incident energy analysis method, with the higher value used to select the PPE
   c. Either the arc flash PPE category method or the incident energy analysis method
   d. It is never necessary to determine arc flash PPE as part of an arc flash risk assessment

6. **The requirements in 130.7(C)(15)(a) stipulate when the arc flash PPE category method is permitted to be used for AC systems. Which is not a condition of use that must be met to use this method?**
   a. The estimated available fault current at the equipment to be worked on must be equal to or less than the maximum available fault current value shown in Table 130.7(C)(15)(a) under the parameters for the type of equipment and voltage level.
   b. The incident energy calculation must be 1.2 cal/cm^2 at the point where the worker reaches into the panel per Table 130.7(C)(15)(a) under the parameters for the type of equipment and voltage level.
   c. The fault clearing time has to be equal to or less than the maximum fault clearing time value in Table 130.7(C)(15)(a) under the parameters for the type of equipment and voltage level.
   d. The working distance must not be less than that shown in Table 130.7(C)(15)(a) under the parameters for the type of equipment and voltage level.

7. **The most commonly-used means to calculate incident energy discussed is ___?___.**
   a. FC^2 Arcing Fault Current Calculator
   b. Point-to-point available short-circuit current method
   c. *IEEE 1584*
   d. Table 130.7(C)(15)(c)

8. **When determining if the arc flash PPE category method can be used for a 480-volt panelboard, if the fault current calculation is greater than the 25,000-ampere parameter value in Table 130.7(C)(15)(a), the arc flash PPE category method could not be used for this situation, unless a more accurate calculation could be done and that value is equal to or less than 25,000 amperes.**
   a. True   b. False

9. **It is safe to assume that the higher the available fault currents and corresponding higher arcing fault currents, the greater the AFB and incident energy.**
   a. True   b. False

10. **There are many variables involved with arcing fault current. Even so, in the case of the *IEEE 1584* testing, which was done under controlled and specific staged conditions, the results were always consistent. The exact same test run later will always produce the same incident energy result.**
    a. True   b. False

Maintenance Considerations

Historically, maintenance of electrical devices and systems focused on reliability to prevent fires and preserve continuity of power. However, *NFPA 70E* also has maintenance requirements which are necessary for the safety of employees who work where exposed to electrical hazards. It is important to be familiar with the key *NFPA 70E* maintenance requirements and to be familiar with why maintenance is important for safety-related work practices.

Objectives

» Understand the value of electrical maintenance and how it can affect safety.

» Recognize that incident energy is related to OCPD design and the condition of maintenance.

» Understand that electrical safety includes the condition of maintenance of electrical equipment.

» Apply the *NFPA 70E* Chapter 2 maintenance requirements.

Chapter 10

Table of Contents

Case Study

Background

An outage was scheduled at a large semiconductor facility to conduct maintenance on the electrical distribution equipment. The cost of conducting an outage at the plant is over $1,000,000 just due to lost production. Based on these costs, the facility management stretched out their scheduled electrical shut-down maintenance period from three to five years. The service company that had been performing the shut-down maintenance for this facility for many years advised the facility management to retain a three-year shut-down maintenance schedule, since a five-year schedule increased the probability of an unplanned outage. However, the facility management believed that the cooled and controlled environment where the electrical equipment was located would permit delaying the electrical maintenance two additional years.

Outage Actions

The initial step of the outage procedure was to de-energize the main power circuit breaker in each low-voltage substation to reduce the load before de-energizing the main substation. To perform this step, the Electrical Worker wore PPE in accordance with the facility Incident Energy Analysis.

The Electrical Worker actuated the "trip" button on the door of the main power circuit breaker and nothing happened. The power remained on, the circuit breaker flag did not change state, and the discharge of the stored energy mechanism was not heard. The Electrical Worker stepped out of the room and reviewed as-built drawings of the switchgear with the maintenance service company representative and the facility engineer. While they were reviewing the drawings, looking for any additional interlocks that may be blocking the "trip" signal to the circuit breaker, the power finally went off and the discharge of the circuit breaker stored energy mechanism was heard, indicating that the circuit breaker finally opened.

Outage Findings

The main power circuit breaker was dis-assembled and inspected during the outage. The main latch release mechanism lubrication had hardened and was no longer malleable. When the initial trip signal was received, the spring mechanism was unable to apply enough force to open the circuit breaker due to the hardening of the lubrication. Over a few minutes, the spring eventually overcame the hardened lubrication, thereby opening the circuit breaker.

Conclusions

The power circuit breaker's instruction manual recommended "exercising" the circuit breaker every six months. The purpose of this recommendation is to keep the lubrication in the operating mechanism malleable. If a fault had occurred on the load side of the circuit breaker, the circuit breaker would not have operated as anticipated, resulting in a higher-than-calculated clearing time. The estimated resulting incident energy would have been greater than 42 calories/cm^2 before the upstream fuse on the primary of the transformer would have cleared the fault. As a result of this incident, the semiconductor company modified their maintenance practices to incorporate regular "exercising" of their circuit breakers and reduced their outage interval back to three years.

Source: Courtesy of Eaton

INTRODUCTION

Maintenance plays a role in *NFPA 70E* in at least two ways:

1. *NFPA 70E* requires owners to maintain their electrical equipment in *NFPA 70E* Chapter 2. The purpose of *NFPA 70E* maintenance requirements is "safety of employees who work where exposed to electrical hazards." (*NFPA 70E* 200.1(3))
2. Electrical equipment condition of maintenance is an important consideration for safety-related work practices.

Specific discussions are presented to demonstrate how the lack of maintenance can impact the operation of overcurrent protective devices (OCPDs) and present situations of elevated risk to the Electrical Worker. Examples of real-world maintenance issues are demonstrated, focusing on how they have or might have resulted in safety issues for the Electrical Worker. The topic of determining the condition of maintenance of OCPDs is discussed to allow those conducting a risk assessment to have additional information to consider to evaluate the risks involved. The frequency of maintenance for specific OCPDs is covered to provide some insight into some factors related to providing proper maintenance for electrical power systems.

THE VALUE OF ELECTRICAL SAFETY-RELATED MAINTENANCE

The first sentence of 90.2, which is the Scope for *NFPA 70E*, states, in part, that "This standard addresses . . . safety-related maintenance requirements . . ."

Refer to Article 100 where "condition of maintenance (Maintenance, Condition of)" is defined.

The evolving awareness that the condition of maintenance of electrical equipment is directly related to electrical safety-related work practices is evident by 110.5(C). This requirement mandates that the employer's electrical safety program includes consideration for the condition of maintenance of electrical equipment. However, it is important to recognize that electrical maintenance is not just about minimizing costly breakdowns and unplanned outages. *NFPA 70E* emphasizes that maintaining electrical equipment is an important element for electrical safety-related work practices.

The purpose of maintenance requirements in *NFPA 70E* is stated, in part, in 200.1(3) as ". . .preserving or restoring the condition of electrical equipment for the safety of employees who are exposed to electrical hazards." It is common knowledge that performing discretionary regular maintenance of electrical equipment is proven through IEEE studies to significantly reduce electrical failure rates and results in increased reliability and reduction in repair costs while allowing efforts to be concentrated on improving operation rather than responding to emergency repairs. Electrical maintenance is also required to also reduce hazards to which Electrical Workers are exposed.

NFPA 70E Maintenance Requirements for OCPDs

The following are sections in Chapter 2 of *NFPA 70E* that address OCPD maintenance:

- **205.4:** requires OCPDs to be maintained per manufacturers' instructions or industry consensus standards. "Maintenance, tests, and inspections shall be documented."
- **210.5:** requires OCPDs to be maintained to safely withstand or be able to interrupt the available fault current. Note that the informational note makes mention that improper or lack of maintenance can increase arc flash hazard incident energy.
- **225.1:** requires fuse body and fuse mounting means to be maintained. Mountings for current-limiting fuses cannot be altered to allow insertion of non–current-limiting fuses.
- **225.2:** requires molded case circuit breaker cases and handles to be maintained properly.

- **225.3:** requires inspection and testing of circuit breakers that interrupt fault current approaching their interrupting rating.

NFPA 70E Maintenance Requirements for Electrical Equipment

In addition to maintenance requirements for OCPDs, *NFPA 70E* contains requirements for other parts of the electrical power system:

- **205.3:** requires electrical equipment to be maintained per manufacturers' instructions or industry consensus standards. The owner or their representative is responsible for maintenance and documentation.

The following are Articles of *NFPA 70E* Chapter 2 that have maintenance requirements for various types of equipment:

- 200 Introduction
- 205 General Maintenance Requirements
- 210 Substations, Switchgear Assemblies, Switchboards, Panelboards, Motor Control Centers (MCC), and Disconnect Switches
- 215 Premises Wiring
- 220 Controller Equipment
- 225 Fuses and Circuit Breakers
- 230 Rotating Equipment
- 235 Hazardous (Classified) Locations
- 240 Batteries and Battery Rooms
- 245 Portable Electric Tools and Equipment
- 250 Personal Safety and Electrical Equipment

Some electrical arc flash incidents are the result of poorly or improperly maintained electrical equipment. For instance, as an Electrical Worker removes a panel trim, a tool or scrap of bare conductor left behind from prior work may become dislodged and fall across a bare energized bus or terminations, initiating an arcing fault. Or perhaps where dust and dirt have been permitted to accumulate inside an electrical enclosure, a vibration disturbance can result in an arc flash incident. In some cases, loose conductor terminations cause thermal damage to

> **OSHA Tip**
>
> **1910.303(g)**
> *600 Volts, nominal, or less.* This paragraph applies to electric equipment operating at 600 volts, nominal, or less to ground.
>
> **1910.303(g)(1)**
> *Space about electric equipment.* Sufficient access and working space shall be provided and maintained about all electric equipment to permit ready and safe operation and maintenance of such equipment.

device electrical insulation properties, and a physical disturbance initiates a high thermal energy arc flash release.

Good housekeeping, such as ensuring electrical equipment interiors are clean and free of dust, dirt, animals, tools, loose parts, or conductor trimmings, is an important maintenance item.

THE IMPORTANCE OF "CONDITION OF MAINTENANCE"

Lack of proper maintenance introduces multiple modes of potential failure into the electrical system that often are not noticed until problems are proactively eliminated through maintenance—or until there is a system failure.

Not performing maintenance on an electrical system can have similar consequences to not performing maintenance on a car. A driver may skip checking the brakes, regularly inflating the tires, or changing the oil, and the car seems to run fine. But if regular maintenance is not performed on the car, the driver risks not being able to brake in time to avoid an accident; tires failing due to lack of pressure, causing the car to lose control; or the engine burning up. The mechanical and insulation systems in an electrical system also need periodic inspection, testing, and maintenance to perform in accordance with their design.

So why is the condition of maintenance important to the Electrical Worker? One example includes improper or lack of maintenance of an OCPD. An OCPD that is not maintained can lead to higher arc flash incident energy and a larger arc flash boundary due to longer-than-expected clearing times that may have been used when performing the arc flash risk assessment. If the incident energy for an actual arc flash event is higher than the incident energy determined as part of the arc flash risk assessment, the Electrical Worker may not be wearing sufficient PPE. In addition, workers who thought they were outside the arc flash boundary may be wearing flammable garments subject to clothing ignition and other unanticipated consequences.

Yet another example where condition of maintenance can lead to longer clearing times of an OCPD include when other unexpected sources of impedance are introduced into the circuit. During fault conditions of a power system, magnetic forces will put stress on the power system testing terminations and cause vibrations. When performing an arc-flash risk assessment, there is a level of expectation that the power distribution system will perform as expected in many ways. It is not expected that a fault condition would cause multiple other fault conditions elsewhere in the power system. Multiple faults in the power system will introduce unexpected impedances that can act to reduce the level of fault current, which in turn reduces arcing currents, causing longer clearing times. Longer clearing times of an OCPD lead to higher-than-expected incident energy values and larger arc flash boundaries.

NFPA 70E Chapter 2, "Safety-Related Maintenance Requirements," specifically requires OCPDs to be maintained properly and inspection documented (205.4). *NFPA 70E* stresses the importance of maintaining all electrical equipment in accordance with manufacturer's instructions or industry consensus standards as part of 205.3. Electrical equipment must perform as expected. After all, when a worker has to remove the trim from an energized electrical panel to perform troubleshooting diagnostics,

that worker may be at greater risk of injury or death if the internal wiring, terminations, devices, etc. have not been properly maintained.

The importance of "properly maintained" as a condition of safe work practices is stated in many *NFPA 70E* requirements and Informational Notes. For example, see:

- Informational Note No. 1 to the Article 100 definition of "Arc-Flash Hazard"
- Article 100 definition of "Condition of Maintenance"
- 110.4(D) and the related Informational Note
- 130.5(B)(2)
- Table 130.5(C), under the column heading "Equipment Condition" where superscript note a refers to 110.4(D). "Properly maintained" is covered in 110.4(D)(2).
- Informational Notes No. 2 and No. 5 located after Table 130.5(C)
- 130.5(G) (second paragraph)
- 130.5(H), including Exception No. 2

It stands to reason that a fundamental principle of safety-related work practices requires electrical equipment to be in good condition and properly maintained.

To investigate the consequences of OCPDs not operating as designed when needed for arc flash mitigation, a large industrial facility conducted a simulation and published a technical paper. In this simulation, the nearest upstream OCPDs supplying the equipment were turned "off" in the commercial arc-flash analysis software package as if the OCPDs would not operate. In this state, the arc flash mitigation was then relegated to the next OCPD further upstream, which is a larger ampere rated device. The IEEE paper, "Prioritize Circuit Breaker and Protective Relay Maintenance Using an Arc-Flash Hazard Assessment" (*IEEE Paper No. ESW-2012-11*) by Dan Doan, examines the effects on an arc flash hazard assessment in an industrial facility if the upstream protective devices do not operate correctly. The study determined that if the closest upstream circuit breaker relay did not operate and the next upstream OCPD cleared the arcing fault current, in approximately $2/3$ of the cases, the worker would not have adequately rated arc-flash PPE.

HOW A LACK OF MAINTENANCE CAN INCREASE HAZARDS

As part of the arc flash risk assessment, as required in *NFPA 70E* 130.5, the arc flash boundary (AFB) and arc rated PPE need to be determined for Electrical Workers to perform work within the AFB where additional protective measures are required and include the use of PPE. **See Figure 10-1.** This table shows how the magnitude of the arcing fault current and/or OCPD clearing time will affect incident energy when the working distance is held constant at 18 inches from the arcing fault.

Note: The incident energy calculations were performed using the 2018 *IEEE 1584 Guide for Performing Arc-Flash Hazard Calculations* basic equation method for "Arc in a Box." The calculations assume the following with regard to key parameters that impact the calculation of arcing current and incident energy:

Figure 10-1	Incident Energy for Various Scenarios							
Distance (inches)	**18**	**18**	**18**	**18**	**18**	**18**	**18**	**18**
Clearing time (cycles)	**3**	**6**	**10**	**20**	**30**	**40**	**50**	**60**
Seconds	**0.05**	**0.10**	**0.17**	**0.33**	**0.50**	**0.67**	**0.83**	**1.00**
SC kA	cal/cm²	cal/cm²	cal/cm²	cal/cm²	cal/cm²	cal/cm²	cal/cm²	cal/cm²
16	1.6	3.3	5.6	10.8	16.3	21.9	27.1	32.7
18	1.9	3.7	6.4	12.4	18.7	25.1	31.1	37.5
20	2.1	4.2	7.2	13.9	21.1	28.3	35.1	42.3
22	2.4	4.7	8.0	15.5	23.5	31.5	39.0	47.0
24	2.6	5.2	8.8	17.1	25.9	34.7	43.0	51.8
26	2.8	5.6	9.6	18.6	28.2	37.8	46.8	56.4
28	3.0	6.1	10.4	20.1	30.5	40.8	50.6	60.9
30	3.3	6.5	11.1	21.6	32.7	43.8	54.3	65.4
32	3.5	7.0	11.8	23.0	34.8	46.7	57.8	69.6
34	3.7	7.4	12.5	24.3	36.9	49.4	61.2	73.8
36	3.9	7.8	13.2	25.7	38.9	52.1	64.5	77.8
38	4.1	8.2	13.9	26.9	40.8	54.6	67.7	81.6
40	4.3	8.5	14.5	28.1	42.6	57.1	70.7	85.2
42	4.4	8.9	15.1	29.2	44.3	59.4	73.6	88.6
44	4.6	9.2	15.6	30.3	45.9	61.6	76.3	91.9
46	4.7	9.5	16.1	31.3	47.5	63.6	78.8	95.0
48	4.9	9.8	16.6	32.3	48.9	65.6	81.2	97.9
50	5.0	10.1	17.1	33.2	50.3	67.4	83.5	100.6

Figure 10-1. The incident energy for various available fault currents (left vertical axis) is related to the various OCPD clearing times (horizontal axis). These values assume an enclosure size of 5.75 inches deep, 20 inches wide, and 36 inches tall. Vertical bus with barrier (VCBB) configuration is also assumed, which yields the worst-case incident energy for panelboards.

Enclosure size: 20 inches wide × 36 inches tall × 5.75 inches deep

Electrode gap: 1 inch (25 mm)

Electrode configuration: Vertical bus with barrier (VCBB)

Voltage: 480 volts

Looking at the table in Figure 10-1, if the available fault current is 22 kA, an upstream protective device that could operate and clear the fault in 0.05 seconds would result in an incident energy of 2.4 cal/cm². In comparison, if the upstream protective device was required to clear the fault, the resulting incident energy is 47.0 cal/cm². It is clearly evident that the "clearing time" of the protective device has a major influence on the resulting incident energy during an arcing fault event. If the protective device fails to operate as designed, or does not operate at all, the incident energy that the Electrical Worker will be exposed to may be much higher than calculated.

In addition, Figure 10-1 can be used to demonstrate that lower-than-expected fault currents yielding longer clearing times could also present a hazard to the Electrical Worker. If, for example, an available fault current of 30 kA is estimated based on a properly installed and maintained power distribution system yielding a clearing time of 3 cycles, 3.3 cal/cm² would be expected. Should an event occur and, due to lack of maintenance, should additional impedance sources be included in the system, the available fault current could be reduced, yielding longer clearing times of the upstream OCPD. For example, in this case, should the fault current be 16 kA instead of 30 kA due to these added impedances, and should 27 cycles be added to the clearing time due to the lower arcing currents being in the short-time delay region of the time-current curve, the expected 3.3 cal/cm² would now in reality be 16.3 cal/cm² and the Electrical Worker may have inadequate PPE due to this higher value.

LACK OR IMPROPER MAINTENANCE CONCERNS FOR THE ELECTRICAL WORKER

Electrical power distribution equipment that is not properly maintained can create a dangerous situation for the Electrical Worker. The following are examples from a reconditioning facility that consistently services circuit breakers, bus systems, conductor terminations, conductors, insulators, contactors, starters, switches, and other equipment that may suffer from a lack of proper maintenance.

Example 1

Consider the case of a circuit breaker less than ten years old where the lubrication had dried out and been contaminated by dirt. The lack of lubrication caused the shutter mechanism to freeze, broke a spring, and rendered the circuit breaker inoperable. **See Figure 10-2.**

Many equipment owners do not realize that the operating mechanisms of circuit breakers and many switches are lubricated when they are built and that the lubrication dries out over time, even if the breaker (or switch) has not been operated. Just because the device has not been required to open does not mean that it does not need to be maintained.

Example 2

One performing a risk assessment may be misled regarding the "state" of a

Figure 10-2   Contaminated Lubrication

Figure 10-2. The circuit breaker lubrication is dried out and contaminated. This caused the shutter interlock to stop working, broke a spring, and rendered the breaker inoperable.

Courtesy of Eaton

circuit breaker by lack of maintenance. Consider a case where a dry unlubricated mechanism would cause the "Open/Close" indicator to be stuck in the "Open Condition" even though the circuit breaker is closed. **See Figure 10-3.** This issue creates an extremely unsafe condition, as it may mislead one into thinking a circuit breaker is "open" when it is really "closed." If an Electrical Worker were to try to rack-in or rack-out the circuit breaker while closed, they may be relying on safety interlocks to open the breaker prior to connecting or disconnecting from the stabs.

Example 3

Not only is maintenance necessary, but it is also necessary that maintenance be performed by workers qualified for the task. The following is another example of improper maintenance creating a safety situation for the Electrical Worker. Consider a case where improper lubricant was applied to the finger clusters that make contact with the cell stabs for a drawout circuit breaker mechanism. **See Figure 10-4.**

The improper type lubricant caused the finger clusters to overheat, leading

to a catastrophic failure of the circuit breaker and cell structure. Improperly maintained equipment like this can be a source of an arc flash incident.

Example 4

Harsh environmental conditions require more maintenance than climate-controlled environments. For example, "silver whiskers" have been found to grow on sharp edges of silver coated parts in sulfur-rich, warm, moist environments. **See Figure 10-5.** These

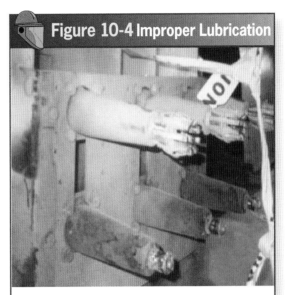

Figure 10-4 Improper Lubrication

Figure 10-4. Improper lubrication of primary stab finger clusters leads to overheating and severe equipment damage.
Courtesy of Eaton

Figure 10-3 Stuck Indicator

Figure 10-3. A completely dry mechanism may cause the "Open/Close" indicator to be stuck in the "Open Condition" even though the breaker is closed.
Courtesy of Eaton

Figure 10-5 Silver Whiskers

Figure 10-5. "Silver whiskers" caused by a contaminated environment and lack of maintenance led to control power transformer failure on this medium voltage switchgear.
Courtesy of Eaton

whiskers have been the cause of many unexpected electrical equipment failures in the petrochemical and food industry.

Example 5

Verifying the proper operation of electrical equipment components is an important part of performing electrical equipment maintenance. Most outdoor electrical installations use "space heaters" to maintain temperature and low moisture levels inside electrical equipment enclosures. If the space heaters are inoperative, moisture can condense on the equipment bus structures and conductor terminations. **See Figure 10-6.** This traps dirt, which leads to tracking and eventual insulation failure. **See Figure 10-7.** Unmaintained equipment like this can be a serious safety concern when workers remove equipment covers or open doors. The vibrations from the workers' actions may be the final action whereby the deteriorating insulation results in a high energy arcing fault.

Example 6

Some electrical equipment, if it is not exercised regularly, can seize and contacts weld shut. In the following example, a bolted pressure switch was never exercised since its original installation. While the operating mechanism worked properly, one of the moving contacts welded to a stationary contact due to lack of maintenance. **See Figure 10-8.** An Electrical Worker opened the switch and assumed all three phases of the switch opened since he heard the mechanism operate. Unfortunately, the worker did not perform a voltage test to verify the switch was open. The worker was injured due to electric shock. The worker should have been wearing shock and arc flash PPE and should have followed proper work practices to verify the equipment was in an electrically safe work condition.

DETERMINING THE CONDITION OF MAINTENANCE

So how does the Electrical Worker determine whether the OCPD is properly maintained? When electrical equipment is installed, it is advisable to

Figure 10-6 Heater Failure

Figure 10-6. Heater failure leads to moisture build-up and bus failure. Regular maintenance would have detected the defective heater.

Courtesy of Eaton

Figure 10-7 Bus Failure

Figure 10-7. Lack of maintenance can lead to bus failure as dirt, moisture, and contaminates cause tracking.

Courtesy of Eaton

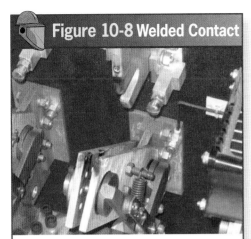

Figure 10-8 Welded Contact

Figure 10-8. A contact pole has become welded on a bolted pressure switch due to a lack of maintenance and exercising (photo shows after switch pole blade had been freed up and opened). The Electrical Worker did not verify that the switch was completely open and, as a result, the worker was injured due to electric shock.

Courtesy of Eaton

conduct site acceptance tests to verify that the electrical equipment is performing in accordance with the design professional's plans and equipment manufacturers' specifications. These tests also verify that components, like circuit breakers and overcurrent relays, are performing within manufacturer's tolerances and industry standards while providing a baseline for future maintenance testing. This service would also include setting these OCPDs per a coordination study and possibly an incident energy analysis to provide the electrical system with the desired level of equipment protection while minimizing incident energy levels. If these settings are not properly implemented, the Electrical Worker may be exposed to a higher incident energy level than anticipated. After these tests are completed, a service sticker is placed on the devices tested to indicate the date of service (condition of maintenance confirmation).

Background

The Hazard Associated with Misapplication of an OCPD - Fuse or Circuit Breakers

Most misapplication problems are avoided when the design professional, equipment suppliers, and equipment installers comply with the installation and design requirements of the *National Electrical Code (NFPA 70)*. An Electrical Worker will often be working at an unfamiliar facility and only recognize the most obvious misapplications of power system components. Proper recognition of misapplication will provide an opportunity to determine if additional protective measures are required, including the use of PPE, even when simply working near the equipment, rather than working on the equipment.

One of the most frequent misapplications of OCPDs is the use of fuses or circuit breakers that have an interrupting rating less than the available fault current that the power sources can deliver. Assemblies such as switchboards, motor-control centers, or switchgear have associated ratings called *short-circuit current rating, short-circuit withstand, momentary current*, or *short-time current ratings*. The rating of the assembly is typically limited to the lowest-rated OCPD in the assembly. For example, if a switchboard assembly has five 65kA interrupting rated circuit breakers and one 35kA interrupting rated circuit breaker, the switchboard assembly is considered to only have a 35kA short-circuit current rating even if the switchboard assembly bus short-circuit current rating is good for 65kA. A catastrophic failure might put the Electrical Worker at risk if a circuit breaker or fuse attempts to interrupt a fault current greater than its interrupting rating.

Courtesy of Eaton

Example: Equipment was retrofitted by adding a surge-protection device into an existing switchboard assembly, but a molded-case circuit breaker that had an inadequate interrupting-current rating was used. The surge-protection device failed, causing a fault current condition. The fault current developed into an arcing fault. Nobody was interacting with the equipment, but if a person had been near the equipment when this arcing fault occurred, that person would likely have been injured if not wearing proper PPE.

See Figure 10-9. An Electrical Worker can use this data, and the corresponding service report, to assist in determining if the equipment has been tested and inspected within a recommended frequency of maintenance for the type of equipment.

Alternative to OCPDs that Are Not Maintained Properly

What if the equipment has never been serviced or documentation is not available? Unfortunately, this is a fairly common occurrence in many electrical system installations. At a minimum, the following inspections should be performed to determine the risk that the equipment may not function as intended.

1. Is the environment in which the equipment is located isolated or protected from the elements and contaminants (dust and chemicals)? Clean and dry equipment is less likely to experience deterioration with insulation and contamination of lubricants used in OCPDs.

2. Are the OCPDs in visibly good condition? Circuit breakers may become discolored if subjected to overheating conditions. Also, cracks or burn marks might be visible, indicating that the OCPD has been subjected to an event that may affect its performance.

3. What is the application of the equipment and how often is it operated? Some applications may put more stress on equipment, including thermal loading, which could lead to deterioration of insulation. While an extreme number of operations might wear out mechanical systems of circuit breakers eventually, some operations provide an indication that the mechanical systems are working and lubricated.

4. What is the age of the equipment? Older equipment, especially if it has not been maintained or operated, is a higher risk due to lack of operation than newer equipment. Newer lubricants used in some circuit breaker brands are more durable and less likely to harden and prevent proper operation.

Even if the environment is controlled and very clean, there is not any way to know if the circuit breaker lubrication has hardened and may prevent the device from operating within its operating parameters.

NFPA 70E does not provide specific requirements or actions to take if an OCPD is maintained inadequately or improperly. There is no single answer to this situation and the action taken may depend on the circumstances of a specific situation. It can be factored into a risk assessment procedure (see 110.5(H), Risk Assessment Procedure, and Informative Annex F, Risk Assessment and Risk Control). If the original objective was to perform justified energized work, it may be advisable to change the job safety plan (see 110.5(I)) and establish an electrically safe work condition rather than work on the equipment while energized. However, the Electrical Worker still has to interface with the equipment to verify the absence of voltage in the process of establishing an electrically safe work condition. If the task is to open a disconnect or rack-out a circuit breaker, using a remote operator or remote racking device may be a more appropriate approach.

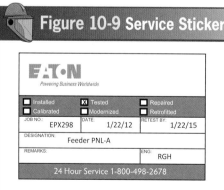

Figure 10-9 Service Sticker

Figure 10-9. *A typical service sticker affixed to electrical equipment indicates the date of service and the retest date, which assist in determining the condition of maintenance.*

Courtesy of Eaton

Again, verifying the absence of voltage still may have to be performed. For example, a maintenance manager for a large automotive industrial facility has a policy to investigate upstream OCPDs to locate an OCPD that has a suitable condition of maintenance and use that device for the arc-flash risk assessment. With this approach, the AFB and arc flash PPE determined will have greater values than if the nearest upstream OCPD is used for the assessment.

FREQUENCY OF MAINTENANCE FOR ELECTRICAL EQUIPMENT

Since maintenance of electrical equipment (other than OCPDs) consists mainly of keeping it clean and maintaining properly tight conductor terminations, the frequency of scheduled inspection and maintenance depends strongly on the cleanliness of the surroundings. Cleaning and preventive measures are a part of any good maintenance program. Facility operating and local conditions can vary to such an extent that the actual schedule should be tailored to the environment where the equipment is located. When the equipment is subject to a clean and dry environment, cleaning is not required as frequently as when the environment is humid with a significant amount of dust and other foreign matter. It is also recommended that maintenance record sheets be completed for the equipment. Careful and accurate documentation of all maintenance activities provides a valuable historical reference on the electrical equipment's condition of maintenance over time.

Background

 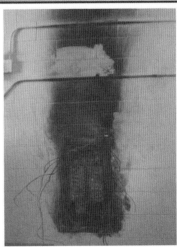

Courtesy of Eaton

Two Electrical Workers were injured as they removed the dead front from a panel that was energized. An arcing fault occurred, with both employees sustaining burns to their hands, and one of the employees receiving burns to his face. They were not wearing PPE. The employees were attempting to identify and relocate a lighting circuit to allow some other crafts to continue to work in the area. It was also discovered that the raceway connector coming into the bottom of the panel did not have a bushing. The conductors had been rubbing on the raceway connector in the panel for an extended time, and when the dead front was being moved the insulation on the conductors finally wore through, making contact with the panel or raceway. It is important not to assume that smaller lighting panels do not have the potential to create a dangerous arcing fault condition. Always verify that equipment has been properly installed and is maintained regardless of the equipment size and rating, and wear proper PPE per an arc flash and shock risk assessment.

Figure 10-10 Power Circuit Breakers

Breaker Frame Size	Interval[1] (Breaker Cycles)
800 amperes and below	1,750
Between 800 and 3,000 amperes	500
3,000 amperes and above	250
[1]Breaker Cycle = one no load open/close operation	

Figure 10-10. *Industry standard for power circuit breakers recommends a general inspection and lubrication after a specified number of operations.*

Frequency of Maintenance for OCPDs

The frequency of maintenance and maintenance recommended can vary by the OCPD type and technology.

Power Circuit Breakers

The industry standard for power circuit breakers recommends a general inspection and lubrication after the number of operations listed. **See Figure 10-10.** The inspection should also be conducted at the end of the first six months of service, even if the number of operations has not been reached.

Almost all power circuit breakers require periodic renewal of lubrication in their operating mechanism. There are four factors that determine the frequency that lubrication should be renewed:

1. The continuous current rating of the circuit breaker
2. The number of close-open operations since the most recent renewal
3. The time since the most recent renewal
4. The circuit breaker's operational environment

Manufacturing Standard ANSI/IEEE C37.13 establishes endurance requirements for low-voltage power AC circuit breakers, and IEEE C37.14 establishes the endurance requirements for DC rated circuit breakers. These requirements relate the minimum number of close-open operations that a breaker must be able to accomplish before requiring service. One of the limiting factors is the need to renew lubrication in a circuit breaker's mechanism. In general, the greater the continuous current rating of the circuit breaker, the fewer operations before required service. The manufacturer's instructional literature is allowed to suggest a greater number of operations than the number given in the manufacturing standard. For example, although an 800-ampere-rated circuit breaker is required by the manufacturing standard to endure 500 operations before service is needed, a manufacturer's instruction book might indicate that an 800-ampere-rated circuit breaker would require renewal of lubrication after 1,750 operations.

The first maintenance inspection should be conducted after the first six months of service to determine the cleanliness of the environment and the number of operations. Subsequent checks should be made at least once a year and may be extended longer if these maintenance inspections indicate that there are no problems. If the maintenance inspection shows a heavy accumulation of dirt, lint, or foreign matter, the service interval should be decreased. Any circuit breaker that has interrupted a fault should be serviced prior to being placed back into operation.

Molded Case Circuit Breakers

Molded case circuit breakers, both thermal magnetic trip and electronic trip types, have proven to be reliable in service. They inherently require little maintenance due to their enclosed design. A molded case circuit breaker must be operated both open and closed with sufficient frequency to ensure that its main contacts are cleaned by wiping action and that the lubrication materials within its mechanism remain evenly spread. For any circuit breaker that is not operated in its normal service, a periodic open-close exercise should be planned. It is recommended that the circuit breaker mechanism is exercised annually. Some studies have shown that the absence of annual mechanical cycling has not impacted reliability, possibly due to advanced Teflon-based lubricants applied in newer designs by some manufacturers. Inspection and maintenance may be required more frequently if adverse operating or environmental conditions exist. There is not a universal recommendation on whether to test or to not test molded case circuit breakers by primary injection at any regular interval. When testing thermal-magnetic molded case circuit breakers in the field, specific ambient conditions and cool-down periods cannot be simulated to produce results that would be comparative to established UL and IEC performance standards. *NEMA AB-4,* "Guidelines for Inspection and Preventive Maintenance of Molded Case Circuit Breakers Used in Commercial and Industrial Applications," provides guidance on testing of molded case circuit breakers in the field, taking into account these limitations.

Electronic trip units were developed to resolve the difficulties in field testing of molded case circuit breakers. The use of an electronic trip unit allows the circuit breaker to be tested by secondary current injection, which simulates the fault current to the trip unit at the secondary of the circuit breaker current transformers. This test verifies the trip actuator, latch mechanism, and electronic circuit of the circuit breaker. Other advantages of secondary injection test sets are that they are lightweight, simple to operate, and have low power requirements, making testing easier and requiring less downtime.

Fuses

Fuses lack moving exterior parts, so physical maintenance is very minimal. However, periodically checking fuse bodies, fuse mountings, and adjacent conductor terminations for signs of overheating, poor connections, or insufficient conductor ampacity is important. Fuses cannot have their performance characteristics tested, but most manufacturers will provide a micro-ohm or millivolt drop test reading that indicates that the fuse would operate within specifications.

Fuses are typically used in conjunction with disconnects that require periodic inspection and maintenance. If a disconnect has lubricated mechanisms, then it is necessary to maintain the lubrication properly. In applications where stored energy type disconnects are equipped with a ground-fault protection relay, the disconnects should be periodically inspected and maintained, and the ground-fault relay calibrated. After a stored energy type disconnect interrupts a ground fault, the disconnect and mechanism should be inspected and maintained, if necessary.

Like all electrical equipment, the frequency of maintenance is highly dependent upon the environment the equipment is subject to. An inspection during the first year of service is recommended to determine the frequency of

OSHA Tip

1910.334(b)(2):

Reclosing circuits after protective device operation. After a circuit is deenergized by a circuit protective device, the circuit may not be manually reenergized until it has been determined that the equipment and circuit can be safely energized. The repetitive manual reclosing of circuit breakers or reenergizing circuits through replaced fuses is prohibited.

Note: When it can be determined from the design of the circuit and the over current devices involved that the automatic operation of a device was caused by an overload rather than a fault condition, no examination of the circuit or connected equipment is needed before the circuit is reenergized.

maintenance based upon observed accumulation of dirt or foreign matter. Deenergized maintenance and cleaning should not exceed three years per the recommendations of *NFPA 70B* 2019. The manufacturer's instruction book should be consulted, as the design of the equipment may require more frequent maintenance.

NFPA 70B Frequency of Maintenance

NFPA 70B, Recommended Practice for Electrical Equipment Maintenance, provides some frequency of maintenance guidelines as well as guidelines for setting up an electrical preventive maintenance (EPM) program, including sample forms and requirements for electrical system maintenance. All users of electrical equipment are encouraged to utilize an electrical preventative maintenance and testing program designed for their particular application. The methods of establishing such a program are covered in Chapter 6 of *NFPA 70B*, and Annex L, "Maintenance Intervals," has recommendations in table form for various types of equipment showing tests and frequencies should manufacturer data not be available.

NFPA 70B recommends that once the initial frequency for inspection and tests has been established, this frequency should be adhered to for at least four maintenance cycles unless unexpected failures occur. If unexpected failures occur, the interval between inspections should be reduced by 50% as soon as the trouble occurs. After four cycles of inspections have been completed, a pattern should have developed, and if the equipment does not require service, the inspection period can be extended by 50%. The adjustment of the interval between inspection and testing should be adjusted for the optimum interval.

Note that the 2019 edition of *NFPA 70B* is a recommended practice. It is currently under revision and it is anticipated that it will become a standard when the 2023 edition becomes effective. There is a significant difference between a "recommended practice" and a "standard," as evidenced by the definitions in Section 3.3.6.1 of NFPA's *Regulations Governing the Development of NFPA Standards*.

SUMMARY

Maintenance of electrical equipment directly associated with worker safety is required by *NFPA 70E*. Improperly maintained equipment or lack of maintenance can create safety hazards for Electrical Workers. Electrical equipment such as panelboards, switchboards, and other assemblies require periodic cleaning of the interiors and checking for signs of loose connections or other abnormalities that could result in an arc-flash incident. Improper maintenance or a lack of maintenance for OCPDs is of particular concern, as it may affect the performance of an OCPD, thereby resulting in increased clearing time and greater-than-calculated incident energy if an arcing fault incident occurs. The frequency of maintenance required for electrical equipment is best determined by reviewing the equipment manufacturers' maintenance manuals. *NFPA 70B* also provides guidelines on recommended maintenance intervals and instructions on how to set up an electrical maintenance program.

REVIEW QUESTIONS

1. After a circuit is deenergized by the automatic operation of a circuit protective device, the circuit shall not be manually reenergized until it has been determined that the equipment and circuit can be ___?___ energized.
   - a. cautiously
   - b. quickly
   - c. safely
   - d. slowly

2. After interrupting a fault approaching its interrupting rating, a ___?___ must be inspected and tested in accordance with the manufacturer's instructions.
   - a. circuit breaker
   - b. fuse
   - c. ground fault protection relay
   - d. motor starter

3. The *NFPA 70E* states that OCPDs shall be ___?___ in accordance with the manufacturer's instructions or industry consensus standards.
   - a. maintained
   - b. replaced
   - c. retrofitted
   - d. sized

4. For the purposes of *NFPA 70E* Chapter 2, maintenance shall be defined as preserving or restoring the condition of electrical equipment and installations, or parts of either, for the safety of ___?___ who are exposed to electrical hazards.
   - a. employees
   - b. employers
   - c. the public
   - d. vendors

5. *NFPA 70E* 205.4 recommends, but does not require, that OCPD maintenance, tests, and inspections be documented.
   - a. True
   - b. False

6. Lack of maintenance on OCPDs is of particular concern, as it may affect the performance of an OCPD, thereby resulting in increased clearing time and greater-than-calculated incident energy if an arcing fault incident occurs.
   - a. True
   - b. False

7. Which of the following is not a way in which maintenance plays a role in *NFPA 70E*?
   - a. Electrical equipment condition of maintenance is an important consideration for safe work practices.
   - b. Maintenance is necessary for continuity of power to keep business processes running.
   - c. Owners are required to maintain their electrical equipment.

8. Improper maintenance or lack of maintenance on an overcurrent protective device can lead to lower incident energy than may have been determined as part of an arc flash risk assessment.
   - a. True
   - b. False

9. Some electrical arc flash incidents are the result of poorly or improperly maintained electrical equipment.
   - a. True
   - b. False

10. The "clearing time" of the protective device has no influence on the resulting incident energy during an arcing fault event.
    - a. True
    - b. False

11. Consider the following situation: On January 21, 2021, an Electrical Worker performed justified energized work on electrical equipment protected by a circuit breaker with the following service sticker affixed to the circuit breaker enclosure. Should the Electrical Worker have solely relied on this label regarding whether the circuit breaker had been properly maintained?

   - a. Yes
   - b. No

12. The condition of maintenance for the bus structure shown in Figure 10-7 could lead to a bus failure.
    - a. True
    - b. False

Eliminating or Reducing Hazards by Design and Upgrades

Several design concepts and system upgrades can be assessed and deployed to eliminate or reduce the risk associated with electrical hazards. A knowledgeable person can identify hazards and, using safety by design concepts, reduce the hazard risk or in some cases eliminate the hazard completely. See F.3 and F.4 in *NFPA 70E* Informative Annex F, Risk Assessment and Risk Control, for insight. Table F.3, The Hierarchy of Risk Control Methods, lists six Risk Control Methods; the lower the number in this table, the greater the effectiveness in reducing the risk.

In addition, it is necessary to be familiar with important safe work practices for overcurrent protective devices.

Objectives

» Understand the important role that system design can play in eliminating or reducing electrical hazards.

» Know that choosing and installing overcurrent protective devices (OCPDs) is an important safety design consideration in regard to arc flash and arc blast hazards.

» Identify other engineering and design practices that can enhance electrical safety for new systems and for upgrading of existing systems.

» Explain OCPD safe work practices.

Chapter 11

Table of Contents

Case Study

An electrician with approximately 10 years of experience was working at a power plant. At about 12:00 p.m., he was electrocuted while replacing a limit switch. The victim had been on vacation up to and including the day before the incident.

Around 11:30 a.m. that day, the victim received a briefing on the need to replace a limit switch. The victim supposedly took a normal lunch break from 11:45 a.m. to 12:15 p.m. At about 12:25 p.m., three workers saw the victim lying face up underneath a conveyor belt. On the ground next to the victim were a pack of cigarettes and two folded one-dollar bills.

The body had no signs associated with a fall and was not in a position that would result from a fall. Examination of the body showed electrical burns on the right hand, aspiration of food into the secondary and tertiary bronchi, a contusion on the left mastoid scalp, and an abrasion of the right mid-tibial area. The medical examiner concluded that the cause of death was electrocution.

The probable sequence of events follows: The victim was standing on the conveyor belt guard installing the new limit switch. Two of the three wires were connected, and the victim was connecting the last wire, the 220-volt energized wire. The wire coming out of the conduit was too short to reach the switch. The victim probably grabbed the wire with his right hand and attempted to pull it farther out of the conduit. As he did, the bottom of part of his hand contacted the limit switch. When the wire hit the upper part of his palm, a circuit was completed. Due to the relatively low voltage, the victim was not killed instantly; his heart probably went into arrhythmia. He probably felt uncomfortable, decided to get down and have a smoke, and died seconds later.

The major causal factor in this fatal incident was the failure of the victim to follow standard procedures for locking out electrical power. The failure apparently resulted from inattention by the victim rather than the difficulty of the procedure or a lack of time to do the job. An explanation for the failure could be a somewhat cavalier attitude of the victim toward relatively low voltages. The research team observed such an attitude in other electricians at the plant.

Source: For details of this case, see FACE Investigation #83PA08. Accessed May 7, 2020.

For additional information, visit qr.njatcdb.org
Item #1201

INTRODUCTION

Implementing safety-related design can significantly impact worker safety. If a system is designed so that an electrical hazard is eliminated, then the worker will not have to contend with the hazard. Also, if the use of a specific design technique mitigates an electrical hazard, the workplace, although not hazard-free, is still a safer environment. Designing for safety provides the opportunity to eliminate or minimize electrical hazards before a worker ever becomes exposed to them. Additionally, there are some design concepts that may not reduce the hazard level, but may still reduce the probability of an incident occurring.

Read *NFPA 70E* Informative Annex O, Safety-Related Design Requirements, which stresses the importance of having risk assessments performed during the design phase. While still in the design stage, various alternative design concepts can be considered so that the most appropriate concepts can be incorporated into the final design and subsequent installation.

There are safety-related design concepts that can be implemented for existing systems resulting in eliminating or mitigating electrical hazards. It may be prudent to have older equipment retrofitted with modern devices. Usually, over the life-cycle of an electrical system, changes are implemented to expand or accommodate different needs. In some cases, these changes may result in more electrical hazards or increasing the level of hazards. For example, available fault currents in electrical systems may increase due to system changes. When a company does a facility-wide incident energy study, including a facility-wide fault current study, it is common to uncover a number of circuit breakers and fuses with inadequate interrupting ratings. These situations are a serious safety hazard and corrective action must be taken.

There are many more design techniques beyond what can be mentioned in a single chapter, and new ideas and products are continually being introduced. Those involved in the design are encouraged to constantly strive to search for, investigate, and implement design techniques that result in safer workplaces. Even those not involved in the design process should be aware of and mention viable design concepts and system upgrades to management, design personnel, and safety personnel to help those who are in the design process understand the value of various alternatives.

OVERCURRENT PROTECTIVE DEVICE CONSIDERATIONS

Choosing and installing overcurrent protective devices (OCPDs) is an important safety design consideration in regard to arc flash and arc blast. Overcurrent protective device selection decisions for new systems and for existing system upgrades may affect arc flash hazards either positively or negatively. The magnitude of the arcing fault current and the length of time the arcing fault current flows are directly related to the arc flash energy released. OCPDs may limit the magnitude of the arcing

OSHA Tip

Appendix E to § 1910.269, Protection From Flames and Electric Arcs, contains information to help employers estimate available heat energy as required by § 1910.269(l)(8)(ii), select protective clothing and other protective equipment with an arc rating suitable for the available heat energy as required by § 1910.269(l)(8)(v), and ensure that employees do not wear flammable clothing that could lead to burn injury as addressed by § 1910.269(l)(8)(iii) and (l)(8)(iv).

fault current that flows and reduce the time duration of the current, thereby potentially mitigating the arc flash hazard. The selection of OCPDs and the performance of proper maintenance can have a significant impact on the level of potential incident energy.

The level of arc flash hazard for a piece of electrical equipment having a specific available fault current is directly related to the protecting OCPD's time-current characteristics. There are a variety of time-current characteristics available for fuses, circuit breakers, and overcurrent relays. In the design stage, the selection of specific OCPD time-current characteristics along with the fault current will determine the incident energy.

Consider the time-current characteristic curves for two 600-ampere time-delay fuses. **See Figure 11-1.** The green fuse curve represents a 600-ampere UL Class RK5 time-delay fuse. The blue curve represents a 600-ampere UL Class J time-delay fuse. For most applications needing a 600-ampere fuse, either one of these fuses could be used. Assuming an available fault current of 16,400 amperes (black vertical arrow) with corresponding arcing fault current of 11,820 amperes (red vertical arrow), the 600-ampere Class RK5 fuse clears in approximately 0.064 seconds (denoted by the red dot). The 600-ampere Class J fuse clears this same 11,820-ampere arcing fault in slightly less than 0.01 seconds (approximately ½ cycle or

Figure 11-1   Time-Current Characteristics of Different Fuses: Different AFB and IE

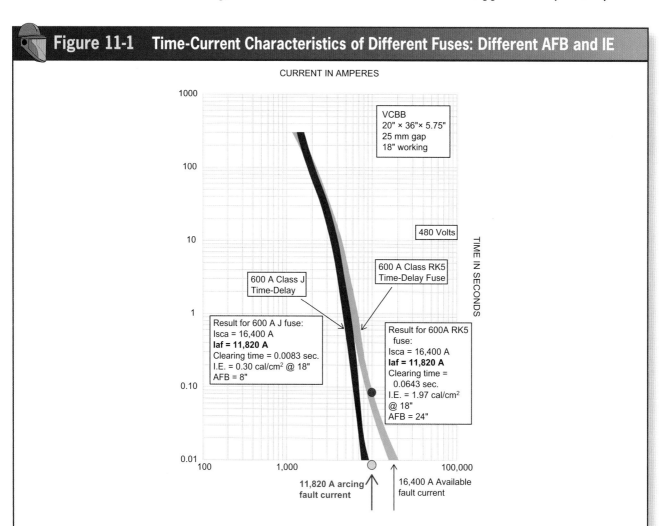

Figure 11-1. Different time-current characteristics for these two fuses may result in different incident energy levels for a specific arcing fault current.

0.0083 seconds), denoted by the yellow dot. This is just at the threshold of entering the current-limiting range of this Class J fuse. An incident energy analysis using an arcing fault current of 11,820 amperes and the clearing times by these two fuses results in 1.97 cal/cm² for the 600-ampere Class RK5 fuse and 0.30 cal/cm² for the 600-ampere Class J fuse. Both scenarios are for an 18-inch working distance in an enclosure 36 inches tall, 20 inches wide, and 5.75 inches deep with a vertical bus with barrier (VCBB) bus configuration. The arc flash boundaries are shown for each scenario. The incident energy and arc flash boundaries were calculated using the basic equation method in the *IEEE*

1584 2018 *Guide for Performing Arc Flash Hazard Calculations.*

Now consider the time-current curve for a 600-ampere electronic trip unit insulated case circuit breaker. **See Figure 11-2.** This may be compared to the

OSHA Tip

1910.333(a)

"General." Safety-related work practices shall be employed to prevent electric shock or other injuries resulting from either direct or indirect electrical contacts, when work is performed near or on equipment or circuits which are or may be energized. The specific safety-related work practices shall be consistent with the nature and extent of the associated electrical hazards.

Figure 11-2 Incident Energy - Molded Case Circuit Breaker: AFB and IE

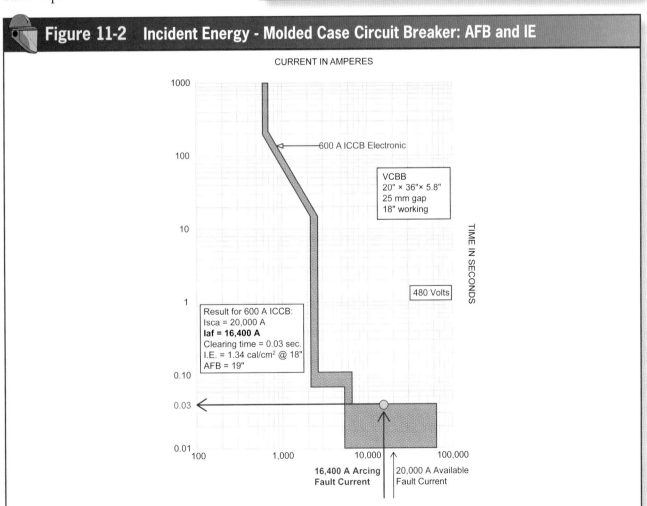

Figure 11-2. The resulting incident energy and AFB for an insulated case circuit breaker with an instantaneous trip is based on 16,400 ampere arcing fault current (20,000 ampere available fault current) and instantaneous trip clearing time of 0.03 seconds. This also assumes the enclosure is 36 inches tall by 20 inches wide by 5.8 inches deep and with a 25-millimeter spacing and VCBB bus configuration. Calculations per 2018 IEEE 1584.

time-current curve for a 600-ampere low-voltage power circuit breaker (LVPCB) with a short-time-delay of 0.5 seconds. **See Figure 11-3.** For a 16,400-ampere arcing fault current, the insulated case circuit breaker interrupts in 0.03 seconds, resulting in an incident energy exposure level of 1.34 cal/cm² at 18 inches working distance, and the LVPCB interrupts in 0.5 seconds, resulting in an incident energy exposure level of 25.6 cal/cm² at 18 inches working distance. These two examples illustrate the benefit of circuit breakers operating in their instantaneous trip range; the faster an OCPD

clears an arcing fault, the less the incident energy. The arc flash boundaries are shown for each scenario.

These examples also illustrate that the selection of OCPDs can make a difference in the incident energy analysis. The incident energies in these examples were calculated using 2018 *IEEE 1584.*

Current-Limiting Overcurrent Protective Devices

A current-limiting overcurrent protective device interrupts a fault current in its current-limiting range in less than $1/2$ cycle and reduces the fault current to something substantially less than

---

Figure 11-3   Incident Energy - Low Voltage Circuit Breaker: AFB and IE

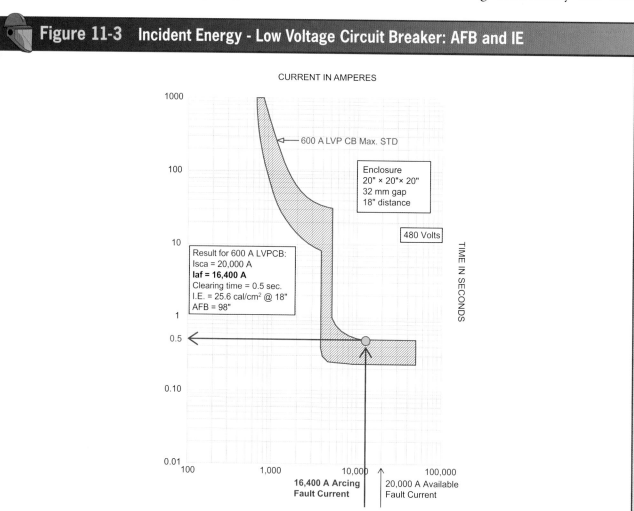

Figure 11-3. *The resulting incident energy and AFB for a low-voltage circuit breaker with a short-time setting and no instantaneous trip is based on 16,400 ampere arcing fault current (20,000 ampere available fault current) and short-time delay clearing time of 0.5 seconds. The enclosure for this power circuit breaker (PCB) is assumed to be 20 inches wide by 20 inches tall by 20 inches deep. The electrode gap is considered to be 32 mm and the bus configuration is assumed to be VCBB. Calculations per 2018* IEEE 1584.

Figure 11-4 Current-Limiting Protection

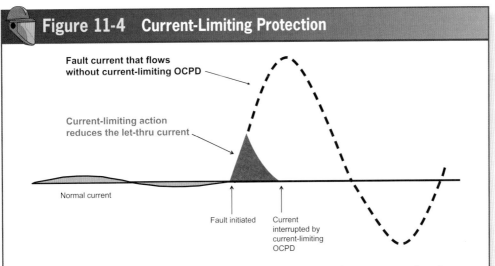

Figure 11-4. The black dashed line curve represents the fault current that flows without protection by a non–current-limiting OCPD and the red triangular shape represents the current flow by the current-limiting action of a current-limiting OCPD.

that which would have flowed if the current-limiting device were not protecting the circuit. **See Figure 11-4.** Overcurrent protective devices that are current-limiting offer superior arc flash mitigation when the available arcing fault current is in the current-limiting range of a current-limiting OCPD. When the fault current is in the current-limiting range of a current-limiting OCPD, the fault current's magnitude and time duration are both reduced, which reduces the energy released by an arcing fault.

Fuses and circuit breakers that are evaluated to be current-limiting per their respective UL product standards are marked on the product as

"current-limiting." **See Figure 11-5.** As part of the UL product standard evaluation criteria, current-limiting fuses or current-limiting circuit breakers must

The IEEE Staged Arc Flash Tests (Tests 4, 3, and 1) provide illustrative examples of the value of current-limiting OCPDs.

For additional information, visit qr.njatcdb.org Item #1223

For additional information, visit qr.njatcdb.org Item #1224

For additional information, visit qr.njatcdb.org Item #1225

Figure 11-5 Devices Marked "Current-Limiting"

Figure 11-5. Overcurrent protective devices 600 volts or less that are current-limiting are marked "Current Limiting."

Courtesy of Eaton

Figure 11-6   UL Limits for 200-Ampere Fuses

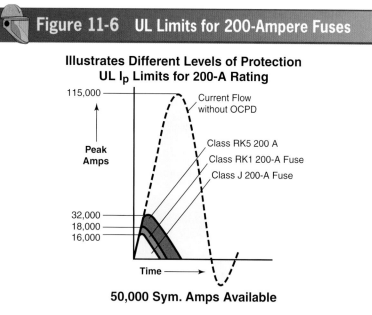

Illustrates Different Levels of Protection
UL I$_p$ Limits for 200-A Rating

Current Flow without OCPD

Class RK5 200 A
Class RK1 200-A Fuse
Class J 200-A Fuse

Peak Amps

115,000

32,000
18,000
16,000

Time →

50,000 Sym. Amps Available

Figure 11-6. *UL I$_P$ limits for fuses rated as "200-ampere" illustrate the different degrees of current limitation and no current limitation.*

perform to specific levels of maximum energy let-through limits. Non–current-limiting fuses or circuit breakers do not have to perform to specific maximum energy let-through limits. **See Figure 11-6.** Consider the UL maximum energy let-through limits for four scenarios

Figure 11-7   UL Limit for 400-Ampere Fuses

Illustrates Different Levels of Protection
UL I$_p$ Limits for 400-A Rating

Current Flow without OCPD

Class RK5 400 A
Class RK1 400-A Fuse
Class J 400-A Fuse

Peak Amps

115,000

50,000
33,000
25,000

Time →

50,000 Sym. Amps Available

Figure 11-7. *UL I$_P$ limits for fuses rated as "400-ampere" illustrate the different degrees of current limitation and no current limitation.*

with an available fault current of 50,000 RMS symmetrical amperes: (1) current flow without OCPD (dashed line black curve); (2) let-through limit for a 200-ampere Class RK5 fuse (purple triangle), (3) let-through limit for 200-ampere Class RK1 fuse (green triangle), and (4) let-through limit for 200-ampere Class J fuse (yellow triangle). Note that the dotted black line represents the asymmetrical fault current that could flow with 50,000 symmetrical amperes available; the instantaneous peak current of that fault could reach 115,000 amperes. The UL fuse product standard instantaneous peak current limit for a 400-ampere Class RK5 fuse is 50,000 amperes; for a 400-ampere RK1 fuse, the limit is 33,000 amperes; and for a 400-ampere Class J fuse, it is 25,000 amperes. The lower the peak current and the smaller the triangle, the lower the energies released during an arcing fault event. UL fuse product standards have established maximum energy let-through limit values for current-limiting fuses at an available fault current of 50,000 RMS symmetrical amperes. Notice that the various classes of 400-ampere fuses have greater let-through currents than the 200-ampere fuses, which is to be expected. **See Figure 11-7.**

It should be noted that the current-limiting performance criteria for circuit breakers is different than for fuses in their respective UL product standards. Devices that are not listed and marked as current-limiting may not significantly reduce the level of fault current, and they may take longer to interrupt. As a consequence, non–current-limiting OCPDs may permit larger amounts of energy to be released during an arcing fault.

Different degrees of current limitation exist. Different OCPDs may become current-limiting at different levels of short-circuit current. Moreover, once in the current-limiting range, different devices are more current-limiting than others. If the arcing fault current is in the current-limiting range of current-limiting fuses, the incident energy released during an arcing fault typically does not significantly increase as the fault current increases. This is an important consideration in mitigating arc flash hazards. This means for certain fuse types and ampere ratings, high fault currents that produce high arcing currents are not a major issue since the fuse's current-limiting ability mitigates the arc flash energies so well.

Class RK5 fuses offer a good level of current-limiting protection. A better choice for applications using Class R fuse clips, however, are Class RK1 fuses; these fuses are more current-limiting and enter their current-limiting range at lower fault levels. As a result, circuits protected by Class RK1 fuses will generally produce a lower incident energy than circuits protected by Class RK5 fuses.

Class J, Class CF, Class RK1, Class CC, and Class T fuses offer the best practical current-limiting protection. They generally have a significantly better degree of current limitation than other alternatives. They also typically enter their current-limiting range at lower currents than the other fuses or limiter alternatives. These types of fuses provide the greatest current limitation for general protection and motor circuit protection.

Overcurrent Protective Device Life-Cycle Consistency

Design criteria for choosing the type of OCPD for new installations or renovations to existing electrical systems should take into account whether the OCPDs will retain their specified fault-clearing operating characteristics over the life cycle of the system. This aspect depends on which type of OCPD is used and whether the appropriate level of maintenance resources, which depends on the type of OCPD, will be allocated throughout the electrical system's life cycle.

The reliability of OCPDs in retaining consistent fault-clearing performance over the system life cycle directly impacts arc flash hazards. *NFPA 70E* recognizes this relationship in 130.5(B)(1) and (2). It is necessary to take into consideration the design of the overcurrent protective device and its opening time, including its condition of maintenance. Additionally, Informational Note No. 2 located after Table 130.5(C) advises that inadequate maintenance of OCPDs can result in increased incident energy, while Informational Note No. 5 points to Chapter 2 as the source of safety-related maintenance requirements. Section 205.4 requires maintaining OCPDs per the manufacturer's instructions or industry consensus standards and states that inspections, maintenance, and tests must be documented. Other notable sections related to OCPDs include 210.5, 225.1, 225.2, 225.3, and 130.8(M).

The opening time of OCPDs is a critical factor for the resultant arc flash energy released when an arcing fault occurs. The longer an OCPD takes to clear a given arcing fault current, the greater the incident energy. When an arcing fault or any fault current occurs, the OCPD must be able to operate as intended. Therefore, the reliability of OCPDs is critical. They need to open as originally specified; otherwise, the arc flash hazard can escalate to higher levels than expected.

OSHA Tip

Appendix E to § 1910.269 - Protection From Flames and Electric Arcs

III. Protection Against Burn Injury

A. Estimating Available Heat Energy Calculation methods. Paragraph (l)(8)(ii) of § 1910.269 provides that, for each employee exposed to an electric-arc hazard, the employer must make a reasonable estimate of the heat energy to which the employee would be exposed if an arc occurs. Table 2 lists various methods of calculating values of available heat energy from an electric circuit. The Occupational Safety and Health Administration does not endorse any of these specific methods. Each method requires the input of various parameters, such as fault current, the expected length of the electric arc, the distance from the arc to the employee, and the clearing time for the fault (that is, the time the circuit protective devices take to open the circuit and clear the fault). The employer can precisely determine some of these parameters, such as the fault current and the clearing time, for a given system. The employer will need to estimate other parameters, such as the length of the arc and the distance between the arc and the employee, because such parameters vary widely.

Figure 11-8   Current-Limiting Fuses

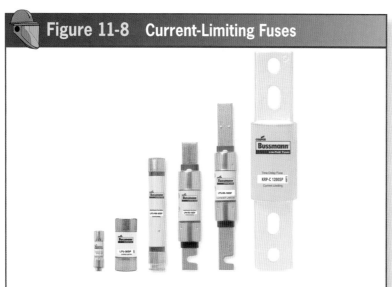

Figure 11-8. *A range of modern current-limiting fuses are available, including: 30-ampere, 600-volt Class CC; 30-ampere, 600-volt Class J; 30-ampere, 600-volt Class RK1; 100-ampere, 250-volt Class RK1; 100-ampere, 600-volt Class RK1; and 1,200-ampere, 600-volt Class L.*

Courtesy of Eaton's Bussmann Division

Two different types of overcurrent protection technology provide different choices in maintenance requirements and might affect the incident energy analysis.

Current-Limiting Fuses

Current-limiting fuses are reliable and retain their ability to open as originally designed under fault conditions. **See Figure 11-8.** When a fuse is replaced, a new fuse is put into service, and the circuit has reliable protection with performance equal to the original specification. Modern current-limiting fuses do not require maintenance other than visual examination and ensuring that there is no damage to fuses from external thermal conditions (such as conductor terminations), liquids, or physical abuse. It is important that when fuses are replaced, the proper fuse types, including interrupting rating and ampere rating, are used as replacements.

Circuit Breakers

Circuit breakers are mechanical OCPDs that require periodic exercise, inspection, testing, and possible maintenance or replacement. A circuit breaker's reliability and operating speed depend on its original specification and its condition. A specific circuit breaker's condition of maintenance is influenced by variables, including the following:

- Length of service
- Number of manual operations under load
- Number of operations due to overloads
- Number of fault interruptions
- Humidity
- Condensation
- Corrosive substances in the air
- Vibration
- Invasion by foreign materials or liquids
- Thermal damage caused by loose connections
- Erosion of contacts
- Erosion of arc chutes
- Maintenance history

When determining what needs to be done and when to perform inspections, testing, and maintenance, follow the manufacturer's instructions and manuals or industry standards. In addition, 225.3 of *NFPA 70E* requires a circuit breaker that interrupts a fault near its interrupting rating to be inspected and tested.

A variety of innovations have made it simpler to determine the cumulative effect of issues that impact the condition of maintenance and thus the performance of circuit breakers. Because circuit breakers are equipped with electronic trip units that are microprocessor based, certain features can be added that use information obtained from the circuit breaker to provide health information important to the Electrical Worker. Breakers on the market today can monitor short-circuits, overloads, operations, temperature, and run-time and can provide a host of individual insights, while the combination of all of this data can provide an overall picture of the condition of the circuit breaker. This information is important for predictive maintenance and system reliability. Specific insights available from these circuit breakers include:

- Operation data provides insight on when the breaker mechanism was last exercised, and if the mechanism was bound or jammed.

- Total number of operations can provide indication of the endurance wear on the circuit breaker mechanism and indication of contact wear.
- Number of interruptions, and the magnitude of the energy interrupted, are vital parameters to the contact wear indication and the arc chute condition.
- Overload interruptions have less of an effect than short-circuits, but they are included in the calculation and affect the circuit breaker's overall health.
- Short-circuits can be damaging to the contacts, integrity, and dielectric strength of the circuit breaker. The magnitude of a short-circuit event is compared to the rating of the circuit breaker and weighed as another factor in the health of the circuit breaker.
- Run-time is also considered and demonstrates how long the breaker has been in use with current flowing through it.
- The environmental temperature is one of the most important measurements; this is the highest temperature recorded. The date and time of that temperature is saved in the analysis.

All of these parameters are saved in the memory of the trip unit. The data may be retrieved locally or remotely via control or communication systems. Alternatively, on some circuit breakers, a summary of this data is available graphically on the circuit breaker's LCD screen in order to easily convey the status of the breaker and to give the Electrical Worker information needed to determine the condition of maintenance of that circuit breaker.

Consideration for Fusible Systems

In addition to current limitation and consistency considerations, there are other important considerations for fusible systems.

Rejection-Style Class J, CF, T, R, G, and L Fuses

It is important to ensure that arc flash protection levels are maintained as a facility ages. Class J, CC, CF, T, R, and L fuses provide an advantage in that these fuse classes each have physical size and/or mounting provisions that are unique to each fuse class. **See Figure 11-9.** A fuse of a given class cannot be inserted into mountings designed for another class. As a result, fuses with lower voltage ratings, interrupting ratings less than 200,000 amperes (100,000 amperes for Class G fuses), or lower current limitation performance cannot be accidentally put into service.

However, the incident energy can vary for a specific ampere-rated fuse of a given class. For a given ampere-rated fuse of a specific class, there may be more than one type of fuse; for

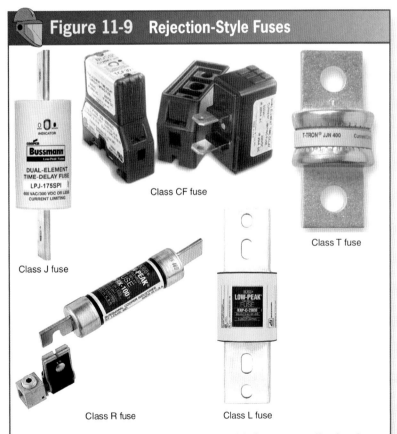

Figure 11-9 Rejection-Style Fuses

Class J fuse

Class CF fuse

Class T fuse

Class R fuse

Class L fuse

Figure 11-9. Class J, CC, CF, T, R, and L fuses are all rejection-style fuses, meaning they cannot be swapped with fuse mountings of a different class.

Courtesy of Eaton's Bussmann Division

example, Class J fuses are available with both non–time-delay characteristics and time-delay characteristics. Each can have different arc flash mitigation capabilities. In addition, there may be differences in performance by fuses of different manufacturers. If an incident energy calculation has been performed for a circuit based on a fuse of a specific type and manufacturer, it is recommended that replacements should be a fuse of the same type and manufacturer. The exception: if the replacement fuse's time-current characteristics are of equal or faster clearing time than the original fuse, the substitution should provide similar or better arc flash mitigation results.

Enhanced Safety of New-Style Fusible Disconnects

Newer generations of fusible disconnects have become even safer. For instance, the branch fusible disconnects in a panelboard may permit servicing of the fuses without opening the panel trim. **See Figure 11-10.** The disconnect is interlocked with the fuses. When extracting or inserting a fuse, place the disconnect handle in the "OFF" position.

Switches Equipped with ERMS

Energy-reducing maintenance switching (ERMS) is one of the most important new technology options to include on larger fusible switching (1,200 amperes and greater) to mitigate the arc flash hazard for lower available arcing fault current situations. When the ERMS option is switched "on," if an arcing fault event were to occur on a circuit with this fusible switch protecting, there is additional enhanced arc flash protection. With the ERMS added to a fusible switch, the result of the ERMS and fuses together can be significantly lower incident energy levels for a wide range of arcing fault currents from low magnitude to high magnitude. For arcing fault currents of lower magnitudes, the ERMS is faster than the fuses, and for higher magnitude arcing fault currents, the fuses will be faster than the ERMS. In some situations, effective in 2020, *NEC* Section 240.67 requires technology that reduces the potential arc flash energy while personnel work on equipment protected by 1,200-ampere or larger fuses.

Reduce Incident Energy Exposure for Existing Fusible Systems

If the electrical system is an existing fusible system, consider replacing or upgrading the existing fuses with fuses that are more current-limiting. This step can reduce incident energy exposure .

Owners of existing fusible systems should consider upgrading Class H, K5, K9, and RK5 fuses to Class RK1 fuses, and should verify that Class J and Class L fuses are the most current-limiting models available. Assessments of facilities have revealed that the installed fuse types are not the most current-limiting, or that fuses were installed decades ago and new fuses with better current limitation are now available. **See Figure 11-11.**

Circuit Breakers

In addition to consistency considerations that have already been discussed for circuit breaker systems, other important points must be considered in relation to electrical safety.

For additional information, visit qr.njatcdb.org Item #4365

Figure 11-10 New Style Fusible Panelboard

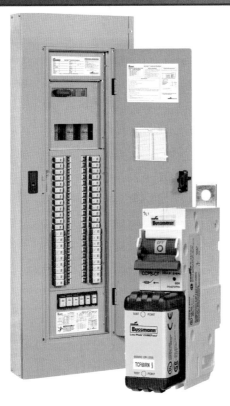

Figure 11-10. *In this fusible panelboard, the branch circuit fuses can be serviced without opening the panel trim.*

Courtesy of Eaton's Bussmann Division

Figure 11-11 Fuses to Reduce Incident Energy

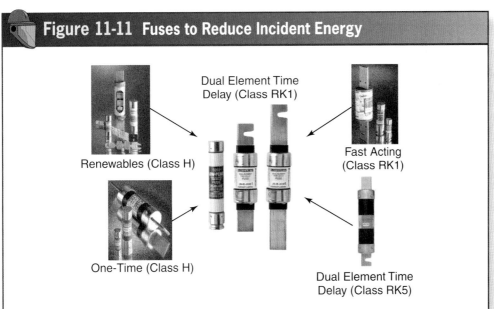

Figure 11-11. *Replacing all existing Class H, Class K, and Class RK5 fuses with Class RK1 fuses can mitigate the arc flash hazard to lower incident energies in many situations.*

Energy-Reducing Maintenance Switching for Circuit Breakers

This is one of the most important options to include on larger circuit breakers to mitigate the arc flash hazard. Energy-reducing maintenance switching (ERMS) for circuit breakers is a fairly recent technology that improves electrical safety for workers who must work on equipment that is not in an electrically safe work condition. When the ERMS is switched "on," if an arcing fault event occurs on a circuit that the circuit breaker protects and the arcing fault current is above the ERMS current pickup, the circuit breaker trips without intentional delay. *NEC* Section 240.87 requires technology that reduces the potential arc flash energy while personnel work on equipment protected by a circuit breaker that can be adjusted to a continuous current rating of 1,200 amperes or higher. A circuit breaker equipped with an ERMS provides a reliable means for compliance. In most cases, an existing installed circuit breaker can be retrofitted with ERMS capability.

Circuit Breaker Instantaneous Trip Settings

Some circuit breakers have adjustable instantaneous trip settings. **See Figure 11-12.** This setpoint establishes the pickup current beyond which the circuit breaker will start to operate in its instantaneous region. This setpoint traditionally is used to help avoid nuisance opening on normal load surges, such as from transformer inrush currents or motor inrush currents, or to improve selective coordination. Selective coordination is required in the *NEC* (620.62, 700.32, and other sections) for some circuits supplying life-safety loads. Where not required by the *NEC*, an owner may still want selective coordination in order to have more reliable power supply and avoid unnecessary power outages. If the arcing fault current calculated falls in the current range between the instantaneous trip low and high pickup settings, the instantaneous trip setting selected for the application can greatly impact the incident energy. If the instantaneous trip level is set to its highest pickup level, the circuit

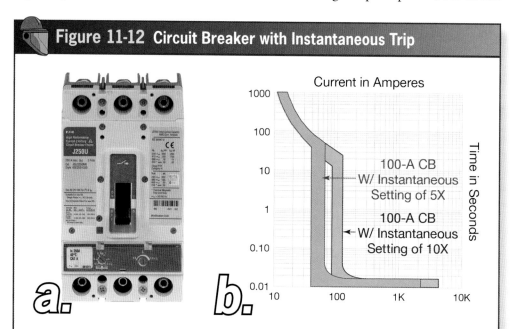

Figure 11-12 Circuit Breaker with Instantaneous Trip

Figure 11-12. *(a) Some circuit breakers have an instantaneous trip setting that can be adjusted by dials.* Courtesy of Eaton's Bussmann Division

(b) A 100-ampere circuit breaker time-current curve shows the instantaneous trip dial setting at 5X = 500 amperes and a different dial setting at 10X = 1,000 amperes.

breaker might not respond with an instantaneous clearing time during an arcing fault. The result is a longer opening time, which in turn means that a much higher level of energy may be released during an arcing fault. Conversely, if the instantaneous trip is set low enough to operate for a low arcing fault condition, the incident energy may be mitigated to a lower level. An assessment is necessary to determine the lowest instantaneous trip setting possible without incurring nuisance tripping.

Maintenance or service personnel should never adjust the trip settings of overcurrent protective devices without getting approval. If adjusting the instantaneous pickup or short-time delay settings of a circuit breaker is necessary to permit a motor to start or transformer to be energized, it must be understood that the ramifications of these changes could be higher incident energy and increased arc flash boundaries. These changes should not be made without approval and review.

Short-Time Delay Circuit Breakers

Some circuit breakers with electronic trip units employ a short-time delay trip curve and associated pickup and time delay settings which offer an interim step of protection for currents less than the instantaneous region of the trip curve before they are left to the long-time clearing region. This feature is only found on circuit breakers with electronic trip units. This portion of the trip curve is demonstrated as that portion of the curve for currents lower than those that would be in the instantaneous region of the trip curve for that circuit breaker. **See Figure 11-13.** The clearing time of the short-time delay region of this circuit breaker is approximately 0.15 seconds and again offers an interim step of a faster clearing time for these lower fault currents.

A short-time delay curve is used to achieve selective coordination between upstream and downstream OCPDs, to provide increased protection of the load, or to provide a reduced clearing time for low arcing currents, improving

the incident energy reduction downstream of the device while still maintaining or meeting other power system design requirements.

A short-time delay setting is very common for large circuit breakers 1,000 amperes and larger as their instantaneous pickup values can be very high. These devices are typically closer to the utility point of common coupling if not the service OCPD themselves and provide an intentional delay so that downstream OCPDs can clear faults to achieve selective coordination, whether to meet design goals or code requirements. Under fault conditions,

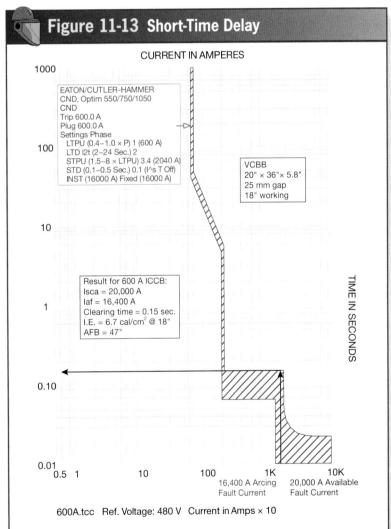

Figure 11-13. The short-time delay portion of the time-current curve is the portion of the curve for currents lower than those that would be in the instantaneous region of the trip curve for the circuit breaker.

a short-time delay trip unit intentionally delays signaling the circuit breaker to open for the time duration setting of the short- time delay. Therefore, a fault is permitted to flow for an extended time. The amount of time that fault currents are permitted to flow will be dependent upon the capabilities of the circuit breaker. For example, molded case circuit breakers (MCCBs) equipped with an electronic trip unit with a short-time delay will not permit high fault currents to persist as long as a low-voltage power circuit breaker (LVPCB) simply due to the construction differences between these two devices. A low-voltage power circuit breaker with a short-time delay and without instantaneous trip can permit a fault up to its interrupting rating to flow for the length of time of the short-time delay setting, which might be 6,

12, 18, 24, or even 30 cycles. **See Figure 11-14.** In addition, MCCBs and insulated case circuit breakers (ICCBs) are all equipped with an instantaneous trip where LVPCBs may or may not have an instantaneous trip.

NEC Section 240.87 was initially introduced into the *NEC* due to the fact that there are some power circuit breakers that do not have an instantaneous trip but yet have a short-time delay capability permitting fault currents to flow for up to and including 30 cycles. This *Code* requirement has changed since its first introduction, which only impacted power circuit breakers that did not have an instantaneous trip, to now include MCCBs and ICCBs which do have an instantaneous trip but still provide delayed responses that cause higher incident energy conditions for the Electrical Worker. These

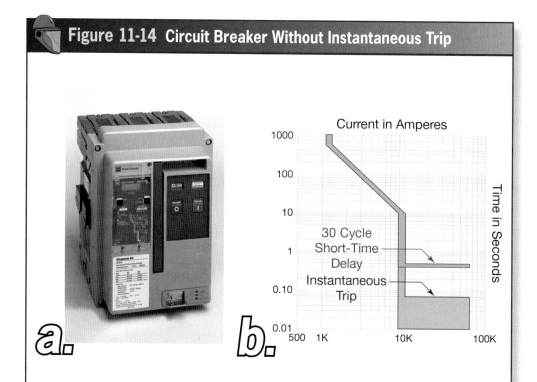

Figure 11-14 Circuit Breaker Without Instantaneous Trip

Figure 11-14. (a.) A low-voltage power circuit breaker (LVPCB) may not have an instantaneous trip. Courtesy of Eaton

(b.) The pink curve represents a LVPCB with a 30-cycle short-time delay setting and no instantaneous trip. The purple curve represents an instantaneous trip for a circuit breaker. A circuit breaker with an instantaneous trip will clear an arcing fault in less time than a circuit breaker with a short-time delay.

changes recognize the fact that these larger OCPDs may not respond instantaneously due to intentional delays to prevent nuisance tripping of the main or to meet selective coordination needs. This section now impacts 1,200-ampere circuit breakers and larger, requiring them to have a means to mitigate the resulting high incident energy due to these intentional delays. An energy-reducing maintenance switch is one option that is often implemented due to it being the most cost-effective technology. Some existing installed low-voltage power circuit breakers, as well as some newly installed LVPCBs less than 1,200 amperes, are equipped with very high instantaneous trip setpoints and may or may not have a short-time delay setting. A circuit breaker does not have to be 1,200 amperes or higher to present an intentional delay that will impact incident energy.

If an arcing fault occurs on a circuit that it is low enough to not be within the instantaneous region of the upstream circuit breaker, significantly more incident energy might be released while the system waits for the circuit breaker long-time delay or even short-time delay to time out. The short-time delay setpoint can provide an interim step to provide faster clearing times than what would be achieved in the long-time trip region of the curve, but setpoints that permit clearing times of upwards of 30 cycles may still let a significant amount of energy through to downstream equipment. The longer an OCPD takes to open, the greater the incident energy due to arcing faults. Experience shows that the incident energy increase is directly proportional with the amount of time arcing current is permitted to flow.

System designers and those exposed to electrical hazards should understand the relationship between arcing currents and clearing times for these OCPDs. Using circuit breakers with intentional delays for any reason could greatly increase the incident energy. Solutions are available for these conditions but may need to be specified during the design process. For new and existing circuit breakers where the arcing currents are low enough to not be within the instantaneous region of the circuit breaker or where circuit breakers are applied without an instantaneous trip, an energy-reducing maintenance switching option either specified before installation or retrofitted to existing circuit breakers, is a viable solution to mitigate incident energy. For new circuit breakers with short-time delay trip and no instantaneous trip, purchase one that has ERMS as part of the circuit breaker.

Zone-Selective Interlocking

While utilizing short-time delay settings may be necessary to achieve selective coordination for a circuit breaker design, short-time delay settings can permit high incident energy levels under arcing fault conditions to occur. Another possible solution to this dilemma is to use circuit breakers equipped with zone-selective interlocking. Zone-selective interlocking is an option for some circuit breaker systems where circuit breakers communicate with each other such that the upstream circuit breaker ignores its setpoints and trips instantaneously when the fault occurs within the zone of protection. Circuit breakers with this option are equipped with communication wiring between the circuit breakers. The benefit is that when a downstream fault is not in a circuit breaker's protection zone, the circuit breaker can be set to operate with a short-time delay to provide selective coordination with downstream circuit breakers. When a fault is within a circuit breaker's protection zone, then the upstream circuit breaker overrides its short-time delay and operates without an intentional delay, thereby providing better equipment protection and less incident energy under arcing fault conditions.

Operating without an intentional delay does not mean that the circuit breaker will operate with the same level of performance as the instantaneous trip. The clearing time is typically

Figure 11-15 ZSI: Fault in Circuit Breaker 3 Protection Zone

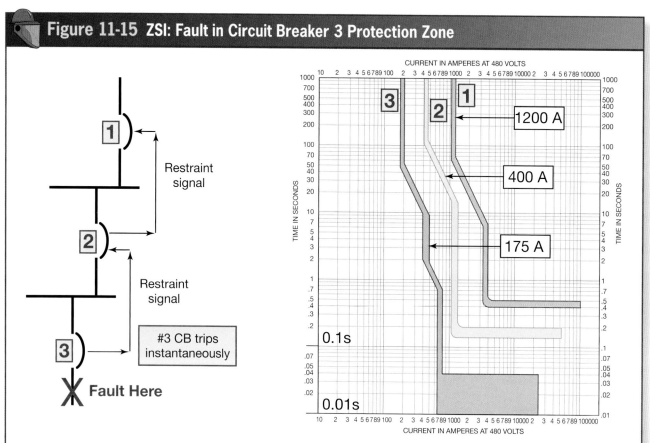

Figure 11-15. *The fault occurs on the load side of circuit breaker 3 (175 A). This fault is not in any zone-selective interlocking region of protection, and if high enough, circuit breaker 3 will operate instantaneously. When circuit breaker 3 senses a fault, it sends a restraint signal to circuit breakers 2 (400 A) and 1 (1,200 A); circuit breakers 2 and 1 will trip based upon their programmed settings and associated trip curves. In this case, the upstream circuit breakers 2 and 1 function with the short-time delay times shown by their time-current curves.*

driven from the fastest short-time delay clearing time, as the level of complexity of the application requires the circuit breaker to process data before it determines to send a trip signal. The upstream circuit breaker, when it sees a fault, must first compare the fault current with its short-time delay pickup setpoint, then check to see if it received a signal from the downstream connected devices; if no signal is received, then it must initiate the trip sequence. This process takes time, and so although no intentional delay is introduced, an unintentional delay of processing time is, which yields a longer clearing time than that which is achieved by the instantaneous trip or instantaneous override function.

Zone-selective interlocking does not enable selective coordination. In order to achieve selective coordination, the circuit breakers must be set to selectively coordinate. Zone-selective interlocking is only intended to reduce damage to equipment when faults occur within the zone of protection.

Consider the three fault scenarios for a system depicted with three circuit breakers zone-selectively interlocked to create two zones of protection. **See Figures 11-15, 11-16, and 11-17.** These three scenarios indicate how these devices will respond to faults at various locations within the system. For this system to selectively coordinate, all breakers must be selected based on the amount of fault current they will see, and none of the fault currents can be high enough to instantaneously trip an upstream device. For this selectively coordinated system, the arcing currents for each of these circuit breakers are not in the instantaneous region of any one of the circuit breakers. Each scenario shows the fault at a particular point in the system and the resulting effective time-current curve for that scenario. Note these three circuit breakers have to selectively coordinate prior to utilizing the zone-selective interlocking function.

Relaying Schemes

Relay schemes can be applied on both new installations and existing systems to mitigate arc flash hazards. When an arc flash event occurs that causes the relay to call for the circuit to be interrupted, the relay output signals a properly rated disconnecting means to interrupt the circuit. The disconnecting means can be a vacuum interrupter, circuit breaker, or disconnect switch with a shunt trip.

Figure 11-16 ZSI: Fault in Circuit Breaker 2 Protection Zone

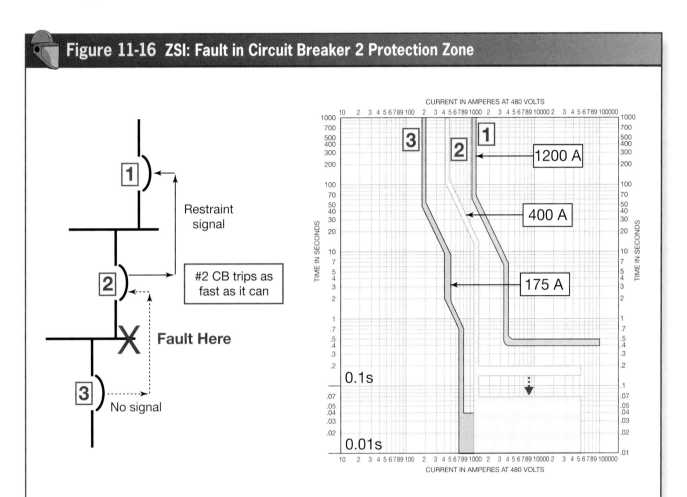

Figure 11-16. *Faults between circuit breakers 2 and 3 are in the zone of protection established by zone-selectively interlocked circuit breakers 2 and 3. Because the fault is on the line side of circuit breaker 3, circuit breaker 3 does not sense the fault current, so it does not send a restraint signal to circuit breaker 2. Circuit breaker 2 senses the fault current and, if the fault current is greater than its short-time delay setting, sends a restraint signal to circuit breaker 1, so that circuit breaker 1 operates based on its programmed settings, which include the short-time delay trip times shown by the time-current curve. Circuit breaker 2 will function without an intentional delay because it does not get a signal from the downstream circuit breaker 3, meaning the fault is within the zone of protection. The clearing time of circuit breaker 2 will be based on its fastest short-time delay clearing time.*

Figure 11-17 ZSI: Fault in Circuit Breaker 1 Protection Zone

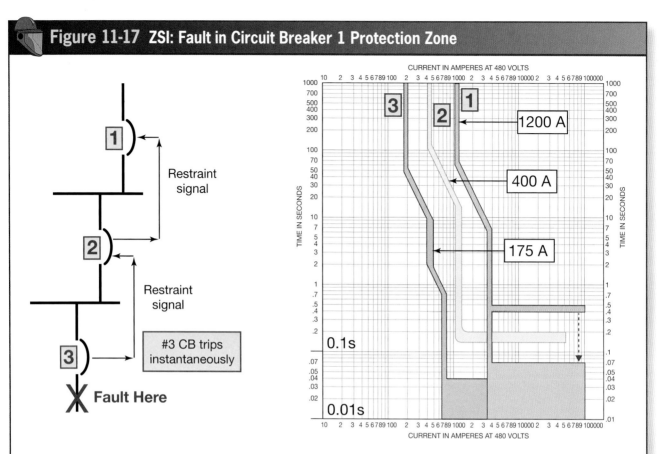

Figure 11-17. *Faults between circuit breakers 1 and 2 are within the circuit breaker 1 and circuit breaker 2 zone of protection. Neither circuit breaker 3 nor circuit breaker 2 senses the fault, and so no restraint signal is sent to circuit breaker 1. Because circuit breaker 1 senses a fault and does not receive a restraint signal from any downstream circuit breaker, it will function without an intentional delay. The time-current curve shows circuit breaker 1 opening as quickly as possible, reducing the arc flash hazard.*

Overcurrent Relays

Overcurrent relays are used for some low-voltage applications, but are more commonly used on medium- and high-voltage systems. The current and time settings to operate are important factors influencing the arc flash hazard with such systems. Coordination for medium- and high-voltage OCPDs is generally more critical from a business continuity basis, because an outage at this level represents a large amount of power. Thus, the objective is to set the relays to minimize the incident energy as well as to provide acceptable coordination levels.

Arc Flash Relays

Arc flash relays can be utilized to mitigate incident energy levels by limiting the time of the fault. **See Figure 11-18.** Typically, these relays monitor for uncharacteristic current, and several light sensors placed at key locations inside an electrical enclosure. Other parameters that could be monitored include sound and pressure. If an arc flash event occurs within the enclosure, the light, sound, and pressure all rapidly escalate to high levels. When an uncharacteristic current flow is combined with one or more of these other parameters, the relay qualifies the event as an arc flash event and then signals a disconnecting means to interrupt. This method is an effective arc flash mitigation means for equipment protected by OCPDs that are too large in ampacity to quickly respond to the arcing fault current.

On installations such as a 480-volt service or unit substation with a large ampacity main OCPD, the arc flash relay technology can be used to signal a medium-voltage disconnect and allow for fast interruption of an arc flash event.

Separate Enclosure for Main Disconnect

Service entrance equipment and the first-level distribution equipment on the secondary of any transformer present similar hazards to the Electrical Worker. These locations typically have high- incident energy due to the fact that the next upstream OCPD is on the line side of the transformer. The primary OCPD on a transformer is selected to ensure energization of the transformer. It must not open based on inrush currents. These devices have an inherent intentional delay which in most cases causes the arcing currents at the secondary first-level distribution equipment to be in the long-time region of the primary OCPD trip curve. To reduce the arc flash hazard exposure at the secondary distribution equipment, some safety by design methods can be put in place.

The design may call for a disconnect to be placed in an enclosure separate from the feeder disconnects and

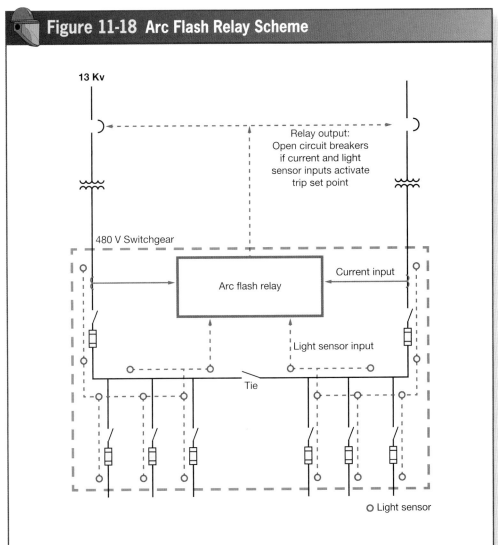

Figure 11-18 Arc Flash Relay Scheme

Figure 11-18. An arc flash relay scheme for double-ended switchgear can mitigate the incident energy to a lower level than is possible with standard OCPDs.

overcurrent protective devices. **See Figure 11-19.** With this configuration, the high incident energy has simply been moved into a separate enclosure with a single OCPD which is much less likely to be accessed and much less frequency accessed. The presence of this disconnect makes it much easier to establish an electrically safe work condition at the feeder equipment. In addition, with this configuration, when justified energized work is being conducted in the distribution equipment with feeder OCPDs, the incident energy is dependent upon the OCPD in the isolated main disconnect on the secondary and not based on the primary OCPD. It is important to remember that if the first-level secondary distribution equipment has a main OCPD as a part of that assembly, the clearing time to determine the arc flash hazard is not based on the main OCPD but rather the next upstream OCPD. A design featuring a separately enclosed main disconnect can also be used for industrial control panels (a separately enclosed disconnect is attached on the outside of the industrial control panel enclosure), motor control centers, branch panels, and distribution panels. This arrangement provides an electrical system designed for safer work practices.

Specify a Main on Each Service

Generally, a single main service disconnect provides for safer work practices than the six-disconnect rule for service entrances as permitted in *NEC* 230.71. The six-disconnect rule is intended to reduce the cost of the service equipment, but this choice typically increases worker exposure to hazards especially where the six disconnects are located in the same equipment. Without a main OCPD, the main bus and line terminals of the feeders are unprotected. In addition, equipment installed under the six-disconnect rule does not allow the bus to be deenergized without the utility being called to deenergize its supply.

The *NEC* limits the locations where six disconnects are permitted to be installed in the same enclosure as part of the requirements found in *NEC* 230.71(B). Four options exist that can be leveraged when a service seeks to employ the six-disconnect rule. These options were arrived upon to facilitate the placement of barriers as required in 230.62(C). *NEC* 230.62(C) recognizes that the line side lugs of the service disconnecting means present an exposure to the electrical worker even when the service disconnecting means is in the open position. This section requires these exposed lugs and conductors to be provided with barriers to reduce the likelihood of coming in contact with these exposed energized parts. The four options of *NEC* 230.71(B) help facilitate the insertion of these barriers for safety and include the following:

(1)   Separate enclosures with a main service disconnecting means in each enclosure.
(2)   Panelboards with a main service disconnecting means in each panelboard enclosure
(3)   Switchboard(s) where there is only one service disconnect in each separate vertical section where there are barriers separating each vertical section.

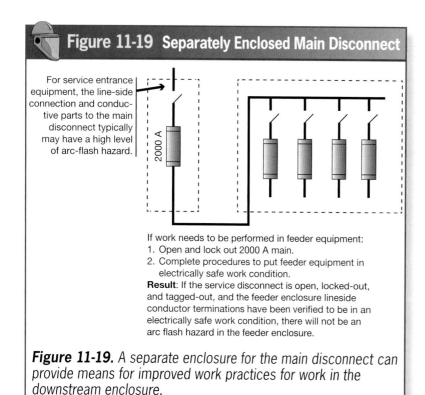

Figure 11-19 Separately Enclosed Main Disconnect

For service entrance equipment, the line-side connection and conductive parts to the main disconnect typically may have a high level of arc-flash hazard.

2000 A

If work needs to be performed in feeder equipment:
1. Open and lock out 2000 A main.
2. Complete procedures to put feeder equipment in electrically safe work condition.
Result: If the service disconnect is open, locked-out, and tagged-out, and the feeder enclosure lineside conductor terminations have been verified to be in an electrically safe work condition, there will not be an arc flash hazard in the feeder enclosure.

Figure 11-19. A separate enclosure for the main disconnect can provide means for improved work practices for work in the downstream enclosure.

(4) Service disconnect in switchgear or metering centers where each disconnect is located in a separate compartment.

A safety by design solution would leverage option (1) of *NEC* 230.71(B) and ensure that the service disconnecting means is in its own enclosure without any other branch or feeder OCPDs. This act essentially separates the service equipment from the equipment that would include the branch and feeder OCPDs and establishes a few important opportunities for Electrical Worker safety:

1. The enclosure with the service overcurrent protective device is less likely to be accessed than the OCPDs in the next downstream enclosure.
2. It is easier for the Electrical Worker to establish an electrically safe working condition in the next level distribution equipment.
3. It is easier for the design to reduce the incident energy level at the first downstream level equipment thus reducing the exposure of incident energy to the Electrical Worker should justified energized work be conducted in that equipment.

When the service overcurrent protective device is placed inside the enclosure that includes the branch and feeder OCPDs, special care must be taken. If a worker must work in the enclosure the compartment where the work is being performed must be closely reviewed to determine if an electrically safe work condition can be established. Providing a main OCPD with line-side barriers can help reduce the likelihood of coming in contact with energized parts which could reduce the likelihood of creating an arc flash event. (There may still be an arc flash hazard due to the service disconnect line-side conductor terminations unless the service disconnect is in a separate enclosure.) **See Figure 11-20.**

If a worker is performing a task within a feeder compartment with an exposed energized conductor, a main OCPD helps protect against arcing faults on the feeder device's line terminals and the equipment's main bus. An incident energy analysis associated with the main device must be performed because large ampere-rated OCPDs might permit high incident energies. In most cases, the main OCPD can provide better protection than the utility OCPD, which is located on the transformer primary.

Figure 11-20 Single Main Disconnect/Overcurrent Protection

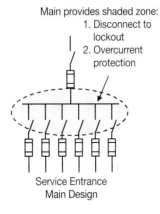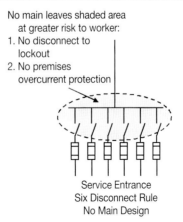

Figure 11-20. Single-line diagrams illustrate systems with and without single main disconnect/overcurrent protection and indicate how each design affects the incident energy level. Note that the system represented by the single-line diagram on the left has a lower incident energy level than the system represented by the one-line diagram to the right, which has no main overcurrent protection.

High-Speed Fuse Assembly

An engineered assembly installed at the secondary of a large transformer or at other locations that may potentially have high incident energy can greatly mitigate the arc flash hazards. **See Figure 11-21.** These assemblies have been used in mining applications, where the transformer secondary has high load current requirements and high incident energy. They incorporate special-purpose high-speed fuses that are very current-limiting. The resulting systems are engineered to carry the normal load currents, but respond very quickly to fault currents. They provide opportunities for electrical design teams to minimize arc flash hazards. Low-impedance transformers provide greater available fault current, a factor that assists in the arc flash mitigation operation provided by this assembly.

Sizing Underutilized Circuits with Lower Ampere-Rated Fuses or Circuit Breakers

When the rated ampacity of a circuit is significantly larger than necessary, the actual load current under the maximum load conditions should be measured, and the most current-limiting fuses should be sized for the load. If an 800-ampere feeder to a motor control center draws only 320 amperes, for example, then 400-ampere current-limiting fuses could be considered. This can lower the arc flash hazard if the lower ampere-rated fuses or circuit breakers result in a lower incident energy for the available fault current. **See Figure 11-22.**

Evaluating OCPDs in Existing Facilities for Interrupting Rating

Fuses, circuit breakers, and other OCPDs must be selected so that their interrupting rating is equal to or greater than the available fault current for the initial installation. Selecting devices with possible future power system changes in mind as well is important increasing the longevity of the design and avoiding system product misapplications.. Changes in an electrical system, including changes made to the supplying utility system, can result in higher available fault currents, which may exceed the interrupting rating of existing OCPDs. For example, when a service transformer is increased in kilo-volt-ampere size or the transformer is replaced with a lower-impedance transformer, the available fault current might increase to levels greater than the OCPDs' interrupting ratings.

In addition to *NEC* Section 110.9, which requires fuses and circuit breakers to have adequate interrupting ratings, *NFPA 70E* Section 210.5 and OSHA

Figure 11-21 Engineered Assembly

Figure 11-21. Engineered assemblies with high-speed fuses can be used to mitigate arc flash hazards.

Courtesy of PACE Engineers Group Pty Ltd.

Figure 11-22 Downsizing

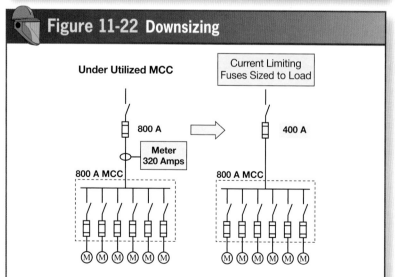

Figure 11-22. On large-ampacity circuits that are lightly loaded, retrofit to lower-ampacity OCPDs.

rules require that OCPDs have adequate interrupting ratings irrespective of the installation date of the system. OSHA 29 CFR 1910.302(b) requires some regulations to be followed regardless of the original system installation date.

OSHA 29 CFR 1910.303(b)(4)

Interrupting rating. Equipment intended to interrupt current at fault levels shall have an interrupting rating sufficient for the nominal circuit voltage and the current that is available at the line terminals of the equipment. Equipment intended to interrupt current at other than fault levels shall have an interrupting rating at nominal circuit voltage sufficient for the current that must be interrupted.

Whenever system changes occur in the power distribution system or changes are made by the utility that might increase the available fault currents, the existing OCPDs must be reevaluated to determine whether they have a sufficient interrupting rating. If a fault current analysis or an incident energy analysis is performed for an existing facility, an evaluation must be made to determine whether all the fuses and circuit breakers have sufficient interrupting ratings for

the available fault current at their line terminals. Fuses or circuit breakers that do not have an adequate interrupting rating must be replaced with fuses or circuit breakers that have an adequate interrupting rating.

The definition for interrupting rating is essentially the maximum fault current that a fuse or circuit breaker is rated to interrupt at rated voltage. An OCPD that attempts to interrupt a fault current beyond its interrupting rating can rupture violently. This misapplication condition can present an arc flash and arc blast hazard, and the violent rupturing can initiate an arcing fault in other parts of the equipment. (Another chapter covers the calculation of the available fault current.) Modern current-limiting fuses have interrupting ratings of 200,000 and 300,000 amperes, which virtually eliminate the hazard of inadequate interrupting rating. However, renewable and Class H fuses have only a 10,000-ampere interrupting rating, some Class K fuses have a 50,000-ampere interrupting rating, and Class G fuses have a 100,000-ampere interrupting rating.

Circuit breakers have varying interrupting ratings, so they need to be assessed accordingly. **See Figures 11-23**

Figure 11-23 Misapplication of Fuse Interrupting Rating

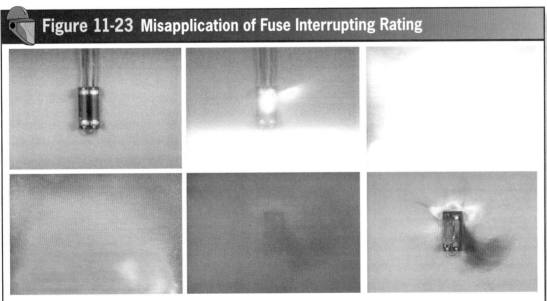

For additional information, visit qr.njatcdb.org Item #1237

Figure 11-23. A laboratory test illustrates what happens when Class H fuses, which have an interrupting rating of only 10,000 amperes, are subjected to a 50,000-ampere fault.

Figure 11-24 Misapplication of Circuit Breaker Interrupting Rating

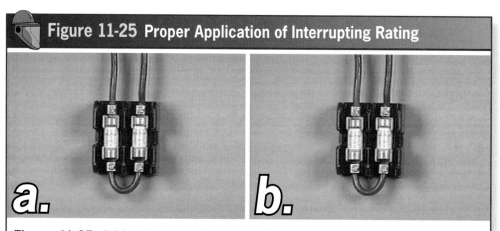

Figure 11-24. A laboratory test illustrates what happens when a circuit breaker with an interrupting rating of 14,000 amperes is subjected to a 50,000-ampere fault.

For additional information, visit qr.njatcdb.org Item #1235

and 11-24. Although these tests depict a violation of *NEC* Section 110.9, *NFPA 70E* 210.5, and OSHA 1910.303(b)(4), they emphasize the importance of a proper interrupting rating for arc flash protection and application of OCPDs. In a fraction of a second, sudden violence can occur.

A fault current can be safely interrupted. **See Figure 11-25.** Note that in this laboratory test, the fuses have an interrupting rating greater than the available fault current; therefore, the current is safely interrupted.

"No Damage" Protection for Motor Controllers

Motor starters that are designated as Type 1 protection are susceptible to violent explosive damage from fault currents. They can be the source of an arc flash or can produce ionized gas that initiates an arcing fault in an enclosure. If an employee needs to work within an

Figure 11-25 Proper Application of Interrupting Rating

For additional information, visit qr.njatcdb.org Item #1236

Figure 11-25. A laboratory test illustrates Class J, low-peak LPJ fuses safely interrupting a 50,000-ampere available fault current. The LPJ fuses have an interrupting rating of 300,000 amperes. (a) Fuses are shown before a laboratory test. (b) Fuses are shown during and after a laboratory test to safely interrupt a fault current.

enclosure that is not in an electrically safe work condition and that contains a motor starter protected by Type 1 protection, he or she may be exposed to a serious safety hazard. Specifying Type 2 motor starter protection can reduce the risk because the level of current limitation typically required to obtain Type 2 protection also provides for excellent arc flash hazard reduction and minimizes the chance that the starter will be the source of the arc flash or contribute to the initiation of an arcing fault.

Type 1 Protection

IEC 60947-4-1, "Type 1 Protection" (similar to requirements for listing motor starters to *UL 508*), requires that, under fault conditions, the contactor or starter cause no danger to persons (with the enclosure door closed) or surroundings, but the contactor or starter might not be suitable for further service without repair and replacement of parts. Note that damage is allowed that may require partial or complete component replacement. It is possible for the overload devices to vaporize and the contacts to weld. Short-circuit protective devices interrupt the fault current but are not required to prevent component damage. **See Figure 11-26.**

Type 2 Protection

Using starters with OCPDs that provide Type 2 protection may mean that the starter elements (heater elements and contacts) will not violently vaporize and result in an arc flash hazard. *UL 508E* (Outline of Investigation) and IEC 60947-4-1, "Type 2 Protection," require that, under fault conditions, the contactor or starter cause no danger to persons (with the enclosure door closed) or the installation and be suitable for further use. No damage is allowed to either the contactor or the overload relay. Light contact welding is permitted, but contacts must be easily separable. "No damage" protection for the National Electrical Manufacturers Association (NEMA) and International Electrotechnical Commission (IEC) motor starters can be provided only by a device that is able to limit the

Figure 11-26 Type 1 Starter Protection

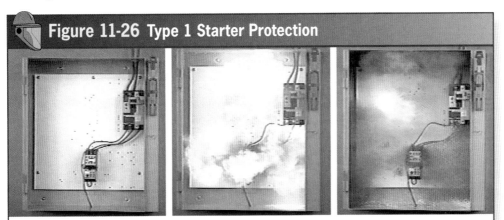

Figure 11-26. *The photos were taken before, during, and after testing a motor circuit protector (MCP) intended to provide motor branch-circuit protection for a 10-horsepower (hp) IEC starter with 22,000 amperes of fault current available at 480 volts. The door was open to visualize the damage level. The heater elements vaporized and the contacts severely welded, contributing vaporized metal to the atmosphere. If a worker had any unprotected or under-protected body parts near such an event, he or she might be injured.*

Figure 11-27 Type 2 "No Damage" Starter Protection

Figure 11-27. *The photos were taken from a video of a motor starter tested to Type 2 criteria (with the door open so as to visualize the lack of a hazard). The photos were taken before, during, and after use of the same test circuit and same type of starter during fault current interruption. The difference is that here Bussmann Series LPJ-SP Class J current-limiting fuses provide the motor branch-circuit protection. This level of protection reduces the risk for workers.*

magnitude and the duration of fault current. **See Figure 11-27.**

Fuses that typically meet the requirements for Type 2 "no damage" protection, as demonstrated by the results of the controller manufacturer's testing, include Class J, Class CF, Class CC, and Class RK1 fuses. As mentioned earlier, these fuses are very current-limiting, which can protect the sensitive controller components.

Selective Coordination

Today, one of the most important parts of any installation is the electrical distribution system and continuity of service. Few things can stop activity, paralyze production, create inconvenience, disconcert people, and possibly cause a panic more than a power outage to critical loads. Selective coordination can be among the means to prevent such an event.

Selective coordination is considered the act of isolating a faulted circuit from the remainder of the electrical system, thereby eliminating unnecessary power outages. The faulted circuit is isolated by the selective operation of only that OCPD closest to the fault condition. An adequately engineered system enables only the protective device nearest the fault to open, leaving the remainder of the system undisturbed and preserving continuity of service.

Personnel safety can be enhanced in a selectively coordinated system because Electrical Workers are not unnecessarily exposed to increased levels of arc flash hazards at upstream panels or switchboards where the actual problem may reside in the power system. In a selectively coordinated system, the OCPD closest to the fault is the only device that will open. This basic principle provides the Electrical Worker with the knowledge necessary to quickly isolate the scope of work and only be exposed at the level of circuit that incurred the problem. In a non-selectively coordinated system, the worker must perform much more troubleshooting to determine the location of the faulted circuit. This needlessly places the worker in upstream equipment, where arc flash energies are often significantly higher.

Consider a case where the arc flash energy at a branch-circuit panel is 1.6 cal/cm². **See Figure 11-28.** If an overcurrent condition on the branch circuit opens only the overcurrent device in the branch-circuit panel, the worker is exposed to 1.6 cal/cm² while troubleshooting the circuit. If the feeder overcurrent protective device unnecessarily opens due to cascading OCPDs, the worker is forced to work within the feeder panel and is unnecessarily

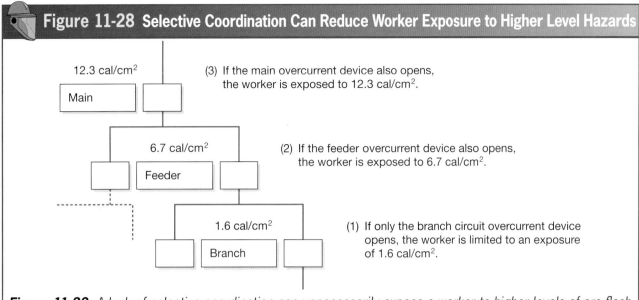

Figure 11-28 Selective Coordination Can Reduce Worker Exposure to Higher Level Hazards

12.3 cal/cm²

Main

(3) If the main overcurrent device also opens, the worker is exposed to 12.3 cal/cm².

6.7 cal/cm²

Feeder

(2) If the feeder overcurrent device also opens, the worker is exposed to 6.7 cal/cm².

1.6 cal/cm²

Branch

(1) If only the branch circuit overcurrent device opens, the worker is limited to an exposure of 1.6 cal/cm².

Figure 11-28. A lack of selective coordination can unnecessarily expose a worker to higher levels of arc flash hazards.

exposed to a higher level of 6.7 cal/cm². If the main also opens unnecessarily, the worker is forced to work within the main panel, thereby exposing the worker to 12.3 cal/cm². Therefore, in this selectively coordinated system example, the worker is exposed to only 1.6 cal/cm², but in the non-selectively coordinated system, the worker is exposed to 12.3 cal/cm². These incident energy levels are merely hypothetical for illustrative purposes; usually the closer the larger ampere-rated equipment is to the service entrance, the higher the incident energy.

ADDITIONAL DESIGN FOR SAFETY CONSIDERATIONS

Beyond overcurrent protective device safety design considerations, there are design techniques for new and existing systems that reduce or eliminate electrical hazards for workers. This section discusses a few of these options; however, a multitude of such design considerations exist.

Remote Monitoring

Specifying remote monitoring of voltage or current, or measurement of other electrical parameters, reduces exposure to electrical hazards by transferring the potentially hazardous troubleshooting activity from the actual live equipment to a display visible with the equipment doors closed, thereby enhancing safe work practices. **See Figure 11-29.** Such remote monitoring can be implemented in many ways. For example, the displays may be mounted so that they are readable from the equipment enclosure exterior; the equipment

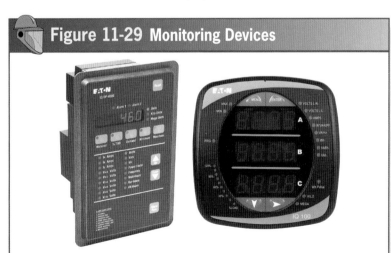

Figure 11-29 Monitoring Devices

Figure 11-29. Remote monitoring devices for electrical system information (for example, voltage and ampacity) provide a means for workers to perform electrical diagnostics with the enclosure doors closed.

Courtesy of Eaton

enclosure exterior may support "plug-in" diagnostic displays, instruments, or computers so that troubleshooting can be performed on the equipment with the doors closed; or remote computers may provide network access to the necessary data. These designs reduce the associated electrical hazards and reduce the number of times that required PPE must be worn by Electrical Workers.

Infrared Thermography Windows

A common practice is to use infrared thermography equipment to assess for abnormally high temperatures in carrying the normal load current. The process normally includes opening the assembly doors or trim to expose the equipment interior. Then infrared thermography images are taken to identify abnormally high-temperature conductor terminations or devices that could

Figure 11-30 Finger-Safe Devices

CUBEFuses™

SAMI fuse covers

Fusible disconnects

Power distribution blocks

Class J fuse holders

Other fuse holders

Figure 11-30. Finger-safe devices can help minimize electrical hazards.

Courtesy of Eaton's Bussmann Division

indicate impending electrical failures.

The task of opening the energized equipment can be an arc flash hazard. To eliminate the need to open the electrical assembly in this process, special small windows are installed in electrical assemblies which allow the infrared thermography imaging of the internal electrical parts to be recorded through these windows. The result is a safer and more efficient process.

Finger-Safe Products and Terminal Covers

One way to minimize exposure to electrical shock hazard is to use finger-safe products and nonconductive covers or barriers. ("Finger-safe" is a generic term but not a product standard criterion for evaluating electrical products' ability to minimize shock hazard.) Finger-safe products and covers reduce the chance of receiving a shock or initiating an arcing fault. If all the electrical components are finger-safe or covered, a worker has a much lower risk of making contact with an energized part (shock hazard). The risk of any conductive part falling across bare, energized conductive parts and creating an arcing fault (arc flash hazard) is also greatly reduced.

Several items have been developed that can help minimize shock hazards and minimize the initiation of an arcing fault. **See Figure 11-30.** All of these devices can reduce the chance that a worker, tool, or other conductive item will come in contact with a live part.

The International Protection (IP) Code rating is an IEC system, detailed in IEC 60529. **See Figure 11-31.** IP20 is often referred to as "finger-safe,"

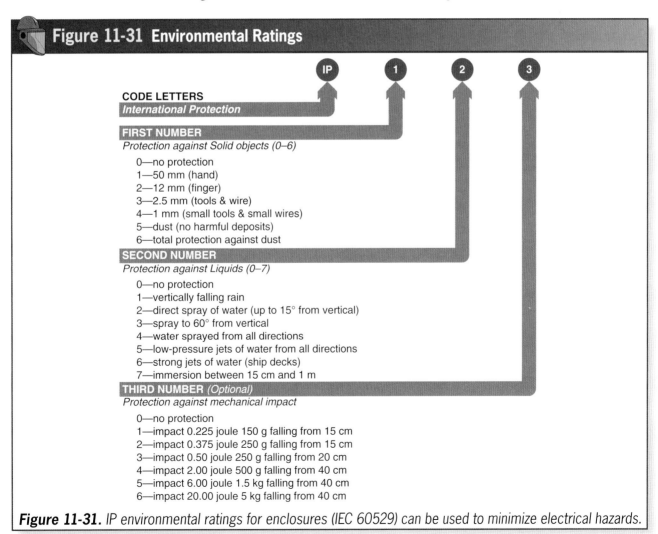

Figure 11-31 Environmental Ratings

CODE LETTERS
International Protection

FIRST NUMBER
Protection against Solid objects (0–6)

0—no protection
1—50 mm (hand)
2—12 mm (finger)
3—2.5 mm (tools & wire)
4—1 mm (small tools & small wires)
5—dust (no harmful deposits)
6—total protection against dust

SECOND NUMBER
Protection against Liquids (0–7)

0—no protection
1—vertically falling rain
2—direct spray of water (up to 15° from vertical)
3—spray to 60° from vertical
4—water sprayed from all directions
5—low-pressure jets of water from all directions
6—strong jets of water (ship decks)
7—immersion between 15 cm and 1 m

THIRD NUMBER *(Optional)*
Protection against mechanical impact

0—no protection
1—impact 0.225 joule 150 g falling from 15 cm
2—impact 0.375 joule 250 g falling from 15 cm
3—impact 0.50 joule 250 g falling from 20 cm
4—impact 2.00 joule 500 g falling from 40 cm
5—impact 6.00 joule 1.5 kg falling from 40 cm
6—impact 20.00 joule 5 kg falling from 40 cm

Figure 11-31. IP environmental ratings for enclosures (IEC 60529) can be used to minimize electrical hazards.

meaning that a probe the approximate size of a finger must not be able to access or make contact with hazardous energized parts. Principally, IEC 60529 defines the degree of protection provided by an enclosure (barriers/guards) classified under the IP Code and the testing conditions required to meet these classifications. IP20-rated products do not offer any protection against liquids. UL product standards are lagging in the adoption of evaluating enclosures and components for shock hazards; however, some UL product standards have the option to evaluate electrical devices (components) for compliance with IP20. In some cases, the manufacturers of components may make self-certified IP20 claims.

Workers should understand the concept underlying the IP20 rating and its benefits and limitations. Some component products with IP20 claims have a "conditional" IP20 rating. For example, the conductor termination may be considered IP20-rated if the conductor is prepared and installed in the terminal properly. This same terminal may be IP20-rated for the larger AWG conductors for which the terminal is rated, but not IP20-rated for the smaller AWG conductors for which the terminal is rated (a bare finger could contact bare energized metal).

Isolating the Circuit: Installation of an "In-Sight" Disconnect for Each Motor

Electrical systems should be designed to support maintenance, with easy, safe access to the equipment. Their design should provide for isolating equipment for repair purposes, with a disconnecting means for implementing lockout/tagout procedures. A sound design provides disconnecting means at all motor loads, in addition to disconnecting means required within sight of the controller location that can be locked in the open position. Disconnecting means at the motor provide improved isolation and safety for maintenance as well as an emergency disconnect.

Horsepower-rated disconnects should be installed within sight (visible and within 50 feet) of every motor or driven machine. **See Figure 11-32.** The provision for locking or adding a lock to the disconnecting means shall be installed on or at the switch or circuit breaker used as the disconnecting means and shall remain in place with or without the lock installed. The *NEC* uses the terms "in-sight from," "within sight from," or "within sight of" to mean that the specified equipment is to be visible and not more than 15 meters (50 ft) distant from the other. See the definition of "In Sight From (Within Sight From, Within Sight)" in the *NEC*.

An "in-sight" motor disconnect is more likely to be used by a worker for the lockout procedure to put equipment in an electrically safe work condition prior to doing work on the equipment. Such a disconnect generally is required as per Part IX of Article 430 even if the disconnect within sight of the controller can be locked out. Some exceptions exist for specific industrial applications.

Breaking up Large Circuits into Smaller Circuits

In the design phase, if preliminary incident energy analysis indicates that equipment in high-ampacity circuits is associated with high arc flash hazards, it may be feasible to divide the loads

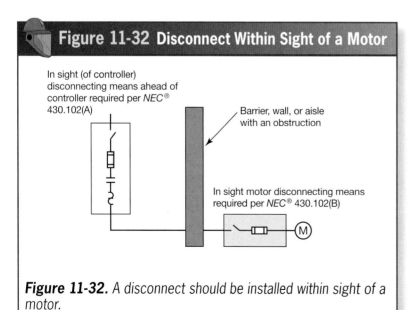

Figure 11-32 Disconnect Within Sight of a Motor

In sight (of controller) disconnecting means ahead of controller required per *NEC*® 430.102(A)

Barrier, wall, or aisle with an obstruction

In sight motor disconnecting means required per *NEC*® 430.102(B)

M

Figure 11-32. A disconnect should be installed within sight of a motor.

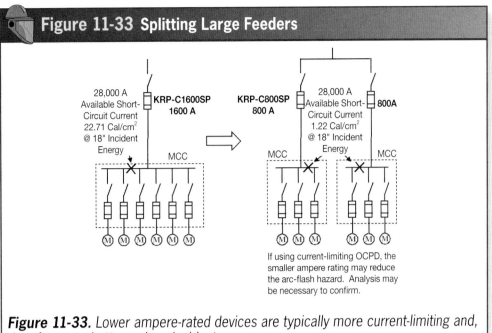

Figure 11-33 Splitting Large Feeders

28,000 A Available Short-Circuit Current 22.71 Cal/cm² @ 18" Incident Energy

KRP-C1600SP 1600 A

MCC

KRP-C800SP 800 A

28,000 A Available Short-Circuit Current 1.22 Cal/cm² @ 18" Incident Energy

800A

MCC

MCC

If using current-limiting OCPD, the smaller ampere rating may reduce the arc-flash hazard. Analysis may be necessary to confirm.

Figure 11-33. Lower ampere-rated devices are typically more current-limiting and, therefore, can better reduce incident energy.

and supply the various pieces of equipment by multiple smaller-ampacity feeders. In many cases, very large ampere-rated fuses and circuit breakers let through too much energy for a practical PPE arc rating.

A 1,600-ampere circuit, for example, might potentially be broken into two 800-ampere circuits. An analysis of the incident energy available in each circuit would then generally indicate that two 800-ampere circuits would be better than one 1,600-ampere circuit.

For specific situations, an incident energy analysis should be completed, as variables can affect the outcome. This is especially beneficial when using current-limiting protective devices, because the lower ampere-rated devices are typically more current-limiting and, therefore, can better reduce the incident energy exposure. **See Figure 11-33.**

Remote Opening and Closing

Opening and closing large switches and circuit breakers have caused serious arc flash incidents when these devices failed while being operated. By opening and closing large switches and circuit breakers remotely, a worker can control the operation from a safe

distance. If an arc flash incident should occur in this scenario, the worker is less likely to be exposed to the hazard. **See Figure 11-34.**

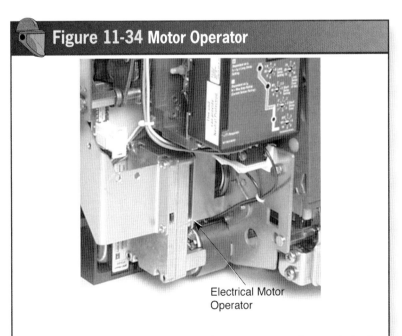

Figure 11-34 Motor Operator

Electrical Motor Operator

Figure 11-34. A motor operator for remote opening and closing of a circuit breaker can permit a worker to operate a circuit breaker at a distance without being directly in front of the circuit breaker.

Courtesy of Eaton

Arc Flash Preventative MCCs

Some motor control centers (MCC) are available with many design features which improve the safety for when maintenance is required. **See Figure 11-35.** With this motor control center, the buckets can be racked in and out remotely.

What makes for arc flash preventative MCCs? Key strategies are used to help safeguard employees against injuries from electric shock, arc flash burns, and arc blasts:

1. Multiple insulations and isolation features enable arc flash prevention.

2. Unlike conventional MCCs, arc-preventative MCC design enables units to be disconnected and reconnected to the vertical bus with the door closed; maintaining a closed door during these operations increases operator safety. Additionally, a remote racking device permits the maintenance personnel to stand at a safe distance. **See Figure 11-36.**

3. A series of safety interlocks ensure that doors cannot be opened and that units cannot be removed from the structure while the stabs are connected to the vertical bus.

4. Each unit contains visual indicators that report the position of the isolation shutters and the stabs, providing maintenance personnel with additional assurance that dangerous voltages are not present inside the unit when service is required.

Arc-Resistant (Arc-Diverting) Medium-Voltage Switchgear

Arc-resistant switchgear can be installed to withstand internal arcing faults. Arc-resistant equipment typically is designed with stronger door hinges and latches, better door gaskets, and hinged enclosure top venting panels. The underlying concept focuses on diversion of the resultant explosive hot gases and pressure from an internal arcing fault via the hinged enclosure top panels. If the switchgear is installed indoors, then a means of exhausting the hot gases to the outside of the building, such as ducts, is required.

Arc-resistant equipment is rated to withstand specific levels of internal arcing faults with all the doors closed and latched. The rating does not apply to any door opened or any cover removed. Therefore, arc-resistant equipment does not protect a worker who is performing a task with an open door or panel.

Figure 11-35 Motor Control Center

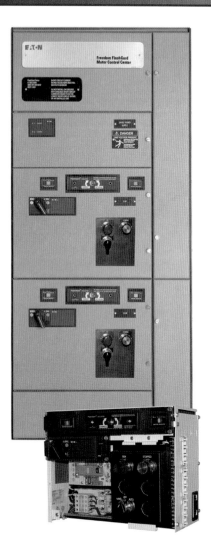

Figure 11-35. *Motor control centers (MCCs) may have the feature to rack the MCC buckets in and out with a remote racking tool.*

Courtesy of Eaton

Figure 11-36 Remote Racking Device

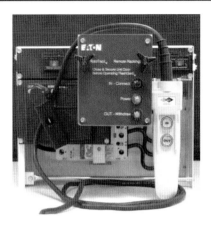

Figure 11-36. A motorized remote racking device permits racking the MCC buckets in and out remotely.

Courtesy of Eaton

The term "arc-resistant" is a bit misleading. The internal switchgear must withstand an internal arcing fault and, therefore, the sheet metal and other components of the equipment must resist or withstand a specified arcing fault. However, a major feature of this equipment is a diversion of the arcing fault by-products (that is, hot ionized gases and blast) via the enclosure top panels. This feature helps to prevent the arcing fault from blowing open the doors or side panels and venting the arcing fault by-products where a worker might be standing. **See Figure 11-37.**

Figure 11-37 Arc-Resistance Switchgear with Venting Above Gear

Figure 11-37. Arc-resistant switchgear diverts the arcing fault gases and pressures out of the top of the gear if all doors are closed and latched properly.

Courtesy of Eaton

Figure 11-38 Service Entrance Panel

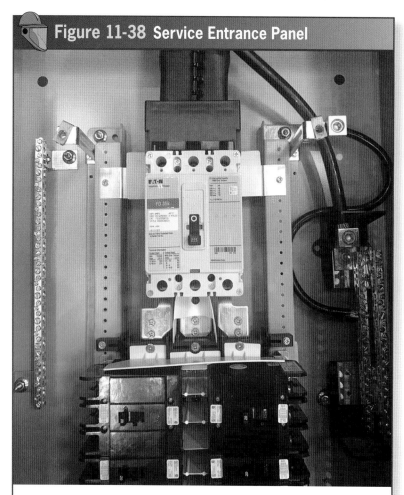

Figure 11-38. *Some panels suitable for service entrance applications have the added feature that the area of the panel where the service conductors terminate to the main OCPD/ disconnect is isolated by the sheet metal barrier.*

Courtesy of Eaton

Service Panel with Isolated Barrier

For these service entrance panels, providing barriers to the line-side lugs of the main OCPD provides a barrier that helps to reduce the likelihood of an Electrical Worker coming into contact with energized parts. **See Figure 11-38.** This feature enhances safety by preventing inadvertent contact with the conductors and terminations in this isolated area and is a requirement in the *National Electrical Code* as part of 230.62. This barrier is not intended for arc flash protection; however, it does reduce the likelihood that an arc flash incident will occur.

Resistance-Grounded Systems

Electrical systems can be designed with resistance-grounded wye systems to increase system reliability and reduce the probability of arc flash incidents. **See Figure 11-39.** In this type of installation, a resistor is intentionally inserted between the center point of the wye of the transformer and the ground, so that the ground fault current is limited by the inserted resistor. For 3-phase systems, this type of system can only be used for a 3-wire system; that is, it is not permitted by the *NEC* for systems such as 277/480-volt, 3-phase, 4-wire.

This type of system can reduce the probability that dangerous or destructive

Figure 11-39 Resistance-Grounded System: System Configuration

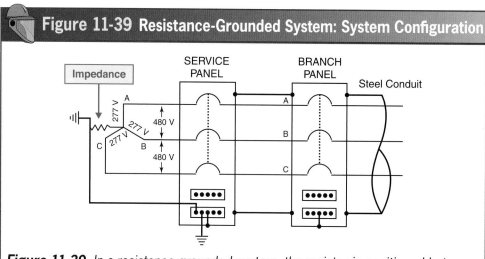

Figure 11-39. *In a resistance-grounded system, the resistor is positioned between the center tap of the wye transformer and the ground.*

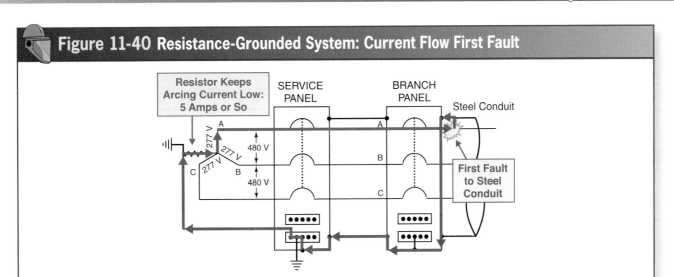

Figure 11-40 Resistance-Grounded System: Current Flow First Fault

Figure 11-40. Because of the resistance, a fault occurring from phase-to-ground does not cause the OCPD to open, since the resistor limits the fault current to approximately five amperes.

arcing faults will occur. For example, with a resistance-grounded wye system, if a worker's screwdriver slips, simultaneously touching an energized bare-phase termination and the enclosure, a high-energy arc fault would not be initiated. **See Figure 11-40.** Instead, the fault current would typically be limited to only a few amperes by the resistor intentionally inserted into the ground return path. This limited fault current is insufficient to create the vaporized metal that would initiate or sustain a 3-phase arcing fault.

A high resistance-grounded system does not eliminate the arc flash hazard,

however. **See Figure 11-41.** For example, if a worker's screwdriver simultaneously touches the energized bare terminations of two phases, a high-level arcing fault might occur because the resistor then is not involved in the faulted current path. If so, it can quickly escalate into a 3-phase arcing fault.

Cautionary Note: If a designer is planning high resistance-grounded wye systems or retrofitting an existing solidly grounded wye system, he or she must consider the single-pole interrupting capabilities of any circuit breakers and self-protected starters to

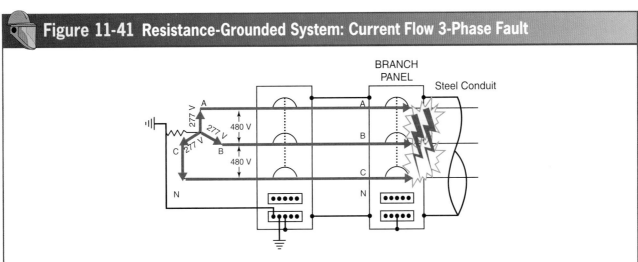

Figure 11-41 Resistance-Grounded System: Current Flow 3-Phase Fault

Figure 11-41. A high energy release arcing fault incident is still possible. If a fault occurs between two phases or all three phases, the resistor is not in the fault current path and high fault currents are possible.

Figure 11-42 Resistance-Grounded System: Current Flow Second Fault

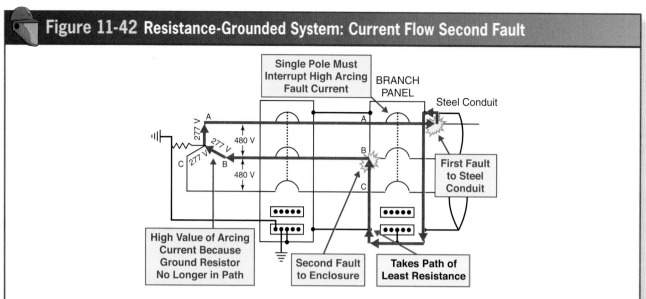

Figure 11-42. *The first fault to ground must be removed before a second phase goes to ground, or a significant fault current can occur across one pole of the branch-circuit device.*

Figure 11-43 Arc Initiator/Absorber Box

<u>Operation</u>

If an arcing fault starts in the switchgear:
1. The current sensor recognizes the arcing-fault signature.
2. Light sensors recognize a flash.
3. The relay processes the inputs and activates the special box to initiate an arcing fault in the specially designed device (this arc is designed to be contained in the box).
4. The relay also signals the main CB to open.
5. The arc initiated in the special box creates low impedance, which results in the fault in switchgear to be extinguished (the voltage at the arcing fault in the switchgear is not sufficient to sustain the arc due to a lower impedance fault in the special box).
6. The main CB opens, which extinguishes the arc in the special box.

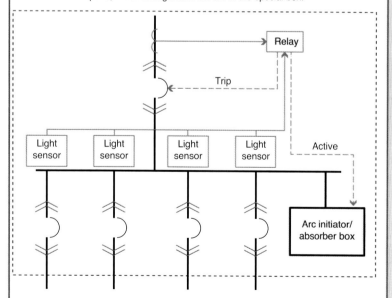

Figure 11-43. *An active arc flash mitigation system can reduce the arc flash hazard.*

be installed or already installed. **See Figure 11-42.** Slash voltage-rated circuit breakers and self-protected starters cannot be used on any system other than solidly grounded wye systems.

Active Arc Flash Mitigation System

An active arc flash mitigation system is a specially designed system made to provide fast response times to clear events that occur within equipment. These systems will often employ a relay, current sensors, light sensors, and an enclosed device that creates a low impedance that all work together to provide very fast clearing times. With this approach, if an arcing fault starts in the switchgear, it is detected, and the enclosed device initiates an arc in the box (crow bar) while simultaneously telling the upstream OCPD to open, which then extinguishes the arcing fault in the switchgear. **See Figure 11-43.**

OVERCURRENT PROTECTIVE DEVICE WORK PRACTICES

There are several important safe work practices that should be implemented when working with circuit breakers and fuses, including maintenance and diagnostic tips.

Resetting Circuit Breakers or Replacing Fuses

A circuit breaker should not be reset, nor should fuses be replaced, until the cause of the problem is known and rectified and it has been verified that it is safe to reenergize the circuit.

NFPA 70E Section 130.8(M) is essentially the same requirement as in OSHA 1910.334(b)(2) with slightly different wording.

This work practice is important for the safety of the workers. If an OCPD opens as a result of fault conditions, damage at the point of the fault could result. If the source of the fault is not located and corrected, reclosing the OCPD into a fault that has not been cleared might result in an even more severe fault. If the protective device is a circuit breaker, it could have been damaged during the initial interruption (see *NFPA 70E* Section 225.3). For this reason, following proper procedures after an OCPD has interrupted a fault is important. If the cause of a circuit breaker or fuse opening is an overload, it is permissible to merely reset the circuit breaker or replace the fuses.

Circuit Breakers

Important work practice considerations should include what to do after a circuit breaker interrupts a fault, how to rack circuit breakers, or how to replace or add circuit breakers to a panel.

Circuit Breaker Evaluation After Fault Interruption

After fault interruption, it is necessary to evaluate a circuit breaker for suitability of use before placing it back into service. This evaluation requires a thorough inspection and may require electrical testing to specifications according to the manufacturer's instruction manual. If the circuit breaker manufacturer's procedures are not available, it is advisable to use an industry standard such as NEMA AB-4. *NFPA 70E* Section 225.3 requires inspection and testing a circuit breaker per manufacturer's instructions after a circuit breaker has interrupted a fault current approaching its interrupting rating.

Racking Circuit Breakers

Racking low-voltage power circuit breakers or medium-voltage vacuum circuit breakers in/out can be a hazardous work procedure. One safe work practice is to increase the working distance when performing this activity. If the incident energy at equipment is 8.8 cal/cm^2 based on a working distance from the potential arc flash of 18 inches, increasing this working distance to 72 inches rather than 18 inches decreases the incident energy to 0.72 cal/cm^2.

After a high level fault has occurred in equipment that is properly rated and installed, it is not always clear to investigating electricians what damage has occurred inside encased equipment. The circuit breaker may well appear virtually clean while its internal condition is unknown. For such situations, the NEMA AB4 "Guidelines for Inspection and Preventive Maintenance of MCCBs Used in Commercial and Industrial Applications" may be of help. Circuit breakers unsuitable for continued service may be identified by simple inspection under these guidelines. Testing outlined in the document is another and more definite step that will help to identify circuit breakers that are not suitable for continued service.

After the occurrence of a faulted circuit, it is important that the cause be investigated and repaired and that the condition of the installed equipment be investigated. A circuit breaker may require replacement just as any other switching device, wiring or electrical equipment in the circuit that has been exposed to a fault current. Questionable circuit breakers must be replaced for continued, dependable circuit protection.

*Written by Vince A. Baclawski,
Technical Director, Power Distribution Products,
National Electrical Manufacturers Association (NEMA)
in Electrical Construction & Maintenance Magazine,
January 1995, p. 10. Copyright EC&M (January 1995).
Reprinted by permission of Penton media.*

Figure 11-44 Remote Racking

Figure 11-44. *A remote racking device permits a worker to rack circuit breakers in or out at a safe distance from the equipment.*

Courtesy of Eaton

Figure 11-45 Racking Tools

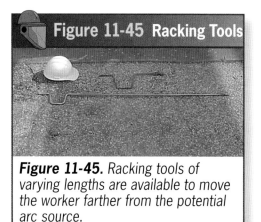

Figure 11-45. *Racking tools of varying lengths are available to move the worker farther from the potential arc source.*

Courtesy of DuPont

Incident energy at 72 inches is typically about $1/12$ what it would be at 18 inches. The following methods can be used to move the worker farther from the potential arc source or outside of the flash boundary for hazardous operations:

1. External and integrated remote-controlled motorized devices are available that rack in and out low- and medium-voltage circuit breakers. **See Figure 11-44.**
2. Extended length, hand-operated racking tools. **See Figure 11-45.**

Figure 11-46 Circuit Breaker Variety

Figure 11-46. *These three circuit breakers are physically interchangeable, but have significantly different voltage ratings, interrupting ratings, and ampere ratings.*

Replacing Circuit Breakers

When adding a circuit breaker to a panel or replacing a circuit breaker, ensure that the circuit breaker is suitable for that panel and the circuit breaker has the proper ampere rating, voltage rating, interrupting rating, and equivalent fault current performance. Circuit breaker frames that are part of the tested listing of the panel are identified on a label provided on the panel or switchboard.

With molded case circuit breakers, there typically are a variety of circuit breakers from the same manufacturer that are physically interchangeable but have different ratings. **See Figure 11-46.** These three circuit breakers are the same frame size and are physically interchangeable. The 240-volt circuit breaker could physically be installed in place of the 600-volt circuit breaker, the 100-ampere circuit breaker could physically be installed in place of the 20-ampere circuit breaker, and the 10kA interrupting rated circuit breaker could physically be installed in place of the 65kA interrupting circuit breaker. Switchgear with drawout power circuit breakers have cell coding plates that prevent the installation of improperly rated circuit breakers.

Fuses

Several work practices should be evaluated when an electrical installation includes fuses. These include testing and replacing fuses.

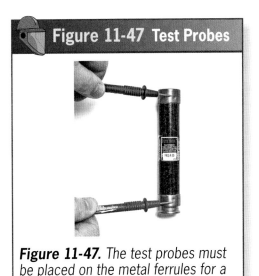

Figure 11-47 **Test Probes**

Figure 11-47. *The test probes must be placed on the metal ferrules for a ferrule fuse.*

Courtesy of Eaton's Bussmann Division

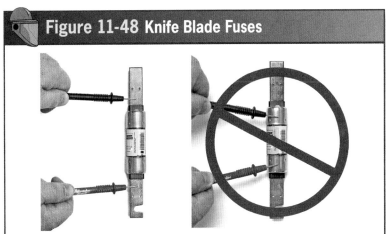

Figure 11-48 **Knife Blade Fuses**

Figure 11-48. *For knife blade fuses, always place test probes on the metal blades as shown on the left. Do not place test probes on fuse end caps as shown on the right.*

Courtesy of Eaton's Bussmann Division

Testing Fuses

When a fuse is suspected of having opened, safe work practices designated by the employer should be followed. One option is to deenergize the fuse from the source of power, including implementing lockout/tagout procedures, followed by removing both indicating and non-indicating fuses from the circuit and checking each fuse for continuity by resistance measurement. If a fuse is being replaced, the replacement fuse should be of a proper type and ampere rating.

When testing a fuse for resistance:
1. For ferrule fuses, place the test probes on the metal ferrules. **See Figure 11-47.**
2. For knife blade fuses, place the test probes on the metal blades, not on the fuse end caps. **See Figure 11-48.**

It is important to properly test knife-blade fuses. Fuse manufacturers do not generally design these types of fuses to ensure electrically energized fuse caps during normal fuse operation. For knife-blade fuses, electrical inclusion of the end caps into the circuit occurs as a result of the coincidental mechanical contact between the fuse cap and terminal extending through it. In most brands of knife-blade fuses, this mechanical contact is not guaranteed; therefore, electrical contact is not guaranteed. One fuse manufacturer has designed some knife-blade fuse versions so that the end caps are insulated to reduce the possibility of accidental contact with a live part. Thus a resistance reading to check for continuity (i.e., that the fuse is open or still usable) taken across the fuse caps is not indicative of whether the fuse is open. For knife-blade fuses, the test probes should always touch the metal knife blades. **See Figure 11-49.**

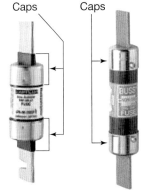

Figure 11-49 **End-Cap Insulation**

Insulated Caps   Noninsulated Caps

Figure 11-49. *The fuse on the left is designed to ensure that the end caps are electrically insulated. The fuse on the right does not have the designed-in end-cap insulation; however, an electrical connection between the fuse blades and end caps is not assured.*

Courtesy of Eaton's Bussmann Division

If, as part of diagnostic testing/troubleshooting, fuses are checked via voltage testing while the equipment is energized, safe work practices and proper PPE must be utilized. The test probes should contact the metal end caps of ferrule fuses and the blades on knife-blade fuses. Refer to the OSHA and *NFPA 70E* requirements related to when such an activity is permitted.

Replacing Fuses

Fuses that open to interrupt a circuit need to be replaced with the proper fuse in terms of both type and ampere rating. Modern current-limiting fuses are always recommended. When using modern current-limiting fuses, new factory-calibrated fuses are installed in the circuit, and the original level of overcurrent protection is maintained for the life of the circuit.

In most newer building systems and utilization equipment, the fuse mountings accept only current-limiting fuses of a specific UL Class fuse. For example, Class J fuse mountings will accept only UL Class J fuses; no other UL Class fuses can be installed in a Class J mounting. This standardization ensures a unique safety system in regard to voltage rating, interrupting rating, and fault current protection capabilities. The reason is that per the UL standard, all Class J fuses are rated as 600 volts AC, have at least a 200,000-ampere interrupting rating, and provide a specific degree of current limitation (at a minimum) under fault current conditions. Thus, when a Class J fuse is replaced, this system ensures that only a Class J fuse can be inserted in its place—that is, it ensures that the fuse has a 600 volt AC rating, at least a 200,000-ampere interrupting rating, and a very high degree of current limitation. In essence, this standardization creates an electrical safety system for overcurrent protection that is unique only for current-limiting fuse classes. Each UL fuse class has its own unique dimensions and specific voltage rating, interrupting rating, and current-limiting performance per the UL standard for fuses.

For older systems, where the fuse clips can accept older-style fuses (Class H), it is recommended to store and use only modern current-limiting fuses (Class RK1) that can be used in Class H fuse clips.

SUMMARY

Electrical system design, whether for a new system or an upgrade, can have a significant impact on personnel safety. The choices made during the design stage play an important role in reducing or eliminating exposure to electrical hazards. Designers should carefully select equipment and circuit designs that provide maximum protection for workers. The selection of the type and characteristics of OCPDs has a significant effect on the incident energy; in addition, other design techniques can affect the incident energy and other hazards. Many design techniques other than those presented are possible.

Worker safety can be enhanced through the implementation of OCPD safe work practices. Various work practices can improve the level of safety when working on electrical equipment; these include not resetting circuit breakers or replacing fuses after a fault until it is safe to re-energize the system, properly evaluating circuit breakers prior to resetting them after a fault interruption, using remote racking devices for circuit breakers, replacing circuit breakers and fuses with devices of the proper type and rating (including interrupting rating), and testing fuses properly.

REVIEW QUESTIONS

1. If a system is designed so that an electrical hazard is eliminated, then a worker will not have to contend with the hazard.
   a. True
   b. False

2. ___?___ may limit the magnitude of the arcing fault current that flows and reduce the time duration of the current, thereby potentially mitigating the arc flash hazard.
   a. Enclosures
   b. Finger-safe products
   c. Overcurrent protective devices (OCPDs)
   d. PPE

3. ___?___ products and covers reduce the chance of receiving a shock or initiating an arcing fault.
   a. Current-limiting
   b. Energy-reducing maintenance switching (ERMS)
   c. Finger-safe
   d. Non–current-limiting

4. The longer an OCPD takes to clear a given arcing fault current, the ___?___.
   a. greater the incident energy
   b. lesser the likelihood of an injury
   c. lower the incident energy
   d. safer the installation

5. ___?___ do not require maintenance other than visual examination and ensuring that there is no damage from external thermal conditions (such as conductor terminations), liquids, or physical abuse.
   a. Circuit breakers
   b. Current-limiting fuses
   c. Protective relays
   d. Vacuum interrupters

6. When the ___?___ is switched "on," if an arcing fault event occurs on a circuit which the circuit breaker protects and the arcing fault current is above the ___?___ current pickup, the circuit breaker trips without intentional delay.
   a. circuit breaker / circuit breaker
   b. electronic trip unit / electronic trip unit
   c. energy-reducing maintenance switching (ERMS) / ERMS
   d. ground fault protection / ground fault protection

7. Fuses and circuit breakers must be selected so that their interrupting rating is equal to or ___?___ the available fault current for the initial installation as well as over the life of the system.
   a. greater than
   b. less than
   c. the same as
   d. weaker than

8. Safety-related design concepts that would result in eliminating or mitigating electrical hazards cannot be implemented for existing systems.
   a. True
   b. False

9. ___?___ provide(s) a means for workers to perform electrical diagnostics with the enclosure doors closed.
   a. Energy-reducing maintenance switching
   b. Finger-safe products
   c. Insulated tools
   d. Remote monitoring devices

10. Disconnecting means at the motor provide improved ___?___ and ___?___ for maintenance as well as an emergency disconnect.
    a. fault protection / visibility
    b. isolation / safety
    c. voltage regulation / safety
    d. voltage regulation / visibility

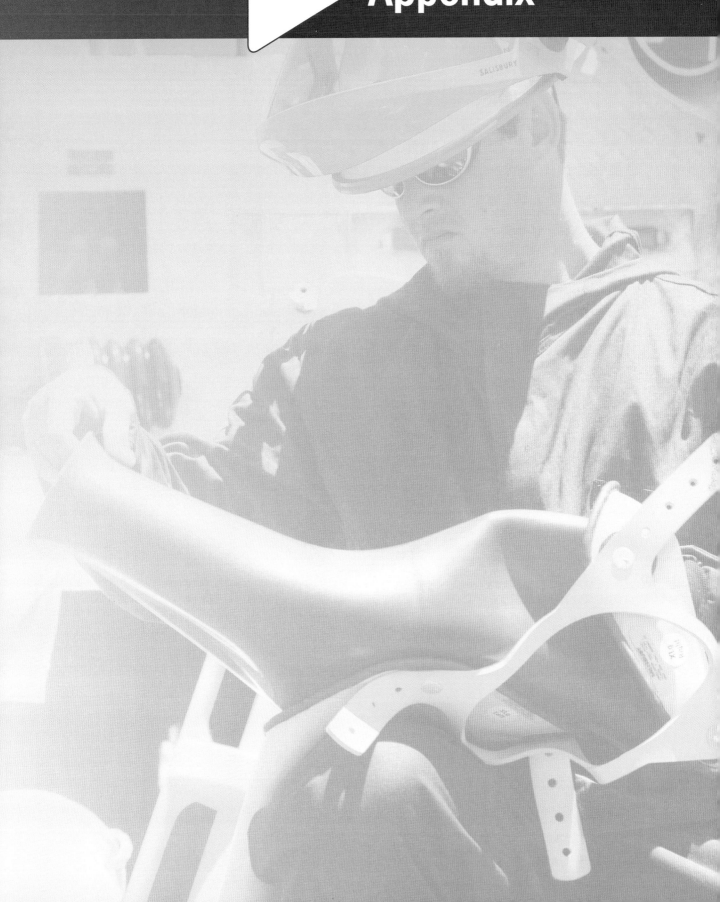

Appendix

Figure A-1   3-Phase Transformer Full Load Currents

3-Phase Voltage (Line-to-Line)	3-Phase Transformer kVA Rating								
	150	**167**	**225**	**300**	**500**	**750**	**1000**	**1500**	**2000**
208	417	464	625	833	1388	2080	2776	4164	5552
220	394	439	592	788	1315	1970	2630	3940	5260
240	362	402	542	722	1203	1804	2406	3609	4812
440	197	219	296	394	657	985	1315	1970	2630
460	189	209	284	378	630	945	1260	1890	2520
480	181	201	271	361	601	902	1203	1804	2406
600	144	161	216	289	481	722	962	1444	1924

Figure A-1. *3-Phase Transformer: Full Load Current Rating (in amperes) values can be used in lieu of the equation shown in Step 1 of the 3-phase fault current calculation procedure.*

Figure A-2   "C" Values for Copper Conductors

AWG or kcmil	Copper Conductors											
	Three Single Conductors Conduit						Three-Conductor Cable Conduit					
	Steel			Nonmagnetic			Steel			Nonmagnetic		
	600 V	**5 kV**	**15 kV**	**600 V**	**5 kV**	**15 kV**	**600 V**	**5 kV**	**15 kV**	**600 V**	**5 kV**	**15 kV**
14	389	—	—	389	—	—	389	—	—	389	—	—
12	617	—	—	617	—	—	617	—	—	617	—	—
10	981	—	—	982	—	—	982	—	—	982	—	—
8	1557	1551	—	1559	1555	—	1559	1557	—	1560	1558	—
6	2425	2406	2389	2430	2418	2407	2431	2425	2415	2433	2428	2421
4	3806	3751	3696	3826	3789	3753	3830	3812	3779	3838	3823	3798
3	4774	4674	4577	4811	4745	4679	4820	4785	4726	4833	4803	4762
2	5907	5736	5574	6044	5926	5809	5989	5930	5828	6087	6023	5958
1	7293	7029	6759	7493	7307	7109	7454	7365	7189	7579	7507	7364
1/0	8925	8544	7973	9317	9034	8590	9210	9086	8708	9473	9373	9053
2/0	10,755	10,062	9390	11,424	10,878	10,319	11.245	11,045	10,500	11,703	11,529	11,053
3/0	12,844	11,804	11,022	13,923	13,048	12,360	13,656	13,333	12,613	14,410	14,119	13,462
4/0	15,082	13,606	12,543	16,673	15,351	14,347	16,392	15,890	14,813	17,483	17,020	16,013
250	16,483	14,925	13,644	18,594	17,121	15,866	18,311	17,851	16,466	19,779	19,352	18,001
300	18,177	16,293	14,769	20,868	18,975	17,409	20,617	20,052	18,319	22,525	21,938	20,163
350	19,704	17,385	15,678	22,737	20,526	18,672	22,646	21,914	19,821	24,904	24,126	21,982
400	20,566	18,235	16,366	24,297	21,786	19,731	24,253	23,372	21,042	26,916	26,044	23,518
500	22,185	19,172	17,492	26,706	23,277	21,330	26,980	25,449	23,126	30,096	28,712	25,916
600	22,965	20,567	17,962	28,033	25,204	22,097	28,752	27,975	24,897	32,154	31,258	27,766
750	24,137	21,387	18,889	29,735	26,453	23,408	31,051	30,024	26,933	34,605	33,315	29,735
1000	25,278	22,539	19,923	31,491	28,083	24,887	33,864	32,689	29,320	37,917	35,749	31,959

See Note at bottom of Figure 8-17.

Figure A-2. *"C" values for copper conductors are used in the Step 4 equation of the 3-phase fault current calculation procedure.*

Figure A-3 "C" Values for Aluminum Conductors

AWG or kcmil	Aluminum Conductors											
	Three Single Conductors Conduit						Three-Conductor Cable Conduit					
	Steel			Nonmagnetic			Steel			Nonmagnetic		
	600 V	5 kV	15 kV	600 V	5 kV	15 kV	600 V	5 kV	15 kV	600 V	5 kV	15 kV
14	237	—	—	237	—	—	237	—	—	237		
12	376	—	—	376	—	—	376	—	—	376		
10	599	—	—	599	—	—	599	—	—	599		
8	951	950	—	952	951	—	952	951	—	952	952	
6	1481	1476	1472	1482	1479	1476	1482	1480	1478	1482	1481	1479
4	2346	2333	2319	2350	2342	2333	2351	2347	2339	2353	2350	2344
3	2952	2928	2904	2961	2945	2929	2963	2955	2941	2966	2959	2949
2	3713	3670	3626	3730	3702	3673	3734	3719	3693	3740	3725	3709
1	4645	4575	4498	4678	4632	4580	4686	4664	4618	4699	4682	4646
1/0	5777	5670	5493	5838	5766	5646	5852	5820	5717	5876	5852	5771
2/0	7187	6968	6733	7301	7153	6986	7327	7271	7109	7373	7329	7202
3/0	8826	8467	8163	9110	8851	8627	9077	8981	8751	9243	9164	8977
4/0	10,741	10,167	9700	11,174	10,749	10,387	11,185	11,022	10,642	11,409	11,277	10,969
250	12,122	11,460	10,849	12,862	12,343	11,847	12,797	12,636	12,115	13,236	13,106	12,661
300	13,910	13,009	12,193	14,923	14,183	13,492	14,917	14,698	13,973	15,495	15,300	14,659
350	15,484	14,280	13,288	16,813	15,858	14,955	16,795	16,490	15,541	17,635	17,352	16,501
400	16,671	15,355	14,188	18,506	17,321	16,234	18,462	18,064	16,921	19,588	19,244	18,154
500	18,756	16,828	15,657	21,391	19,503	18,315	21,395	20,607	19,314	23,018	22,381	20,978
600	20,093	18,428	16,484	23,451	21,718	19,635	23,633	23,196	21,349	25,708	25,244	23,295
750	21,766	19,685	17,686	25,976	23,702	21,437	26,432	25,790	23,750	29,036	28,262	25,976
1000	23,478	21,235	19,006	28,779	26,109	23,482	29,865	29,049	26,608	32,938	31,920	29,135

Note: The values for Figures 8-16 and 8-17 are equal to 1 over the impedance per 1000 feet and based upon resistance and reactance values found in IEEE Std 241-1990 (Gray Book), IEEE Recommended Practice for Electric Power Systems in Commercial Buildings, and IEEE Std 242-1986 (Buff Book), IEEE Recommended Practice for Protection and Coordination of Industrial and Commercial Power Systems. Where resistance and reactance values differ or are not available, the Buff Book values have been used. The values for reactance in determining the "C" value at 5 and 15 kV are from the Gray Book only (values for 14-10 AWG at 5 kV and 14-8 AWG at 15 kV are not available, and values for 3 AWG have been approximated).

Figure A-3. "C" values for aluminum conductors are used in the Step 4 equation of the 3-phase fault current calculation procedure.

Figure A-4   "C" Values for Busway

Ampacity	Busway				
	Plug-In	Feeder		High Impedance	
	Copper	Aluminum	Copper	Aluminum	Copper
225	28,700	23,000	18,700	12,000	—
400	38,900	34,700	23,900	21,300	—
600	41,000	38,300	36,500	31,300	—
800	46,100	57,500	49,300	44,100	—
1000	69,400	89,300	62,900	56,200	15,600
1200	94,300	97,100	76,900	69,900	16,100
1350	119,000	104,200	90,100	84,000	17,500
1600	129,900	120,500	101,000	90,900	19,200
2000	142,900	135,100	134,200	125,000	20,400
2500	143,800	156,300	180,500	166,700	21,700
3000	144,900	175,400	204,100	188,700	23,800
4000	—	—	277,800	256,400	—

Note: These values are equal to 1 over the impedance per foot for impedance in a survey of industry.

Figure A-4. "C" values for busway are used in the Step 4 equation of the 3-phase fault current calculation procedure.

Figure A-5   Multiplier = $1/(1 + f)$

f	M	f	M
0.01	0.99	1.5	0.4
0.02	0.98	1.75	0.36
0.03	0.97	2	0.33
0.04	0.96	2.5	0.29
0.05	0.95	3	0.25
0.06	0.94	3.5	0.22
0.07	0.93	4	0.2
0.08	0.93	5	0.17
0.09	0.92	6	0.14
0.1	0.91	7	0.13
0.15	0.87	8	0.11
0.2	0.83	9	0.1
0.25	0.8	10	0.09
0.3	0.77	15	0.06
0.35	0.74	20	0.05
0.4	0.71	30	0.03
0.5	0.67	40	0.02
0.6	0.63	50	0.02
0.7	0.59	60	0.02
0.8	0.55	70	0.01
0.9	0.53	80	0.01
1.0	0.5	90	0.01
1.2	0.45	100	0.01

* $M = 1/(1 + f)$

Figure A-5. This table can be used to determine "M" (multiplier)* rather than doing the calculation in Step 5 or Step B when "f" is known from Step 4 or Step A.

Figure A-6   Highest Available Fault Current for Transformers from Survey

Voltage and Phase	kVA	Full Load Amps	% Impedance †† (Nameplate)	Fault Amps †	Voltage and Phase	kVA	Full Load Amps	% Impedance †† (Nameplate)	Fault Amps †
277/480 3-phase**	112.5	135	1	15,000	120/208 3-phase**	25	69	1.6	4,791
	150	181	1.2	16,759		50	139	1.6	9652
	225	271	1.2	25,082		75	208	1.11	20,821
	300	361	1.2	33,426		112.5	278	1.11	27,828
	500	601	1.3	51,362		150	416	1.07	43,198
	750	902	3.5	28,410		225	625	1.12	62,004
	1000	1203	3.5	38,180		300	833	1.11	83,383
	1500	1804	3.5	57,261		500	1388	1.24	124,373
	2000	2406	5	53,461		750	2082	3.5	66,095
	2500	3007	5	66,822		1000	2776	3.5	88,167
	–	–	–	–		1500	4164	3.5	132,190
	–	–	–	–		2000	5552	5	123,377
	–	–	–	–		2500	6950	5	154,444

**3-phase available fault currents based on "infinite" primary.

††UL-listed transformers 25 kVA or greater have a ±10% impedance tolerance. Available fault amps reflect a "worst-case" condition.

†Fluctuations in system voltage will affect the available current. For example, a 10% increase in system voltage will result in a 10% increase in the available fault currents shown in the table.

Figure A-6. These generalized worst-case or highest available fault current for 3-phase transformers of given kVA and secondary voltage provide some guidance. The lowest impedance of transformers is assumed based on a survey, infinite primary available fault current, as well as worst-case adjustment values for transformer impedance tolerance and system voltage fluctuations.

Index